Demanding Democracy

REFORM AND REACTION IN COSTA RICA
AND GUATEMALA, 1870S–1950S

DEBORAH J. YASHAR

Demanding Democracy

REFORM AND REACTION IN

COSTA RICA AND GUATEMALA,

1870S–1950S

STANFORD UNIVERSITY PRESS

STANFORD, CALIFORNIA

Stanford University Press
Stanford, California
© 1997 by the Board of Trustees of the
Leland Stanford Junior University
Printed in the United States of America

CIP data appear at the end of the book

Stanford University Press publications are
distributed exclusively by Stanford University
Press within the United States, Canada, Mexico,
and Central America; they are distributed
exclusively by Cambridge University Press
throughout the rest of the world.

To John Gershman

Preface

Two Central Americans have been awarded the Nobel Peace Prize for their attempts to replace authoritarian rule with democracy. Oscar Arias Sánchez, then president of Costa Rica, received the prize in 1987 for his diplomatic efforts to negotiate an end to the civil wars raging in Guatemala, El Salvador, and Nicaragua. Rigoberta Menchú Tum, an indigenous Guatemala peasant leader, received the same award in 1992. Honored for her role in organizing peasants and promoting indigenous rights, she emerged as a symbol of the ongoing fight against political and economic violence in Guatemala.

Arias and Menchú are an unlikely pair. The former president and the indigenous peasant organizer highlighted diplomatic and grassroots efforts to secure a space for democracy. By demanding democracy, they gave voice to those seeking basic political, social, and economic freedoms denied to so many in the Central American isthmus. But in demanding democracy, this pair also highlighted the demands *of* democracy. For indeed, democracy demands, among other things, a military subordinated to civilian rule, universal respect for political rules and institutions, and the creation of spaces for effective and meaningful political participation. Through diplomacy and organizing, Arias and Menchú demanded institutional changes and met the challenge of effecting these changes in the face of authoritarian reactions.

If Arias's and Menchú's actions and words made clear the duality of demanding democracy, their countries of origin embodied the widely divergent types of experiences that could emerge in the process. Costa Rica has sustained Latin America's oldest political democracy in the postwar period. Founded in 1948, Costa Rica's contemporary political democracy has maintained competitive and honest political elections, has no centralized standing military, and has largely respected human rights. When Latin America's other political democracies gave way to military rule in the 1960s and 1970s, Costa Rica maintained its democratic practices and institutions. Guatemala, on the other hand, has experienced the region's most egregious human rights abuses at the hands of the military. Arguably, it has sustained the region's longest-standing and most brutal postwar experience with authoritarian rule.* Against a shared historical legacy of colonial rule, the contemporary differences between Costa Rica and Guatemala appear all the more striking.

How can one begin to explain why these two small countries could emerge with such radically divergent and enduring political regimes? It is this central question that has consumed me intellectually and politically for the past decade. While the examples provided by Arias and Menchú prove inspiring, this study puts forth the idea that even exemplary leaders such as these are largely insignificant to an explanation of why some countries are democratic and others are authoritarian. Historical legacies, coalitions, and the politics of reform have proven far more consequential, as this study will argue.

If individual actions cannot explain the founding of enduring democracy and authoritarianism, individuals did prove immensely important in sustaining, encouraging, and challenging me in the process of writing this book. The life of an author is quite solitary. Nonetheless, as I finish this work I am struck by the extraordinary collective effort that has gone into its making. The process of researching and writing has generated colleagues, friendships, and perhaps even some foes. I warmly thank those who have provided their time, insight, and goodwill.

The intellectual terrain charted by David Collier, Ruth Berins Collier, and the late Gregory Luebbert first inspired me to undertake this project. They carried out interrelated projects addressing the comparative historical and structural origins of regime development and state-society relations in Latin America and Europe. With their encouragement, I decided to compare the origins of Guatemala's repressive state-labor rela-

---

*Mexico's hybrid electoral-authoritarian regime has endured longer than any other Latin American regime. However, it was established prior to World War II, has not achieved Guatemala's level of human rights abuses, and has largely subordinated the military to civilian rule.

tions and authoritarian rule with Costa Rica's more open state-labor relations and political democracy. In the process, I developed a passion for researching Latin American politics and a comparative method for doing so.

As always, the greatest process of learning and growth took place, however, in the field during a year and a half of research in Guatemala, Costa Rica, and Mexico, followed by three additional but shorter research trips. I extend my deepest gratitude to the activists, politicians, and friends who so generously offered their time, opened up their homes, and shared their political analyses and/or personal experiences. I especially thank those who offered a measure of sanity in Guatemala, amidst the repression and the fear embedded in daily life. And I am indebted to all of the people I interviewed, some three, four, and even five times. I also thank Marta Samayoa and Virginia Mora, along with the staff at the Guatemalan and Costa Rican national archives and *hermerotecas*, who assisted me in gathering endless lists of material and scouring close to a decade of newspaper sources. Most of these people would most likely disagree with statements made in this study, as they would most likely distance themselves from me politically.

On my return, I benefited greatly from the working group Democracy and Development Association (DADA). At various stages, DADA included John Gershman, Michael Gorges, Andrew Gould, Ollie Johnson, Karen Kampwirth, Deborah Norden, Robin Silver, Arun Swamy, and myself. DADA provided a supportive and challenging arena for exchanging war stories about research and writing on diverse parts of the world—Central and South America, Western Europe, and South Asia. As friends and colleagues, they painstakingly read different parts of what then was a dissertation and consistently posed thought-provoking questions and critiques; they only occasionally moaned about the length of the chapters and the obscurity of the prose.

Victor Hugo Acuña, Gabriel Aguilera Peralta, Robert Bates, Nancy Bermeo, Judith Biewener, Robert Bullock, Isaac Cohen, Javier Corrales, Grzegorz Ekiert, Peter Evans, Cindy Forster, Jonathan Fox, Daniel Goldhagen, Jim Handy, Raymond F. Hopkins, Fabrice Edouard Lehoucq, David McCreery, James Mahoney, Hector Pérez-Brignoli, Mario Samper, Mina Silberberg, Theda Skocpol, Arturo Taracena, Paul Thomas, Edelberto Torres Rivas, and Robert Williams also commented on research designs, chapters, or talks. Their collegiality and insight were cricial as I revised my argument and rewrote the book.

I extend particular thanks to Jorge I. Domínguez, John Gershman,

Peter A. Hall, Peter Kingstone, Margarita Melville, Barrington Moore, Jr., María Victoria Murillo, and Timothy R. Scully, who carefully read and commented on the entire manuscript in one form or another. Their incisive and stimulating critiques helped place this study in sharper comparative perspective, to tighten the argument, and to make it better than it otherwise would have been. Their comments, individually and collectively, challenged me to move this manuscript in new directions and encouraged me to travel down new roads—not all of which I was able to take.

Research abroad was generously supported by a Fulbright grant administered by the Institute for International Education, two travel grants offered by the Center for Latin America Studies at the University of California, Berkeley, a Phi Beta Kappa grant extended by the U.C. Berkeley chapter, and the Samuel P. Huntington Fund of the Center for International Affairs at Harvard University. The Centro para Investigaciones Regionales de Mesoamérica (CIRMA) in Antigua, Guatemala, and the History Department in San Pedro, Costa Rica, graciously provided affiliations and access to their resources while I was conducting research. A Graduate Opportunity Fellowship from the University of California, Berkeley offered generous assistance as I was writing the dissertation.

The Center for International Affairs at Harvard University supported me as I revised the manuscript for publication. I was aided in this process by two excellent researchers. Anna Dahlstein and Hilary Burger conducted research with great persistence, wisdom, and humor. I also thank The Helen Kellogg Institute for International Studies at the University of Notre Dame for its support at the final stages of this project; in particular, Caroline Domingo for lending her ear as I worked through the final revisions and Caroline J. Richard for lending a hand as I tracked down final sources. Debra-Lee Vasques and Jim O'Brien provided invaluable assistance in the last days of proofing and indexing. Unless stated otherwise, all translations are my own.

Muriel Bell and Ellen F. Smith at Stanford University Press were professional and generous as they ushered the manuscript through its various stages. I greatly appreciate their expertise, encouragement, and humor. I also thank the reviewers of this manuscript for their invaluable comments and suggestions.

To my parents, Audrey and John Yashar, I owe my commitment to education and love of politics. They have together highlighted the importance of blending a commitment to work and community, family and self. In turn, my siblings Beverly, Susan, Gail, and Stephen have, by their examples, demonstrated that one can choose different paths with the same strength of character, creativity, dedication, and determination. And to Zachary Yashar Mesberg, Rachael Yashar Brown, Alexander Yashar Mesberg, and Leah Yashar Brown, I thank you for reminding me with your every birthday that life goes on and that indeed it is due time that I finished this book.

John Gershman saw more sides of this book than he or I care to remember. He has traveled with me intellectually as I wrestled with this material, geographically as we bounced around the globe, and emotionally, as is required in these long endeavors. His political commitment inspired me. His curiosity challenged and encouraged me. His humor reminded me of the importance of mixing hard work with laughter. And his insight made this a much better book than it could have been otherwise. I dedicate this book to him.

D. J. Y.

Contents

Contents

Figures, Maps, and Tables

Figures

Maps

Tables

Acronyms

AFL	American Federation of Labor (U.S.)
CIO	Congress of Industrial Organizations (U.S.)
CIT	Confederación Interamericana de Trabajadores
CTAL	Confederación de Trabajadores de América Latina
ILO	International Labor Organization
IRCA	International Railways of Central America
UFCO	United Fruit Company
UFSCO	United Fruit Steamship Company

In Guatemala

AEU	Asociación de Estudiantes Universitarios
AFG	Alianza Femenina Guatemalteca
AGA	Asociación General de Agricultores
AGIG	Asociación General de Industriales de Guatemala
CACIF	Comité Coordinador de Asociaciones Agrícolas, Industriales y Financieras
CAN	Central Auténtica Nacionalista
CAO	Central Aranista Organizada
CCIG	Comité de Comerciantes e Industriales de Guatemala
CEUA	Comité de Estudiantes Universitarios Anticomunistas
CGTG	Confederación General de Trabajadores de Guatemala
CNCG	Confederación Nacional Campesina de Guatemala
CNUS	Comité Nacional de Unidad Sindical

CTG	Confederación de Trabajadores Guatemaltecos
CUC	Comité de Unidad Campesina
DAN	Departamento Agrario Nacional
FPL	Frente Popular Libertador
FRCT	Federación Regional Central de Trabajadores
FSG	Federación Sindical de Guatemala
IGSS	Instituto Guatemalteco de Seguridad Social
IIN	Instituto Indigenista Nacional
INFOP	Instituto de Fomento de Producción
MDN	Movimiento Democrático Nacional
MLN	Movimiento de Liberación Nacional
PACs	Patrullas de Autodefensa Civil
PAR	Partido de Acción Revolucionaria
PC	Partido Comunista
PGT	Partido Guatemalteco del Trabajo (communist party)
PID	Partido Institucional Democrático
PIN	Partido de Integridad Nacional
PR	Partido Revolucionario
PRG	Partido de la Revolución Guatemalteca
PROG	Partido Revolucionario Obrero de Guatemala
PS	Partido Socialista
PUA	Partido de Unificación Anticomunista
RN	Renovación Nacional
SAMF	Sociedad de Auxilio Mutuo Ferrocarrilero
STEG	Sindicato de Trabajadores de Educación de Guatemala
USAC	Universidad de San Carlos
VD	Vanguardia Democrática

In Costa Rica

AD	Acción Demócrata
CCTRN	Confederación Costarricense de Trabajadores Rerum Novarum (Rerum Novarum)
CEPN	Centro para el Estudio de los Problemas Nacionales (Centro)
CNP	Consejo Nacional de Producción
CP	Costa Rican communist political party, whose name changes from Bloque de Obreros y Campesinos to Partido Vanguardia Popular (PVP) in 1943.
CSCRN	Confederación de Sindicatos Costarricenses Rerum Novarum

CTCR	Confederación de Trabajadores de Costa Rica
CU	Coalición Unidad
IDECAFE	Instituto de Defensa del Café
JOC	Juventud Obrera Católica
PD	Partido Demócrata
PLN	Partido Liberación Nacional
PRN	Partido Republicano Nacional
PRNI	Partido Republicano Nacional Independiente
PSD	Partido Social Demócrata
PUN	Partido Unión Nacional
PUnN	Partido Unificación Nacional
PUSC	Partido Unidad Social Cristiana
PVP	Partido Vanguardia Popular; also referred to as communist party (CP)

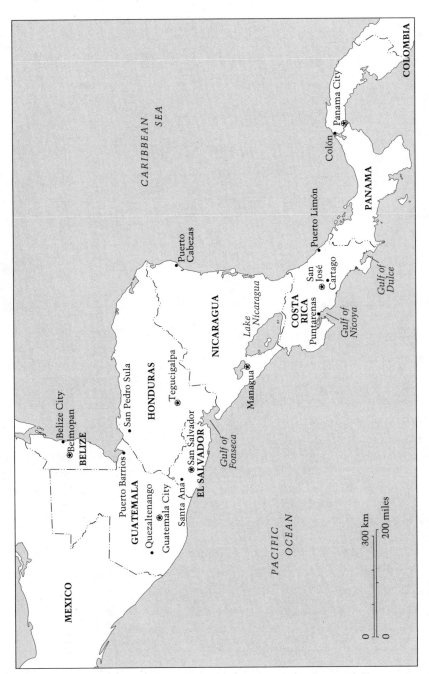

Map 1. Central America

Map 2. Guatemala, showing provinces and major towns

Map 3. Costa Rica, showing provinces and major towns

Demanding Democracy

REFORM AND REACTION IN COSTA RICA
AND GUATEMALA, 1870S–1950S

CHAPTER I

Introduction

This book examines the origins of democracy and authoritarianism. It explains the conditions under which actors found democracy and the conditions under which they are able to sustain it. It explores this question by analyzing the cases of Costa Rica and Guatemala. While today these two countries represent Latin America's most divergent political regimes, this was not always the case. Why did Costa Rica emerge with an enduring political democracy and Guatemala with authoritarian rule? This is the central analytical question posed by this book. In the process of excavating an answer, this book develops a distinct theoretical approach that integrates an analysis of the conditions fostering democracy's founding with those conducive to its endurance.

A long and rich scholarly tradition has dedicated itself to the study of democracy. Like medieval sorcerers, scholars have attempted to surmise the magical conditions that give rise to democracy. As philosophers, they have sustained a probing debate about democracy's social meaning and relevance. As humanists, they have searched for ways to advance democracy's cause. And as social scientists, they have attempted to discern the conditions that foster and nurture democracy in some conditions over others.

Yet, at century's end, this ongoing exploration and explanation has left unresolved why some countries are able to create and sustain democracy while others are not. For, while democracy was once seen as a natural by-product of modernization, today we have come to see democracy as a much more fragile entity, one difficult to create and to sustain.

In Guatemala, demands for democracy have often met the repressive fist of the state. Cases as diverse as Haiti, China, and Iran have also failed to initiate a meaningful transition to democracy. Although Costa Rica's democracy has endured, most other developing countries with histories of democratic government, including Chile, Uruguay, Nigeria, and the Philippines, have been militarily challenged at one point or another. These examples underscore that not only are demands for democracy rarely met, but the demands of abiding by existing democratic rule have too often led elites to overthrow democracy itself.

How do we explain the founding of democracy over authoritarian rule? When do newly founded democracies endure? This book does not offer a universal theory. Indeed, it is doubtful whether any theory can realistically offer an explanation across cases and across time. Grand theorizing at one time attempted to do so, by focusing on structural patterns of agrarian capitalism, industrialization, levels of development, and international capital. Subsequent middle-range theorizing maintained an emphasis on structural patterns but focused on particular sets of cases. While these grand and middle-range theories delineated general patterns that were particularly inimical to or supportive of democracy, they were less clear about the process and causal mechanisms by which particular democracies were founded. More recently, scholars have attempted to redress these problems by focusing on the particular actors involved in founding and overthrowing democracies. These agency- and process-oriented explanations, however, have assumed a largely descriptive cast and have proven less than successful in explaining the conditions under which newly founded democracies endure.

These structural and agency-based approaches to democratization have broadly defined contemporary studies of democracy and authoritarianism. Indeed, the literature has asked us to choose between the two different types of causal mechanisms. In the pursuit of methodological purity and analytical clarity, we have unwittingly, however, neglected to underscore the simple point that the two approaches, in fact, address two different questions. On the one hand, structural arguments have underscored the conditions most conducive for democracy's endurance—without explaining how and why countries transit toward democracy. On the other hand, agency-based arguments have emphasized the actors who found political democracies—with limited attention paid to how newly founded democracies endure. The cases explored in this book underscore the limitations of focusing on only one part of the question and only part of the explanation. Yet the contemporary literature on regime politics has, by example, urged us to do precisely that.

The question posed by this book prevents us from choosing simply between these two camps of the regime literature. By linking the question of why a regime is founded with why it endures, this book advocates an integrative approach. It assumes neither that historical institutions dictate future political outcomes nor that political actors forge political regimes on the basis of will alone. To the contrary, it assesses the historically constructed conditions that have undergirded authoritarianism and the actors that have set out to overcome them. It takes structures seriously insofar as the organization of states, the economy, and society often institutionalize a given distribution of power, set of vested interests, and modes of interaction. These institutions provide the constraints within which and against which actors maneuver. They are also likely to provide the conditions to predispose actors to favor one political outcome over another. But individuals are the ones who take action. And, at times, individuals are innovative and brave; they challenge the very structures in place; they take to the street to protest, they stand in front of tanks, and they fight for change. Politics, therefore, is not only about defining what is just but also about redefining what is possible. Individuals, however, have neither total discretion in defining their options nor total control over the consequences of their actions. In short, they do not act under conditions of their own choosing and rarely produce the outcome for which they had hoped.

The approach developed here, therefore, agrees with those of Kitschelt (1992) and Karl (1990), who suggest that we need to develop a more nuanced understanding of the interaction between historical conditions and political agents, but it does not take its explanatory or analytical cue from them. While Kitschelt admittedly does not outline a framework for doing so, Karl focuses on modes of transition and cross-national correlations of these transition moments. Yet her approach does not incorporate the historical structural factors that she argues need to be incorporated; it sidesteps the issue of what causes the transition, how historical structures condition the transitions that she studies, and how historical processes shape regime outcomes. Rather, this study draws on the comparative historical examples offered by Collier and Collier (1991: 5) and Scully (1992). These studies focus on critical junctures or transitions but analyze them both against a historical backdrop and with an eye toward discerning newly constituted institutional legacies.[1] They outline general causal patterns, which are evaluated and probed through a careful analysis of particular historical cases and the actions of individuals.

To analyze the interaction between historically constituted structures

that favor authoritarian rule and the political actors who work to re-
make those institutions in ways consonant with political democracy,
this book emphasizes the role of political coalitions. Political coalitions
serve as an analytic optic to assess the ways in which structures condition political options and the futures to which actors aspire. Coalitions
are the nexus at which structure and agency meet to modify individuals'
options and capacities to effect change. This book analyzes which conditions tend to generate coalitions that will build democracy, that will
reform institutions and structures in a way consonant with the maintenance of democracy, and that will be strong enough to sustain the democratic changes in the face of opposition.

This chapter lays out the book's empirical and theoretical approach,
moving from the more specific to the more general. The first section
introduces the reader to Costa Rica and Guatemala. It delineates the
analytic puzzle posed by these two cases and the methodological reasons
for which they are salient to a larger theoretical discussion of democracy
and authoritarianism. It then explores prevailing explanations of democracy and authoritarianism, elaborating on the critiques of structural
and agency arguments alluded to here. The final section lays out the
comparative theoretical approach developed in this book to explain the
founding of Costa Rica's contemporary democracy and Guatemala's authoritarian rule. The cases of Costa Rica and Guatemala suggest that
democratizing coalitions emerged in the context of a publicly divided
elite and the rising organization of marginalized sectors demanding political inclusion. The ability to sustain these democratizing coalitions,
however, rested on their capacity both to redistribute elite property and
to develop political control of the countryside. Rapid but bounded redistributive reforms implemented during the transition to democracy were
more conducive to democracy's endurance than their implementation
after democratic institutions were assumed to be in place.

The Cases

From the vantage point of the 1990s, Costa Rica and Guatemala pose
a striking contrast. Costa Rica is the only country in Central and South
America that has sustained a stable political democracy and a competitive party system in the post–World War II period. Since its 1948 civil
war, Costa Rica has experienced honest, competitive elections combined with a basic respect for human and civil rights. While one party
has dominated the legislature, there has been regular alternation in

power in the executive. Moreover, civilians abolished the national army in 1948 and have established control over decentralized military forces since then. The political democracy that emerged from the 1948 civil war, in short, has far surpassed that in other Latin American countries, both in quality and in longevity. Even though Chile and Uruguay had longer historical traditions of democracy, they underwent coups in 1973 that initiated over a decade of military rule. Despite comparisons with Venezuela and Colombia, Costa Rica has not endured the formal restrictions on participation experienced by the former countries—although, as we will see, restrictions did occur. Nor has it suffered recent coup attempts, as has Venezuela in the 1990s, or widespread political violence, as in Colombia.

Guatemala's political trajectory has differed substantially from that of Costa Rica. Guatemala has experienced four decades of direct or indirect military rule. Between 1954 and 1985, military officers assumed the presidency for all but one term, during which a civilian, dominated by the military, had almost no room to maneuver. The transition to civilian rule in 1986 has occurred in the shadow of a military that organized at least four coup attempts between 1986 and 1995. Military rule, however, has not been limited to control over governing institutions. The Guatemalan military has emerged as one of the more economically powerful and politically repressive in the region, using military and paramilitary institutions to control the civilian population as if it were an external enemy and dispensable labor pool. Consequently, Guatemala's human rights record has been notorious for its brutality. After the 1954 coup, the Guatemalan military perfected a system of repression in which military or paramilitary forces killed an estimated 100,000 to 140,000 people, razed 440 villages, and created close to a million internal and external refugees.[2] At the time of this writing, the Guatemalan military retained a disproportionate amount of power in a formally civilian government.

THE PUZZLE

Guatemala and Costa Rica represent Latin America's most divergent political regimes in the postwar period. Whereas Costa Rica has claimed the longest-standing and arguably the most well-regarded democracy in the region, Guatemala has achieved one of the longest and arguably the most brutal authoritarian rules in Latin America. Yet these two countries share a number of similar characteristics; they are roughly similar in terms of regional location, size, position within the world economy, and levels of economic development. The World Bank considers them both "middle-income economies" (see Table 1).

Moreover, we can discern that despite significant contemporary political differences between Costa Rica and Guatemala, the two countries experienced similar periods of political change and development up until the middle of the twentieth century. Following independence from Spain in 1821, the two countries followed broadly similar political-regime tra-

TABLE I

Comparative Data on Costa Rica and Guatemala

	Costa Rica	Guatemala
Population (in thousands)		
1960	1,236	3,964
1970	1,731	5,246
1980	2,284	6,917
1990	3,035	9,197
1994	3,347	10,322
Urban population (% of total)[a]		
1960	33.2	34.0
1980	43.1	37.4
1990	46.8	39.4
1993	48.0	40.6
Gross domestic product (GDP) per capita (in 1986 U.S. dollars)		
1960	1,332	1,020
1970	1,694	1,373
1980	2,222	1,732
1987	2,011	1,376
Percentage of economically active population employed in[b]		
Agriculture, 1960	51.0	66.5
Agriculture, 1970	42.5	61.2
Agriculture, 1980	30.8	56.9
Industry, 1960	18.4	13.5
Industry, 1970	20.0	17.1
Industry, 1980	23.1	17.1
Percentage of GDP from industry		
1960	14.0	13.0
1980	22.0	17.0
1987	23.0	16.0

SOURCE: Booth and Walker (1989:176, Table 2); Inter-American Development Bank (1994); Economic Commission for Latin America and the Caribbean (1995: 40–42, 173).

[a] The percentage of urban population throughout Latin America as a whole compares as follows: 65 percent in 1980, 72.1 percent in 1990, and 74 percent in 1993.

[b] The percentage of Latin America's EAP employed in agriculture compares as follows: 47.9 percent in 1960, 40.9 percent in 1970, and 32.1 percent in 1980. The percentage of Latin America's EAP employed in industry compares as follows: 20.9 percent in 1960, 23.1 percent in 1970, and 25.7 percent in 1980.

jectories, marked by seven decades of Liberal oligarchic and authoritarian rule (1870s–1940s), close to a decade of democratic and socioeconomic reforms (1940s–1950s), and a counterreform movement that overthrew the prior democratic regime in Costa Rica (1948) and Guatemala (1954). Moreover, in the nineteenth century, both countries developed agro-export economies that by the turn of the century revolved around nationally owned coffee production and internationally owned banana enclaves on the Atlantic coast. Yet, despite these parallel political and economic trajectories, by the middle of the twentieth century Costa Rica's and Guatemala's regime trajectories diverged; while the Costa Rican counterreform movement installed political democracy in 1948, the Guatemalan counterreform movement installed authoritarian rule in 1954 (see Figure 1).

From this broadly comparative historical perspective, one can discern that whereas Costa Rica and Guatemala experienced variations *within* broadly parallel regime trajectories of authoritarianism and democracy through the middle of the twentieth century, variations *of* regime outcomes followed on the heels of failed mid-twentieth-century reforms. The cycles of reform and reaction in the 1940s and 1950s were regime-defining moments in Costa Rica and Guatemala; the counterreform regimes that emerged not only diverged markedly from one another but also have endured longer than all other Latin American regimes, except for Mexico, in the post–World War II period.

PREVAILING EXPLANATIONS

Despite these parallels, accounts of Costa Rica and Guatemala have analyzed these historical periods in isolation from one another, arriving at particularistic explanations of Guatemala's and Costa Rica's postwar regime outcomes. The predominant view in the social science literature has concluded, with some notable exceptions, that structural factors— land-tenure patterns and/or the role of U.S. intervention in planning and subsidizing the 1954 coup—explain Guatemala's contemporary authoritarian rule and that culture or domestic leadership—a democratic tradition and/or the role assumed by José Figueres Ferrer in initiating and negotiating the end to the 1948 civil war—explain Costa Rica's political democracy. (Some scholars argue that an agricultural tradition of yeoman farmers explains Costa Rica's democracy, a point discussed and critiqued below.) As Remmer (1991) has remarked about democratization studies in general, these arguments, when viewed together, are incoherent and lead one to conclude that while actors are responsible for

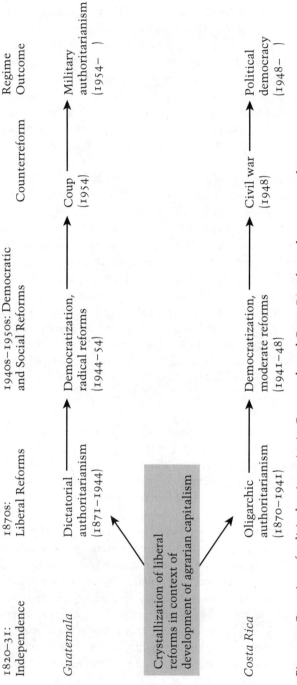

	1820–31: Independence	1870s: Liberal Reforms	1940s–1950s: Democratic and Social Reforms	Counterreform	Regime Outcome

Guatemala

Dictatorial authoritarianism (1871–1944) → Democratization, radical reforms (1944–54) → Coup (1954) → Military authoritarianism (1954–)

Crystallization of liberal reforms in context of development of agrarian capitalism

Costa Rica

Oligarchic authoritarianism (1870–1941) → Democratization, moderate reforms (1941–48) → Civil war (1948) → Political democracy (1948–)

Figure 1. Overview of political trajectories in Guatemala and Costa Rica from the 1820s to the 1990s.

the glory of democratization, they cannot be held responsible for failing to sustain it.[3]

The approach developed here challenges three prevailing arguments. I outline why these explanations provide limited comparative leverage to explain the founding of democracy and authoritarianism in Costa Rica and Guatemala, in particular, and across cases, in general.

Leadership or actor-oriented arguments, overall, have stressed the ability of political leaders to transcend structural constraints in order to found or sustain democracy. This type of argument is commonly cited to explain Costa Rica's founding of democracy in 1948. According to this approach, individuals have the power to effect regime outcomes; they can found democracy and compromise its endurance. Ingenuity and mistakes, therefore, can affect the founding and unfounding of democracy (Linz 1978; Di Palma and Whitehead 1986; O'Donnell and Schmitter 1986; Di Palma 1990; Higley and Gunther 1992). Linz, for example, argues that the failure of political leadership to address polarization has led to the breakdown of democracy. O'Donnell and Schmitter, and Di Palma, moreover, highlight the importance of political actors in military regimes and democratic oppositions who elect to form coalitions designed to transit from authoritarian rule: "The O'Donnell-Schmitter (1986) approach was to focus on the strategies of different actors and explain the outcomes as a result of these strategies. . . . The result was an intuitive micro approach often couched in macro language" (Przeworski 1991: 97). The preceding authors all focus on transition moments and elite interactions. Some focus on leaders, others focus more on individuals who create coalitions. In each case they analyze actors who attempt to sidestep conflict, by overcoming polarization and/or demobilizing civil society at moments of potential regime transition. For each of these theorists, democratic options remain open so long as wise leaders initiate wise moves.

Yet, by focusing on individuals, the moment of change, and efforts to redirect conflict, these choice-oriented approaches theorize neither the source of political conflict that generates democracy's overthrow nor the conditions under which democratization is likely. Broadly speaking, these arguments suggest that inadequate political leadership in polarized political situations leads to the breakdown of democracy, while political ingenuity leads to its foundation. The art of politics may indeed be the ability of certain leaders to overcome constraints. Nonetheless, individuals do not craft political coalitions and institutions in the absence of a historically defined context. Without understanding the shared conditions that generate polarization, these explanations remain ad hoc. They leave unexplained the underlying sources of conflict embedded in state-society and capital-labor relations, as well as the structural conditions within which and against which actors maneuver.

On their own terms, these approaches cannot really address the questions of which conditions tend toward democracy-founding coalitions, what space there is for reform, or why a given political outcome does or does not endure. In fact, agency-oriented approaches have difficulties explaining patterns of change versus continuity. If actors can effect change, why can't they do this all of the time? If change is always possible, then how can one arrive at an enduring outcome? And, if actors only experience the possibility to effect change at certain points, then how does one know that one has arrived at this juncture? Agency-oriented explanations, therefore, highlight the role of actors to make choices that shape the course of politics; in marked contrast with macrostructural discussions, they minimize their discussion of inherited historical institutions and turn Marx's famous statement from "The Eighteenth Brumaire of Louis Bonaparte" on its head.* Actors make choices in conditions they have created and can recreate. Yet to understand when and why an outcome does or does not endure, one needs to look beyond elite and/or social-movement actions to underlying structures of conflict, the ways in which collective actors negotiate or act on that conflict, and the existing political institutions that favor one outcome over another.

A second prevailing argument posits a link between patterns of land tenure and authoritarian outcomes. This argument draws on a tradition of comparative historical analysis that assumes historical institutions cast a powerful hold on the future and can foreclose democratic options for countries with the inappropriate set of historical conditions. The most common version suggests that more equitable land tenure tended toward political democracy in Costa Rica and that more concentrated land tenure tended toward authoritarian rule in Guatemala.

In its more sophisticated form, this type of argument draws from Moore (1966) and suggests that repressive forms of commercial agriculture in Guatemala explain that country's experience with authoritarian rule and that market forms of commercial agriculture in Costa Rica

---

*"Men make their own history, but they do not make it just as they please; they do not make it under circumstances chosen by themselves, but under circumstances directly found, given and transmitted from the past. The tradition of the dead generation weighs like a nightmare on the brains of the living" (from the second paragraph of the opening of "The Eighteenth Brumaire").

explain that country's experience with democracy (Stone 1983; Baloyra Herp 1983; Paige 1990). These overall patterns of agriculture are historically accurate in both countries, as discussed in Chapter 2. Indeed, the organization of agriculture did matter for the severity of authoritarianism in Costa Rica (1870–1940) and Guatemala (1871–1944). In Guatemala, landed oligarchs relied on the state to sustain a repressive labor market, while in Costa Rica the state did not need to repress labor to sustain the financial, commercial, and agricultural markets. These structural differences in the organization of the political economy and state-society relations formed the basis for arguments that Costa Rica had a better chance than Guatemala of establishing and sustaining democracy because of a more-moderate state role in sustaining the authoritarian regime, less-repressive economic relations, and a more-developed civil society—all of which would suggest that conflict would be less severe, multiclass coalitions more likely, and democratic evolution more imaginable.

The narrative developed in this book demonstrates that this was not unambiguously so. Guatemala's political economy was certainly inauspicious to democracy. But Chapter 2 reveals that market forms of commercial agriculture also coincided with authoritarian rule for more than seven decades and engendered a parallel cycle of democratic reforms and reaction. Neither Guatemala nor Costa Rica's nineteenth-century political economy appeared ready to accommodate democratic change; indeed, electoral changes in Costa Rica and Guatemala were accompanied by fraud, while the 1930s witnessed an authoritarian retrenchment in both countries.

As elaborated below, what would matter for regime outcomes was the concentration of economic power and the absence of elite accountability. The monopolization of economic power, whether in land for Guatemala's oligarchy or finance for Costa Rica's, was inauspicious for democracy—in large part because of the power the elite could wield and the interests it was committed to defend. We will see that Costa Rican and Guatemalan elites both mobilized against democracy to defend their economic privileges—despite differences in land tenure, the organization of labor markets, and the repressive nature of the state.

These observations suggest that one cannot simply infer political-regime outcomes from historical domestic structures alone. The organization of the economy matters and does weigh political development in certain directions—but not in any one-to-one relationship with regime outcomes. Most contemporary democracies had historically in-

auspicious structural pasts rooted in repressive agriculture and strong
landed classes, conditions assumed to be adverse to the maintenance of
democratic institutions. Some successfully founded enduring democracies while others did not. Hence, past structures do not simply determine future paths, and democratic outcomes do not just evolve. Political
actors must usher in these political changes. For democracy's endurance,
what mattered most was whether governing coalitions had the political
capacity to reform inauspicious structural conditions in enduring ways.
The second line of argument provides limited insight, however, into the
conditions under which actors can effect the structural changes necessary for democracy's endurance.

The third prevailing line of argumentation to explain Central American regime change draws on dependency theory and arguments about
U.S. imperialism. This analytical tradition has focused on international
factors—multinational firms and U.S. intervention—to explain the development of pervasive and harsh authoritarian rule in the Central
American isthmus. Dependency theory has been harshly criticized in
some cases and jettisoned in others for its failure to provide a clear and
compelling explanation of the diverse patterns of democracy and development in the third world. Nonetheless, studies of Central America often begin with the assumptions outlined by dependency theory. Indeed,
Guatemala is often presented as the clearest example of a dependent
country whose otherwise progressive democratic future was capsized by
an aggressive, anticommunist United States committed to maintaining
the dependent and inequitable basis of the economy.[4] As I discuss in
Chapter 6, the United States was actively involved in the 1954 coup that
toppled Guatemala's decade of democracy. However, it was not the only
or even the most important actor in the 1954 coup or in imposing an
authoritarian regime in the coup's aftermath.

From a comparative perspective, this international-level explanation
becomes even more suspect when analyzing Guatemala's contemporary
authoritarian rule and Costa Rica's political democracy. The two countries are similarly situated in the international political economy and
followed similar regime trajectories prior to the middle of the twentieth
century; arguments pitched at the international level cannot explain
both these similar and different political experiences.

Furthermore, Costa Rica and Guatemala experienced their democratic-
reform periods at different moments in world historical time. Costa
Rica, like most of Latin America, experienced political openings and closures in step with the democratic call in World War II and the backlash

caused by the beginning of the Cold War. Yet dependency theory cannot explain why Costa Rica developed an enduring democratic outcome, despite significant U.S. investment in banana plantations. Indeed, the United States played a minor role in shaping Costa Rica's democratic outcome. Guatemala, by contrast, experienced its political opening just as the rest of the region started to restrict democracy; it launched its most democratic reforms at the height of the Cold War. Had international factors determined regime development, Guatemala would have experienced the reform and reaction at an earlier date and would never have launched comprehensive political reforms in the early 1950s.[5] The narrative developed here argues that a subset of domestic actors created both the conditions and the call for an authoritarian solution. While the United States decided which military officer would first assume political office, it chose from among a group of military officers whom the domestic counterreformers were equally ready to back, in what they had already decided would be a military-governed regime.

In short, international factors did not determine regime outcomes in Central America, although they reinforced already existent counterreform movements in Guatemala. Hence, one needs to analyze domestic factors. This book follows Cardoso and Faletto (1979), who hold that international factors are primarily catalytic. They structure the export economy, shape the international political climate, and often underwrite capital and military alliances. But they do not primarily or singlehandedly cause either democracy or authoritarianism in the absence of domestic conditions that can found and sustain these regimes.

These three prevailing explanations provide limited comparative leverage to explain Costa Rican democracy and Guatemalan authoritarianism. This book does not narrowly embrace any of these approaches. Nor does it entirely reject them. Rather, it attempts to integrate their deepest insights to arrive at a more unified theoretical explanation of the conditions under which democracies are created and sustained in an age of mass politics.

The Framework

The argument developed here begins with the premise that the bread and butter of politics involves the struggle over controlling and gaining access to valuable material resources, political institutions, and ideas. Seen in this context, the most significant axiom for us to recognize about democracy is that it expands access to power and, potentially, to at least some of these resources. With the acquisition of democratic rights—including freedom of expression, freedom of association, and extension of the suffrage (assuming free, fair, and honest elections)—individuals gain, by definition, a political voice. They achieve the right to participate in elections and to try to influence the policy process. Democratization, therefore, provides the institutional mechanisms to try to reconfigure the existing production, allocation, and consumption of scarce resources, the political rules of the game, and the ideologies that are most powerful.

From this a second crucial fact follows, namely, that democratization in the age of mass politics dilutes the relative power of those political and economic elites and institutions that had previously defined the rules of the game and controlled access to resources. From this perspective, democratization poses a potential threat to these same elites. As coalitional members articulate and mobilize behind new ideas and reform policies, this threat appears more vivid. This is particularly so if demands revolve around redistribution. From these observations, we can draw several significant conclusions about what factors are likely to matter most for democratization and its endurance.

POSTULATE I: DISTRIBUTION OF RESOURCES

If we view politics as the struggle over (the production, consumption, and allocation of) resources, then we must begin by identifying the distribution of resources prior to democratization and the ways in which this given distribution privileges some groups over others. States and markets (by which I mean the organization of capitalist economies) have played a dominant role in configuring, institutionalizing, and regulating the distribution of resources and the property rights that uphold it. Analyzing the process of state building and market creation, therefore, can help to delineate these general patterns. State building attempts to concentrate and homogenize political control over a given territory (often at the expense of regional elites) and to develop a monopoly over the legitimate use of force.[6] The successful organization of the market and, more specifically, the means by which economic elites accumulate capital, in turn, can be viewed as dependent on developing state capacity to provide clear political rules, regulate contracts, provide infrastructure, and regulate labor markets.[7]

The first postulate of this work, then, is that one needs to analyze the complex of states and markets and the associated distribution of resources that results. This work makes no assumption that stronger states and more developed markets do or do not lead to democracy. States and markets do not necessarily distribute resources or shape interests in parallel or uniform ways. Nonetheless, an analysis of the ways in which states and markets (differentially) pattern social relations provides a necessary starting point. It helps to delineate the political institutions and distribution of resources that have undergirded authoritarian rule. It also provides insight into the individuals, political groups, or corporate networks that are invested in any given authoritarian regime and, therefore, least disposed toward democratization.

POSTULATE 2: COALITIONS

Coalitions matter. If politics is the struggle over access to resources, then we can understand the politics of founding and practicing democracy in terms of the political coalitions that are forged to control and gain access to those resources. Thus, I put forth a coalitional approach toward the study of regime politics. This is the second postulate of this book.

For the purposes of this study, coalitions are defined as alliances among social sectors or groups. They provide the organizational framework for delineating who sides with whom, against whom, and over what. Coalitions bring together groups or institutions with heterogeneous, divergent long-term goals that they are willing to sacrifice for some intermediate, collective goals. Coalitional members, therefore, do not necessarily espouse a uniform ideological position. The constituent groups do not necessarily intend to sacrifice their allegiance to existing institutional associations for the sake of the coalition itself. Indeed, coalitions draw their numerical strength precisely from the fact that they bring together distinct groups. Coalitions can organize joint electoral candidates or lists or they can initiate collective protests. But, in all cases, they present a reconfiguration of power between and among groups in politics that might in other circumstances take different sides or remain unmobilized.

It follows from the preceding discussion that the existing distribution of resources will provide insight into the coalitions that are likely to form. Historically defined institutions privilege certain social sectors as well as define and mediate the range of interests, distribution of resources, sources of conflict, and range of coalitional opportunities. Certain conditions encourage or discourage coalitions that will build democracy, that will reform institutions and structures in a way consonant with the maintenance of democracy, and that will be strong enough to sustain the democratic changes in the face of opposition.

In particular, the greater the concentration of resources, the more difficult it is to create a democratizing coalition. Dahl (1971) also noted that the more concentrated power is—in a given institution or class—the less likely it will engender or sustain a democratic outcome. This has been the case because where elites monopolized control over the state and/or the capacity to accumulate capital, three conditions obtained. First, these elites were rarely held accountable for their actions. Second, there was generally greater conflict and polarization as the less fortunate struggled for access and elites reacted to protect their status and property. Third, individual and collective actors confronted a limited range of coalitional possibilities for change because elite and nonelite actors shared few if any interests or goals in common; in other words, politics was perceived as zero-sum. Finally, the more concentrated political and/or economic power was for elites, the more likely these same elites were to view democratic politics—theoretically based on the institutional commitment to uncertain outcomes—as too much of a threat to their vested interests.[8]

POSTULATE 3: DIVIDING ELITES AND MOBILIZING MASSES

If the concentration of power has proven inimical to democracy, then it follows that the founding of enduring democracies entails breaking the political unity of the old elites and creating opportunities for new multiclass coalitions that include part of the divided elite and part of the "masses" or "popular sectors."* Neither elites nor the masses on their own can generate an enduring democracy. Elites by definition have disproportionate access to the economic resources, political contacts, and military power that are necessary for the success and stability of any new regime. They are unlikely to initiate a democratic process that provides the opportunity to dilute their status and wealth in the absence of social pressure from other sectors to do so. But the masses on their own cannot initiate democracy, because to exclude the elites as a class is to create a

---

*In Latin America, the term *popular sectors*—*el pueblo* or *lo popular*—refers to those sectors in society that have a tradition of being marginalized politically, socially, and economically. It corresponds to the informal sector—the rural and urban working classes—and parts of the middle class. References to popular classes do not mean that they are the most socially prestigious. As does the word *masses* with regard to European society, *popular sectors* here refers to Latin America's most populous yet historically marginalized sectors. See O'Donnell (1979: 288–91).

Organization of popular sectors and demands for citizenship	Publicly expressed political divisions within elite: YES	Publicly expressed political divisions within elite: NO
YES	Democratizing moment; possibilities to forge multiclass coalitions and initiate change of regime	Marginalization or repression
NO	Potential for transition of kind, from one authoritarian regime to another	Relative status quo

Figure 2. Social conditions and the potential for regime change.

formidable enemy with the power to pose a serious challenge to the regime itself. Hence, a regime-founding coalition including a portion of the elites and part of the masses is a precondition for founding an enduring political democracy. Moore (1966) expressed a similar insight when he said that one of the fundamental problems in the path to democracy in Europe was to ensure that the coalition among the crown, aristocracy, and bourgeoisie against the peasant and workers was not sustained.

It is important, therefore, to look at those factors that impinge on the political unity of the elite and those that foster or militate against a coalition between some portion of that elite and the populace at large. Figure 2 presents four stylized configurations that follow from this. Where the elite remains publicly united in support of the regime, a change of regime is unlikely; elites in authoritarian countries frequently hold widely differing positions, but they rarely express these differences in public forums. Confronted with a populace demanding change, a publicly united elite is more likely to engage in repressive than liberalizing tactics (as illustrated by the repression in China's Tienanmen Square in 1989 in contrast to the political liberalization in Eastern Europe in that same year).

A publicly divided elite, on the other hand, creates the possibility for change. The particular conditions under which elite unity breaks vary from case to case; disagreement over policies, struggles over leadership, ideologies, and revolutionary upheaval has divided elites that otherwise might have presented a publicly unified political position. What remains central, however, is that elites express these divisions in public forums—for example, by founding new parties or publishing an open letter—thereby creating additional latitude for opposition groups and a political opening to construct new coalitions.

Where the elite has divided, there is likely to be jockeying for power. Coup attempts and elite bargaining, for example, have effected a change of regime from one (form of) authoritarianism to another, but they have rarely led toward democracy in the absence of mobilized or mobilizable coalition partners. Where, however, a publicly salient division within elite ranks occurs in the context of a mobilized or mobilizable populace demanding inclusion, a democratizing moment is possible. Under these conditions, a divided elite has the opportunity to reach out to the masses to achieve a more competitive position vis-à-vis other elite sectors. Cross-class political alliance building, therefore, offers a rare opportunity for democratic reform when organized popular sectors are able to exact democratic changes in exchange for their political support while different factions of the elite compete to emerge on top. From this perspective, democracy is not granted by elites—even if elites play a central role in its formation—but is created in the process of struggle and multiclass coalition building to arrive at the most auspicious political arrangements, on which coalition partners rarely agree.

Hence, elites have rarely opted for democracy, and social mobilization by itself has not proven sufficient for the overthrow of authoritarian regimes. The analysis developed in this book challenges two commonly cited hypotheses about democratization, elite action, and popular mobilization: first, to the extent that political leaders create political institutions to channel popular participation *before* the rise of mass mobilization, they will ensure political stability; second, once popular participation is so channeled, political leaders will identify and/or create the political space to oversee the eventual transition to democracy. Political elites have used this line of argument to legitimate authoritarian rule and repression. However, comparative political history suggests that when political leaders have created institutions to restrict participation—either through co-opting mechanisms or through coercive means—popular organizations rise up, often with arms, with the hopes of transforming or overthrowing these leaders. Representative and stable democratic institutions are formed in tandem with mass struggles that shape the form and content of those institutions.[9]

The third postulate of this work, therefore, is that a move toward democracy is unlikely to occur without a simultaneous division within the elite and a mobilized populace. These conditions create the space for a democratic class compromise.[10]

POSTULATE 4: CIVIL SOCIETY

If a mobilized population can propel a divided elite toward democracy, then it also follows that a tradition of civil society augurs well for democracy.[11] *Civil society* refers here to the sphere of associations and social movements, which are independent of the state even while they may try to influence it. The development of civil society suggests that there will be demands for democracy that are necessary for a transition to democracy (assuming that democracy is not imposed by a foreign power as in postwar Germany and Japan).

Moreover, a tradition of civic organizing suggests that democratization can appear less threatening to the old elites than the image of a newly mobilized mass, new organizations, and new demands—some of which are likely to make more radical redistributive demands. When civil society is deep, elites have the option of forming alliances with middle-class sectors that are less likely to challenge property rights or to demand expanded rights for urban or rural working classes. When civil society is shallow, old elites are less likely to identify coalitional partners and more likely to identify an emerging civil society as a threat; in this setting, old elites are more likely to support if not engineer democracy's overthrow.

Finally, a tradition of civic organizing suggests that society, as a whole, has developed and normalized a certain set of practices—such as participation, compromise, and social trust—that are supportive of democracy. These practices are constitutive of enduring democracies and appear to be transitive from civil to political society.

THE DILEMMA OF DEMOCRATIC REDISTRIBUTION: POLITICAL SURVIVAL VERSUS SUICIDE

The previous postulates raise a dilemma. If democracy enables the open struggle over resources, new democracies confronted with the monopolization of economic power and high levels of inequality are likely to experience rising demands for redistribution—for example, land and tax reforms. The previous discussion suggests that redistribution can be both necessary and detrimental to democracy's endurance. On the one hand, the dilution of concentrated economic resources or power favors democracy—not least because it can result in making elites more accountable. On the other hand, these types of reforms necessarily impinge on the economic privileges of elites who are most capable of precipitating democracy's demise. Lowi (1964) anticipated this dilemma in his discussion of the American policy process. He wrote that redistributive issues engender polarizing conditions. They demarcate and crystallize antagonistic and enduring political coalitions, as elites battle to secure the existing distribution of resources while less-endowed groups mobilize to secure what they see as their due. Przeworski, writing about Latin America, also anticipated this dilemma by arguing that elite interests must be secured: "Successful transitions to democracy are necessarily conservatizing, because only institutional arrangements that make radical social and economic changes difficult provide the security that induces actors to play by democratic rules of the game. For democracy to be established, it must protect to some degree the interests of the forces capable of subverting it, above all capitalists and the armed forces."[12]

How does one reconcile the arguments that the concentration of resources is inimical to democracy and that democracy's endurance rests on leaving property relations intact? One argument, already discussed, contends that democracy is only possible in cases where resources are not concentrated. In this argument, the foundation of democracy is *easier* (although not automatic) under these conditions. Elites have less to lose, politics is less polarized, and demands are likely to be less threatening; structurally, redistribution is likely to be a less-demanding issue. The potentially polarizing conditions working against democracy's founding and endurance appear less onerous.

A second argument posits that elites retain a dominant position at the moment of democratization and hence help to define and delimit the appropriate political institutions and policy agenda. They secure protection of property rights in exchange for supporting democratization;[13] coalitional bargains take redistributive issues off the policy agenda and create institutional boundaries to delimit policy innovation. Both the first and second arguments assume that redistribution is political suicide for new democracies. Either redistribution is not a pressing structural issue (argument 1), or elites prevent it from becoming one (argument 2).

But democracies have occasionally emerged from inauspicious structural conditions, and elites are not always in a position to secure their property interests. This book explores a third argument to complement the first two. Reformers have successfully initiated redistributive reforms *in tandem with regime founding.* This book analyzes two cases where redistributive reforms contributed to the overthrow of the regime and one where it did not. In Costa Rica (1946–48) and Guatemala (1952–54), reformers implemented redistributive policies that contributed to their regimes' overthrow. In 1948, the Costa Rican regime-founding coalition implemented a redistributive reform and endured. The cases explored in this book suggest that redistributive reforms have been most successful when implemented during democratic transitions.

Regime-founding coalitions or transitional juntas had the political space and capital to act in extraordinary ways in these extraordinary times: political coalitions were still in flux, social pacts were being negotiated, the oligarchy was generally divided, institutions were being restructured, and the policy agenda was still being defined. Hence, governing coalitions could credibly dangle carrots on sticks. They could implement redistributive reforms that challenged elite property rights during the transition while promising to respect property relations thereafter. The promises appeared credible only insofar as elites believed that they would not be excluded subsequently from the policy process itself. In this sense, discrete and rapid reforms at transition moments assured the old elite that losses and policy initiatives were bounded, the price of a transition in which the limited losses of the present appeared more palatable than the more comprehensive and unlimited reforms they had feared under the regime that they had helped to overthrow.[14]

The rapid implementation of redistributive reforms, therefore, had to coincide with a process of inclusion that involved both the creation of and belief in formal and informal institutions for multiclass contestation, representation, and participation in political decision making and the trust on the part of these sectors that the state would continue to respect the institutions, rules, and regulations of inclusion. As a corollary, politically powerful sectors could not believe, therefore, that these institutions consistently favored one sector over others; in other words, this is an argument about believing that even if one lost out during the transition, one could still win later (Przeworski 1991: 30–31). Hence, structures of representation and elite perceptions of opportunities overlapped in the Costa Rican democracy that endured. From this perspective, rapidly implemented redistributive reforms plus assurance of elite inclusion were necessary to the endurance of new democracies born with concentrated economic power.

Whether governing coalitions pursued the strategy of rapid or delayed reforms depended on the organized interests, ideologies, and institutional support for any given set of reforms. Leaders could act only when they could capitalize on these factors. In their absence, no leader could push redistributive reforms through.

INTEGRATING THE POSTULATES AND PROPOSING A COALITIONAL FRAMEWORK

Democracy, therefore, is invariably determined by many factors. It is affected by the legacy of historical institutions, the organizational dynamic of political coalitions, and the context of reforms. This book will delineate the conditions under which each holds sway. In the process, it will argue that, while most historical conditions tend to push countries down one path, there are discrete moments at which coalitions of actors can reconfigure power. How is this the case?

To reiterate, a structural logic explains the conditions that have proven inimical to the founding and endurance of democracy: when economic and political power is concentrated, interests of various groups are sharply defined, politics is zero-sum, and powerful elites have many incentives to subvert or sidestep the democratic process when it threatens their property and influence. A coalitional logic explains when democratic transitions are possible: a political division of elites, confronted with organizing popular sectors, creates the conditions for democracy-founding coalitions; the longer the legacy of civic organizing, the better the chances for democracy's endurance. Coalitional politics, and not the agency of individuals or leaders, therefore, explain the politics of regime founding. As we will see in ensuing chapters, the nature of any new democracy rests on the distribution of power within the given founding coalitions.

These structural and coalitional arguments appear to leave little room for individual actors to reshape historical pathways. However, agency can prove paramount precisely at the political moment offered with a transition to democracy. It is during these brief and extraordinary times that actors are best able to redistribute otherwise concentrated *economic and political* resources. Sequencing matters. If actors do not reform these economic institutions as political ones are being reconstructed, they generally lose the capacity to do so without precipitating democracy's demise. From this perspective, it is best to reform and redistribute rapidly rather than to wait to do so. In the event that actors do not act at the moment of democratic transition, they will lose a historic opportunity to reshape institutions in an enduring way. In newly formed democracies, efforts to redistribute property after political institutions were reconstructed exacerbated political conflict, more clearly delineated democracy's enemies, and served as a catalyst for democracy's overthrow.

This book, therefore, does not accept the binary ways of thinking about democracy characteristic of much of the democratization literature that has urged theorists to choose whether structure or agency is responsible for democracy and whether all countries have a democratic future toward which the next generation can aspire. This study, rather, attempts to discern the conditions under which democratic options are possible or foreclosed. It identifies the successful and failed efforts by actors to overcome these constraints. Coalitions created at moments in which the elites are divided and the popular sectors mobilized provide an analytical fulcrum for mediating between the weight of structural conditions and the possibilities of individuals to initiate an enduring regime change. The cases of Costa Rica and Guatemala bear this argument out.

Organization

This book explores the origins of Costa Rica's transition to political democracy in 1948 and Guatemala's transition to authoritarian rule in 1954 by exploring three comparative historical frames. Part I analyzes the commercialization of agriculture and state building in the nineteenth century. These processes generated authoritarian rule and consolidated agro-export markets in each case but did so on the basis of a different role for the state in organizing economic production and different political spaces for the development of civil society. These differences explain the tendency toward military solutions in Guatemala and civilian solutions in Costa Rica, but do not explain regime outcomes. Rather, they prefigured the range of coalitional allies (particularly whether the rural sector was available for mobilization), strategies deployed, target of reforms and counterreforms, and depth of political and civil society by the middle of the twentieth century.

Part II analyzes the emergence in Costa Rica and Guatemala of parallel reform movements that attempted to replace nineteenth-century Liberal institutions with democratic ones. The three chapters in Part II present different but parallel analytical narratives for the mid-twentieth-century reform periods in Costa Rica and Guatemala. Chapter 3 analyzes the origins, strategies, and evolution of the democratizing coalitions that ushered in the age of mass politics—highlighting, in particular, their emergence once the traditional oligarchy had divided politically and popular sectors had formed incipient organizations. Chapter 4 addresses the varied democratic and socioeconomic reforms that these new coalitions legislated. While discussing the significant differences in the target and scope of reforms, I underscore parallel efforts to redistribute resources and challenge the economic power of each country's oligarchy. Chapter 5 focuses on the popular organizing that accompanied these reforms, demonstrating the ways in which the democratizing reform coalition engendered popular mobilizing and came to depend on it. Together, Chapters 3, 4, and 5 work as a unit to analyze how democratizing coalitions tried to effect change and why they were unable to sustain it in the face of opposition.

Part III analyzes the counterreform coalitions that founded and sustained political democracy in Costa Rica and authoritarian rule in Guatemala. In both cases, parallel counterreform coalitions overthrew democratizing coalitions, limited popular mobilization, and attempted to place limits on social and redistributive reforms. In this sense, the Guatemalan and Costa Rican counterreform coalitions were analytically equivalent. Yet they founded different political regimes. Ultimately, differences in the composition of the counterreform coalition—conjunctural differences in the unity of national elites, historically defined organizational capacities and interests, and the commitment to shared ideological goals—determined the founding of political democracy in Costa Rica in 1948 and authoritarian rule in Guatemala in 1954. The endurance of these two regimes, however, depended in large measure on the politics of the countryside, the focus of the final comparative chapter.

The chapters that follow, therefore, examine the successive phases of political development in Costa Rica and Guatemala with a view to indicating how the conditions conducive to or destructive of democracy were established in each phase and, more important, how these conditions interacted to produce quite different outcomes.

This book seeks a balance between modest and grand claims. On the one hand, it sets out to explain the origins of democracy and authoritarianism. It does so by putting forth a novel interpretation of Latin America's prototypical case of each, one that focuses neither on leadership nor on foreign intervention. These may play some marginal role, but this analysis contends that it can only be marginal—because democracy must be founded on domestic coalitions if it is to be sustained over any length of time—and that the crux of the issue is whether the conditions for such coalitions do or do not exist. Certainly a skillful leader can expedite or exploit these conditions, and an unskillful one can fail to do so, but most basic are the conditions themselves. And they are ultimately determined more by domestic circumstances, often with deep historical origins, than by international intervention.

On the other hand, this work attempts to transcend arguments that analysis must focus on either constraining conditions or mobile actors; rather, both matter. The basis of this unitary analysis—that is, the basis on which I argue democracy is founded—is the unity or division of elites and the coalitions among social groups. These can be affected by long-term structural conditions and by short-term arrangements, policies, or events. Thus, this analysis shows that both can be important and why they are important. It suggests that neither should be neglected: one cannot be a substitute for the other.

It is up to the reader to decide which of these claims is the more modest or grand. To the social scientist the theoretical claim will certainly appear more ambitious. To the Costa Ricans and Guatemalans with whom I spoke, however, the explanation of why one country went down the democratic path while the other took an authoritarian one appears the most important question of all.

PART I

The Liberal Authoritarian Period, 1870s–1940s

CHAPTER 2

Between Building States and Agricultural Export Markets

Costa Rica's political democracy and Guatemala's authoritarian rule were founded in the decade following World War II. The coalitions that engendered these different regimes, however, mobilized around vested interests and conflicts that had been institutionalized with the late nineteenth-century Liberal reforms.* This chapter explores the Liberal reforms in Guatemala and Costa Rica that institutionalized 70 years of authoritarian rule. The analytic narrative provides the comparative historical background to explain similar demands for democratic reform at the middle of the twentieth century and the different organized interests that were at stake.

The comparative historical argument of this chapter operates at three levels. First, this chapter argues that Costa Rican and Guatemalan Liberals pursued similar goals and initiated similar processes between 1870 and 1940. Liberal reformers founded authoritarian regimes in Costa Rica and Guatemala, which promoted state building and agro-export, coffee-

---

*The term *liberal* remains contested, with varied meanings over time and place. In this book I use the term in a historically and geographically delimited sense to refer to those political parties in Latin America—and more specifically Guatemala and Costa Rica—that used this name, the reforms initiated by these parties during the 1870s and 1880s, and the regimes that emerged from and rested on those reforms. When using the term with any of these three meanings, I capitalize it. Further, I refer to the decades from the 1870s to the 1940s as the "Liberal period" to identify the political group that originated these enduring institutional reforms—authoritarian rule, state building, and agro-export, coffee-based economies—rather than to highlight Liberal party hegemony throughout this period.

based economies. These broadly parallel regimes would spawn cycles of reform and reaction by the middle of the twentieth century as political coalitions emerged to challenge and defend the institutions established in the nineteenth.

Second, this chapter highlights differences in the types of states, markets, and societies that developed with the Liberal period. The role that the state assumed in upholding each economy affected the severity of authoritarianism in Costa Rica (from 1870 to 1940) and Guatemala (from 1871 to 1944). In Guatemala, a landed oligarchy relied on a repressive state to sustain a repressive labor market, while in Costa Rica the oligarchic state created institutional spaces for the growth of an incipient civil and political society. These differences led to a more coercive form of authoritarian rule in Guatemala than in Costa Rica. By the end of the Liberal period, the Guatemalan state politically subordinated the oligarchy alongside other social sectors, in contrast to the Costa Rican state, which created institutional arenas for elite organization and accommodation.

Third, despite varied markets and states, the organization of the economy does not explain the founding of political democracy in Costa Rica and authoritarian rule in Guatemala. In both countries nonrepressive and repressive forms of commercial agriculture coincided with authoritarian rule for more than seven decades; in the following chapters we will see that these divergent economies also engendered a parallel cycle of democratic reforms and reaction. Neither Costa Rica's nonrepressive labor market nor Guatemala's repressive labor market appeared ready to accommodate a democratic change in the late nineteenth and first half of the twentieth centuries. Hence, while the states and markets that emerged in Costa Rica and Guatemala between 1870 and 1940 would define the level of coercion during the Liberal period, they would also prove compatible with authoritarian rule, which endured for seven parallel decades.

With these three interrelated arguments in mind, this chapter examines the divergent markets, states, and societies that developed alongside parallel Liberal authoritarian regimes.

The Comparative Context

Liberal reforms institutionalized states and markets throughout Latin America in the nineteenth century. Drawing on ideas from the European Enlightenment, Liberals set out to build states capable of commanding a national military, governing a capitalist market, and integrating disparate political regions. While the ideas of Liberalism fostered a process of democratization in Europe and parts of Latin America, its institutions undergirded seven decades of authoritarian rule in Guatemala and Costa Rica.[1]

Liberal politicians in Costa Rica and Guatemala oversaw the foundation of a new cycle of authoritarian regimes, which would survive from the 1870s until the 1940s. Despite constitutional commitments to republican principles and institutions, such as unicameral legislatures and judicial branches, dictators came to dominate many of the Liberal governments. Three Guatemalans, Justo Rufino Barrios (1873–85), Manuel Estrada Cabrera (1898–1920), and Jorge Ubico (1931–44), as well as the Costa Rican Tomás Guardia (1870–82), promoted dictatorial political rule and the growth of a national military while disregarding electoral and constitutional procedures (Woodward 1985:166–67). Despite the existence of legislative and judicial institutions, ruling elites effectively circumscribed political participation through electoral fraud and a disregard for the rule of law. In both cases, Liberals engaged in an active process of state building and organizing the coffee economy.

These broad similarities in Guatemala and Costa Rica coincided, however, with significant and interrelated differences that would distinguish the countries' Liberal periods from one another and indirectly shape the cycles of reform and reaction in the middle of the twentieth century. Differences included the patterns of accumulating capital in the coffee export economies, the role assumed by the state in sustaining the economy and political order, and the ensuing spaces allowed for the development of civil society. These combined differences led to variations in Guatemala's and Costa Rica's Liberal political regimes, with dictatorial authoritarian rule in Guatemala (1871–1944) and oligarchic authoritarian rule in Costa Rica (1870–1940). As discussed in subsequent chapters, these differences provided the structural conditions within which and against which democratizing movements would emerge in the mid-twentieth century and attempt to implement political and social reforms (see Table 2).

The first significant institutional difference grew out of the organization of the coffee export economies that developed in the nineteenth century and that Liberals helped to consolidate.[2] In particular, the two countries developed divergent regimes of accumulation, that is, the primary ways in which each national elite accumulated capital and the state regulated labor markets.[3] Many studies of Central American devel-

TABLE 2

Attributes of State-Society Relations in the Liberal Periods of Guatemala and Costa Rica, 1870–1940

Attribute	Guatemala	Costa Rica
Authoritarian regimes	Dictatorial; politics is the preserve of one man	Oligarchic competition and collusion within oligarchic circles
Coffee economy: regimes of accumulation	Capital accumulation based on control of land; repressive labor markets; primary conflict between landed elite and rural labor force	Capital accumulation based on control of finance, coffee processing, and commerce; nonrepressive labor markets; primary rural conflict between elites in finance, processing, and commerce versus smallholders
State's role in establishing and sustaining economic order	State delivers land and labor to elite and represses conflict	State creates institutions to mediate and channel conflict; infrequently resorts to violence
Civil society	Restricted space for civil society, particularly in the 1930s	Incipient civil and political society; political input limited through electoral fraud

opment have focused on differences in Costa Rica's and Guatemala's land tenure and labor markets as a way to elucidate Guatemala's more conflictual and Costa Rica's more accommodationist histories. While differences in land tenure have been significant, scholars and politicians have tended to exaggerate the democratic basis of the Costa Rican economy by obscuring the bases of capital accumulation from which elites have derived economic, political, and social power. I analyze regimes of accumulation in the respective coffee economies to discern and compare the different bases of elite power and the associated distribution of resources, vested interests, and the role of the state in sustaining and mediating agricultural conflicts.[4]

The Guatemalan coffee oligarchy accumulated capital through control and ownership of newly confiscated land and through state-organized debt peonage of the largely indigenous rural population. Conflict emerged primarily between landowners versus rural workers and sub-subsistence peasants. The Costa Rican oligarchy, on the other hand, accumulated capital primarily through control over coffee processing and financial markets. The state regulated what were largely market-managed labor patterns. Conflict emerged between processors and financiers versus smallholders. In both cases, the concentration of economic power and ties to the state would prove inimical to democracy. Nonetheless, the types of rural conflicts that grew out of these divergent types of capital accumulation would appear rigidly zero-sum in Guatemala, with its struggle over land and access to labor, and more fluid in Costa Rica, where conflicts revolved around the terms of access to credit.[5] The ensuing differences in production relations would shape the associated rural conflicts and the types of Liberal states that would develop to sustain these divergent production relations.

The second significant difference, therefore, revolved around the emergence of different kinds of states in Costa Rica and Guatemala. With the Liberal reforms, Guatemalan and Costa Rican states centralized political power and assumed a more active role in managing social and economic affairs. In both cases, political rulers occasionally relied on the military to assert political control over other politicians and electoral contests. In Guatemala, however, dictators relied more heavily on the military as a means to maintain order in the countryside and underwrite the development of agrarian capitalism. The Guatemalan state deployed a coercive military apparatus to control or quash political and social organizing, to promote land concentration, and to deliver labor to coffee plantations. In the process, dictators came to dominate the Guatemalan state with respect to policy making and implementation. By contrast, the Costa Rican state did not actively repress the population in the name of agrarian elites. Rather, political elites primarily relied on civilian-dominated institutions to regulate production and to diffuse or channel conflict. In the process, the Costa Rican state became an arena for oligarchic competition, collusion, and accommodation; while the terms of this interaction could not be called democratic, they did create an institutionalized legacy of interaction between members of the oligarchy, who resorted to force in the last instance as opposed to relying on the military and the power of a dictator in the first.

Finally, between markets and states emerged a third significant difference between Costa Rica and Guatemala: the politically sanctioned space for the organization of an emerging civil society. The coercive state and its role in sustaining agrarian capitalism and authoritarianism impeded the growth of civil society in Guatemala among both popular and elite social sectors. By contrast, the nonrepressive form of capitalism and authoritarianism in Costa Rica permitted the growth of organized sectors, first among elites and later among others. In Guatemala, the powerful coffee barons ironically became extremely dependent for their economic livelihood and position on a succession of dictators who sustained repressive labor markets; elites were less likely to form participatory political and economic organizations. Throughout this period, the state inhibited the growth of popular organizations or civic organizations and, in the 1930s, actively repressed any attempts at popular or elite organizing, demonstrating the increased autonomy of the state from the elite itself. By contrast, the Costa Rican coffee elite became more economically independent from the state and played a more direct role in national politics. It formed nascent, if ephemeral, political parties and chambers during the Liberal period. Throughout this period, middle and popular sectors created civic associations—which were repressed much less frequently than their counterparts in Guatemala.

The Liberal period endured for seven decades. Indeed, with the economic crisis and political mobilization resulting from the 1929 depression, Guatemalan and Costa Rican authoritarian rulers in the 1930s continued to maintain a facade of democratic politics in which the citizenry elected a president as well as representatives to a unicameral legislature. In both countries, the Liberal regime attempted to bolster the shaken economy and, in the process, to diffuse the rural conflicts that had developed. The respective executives continued to manipulate elections and to employ massive fraud. In Guatemala, a dictator and his military apparatus staged periodic elections. In Costa Rica, a civilian oligarchy controlled regularly scheduled elections. Political differences in the 1930s between Guatemala and Costa Rica continued to reflect the respective state-society relations constructed with the 1870s Liberal reforms.[6] The coercive mechanisms to control political participation and civil society in Guatemala contrasted with civilian oligarchic efforts to minimize political participation in Costa Rica. The Guatemalan dictator, General Jorge Ubico y Castañeda (1931–44), was suspicious of the growth of civil society and repressed all forms of civic, economic, and political organizing through an increase in military control. This policy affected members of all classes, including the oligarchy. By contrast, in Costa Rica, the 1930s witnessed a rise in labor organizing and the founding of a communist party. Unions waged strikes and communists participated in elections. The authoritarian regime permitted this level of social activity but often prevented political popular leaders from assuming office or influence over political and economic decision making. This different construction of state-society relations set the terms for the strategies the mid-twentieth-century Guatemalan and Costa Rican reformers adopted, as well as the types of reform agendas they produced.

Guatemala

In Guatemala, Miguel García Granados and Justo Rufino Barrios together led the rebellions in 1871 that toppled 30 years of Conservative power and initiated 70 years of Liberal rule.[7] These men mobilized urban merchant capitalists and coffee planters from the western regions, who confronted what they considered to be unfair economic obstacles and insufficient Conservative commitment to the expansion of coffee production. This economic alliance placed the Liberals in opposition to the more established plantation owners and merchant elite who had benefited from and supported Conservative rule (Kauck 1988:146; Palmer 1990:124; McCreery 1994:172–73). As the Liberal period progressed, the coalition of interests that came together under the Liberal banner made demands for increased infrastructure, state aid in controlling and gaining access to labor, titling of unregistered lands, and government services (McCreery 1983:736 and 1990:105; Cambranes 1985:115; Dunkerley 1988:25).

Liberal reforms institutionalized a new and more coercive state role in promoting agrarian capitalism. The militarization of state power left the new oligarchy debilitated and dependent on a growing state bureaucracy to secure labor, promote land concentration, build financial institutions, and maintain "law and order." In short, these reform measures served to create the basis for an increasingly autonomous and coercive state, an economically powerful but politically weak coffee oligarchy, and a politically excluded and exploited majority (Handy 1984:50–58; Woodward 1985; Pérez Brignoli 1985; McCreery 1990). These institutions initially pitted landed elites against peasants and rural workers; they would eventually pit most of society against the state.

STATE BUILDING

Barrios ruled Guatemala from 1873 until 1885, when he was killed in a battle for Central American unification. His administration and those that followed introduced reforms that centralized power within the Guatemalan state. In contrast to state building in Costa Rica, Guatemalan Liberals consolidated the power of dictators (Barrios, Estrada Cabrera, and Ubico), providing few channels for organized and sustained elite participation in state offices and institutions. The Guatemalan elite supported this centralized state power, which sustained a redistribution of economic power that favored them.

To consolidate this state power, Liberals undermined the Catholic Church, the one institution that could challenge the Liberals' right to rule. The Guatemalan Catholic Church had been a formidable political institution, with a presence throughout much of the country. During the colonial period (before 1821) and Conservative rule in the mid-nineteenth century, the Catholic Church assumed a de facto role in the rural areas as a surrogate state. Indeed, Conservative governments had depended on the Church for its contact with the rest of the population (Woodward 1985:168; McCreery 1994:130–31). Liberals sought to undermine the Church's power, which had become fused with state power. In line with Liberal ideology overall, they accordingly forbade Church intervention in politics and asserted the state's responsibility to regulate education, marriage, and birth registrations—areas the Church had previously and traditionally dominated. Indeed, by wresting education from Church control and secularizing the University of San Carlos, President Barrios argued that one could build a moral, productive, and stronger society.

Liberals also oversaw the expropriation of Church property, including land and endowments, which undermined the Church's powerful economic position and ultimately benefited the coffee elites, who purchased many of these lands. Finally, Barrios sought to undermine the spiritual monopoly of the Catholic Church. He expelled some orders; some of the expelled clerics went to Costa Rica. He forbade the remaining foreign clerics from donning clerical garb in public and holding religious ceremonies in public. He monitored and, at times, banned religious processions. And, in the name of religious toleration, Barrios invited protestants to immigrate to the country. In response, the Guatemalan archbishop excommunicated Barrios, who, in turn, exiled the archbishop and bishops.[8] The Guatemalan Liberal state treated the Church more harshly than did the other Central American Liberal republics (Holleran 1949; Chea Urruela 1988; Handy 1984:62–63; Pérez Brignoli 1985:76; Woodward 1985:167–71; Dunkerley 1988:25).

The Liberal dictators sought to replace the Church's dominant role in the countryside through the centralization and institutionalization of military power. Barrios, for example, increased the policing capacities of local military chiefs and state political agents, who monitored local events on behalf of the dictator (McCreery 1990:110–11). Moreover, he professionalized the military with the founding of the military academy, the Escuela Politécnica, in 1873. The Escuela Politécnica subsequently trained young cadets and attempted to create a more skilled and loyal armed services.[9]

The Liberal period, as a whole, resulted in an increased commitment to a stronger military. Government expenditures for the Ministry of War increased more than ten times, from 327,779 pesos in 1870 to 3,737,657 pesos in 1910 (McCreery 1994:178). With a stronger and better financed military, the state penetrated further into rural areas to impose order at the same time that it regulated the labor market. This stronger military remained subordinate, however, to dictators, who continued to centralize state power in the hands of the executive himself.

PROMOTING AGRO-EXPORT PRODUCTION

If the Liberal period centralized political power in the Guatemalan state, it also strengthened a new commercial, coffee-based oligarchy.[10] With the increase in coffee prices (which had tripled in the four years prior to the Liberal reforms) and the decrease in cochineal prices, coffee producers rallied for increased support (see Table 3). By 1871, coffee totaled one-half of the country's total sales abroad (McCreery 1994:129, 161. By the end of the next decade, Guatemala emerged as the fourth largest coffee producer in the world (Handy 1994:9). Liberal reformers helped to create the infrastructure and context for the success of this new coffee elite.

In the 1860s and early 1870s, coffee growers had faced significant obstacles, including inadequate infrastructure, a scarcity of capital, and chronic labor shortages. Despite commonly held images of large land-

TABLE 3

*Guatemala's Coffee and Cochineal
Exports by Value, 1867–71*

(in pesos)

Year	Coffee	Cochineal
1867	415,878	1,068,047
1868	788,035	891,513
1869	790,227	1,266,613
1870	1,132,298	865,414
1871	1,312,129	876,025

SOURCE: McCreery 1994:129.

holdings in Guatemala, the late colonial and early national periods had not contributed greatly to hacienda expansion, and few elites seemed committed to the accumulation or modernization of property. Indeed, land values generally declined substantially in the period 1760 to 1860, as indicated by the resale of properties from this period (McCreery 1994:69–74).

Liberals sought to overcome these obstacles and to establish incentives to promote coffee production. They improved the country's infrastructure, including its roads, railways, dams, bridges, and communication networks.[11] By the end of the 1880s, telegraphic communication was possible throughout the country (McCreery 1990:110). Liberals also founded an agricultural bank and invited foreign investment. But most significantly, the government issued a series of measures to enhance the emerging coffee producers' access to lands and labor.

Coffee producers sought rich agricultural lands in the west and the Verapaces provinces to the north of Guatemala City. These regions proved particularly well-suited for coffee production. Indigenous communities, however, largely owned and/or cultivated these lands. Consequently, the Liberal reformers enacted a land reform, Decree 170 (January 1877). The decree abolished *censo enfiteusis*, which had enabled tenant farmers to rent communal land in perpetuity in exchange for a 3 percent annual tax (Pérez Brignoli 1985:76–77; Kauck 1988:89; McCreery 1990:106, and 1994, ch. 6). Liberals argued against communally held lands and claimed that the privatization of property would promote efficiency and agricultural development (McCreery 1994:51). Decree 170 led to the titling of much of the previously untitled, communal lands held in *censo*. Although the decree formally offered tenants the ability to buy the land they had been cultivating, the interest rates were too onerous for most indigenous cultivators. The decree, therefore, enabled the privatization and concentration of lands.

Decree 170 had its greatest initial impact in the areas most conducive to coffee production, along the Pacific slopes.[12] In these areas the coffee oligarchy displaced largely indigenous *campesinos*, absorbed their lands, and employed their labor (Pérez Brignoli 1989:84). Adding insult to injury, the money received for the sale of community lands was deposited in the national coffer; the community whose land had been sold did not receive any monetary compensation for these sales (McCreery 1990:106). Between 1871 and 1883, the state sold between 958,143 and 970,522 acres of legally untitled lands, or roughly 3.6 percent of the country's total area (Stone 1982:27; Dunkerley 1988:27–28; Pérez Brignoli 1989:84).[13] While Liberal reforms did not strip the indigenous communities of all forms of autonomy, they effectively limited land access and assured their availability as a temporary labor force.[14]

A foreign population, one neither indigenous, ladino, nor creole, overwhelmingly benefited from this increased access to land.* A foreign commercial sector grew in response to Liberal initiatives to increase the role of foreign capital in Guatemala. Miguel García Granados had argued against a strong role for foreign capital in Guatemalan commerce. Barrios's position, however, drew on the Liberal belief that foreign capital would promote economic growth and progress through investment in land as well as infrastructure. In 1877 Barrios stated, "One hundred foreign families were worth as much as 20,000 indians."[15] Liberals were successful in attracting U.S. investment in banana production, railways, and shipping, as well as German investment in coffee production. By 1885 foreigners constituted 83.5 percent of active import traders (Cambranes 1985:64–65).[16] And by the early twentieth century, Germans claimed the largest and most productive coffee plantations (Handy 1984: 66; Dunkerley 1988:29; McCreery 1994:233–34).

The growth of commercial coffee estates, in particular, required steady access to rural labor. The state coupled its land policy with efforts to create a larger labor pool. The regime sought unsuccessfully to attract European wage earners (Handy 1984:64). With the failure to attract immigrant labor, the Liberal state relied more heavily on coercive labor control of the largely indigenous, rural population, which constituted an estimated 64 to 69 percent of the total population between 1870 and 1880.[17] Liberals argued that the development of a capitalist economy with forced labor would civilize Mayan Indians. A government document from this period illustrates how Liberals justified this repressive labor strategy: "The only method of improving the situation of the Indians, of taking them out of the state of misery and abjection in which they exist, is to create in them the needs they will acquire by contact with the ladino class, accustoming themselves to work by which they can fill them, thus becoming useful to national agriculture, commerce and industry."[18]

To this end, the state decreed two important labor laws between 1877 and 1894—Decrees 177 and 243—that relied on different combinations of coercive labor control, including *mandamientos* (which organized

---

*In this book, *creole* refers to self-identified European descendants, *indigenous* refers to self-identified Indians, and *ladino* refers to mestizos (of mixed European and indigenous descent) or those who identify themselves as such. In Guatemala these terms have historically contingent meanings.

conscripted labor gangs for military service and road construction), vagrancy laws (which regulated those who did not work a given number of days per year for minimal wages), and debt peonage.[19] These three methods secured a cheap labor force for both the state and the coffee estates. They demonstrate the increased capacity of state institutions to penetrate the countryside as well as the increased dependence of the oligarchy on the state.

Guatemalan *mandamientos* and vagrancy laws enforced harsh working conditions. State projects led to increasing labor demands to build infrastructure and to serve in the military. The only legal alternative to working on these demanding state projects was to work for a plantation owner, one of the few employers who could afford to pay the money required to exempt rural workers from conscripted labor gangs. But the Guatemalan Liberal state also assumed an active role in providing a cheap labor force for the coffee plantations. Guatemala actively regulated and enforced debt peonage to a degree unobserved in other Latin American countries. General Barrios even obliged local political chiefs to aid landlords in their attempts to draft indigenous workers. State officials, such as the president, a minister, or a chief, commanded municipal officials, sometimes from the Indian communities, to deliver a determined number of workers who would labor for a predetermined wage, time period, and plantation.

Indigenous communities, however, also needed additional work. Given decreased access to communal lands, many peasants could not produce enough to sustain themselves throughout the year. As a result, they often incurred debts, which they then paid by working on coffee plantations.[20] The supply of peasants to plantations was facilitated by the fact that the season for coffee harvest occurred at about the same time as the dead season for corn cultivation in the highlands.[21] Low wages made repayment of debts virtually inconceivable, leading to a lifetime of indebtedness and a life of squalor. Debt peonage became the principal means to secure labor for the Guatemalan plantations (McCreery 1983:742). This process fostered the plantation owners' increasing dependence on the state to help provide needed labor and to build the infrastructure to transport their crop for export.

By the 1890s, the Liberal state regulated the labor force by mandating a work pass system. Those exempted from public work or military service had to carry the work pass, called a *boleto de camino*. If the authorities found an indigenous man without his pass, they would arrest him, send him to prison, and order him to perform public work. This system further bound workers to the plantations, since members of the landed oligarchy often bought *boletos* for those working on their plantations, running rural workers further in debt (Cambranes 1985 : 224). By the end of the nineteenth century, this policy depleted the labor source available for public works and the military. Consequently, only two types of rural workers—those who worked a subsistence plot of land on a plantation in exchange for the year-round labor and those who needed to work on a plantation to pay off debt—had to carry work passes (Cambranes 1985 : 277). Under these conditions, the state reintroduced conscripted labor gangs in 1897 (only three years after it had suspended them), a practice that lasted until 1920.[22]

Labor laws, therefore, compelled the indigenous population to work for the state or for plantation owners, which essentially became functional equivalents to the indigenous rural work force. Those who sought to avoid work on the plantations had three "options": pay off their debts (practically impossible for most), work on public projects, or try to escape the system (Cambranes 1985 : 224).

Despite harsh conditions associated with the system of labor control, overt incidents of indigenous resistance decreased in the late nineteenth century. Indigenous resistance generally became manifest less in collective protest or violence than through such everyday forms of resistance as evasion and negotiation.[23] Barrios effectively supplemented repression with tactics to co-opt and divide indigenous communities (Dunkerley 1988 : 26; McCreery 1990 : 108–10, and 1994, conclusion; R. G. Williams 1994 : 61–64). During the dictatorships of Barrios and his successor Estrada Cabrera, the state effectively secured and sustained a cheap labor force in times of labor shortage; through its local and national institutions, it seized many of the indigenous lands, coerced the population into debt, and enforced debt peonage. The Liberal reforms, therefore, increased state penetration of rural areas, decreased indigenous communal autonomy, and concentrated economic resources in the hands of the coffee oligarchy. In the process, the oligarchy came to depend increasingly on the Guatemalan Liberal state and its dictators to sustain the regime of accumulation in coffee production.

THE DEPRESSION: REPRESSING RURAL CONFLICT

The worldwide depression that began in 1929 highlighted the oligarchy's exaggerated dependence on the state to sustain repressive labor markets. A centralized state apparatus and the absence of developed civic associations enabled General Jorge Ubico y Castañeda to assume dictatorial powers. Although he won the 1931 presidential election in an unopposed race, he ruled as a dictator until 1944 (Grieb 1979:11).[24] As dictator, he addressed the economic crisis with increasingly repressive measures and, in the process, further centralized state power at the expense of even the oligarchy's right to form political or social organizations. Indeed, while the Liberal state continued to coerce an indigenous labor force in the countryside, it also repressed incipient urban attempts to form civic organizations. Eduardo Galeano's literary depiction of Ubico takes creative license to highlight the dictator's very real narcissistic and coercive efforts to govern Guatemala:

> General Jorge Ubico, Chief of State of Guatemala, governs surrounded by effigies of Napoleon Bonaparte, whom he resembles, he says, like a twin. But Ubico rides motorcycles, and the war he is waging has nothing to do with the conquest of Europe. His is a war against bad thoughts. . . . Against bad thoughts, military discipline. Ubico militarizes the post office employees, the symphony orchestra musicians, and the school children. . . . To expel the bad thoughts from the minds of the revolutionaries, he invents a steel crown that squeezes their heads in police dungeons. (Galeano 1988:104–5)

Ubico's showcase elections became a transparent effort to legitimate his dictatorial rule. On one occasion, in 1935, he engineered a constitutional reform in order to overcome limitations on serving two consecutive terms in office. The legislature received thousands of allegedly spontaneous petitions from 246 municipalities. These identically worded petitions called for a constitutional amendment to extend Ubico's term in office. Ubico therefore called for a national referendum on whether he should remain in office despite the constitutional article preventing reelection. The official results reported a near 100 percent popular mandate to suspend the constitutional article and allowed Ubico to serve an additional six-year term (Grieb 1979:119–21). On a second occasion, in 1941, the regime orchestrated another public call for Ubico's continuation in power. Ubico's cronies in the legislature voted to extend his term for another six years (Grieb 1979:270) (see Table 4).

If Ubico sought to construct an image of popular legitimacy, he also sought to ensure it with the centralization of state institutions at the national, regional, and local level. Engaging in what Joel Migdal calls the politics of survival, the dictator weakened competing branches of the state at the same time that he replaced elected officials with appointed ones. Afraid of losing power, he attempted "to prevent threatening centers of power from coalescing" (Migdal 1987:407). Ubico appropriated

TABLE 4

Estimated Percentage of Population Voting in Guatemalan Presidential Elections, 1865–1941

Year	Reported percentage of population voting	President elected
1865	0	Vicente Cerna
1869	0	Vicente Cerna
1873	0	Justo Rufino Barrios
1876	0	Justo Rufino Barrios
1880	3	Justo Rufino Barrios
1886	0	Manuel Lisandro Barillas
1891	4	José María Reyna Barrios
1898	0	Manuel Estrada Cabrera
1904	4	Manuel Estrada Cabrera
1910	4	Manuel Estrada Cabrera
1916	4	Manuel Estrada Cabrera
1920	13	Carlos Hererra
1921	13	José M. Orellano
1926	13	Lázaro Chacón
1931	14	Jorge Ubico
1935	39	Jorge Ubico
1941	0	Jorge Ubico

SOURCE: Ochoa (1987:884).
NOTE: Ochoa calculated percentages according to estimates of numbers of total voters over estimated total population.

power from the legislature, which became a forum to air and legislate his ideas. The dictator came to designate members of the legislature, who handily won state-controlled and orchestrated elections:

> The Legislature became primarily a rubber stamp, selected under carefully controlled balloting. The President personally designated its members, and the governmental apparatus assured their "elections" in accordance with what its officials regarded as the normal tradition of the nation. . . . As the regime wore on, only the official Liberal Progressive Party [Ubico's political party] bothered to nominate candidates. . . . Congress dutifully approved the bills submitted by the Executive, and then adjourned. (Grieb 1979:22)

Ubico ultimately suspended legislative assemblies, the last of which was held in 1932 (Villamar Contreras 1985:28), and replaced public officials—appointed and elected—with those personally loyal to him.

The dictator also created institutions to extend his jurisdiction over policy implementation and political officials at the provincial and municipal level. (Administrative regions in Guatemala are called *departamentos*, which I translate as provinces.) Different ministries nominally oversaw provincial politics, but in reality the president held the provinces directly responsible to himself. All provincial services, including revenues, the police, and public education, eventually came under the jurisdiction of the presidency (Cruz Salazar 1987:4). Moreover, Ubico reinstated laws that reinforced the role of the state in the regulation and supervision of labor. At the local level, he similarly undermined municipal powers with the 1935 Municipal Law, which replaced elected local officials with those appointed by the central government as *jefes políticos* or *comandantes de armas* (Villamar Contreras 1985:28; Gleijeses 1989a:35).

The centralization of power and assumption of authoritarian rule paralleled the penetration and control of people's daily lives, including that of workers, *campesinos*, and elites alike. Ubico, like Estrada Cabrera (1898–1920) before him, sought to control and weaken an incipient civil society both at the level of organization and of discourse.[25] Ubico justified the limitations placed on social, political, and economic organizing as a response to the threat of communism. He suspected subversive organizing everywhere, particularly among workers and intellectuals. This suspicion was taken to such an extreme that he opposed industry for fear of creating a working class that could foster a communist conspiracy to overthrow the Liberal regime (Quan 1972:218; Gleijeses 1989a:40). His opposition to industrialization was ironic insofar as Liberals generally equated industrialization with progress.

Ubico used the failed 1932 Salvadoran peasant uprising as an excuse to repress the weakly organized Guatemalan urban workers. He argued that workers' associations had prepared to overthrow the Guatemalan state. In light of the objectives and resources of the incipient workers' organizations, however, this hardly appears credible. In 1934, after a real but failed attempt to overthrow Ubico, the Guatemalan military and police again cracked down on workers, intellectuals, and suspected subversives. The security apparatus subsequently became more pervasive and oppressive (Grieb 1979:49, 118; Gleijeses 1989a:39; Pérez Brignoli 1989:109).

The dictator's efforts to delimit an emerging civil society also affected the oligarchy. He banned the elite agrarian associations that had formed in the 1920s while simultaneously promoting economic policies designed to improve the economy. Elites, therefore, remained politically subordinate to a state that acted to promote capital accumulation. Efforts to contain civil society coincided with limitations placed on discourse after 1932. Ubico banned from public discourse words that seemed to imply class struggle—including *obreros* (workers), *sindicatos* (unions), and *huelgas* (strikes) (López Larrave 1976:24; Gleijeses 1989a: 25–32). In fact, Ubico declared that from then on "workers" did not exist in Guatemala (Gleijeses 1989a:32). Those overheard using this vocabulary were often thrown in jail. Essays and literature produced during that time period illustrate the seriousness with which this mandate was taken and implemented as well as the fear that it generated.

Restrictions on social gatherings of any size and on discourse engendered a climate of fear that counteracted the idea of citizenship in Guatemala: "[In the thirties] there was no . . . citizenship. The dry rot of fear and of servility had infested everything" (Galich 1977:39). Guatemalans of all classes expected that anyone and everyone was a spy, actively listening to conversations and eagerly waiting to report on anything that could be construed as subversion. People began to refer to government spies as *orejas*, ears, to indicate the existence of a pervasive, semi-invisible spy network.

The dictator's interest in absolute control of state mechanisms and in demobilizing popular and oligarchic organizations coincided with his populist effort to generate support among the peasantry. In the first years of his regime, he commonly traveled throughout the countryside on his Harley-Davidson motorcycle. His occasional, friendly, and much publicized visits belied the existence and consolidation of a repressive state apparatus that controlled rural labor patterns.

Ubico increased militarization in his effort to centralize authoritarian rule and to control society, appointing military officers to replace local civilian officials and militarizing the schools, the post office, and even the symphony. In the schools, for example, he feared that intellectuals would instigate rebellion. Consequently, army officials became school principals, restricted curricula, taught students how to perform military drills, and commissioned graduates as lieutenants. The dictator similarly sought to stifle university activity by limiting the types of professional degrees offered (Palacios 1950:9–19; Grieb 1979:267–68; Gleijeses 1989a:36–39).

In short, Ubico strengthened the coercive branch of the state but essentially did so within the institutional parameters founded with the Liberal reforms, as practiced by Barrios and Estrada Cabrera before him. Ubico further entrenched authoritarian rule by simultaneously centralizing state power in the hands of a dictator and stifling efforts to form civic associations. While delimiting the political power of the oligarchy, a power briefly achieved in the 1920s, Ubico revived the practice by Guatemalan Liberal rulers of subordinating the formal presence of the oligarchy in the regime while implementing economic policies in its name.

Ubico's commitment to centralizing state power at the expense of civil society coincided with a commitment to strengthen Guatemala's economy. The Great Depression had provoked a precipitous decline in coffee prices. Given that coffee and bananas combined accounted for over 90 percent of export earnings in the 1920s, the collapse of international commodity prices and markets reverberated harshly in Guatemala; coffee prices, which had peaked in the 1920s, fell to one-third their market value by the first few years of the 1930s and remained low throughout the decade (Bulmer-Thomas 1987, ch. 3; Dunkerley 1988, ch. 3; Torres Rivas 1991:71). Faced with the economic crisis and significant financial obligations, it appears that many Guatemalan landholders were forced to sell their properties (R. G. Williams 1994:172–73). In addition to this dramatic drop in market prices a contraction in monetary circulation occurred. By 1931, Guatemala's deficit had risen to $2,518,857, totaling about 20 percent of total expenditures (Poitevin 1977:49; Grieb 1979:56). The government, behind on payments, had amassed a large floating debt of around $5 million. At the end of 1930 a newspaper report indicated that the National Treasury had only $27 (Grieb 1979:56).

Confronted with this disastrous economic situation, Ubico pledged in his 1931 presidential campaign to overcome the detrimental consequences of the Depression. He called for an honest and efficient fiscal reorganization of the country, a balanced budget, and the development of infrastructure to spur economic development through the expansion of areas previously uncultivated and/or inaccessible to the market (Grieb 1979:10–11).[26] Ubico argued that private initiative on the part of the landowners would increase agricultural production, and he limited government services to ad hoc measures, including the distribution of better seeds and agricultural implements (Grieb 1979, ch. 10). Nonetheless, Ubico did implement new coercive state mechanisms to control the indigenous rural population and to secure access to an ample and cheap work force.

State efforts to regulate labor patterns reinforced rather than muted conflict between the rural work force and the landed oligarchy, while increasing the latter's dependence on the state for capital accumulation. The state legislated three new measures that provided virtually free labor to the state and to the coffee plantations. The new highway tax required that every man provide two weeks of free labor to build or maintain the roads. The state exempted those who paid two quetzales, equivalent to two dollars. Rural day workers, primarily indigenous, received on average about one quetzal a week for their labor. Consequently, most indigenous men, unable to afford the exemption fee, had to provide two weeks of free labor to the state. Those who worked on the public roads received neither a wage for their two weeks of labor nor any meals during the daily work hours of their public service (Grieb 1979:129; Bulmer-Thomas 1987:72). Along with the highway tax, Ubico enacted a public-works program that increased state regulation of labor. The state sought to construct government buildings, including the national palace, the post office, and the police station, that were elaborate structures and entailed substantial labor and resources. Although the government did pay for over half of the labor force, it required that municipalities provide volunteers to the construction efforts, thereby alleviating the construction cost of these large, ornate government buildings (Grieb 1979:165).

Finally, Ubico issued two decrees in 1934 that ostensibly liberated the indigenous from the vagaries of previous labor practices and regulated labor delivery to the coffee farms. Decree 1995 set the terms for the abolition of debt peonage. It stipulated that plantation owners had two years to exact debt payment from rural workers; after that two-year period, debts incurred through debt peonage would be cancelled (McCreery 1983:757, and 1994:315). The regime declared that the abolition of debt peonage would benefit workers, and, in fact, wages increased for a brief time, although these increases did not substantially improve the material conditions of workers (Grieb 1979:40; Handy 1984:98). Jim Handy argues that a number of plantation owners no longer perceived debt peonage as the most efficient system and were therefore calling for a change of labor practices: "Debt bondage was not particularly effective and proved costly in the initial outlay of cash required to entrap the workers" (Handy 1984:98).

Decree 1996 replaced the practice of debt peonage with a vagrancy law that ultimately created a more systematic and cheaper form of labor delivery to the plantation owners. The law stated that all men, indigenous and ladino, must have the capability to support themselves. Those men who did not work in certain professions, did not attain a certain level of income from business, or who did not cultivate a fairly large amount of land, were considered vagrants. Vagrants identified by the state had to deliver their labor for 100 to 150 days a year to any plantation owner.[27]

Given that the coffee harvest took place during approximately a three-month period, the delivery of 100 days of labor in exchange for sub-subsistence wages proved more than ample for the coffee oligarchy (Handy 1984:98). "Labor had become 'free' and obligatory" (McCreery 1983:757). The state obliged "vagrants" to carry small books, *libretos*, in which plantation owners were to enter the number of days worked. The booklet provided a means for the state to control rural labor patterns and for plantation owners to exact additional free labor simply by refusing to enter the correct number of days worked. The new law also required all indigenous men to carry a registered identity card (*cédula de vecindad*) (McCreery 1994:304). The vagrancy law affected all poor rural workers, both indigenous and ladino.

The state assumed additional responsibility for coercively enforcing the vagrancy law. Guatemala developed a full-time rural police in addition to its already-established militia and treasury police. Policemen could and often would detain indigenous men to examine their booklets. If state officials found that workers had not worked the required number of days, they sentenced rural laborers either to work on a plantation or to jail (McCreery 1994:304, 317–18), where they had to perform forced labor anyway.

In short, the vagrancy laws assured an ample and cheap labor supply for the landowners and state while simultaneously increasing state-coerced control over the rural indigenous population. This extreme control over rural labor, coupled with efforts at state centralization and control over civil society, effectively limited rural organizing, political participation, and attempts to voice discontent. Ubico further restricted the space for organizing rural workers by granting the oligarchy additional leeway to act as it pleased on its own farms. Decree 1816, in April of 1932, extended landowners' legal right to carry and use arms in order to protect their lands and safety. The decree legalized the right of agricultural elites to kill rural laborers, as long as the murder occurred on the former's private property (Grieb 1979:40; Handy 1984:98; Gleijeses 1989a:34, and 1991:13).

Finally, Ubico, like his Liberal predecessors, maintained a firm commitment to maintaining and attracting foreign investment, particularly by the U.S.-owned banana company, the United Fruit Company (UFCO).[28] Indeed, private U.S. firms came to control the banana sector, railroads, ports, and electricity companies.[29]

The Guatemalan Liberal reforms institutionalized dictatorial authoritarian rule and agro-export markets predicated on extreme inequality of resources and a coercive state. To consolidate dictatorial powers and oligarchic regimes of accumulation, the state coerced the majority of the indigenous population and quashed most efforts to form urban and rural civil associations. The landed elite, however, never assumed political control, despite its extensive socioeconomic power, but instead depended on dictators and their militaries to provide the needed infrastructure to transport harvests and to control labor. In the end, the Guatemalan landed coffee-elite became extremely dependent on the state, not only for the initial agrarian reforms that led to increasing privatization and concentration of lands, but even more so for rural labor control and delivery. From 1873 to 1944, these conditions supported three dictators—Barrios (1873–85); Estrada Cabrera (1898–1920); and Ubico (1931–44)—who jointly ruled for 47 out of the 71 years of the Liberal period.

While the alliance between Guatemala's landed elite and its military dictators tended inevitably toward authoritarian rule, this was not the only condition that could lead in that direction. As the next section emphasizes, less-coercive forms of capital accumulation and labor control, and other types of elite-state relations, undergirded 70 years of authoritarian rule in Costa Rica as well. The next section illustrates that the less-coercive form of commercial agriculture shaped and was supported by the emergence of authoritarian rule by Costa Rica's collusive oligarchy.

Costa Rica

General Tomás Guardia launched a successful coup on April 27, 1870, and assumed dictatorial power in Costa Rica for the next 12 years (1870–82). As the country's military hero in the 1856 war against William Walker, and later as the first Liberal leader, Guardia developed a historical legacy as a progressive dictator, particularly when compared with General Barrios in Guatemala. From a comparative perspective, both Liberal dictators stand out for having engaged in a process of state building that strengthened the state's coercive apparatus and increased its capacity to generate revenues. These political institutions sustained seven decades of authoritarian rule in each country.

Costa Rican Liberals followed a more moderate course than their Guatemalan counterparts. In governing the polity, economy, and society, the state created institutional arenas to channel and address conflict. This institutional arrangement allowed for the formation and expression of varied interests and the diffusion of conflict in rural areas. In the process the Costa Rican oligarchy managed to develop both as an economic and political class. Like its Guatemalan counterpart, it had developed an economic monopoly in coffee—although it did so on the basis of finance, commerce, and coffee processing. But unlike its Guatemalan counterpart, it did not depend on state coercion to sustain its economic position. Less dependent on the military, the Costa Rican coffee oligarchy began to organize in and through the state to sustain its privileged economic and political standing. Throughout the Liberal period, the Costa Rican oligarchy succeeded in blending Liberal discourse with oligarchic control and electoral fraud. In short, even with a less-coercive state and form of agriculture, the Liberal reforms institutionalized authoritarian rule for seven decades.

In the 1940s Costa Ricans would demand democratization. To explain the origin of these demands and the direction they took, it is essential to analyze the institutions against which they reacted and the interests that were at stake.

STATE BUILDING

In the decade following his assumption of dictatorial powers, General Guardia professionalized and strengthened the military to increase his capacity to check against internal (personal) and external (national) enemies. He increased the percentage of the state budget directed to the military from 15 in 1875 to 36 in 1879. And, in conjunction with Lorenzo Montúfar, his minister of war, he set out to professionalize the military, composed then of a small core of 500 men and supplemented by a militia of 20,000. While he strengthened the military as a force against Nicaragua and Guatemala, he also used it to defend himself against occasional coup attempts (Vega Carballo 1981:251, 269). While the size of the military would in subsequent years eventually increase and then return to its 1870 levels, the police force increased incrementally throughout the Liberal period (see Table 5).

As a reflection of this increased but comparatively mild militarism, military men—General Tomás Guardia Gutiérrez, General Próspero Fernández Oreamuno, and General Bernardo Soto Alfaro—assumed the executive office during the first decades of the Liberal reform period. Guardia was the only one to see battle, but all three wore military uniforms at all public events (Stone 1982:125).

If Guardia successfully increased the power of the military during the first Liberal decade, the Costa Rican army assumed a limited role in Costa Rican politics for the rest of the Liberal period. The military tended to intervene at moments of intra-oligarchic conflict and often

TABLE 5

Estimated Number of Members in Costa Rica's
Army and Police, 1870–1940

Year	Army	Police	Year	Army	Police
1870	500	n/a	1921	500	828
1915	1,000	695	1922	500	822
1918	5,000	782	1932	500	753
1920	1,000	846	1940	544	947

SOURCES: Archivos Nacionales de Costa Rica, Congreso Constitucional 19570, *Acuerdo* 3, Aug. 24, 1940; Vega Carballo (1981); Muñoz Guillén (1990); Lehoucq (1922:76).

tilted the political balance in favor of candidates favored by Liberal politicians. However, unlike its Guatemalan counterpart, the Costa Rican military did not penetrate the countryside or the cities to check the emergence of civil society or to enforce coercive labor markets. As discussed below, Costa Rican political parties came to dominate the authoritarian politics that emerged in the decades following Guardia's dictatorship. In the process, Liberals created largely noncoercive mechanisms to contain the influence of the increasingly organized civil society that they had fostered.

The process of state building during the Liberal period also dramatically increased the state's capacity to collect revenues: from 1,663,774 colones in 1871 to 3,164,051 colones in 1880 (see Table 6). In turn, this increase in state revenues helped to fund the construction of infrastructure necessary for the state to govern the country effectively and to expand coffee markets. Railroad tracks to the Atlantic were completed by 1890. The port of Limón was completed in 1870. Moreover, increased state revenues allowed for the expansion of the small public sector; from 1,683 government workers in 1875, Guardia oversaw an increase to 2,118 in 1881 and 2,310 in 1882; in the years following his dictatorship, the public sector continued to grow to 3,390 workers in 1900, 5,557 in 1920, and 7,173 public employees in 1930. Guardia also oversaw an increase in the number of state ministries and secretariats in such areas as foreign relations, development, commerce, war, and marinas. This process of state building depended on a strong economy. With the economic contraction between 1882 and 1887, the state was forced to reduce the salary of public employees by 10 percent and to decrease the number of ministries and military expenses (Vega Carballo 1981 : 271–75, 306).[30]

Finally, a fundamental tenet of Liberal parties and the process of state building consisted of the commitment to separate church and state. Costa Rican Liberals pursued this goal by guaranteeing religious tolera-

TABLE 6

Costa Rican State Revenues, 1866–90

(*in colones*)

Year	Revenues	Year	Revenues
1866	1,095,465	1879	2,525,726
1867	1,295,884	1880	3,164,051
1868	1,000,172	1881	n/a
1869	1,001,567	1882	1,550,020
1870	1,078,123	1883	1,730,794
1871	1,663,774	1884	2,611,693
1872	2,500,426	1885	2,387,290
1873	2,812,584	1886	2,435,189
1874	2,588,027	1887	n/a
1875	2,396,156	1888	n/a
1876	2,379,432	1889	4,184,846
1877	3,924,956	1890	5,624,577
1878	2,803,851		

SOURCE: Vega Carballo (1981:271–72).

tion in the 1871 Constitution and, therefore, adopted a more moderate position toward the Catholic Church than did Guatemala; the Catholic Church in Costa Rica had not wielded the same type of economic or spiritual power as it had in Guatemala, where it had developed a stronger base during the colonial period in Guatemala City, the center of the colonial administration for the Central American isthmus. Early Costa Rican Liberals, therefore, initiated the process of state building and the construction of infrastructure without undermining the Church. In fact, some of the clerics from other countries in the isthmus traveled to Costa Rica to take advantage of political exile offered by Costa Rica's Liberal dictator Tomás Guardia.

BETWEEN MARKETS AND STATES: A NASCENT POLITICAL AND CIVIL SOCIETY

Guardia's Liberal dictatorship gave way to an authoritarian regime defined by oligarchic politics. The Liberal leaders who rose alongside and following the Guardia dictatorship are commonly referred to as the "Olympians" or the "Generation of 1888." They came to dominate politics over the five decades following Guardia's death. In the process, they successfully appealed both to the Costa Rican coffee oligarchy and to other social classes: "Their commitment to free enterprise won the support of the coffee barons, while the popular classes venerated them as new patriarchs" (Ameringer 1982:20). While they adopted harsher anticlerical positions following Guardia's death in 1882, and relied less on the military than had Guardia, they sustained the basic institutional parameters for authoritarian rule and legitimated these practices with reference to the Liberal constitution.[31]

The Costa Rican Liberals, however, struck a different balance between restrictive oligarchic and more inclusive mass politics than did the Guatemalan Liberals. In Guatemala, the authoritarian regime following the Liberal reforms restricted political participation among the popular sectors, and at times among the oligarchy, and reserved politics for a succession of dictators. In Costa Rica, by contrast, the Liberal dictatorship of Tomás Guardia gave way to an authoritarian regime characterized by oligarchic collusion, ephemeral political parties, and fraudulent electoral politics. Hence, a number of Costa Rican oligarchs, rather than a single dictator, dominated politics during the Liberal period. Rodrigo Facio, a renowned Costa Rican intellectual, argued that Liberals put an end to "nascent militarism."[32] However, this too would be an exaggeration of the ability and desire of the Liberal politicians to transcend occasional reliance on the military when convenient and politically advantageous to do so. Presidents declared states of siege seventeen times within the first 22 years of the Liberal period. Indeed, the military intervened sporadically throughout the Liberal period. At least four coup attempts and between 11 and 22 revolts attempted to overthrow the central government between 1889 and 1948. Furthermore, presidents regularly resorted to violence and fraud to shape electoral outcomes (Creedman 1971:32–36; Oconitrillo 1981; Vega Carballo 1981; Lehoucq 1991, and 1992:30, 33, 85). Theodore Creedman (1971) points out that

> in summation, of the twelve elections between 1889, when the big change [toward democracy] supposedly took place, and 1936, only four elections (1910, 1920, 1928, and 1936) could be said to have been untainted. Three (1890, 1984, and 1932) were accompanied by revolution or serious uprisings. The remaining five (1898, 1902, 1906, 1914, 1924) were the results of continuismo (the unconstitutional prolongation of a term of office), illegal imposition of candidates, or other illegal procedures. (52–53)

It should be emphasized, however, that in contrast to other Latin American countries, Costa Rica never had a large military. The active armed forces claimed a meager 500 people by 1940 out of an estimated population of 300,000.[33]

The formal political arena in Costa Rica institutionalized both a public commitment to more inclusive participation and yet a limitation on that influence through oligarchic collusion and electoral manipulation. With political institutions weighted in their favor, the Olympians dominated the Liberal period until the early 1940s. Between 1906 and 1936, two men alone, both from the Generation of 1888, dominated the presidency: Cleto González Víquez and Ricardo Jiménez Oreamuno, who served three terms each as president. The Liberal period did include presidents from a range of parties, including Partido Civilista, Partido Unión Nacional, and Partido Republicano Nacional. Indeed, citing the Conservative Party's victory in the 1889 elections, traditional historiography has argued that the Liberal period was truly democratic. However, the victorious parties differed little on ideological grounds, and, more important, they generally followed the dictates of those who had nominated them for office, perpetuating a Liberal hegemony throughout this period. Oconitrillo (1981:43–48) recounts, for example, the intrigue surrounding the 1906 presidential elections:

> In this campaign, the political parties did not have well-defined platforms or principles. The political groups lacked cohesion. They were looking primarily for the predominance of a social club rather than ideological principles. They did not worry about social issues. Liberalism satisfied everyone. . . . In 1905, there was no struggle for principles, much less ideologies. Politics revolved around the personality of each of the five candidates. (Oconitrillo 1981:43)

When it became unclear whether Cleto González Víquez would win the 1906 elections, the government suspended individual guarantees, imprisoned and then exiled three of the presidential candidates on alleged charges of military conspiracy, and held a second round of elections, which González Víquez won. It was subsequently rumored that a secret pact had been signed in which former president Rafael Iglesias had agreed to hand the presidency over to Ascensión Esquivel in 1902 with the proviso that Esquivel would turn the presidency over to González Víquez in 1906.

Recent historiography has further highlighted the recourse to fraud and absence of elite accountability. Samper's (1988) essay on sociopolitical forces and electoral processes analyzes Costa Rican elections up to 1936 and concludes that electoral fraud, far from an aberration or imperfection, was an integral part of the electoral process. Political parties first emerged in Costa Rica in 1889 around election time. These parties, however, were not permanent, ideologically defined organizations but rather temporary vehicles created to mobilize electoral support around a candidate from the dominant agro-export class (Stone 1982:40; Woodward 1985:167; Samper 1988; Lehoucq 1992). In this context, the oligarchic political parties that had emerged following the Liberal reforms remained personalistic vehicles that vied for access to state resources and for influence over decision making. They emerged with the announcement of elections and just as quickly receded after the elections. Fraud continued to constitute an integral part of the electoral process in Costa Rica, most often through the annulment of votes. The party in power often used state officials to advance its campaigns, and elites remained unaccountable for their fraudulent actions (Creedman 1971:32–36; Stone 1982; Bulmer-Thomas 1987:18; Samper 1988; Cerdas Cruz 1991: 278). Oconitrillo (1981), in his anecdotal discussion of the elections that transpired during the Liberal period, highlights one example of elite collusion in electoral fraud after another.

Despite the elite nature of politics, the Costa Rican regime sustained an aura of democracy in the 1930s. In contrast to Guatemala's, Costa Rica's government respected alternation in power, maintained civilian control, and allowed more space for civic, political, and economic organizing by all classes, including the working class. This nonmilitarized, more open and inclusive political space institutionalized white male participation in a political system that successfully channeled popular participation but prevented any substantive popular access to political resources or decision-making arenas.

Liberal attitudes toward suffrage highlighted this internal tension between expanding mass politics and state control. Oligarchic political parties passed legislation extending the suffrage and the terms of participation. Legislation in 1909 replaced the prior practice of national appointment of municipal leaders with local elections (Stone 1982:222– 23; Winson 1989:26). Liberals passed the direct vote in 1913 and the secret vote in 1928, although universal suffrage would have to wait until 1949. While these changes expanded the electorate, as illustrated by Table 7, their effective impact on electoral outcomes was limited by the continued resort to fraud.

PROMOTING AGRICULTURAL EXPORT

Costa Rican Liberals articulated a commitment to economic progress, focusing particularly on the development of the coffee export economy. This commitment was not surprising, given Costa Rica's historically impoverished economy prior to the introduction of coffee in the 1820s and 1830s and the central place it had assumed thereafter.[34] Indeed, by the second half of the nineteenth century, coffee had come to dominate Costa Rican exports, representing 75 to 95 percent of the total value (Dunkerley 1988:20).

TABLE 7

Estimated Percentage of Population Voting in
Costa Rican Presidential Elections, 1872–1940

Year	Reported percentage of population voting	President elected
1872	0.2	Tomás Guardia
1876	0.2	Aniceto Esquivel Sáenz
1882	0.2	Próspero Fernández Oreamuno
1886	0.2	Bernardo Soto
1890	0.2	José Joaquín Rodríguez
1894	0.2	Rafael Iglesias
1898	0.2	Rafael Iglesias
1902	0.2	Ascención Esquivel Ibarra
1906	0.2	Cleto González Víquez
1910	0.2	Ricardo Jiménez
1914	0	Alfredo González Flores
1919	11.3	Julio Acosta
1923	15.7	Ricardo Jiménez
1928	14.6	Cleto González Víquez
1932	14.7	Ricardo Jiménez
1936	15.6	León Cortés Castro
1940	17.2	Rafael Angel Calderón Guardia

SOURCE: Ochoa 1987:876, Table 3405.
NOTE: These are estimated figures, which do not coincide with those provided by Stone (1982:236–37), particularly when comparing pre-1919 figures. Because Ochoa provides figures for both Costa Rica *and* Guatemala, I include his data for comparative reference.

Yet the relationship between the Liberal reforms and the role that the state assumed in promoting agricultural export markets distinguished Costa Rica's Liberal period from that of Guatemala. First, the initial development of the coffee market in Costa Rica preceded the onset of the Liberal reforms. The Liberal reforms, in turn, reinforced the economic predominance of an already-established, coffee-based political economy. They accelerated the distribution of land for coffee production and increased the regulation of coffee markets. Second, the Costa Rican oligarchy did not produce coffee on large estates. Instead, it primarily accumulated capital and derived its economic, political, and social power through control over coffee processing, credit, and commerce (Cardoso 1977; Stone 1982:40, 215–21; Pérez Brignoli 1985:90; Winson 1989:25; Samper 1990). As a result, Costa Rica's oligarchy depended less than Guatemala's on control over land and access to a cheap labor supply. Indeed, peasants produced coffee on small and medium-sized farms, although, as we will see, they developed a conflictual relationship with the coffee elite, on whom they depended for credit, commerce, and the processing of their crop. This discussion, therefore, does not focus on land

distribution per se, because this would obscure the dependent relationship between Costa Rica's elite and smallholders. Third, and related to
the second point, the Costa Rican oligarchy did not call for a coercive
state role in the countryside to establish the basis for capital accumulation. Rather, it depended on the state primarily to regulate the market.[35]

The overview developed here of Costa Rica's coffee markets challenges traditional historiography, which has assumed that Costa Rica
enjoyed a rural democracy prior to the introduction of coffee and that
Liberals did not actively promote coffee production.[36] While historians
generally agree that Liberal state intervention to promote agricultural
markets did occur in the mid-nineteenth century, an assessment of
the data presented in Ciro Cardoso's classic 1977 essay on Central
America suggests that the state assumed a significantly more active role
during this period than previously assumed. Out of 191,630 hectares of
land granted between 1584 and 1890, 120,952 hectares, or an estimated
63 percent, were granted between 1871 and 1890 (the period coinciding
with the Liberal reforms), in contrast with 44,665 in the period between
1840 and 1870.[37] In fact, the average amount of land granted per decade
in the first two decades of the Liberal period (60,476 hectares) was more
than three times the decade average in the prior years of coffee growing
(14,888 hectares). The amount of land sold in the first two decades of the
Liberal period increased around 36 percent per decade when compared to
the years from 1840 to 1870.[38] And by 1890, coffee was produced on a
third of the land in Costa Rica's central valley, where four-fifths of its
population lived (Dunkerley 1988:20). The shift of land use from cattle
and subsistence production to coffee production led by the end of the
nineteenth century to the displacement of many peasants from their
lands, the displacement of many who had used lands that they did not
technically own, and the increasing domination of coffee production in
previously more-diversified though less-wealthy rural areas (Gudmundson 1989a:228–29).[39] Ciro Cardoso (1977:177) states that "with respect
to the Meseta Central, the physical expansion of the coffee estates had
more or less come to an end by the late 1880s, with the occupation of all
the waste lands (the *terrenos baldíos*). Subsequent expansion took place
on farms already established, by the steady substitution of coffee production for alternative types of agricultural activities."

Costa Rican coffee producers developed effective coffee estates comparable in size to those in Nicaragua and El Salvador, even if they did not
own land in the same proportions as agricultural elites in Guatemala, El
Salvador, or Nicaragua (Paige 1987:164). Indeed, Costa Rican land concentration increased with each economic crisis (Williams 1994:50). The

most significant estate formed between 1882 and 1938 claimed an estimated 604 acres, or 875 *manzanas* (C. Cardoso 1977:176). These large estate owners coexisted with smallholders and sub-subsistence farmers, who had also benefited from the privatization of land in the nineteenth century (Dunkerley 1988:22; Paige 1987:162–69).

Yet, if Costa Rican economic elites held sizable coffee estates, by the 1870s they derived their economic livelihood and power primarily from control over financial markets and *beneficios* (machinery that processes or prepares the bean for roasting), taking advantage of the smallholders producing coffee for the international market. As Ciro Cardoso has stated,

> There is no doubt, however, that it was not control over the land which enabled the coffee bourgeoisie to achieve a high degree of economic, social, and political dominance. Rather it lay in their ability to manipulate and combine the three basic monopolies which were fundamental to the coffee trade: the control of rural credit and the processing and marketing of the crop. . . . To summarize, the particular demographic, historical, and ecological conditions of the country permitted the survival and even the expansion of the smallholding property structure, at the same time as the control of rural credit and the processing and marketing of coffee underwrote the economic, social, and political supremacy of the small ruling group. (C. Cardoso 1977:192–93)

The increasing international demand for coffee during these years, particularly in London, began to outstrip the Costa Rican coffee oligarchy's production capabilities. This created an interdependent albeit unequal relationship between large estate owners and smallholders. Members of the oligarchy came to depend on smallholders to supplement the production of the large estates, adding smallholders' yields to theirs in the processing stage. The smallholders, in turn, depended on the large coffee producers to sell and process their crop. Smallholders also became increasingly dependent on the large coffee and financial elites for cash or credit advances. Commercial capitalists advanced credit to coffee-producing smallholders in installments before and during the growing season and at the sale of the harvest. This financial relationship enabled creditors to transfer losses to smallholders, who generally bore the costs of a poor market.

In the decade before the Liberal reforms, there was one significant effort to challenge the oligarchy's commercial oligopoly, which Costa Rica's economic elite thwarted. President Juan Rafael Mora (1849–59), a leading coffee producer, and the merchant Crisanto Medina founded Costa Rica's first commercial bank, Banco Nacional Costarricense, in

1858. The bank offered contracts and low interest rates for land and, therefore, affected the ability of other elite merchants and coffee growers to sustain their advantageous credit relations with smallholders. For this reason Costa Rica's coffee elites viewed the bank as a threat to the usurious credit relations they had established; some historians contend that as a consequence they arranged a coup d'état and overthrew the government. In the following decades, Costa Rican coffee exporters founded commercial banks that continued to lend to smallholders at very high rates. Indeed, smallholders' dependence on the financial elite remained onerous and became particularly apparent with the Great Depression (C. Cardoso 1977:183–84, and 1991:44; C. Hall 1982:38–40, 45–46; Dunkerley 1988:22; Williams 1994:156–58; Gudmundson 1995:153). Ciro Cardoso tells us that

> during the following decade credit-giving establishments multiplied in numbers; the most important was the Banco Anglo-Costarricense, established in 1863. Limited companies also grew up in the fields of interest-bearing loans, coffee financing, and the purchase of landed property. However, it is important to point out that in nineteenth-century Costa Rica these banks never functioned as dispensers of short- and medium-term rural credit, which continued to be advanced through the established mechanisms of advance payment for the crop by British importers to the large growers, processors, and merchants, who in turn extended credit at high rates of interest to the smallholders. (1977:183–84)

It is against this backdrop that the Liberal dictatorship initiated bank reform to regulate commercial markets. In January of 1871, Guardia approved the statutes for the Banco Nacional de Costa Rica. Later, the Liberal state set out to establish stability in the currency and financial markets with the 1900 General Law of Banks, along with other regulations (Stone 1982:30). While these measures secured economic space for the oligarchy as a whole, this same oligarchy interpreted the government's efforts to tax it as a transgression of state authority. In 1917, the one time a Liberal government (that of Alfredo González Flores) attempted to impose an income tax, the oligarchy overthrew it. Another attempt to do the same, in 1947, also heightened the oligarchy's opposition to the existing government and its support of the armed antigovernment movement.

Alongside financial lenders, *beneficio* owners (those who processed the coffee) assumed powerful economic positions vis-à-vis the smallholders.[40] Williams (1994:158) argues that "because of the higher rates of profit in processing as opposed to cultivation, Costa Rican capital was systematically drained from the cultivation phase (through price differentials and high interest rates) and flowed into the processing phase." Germans and their descendants living in Costa Rica, in particular, became owners of powerful *beneficios*. While the foreign coffee elite was numerically small, its influence and economic weight far surpassed its size. Foreigners or their descendants constituted only around 1 percent of the population in 1935. Nonetheless, they owned around 14.5 percent of the land. Moreover, by the end of the nineteenth century, they constituted more than 20 percent of the processors and exporters. By 1935, German descendants owned a third of the Costa Rican *beneficios* and they processed 40 percent of the crop (C. Hall 1982:51–53; Paige 1987: 150). Hence, Germans in both Costa Rica and Guatemala developed pivotal economic roles in each country's coffee economy, in accord with different patterns of capital accumulation. While Germans in Costa Rica played a pivotal role in processing, Germans in Guatemala primarily became powerful landowners.

Given the comparative lack of emphasis on landholding, Costa Rica's coffee elites were less concerned about securing a rural labor force. Even though labor scarcity existed in both Costa Rica and Guatemala in the nineteenth century, Costa Rican Liberals did not deploy coercive military or paramilitary forces to control and deliver rural labor to coffee plantations. The labor markets in the two countries, therefore, developed differently. Whereas Guatemalan elites and the state unambiguously indebted and exploited rural labor, the Costa Rican elites and state passed measures that triggered market pressures and provided incentives for mestizo smallholders to sell their land and ultimately their labor, legislation recalling the enclosure laws in England. Neither did Costa Rican elites coercively create indigenous work gangs, an unrealistic proposition insofar as Costa Rica's Indian population had become numerically insignificant by the nineteenth century (Gudmundson 1986a: 47–54).

Two additional factors conditioned labor relations between rural workers and landowners in Costa Rica's coffee economy: patterns of kinship support and ethnic homogeneity. Seasonal workers often labored on medium-sized farms owned by relatives. Consequently, landowners and laborers often characterized the hired hands as familial "help." Given the conjunction of a labor shortage and the established practice of and dependence on wage labor, coffee landowners developed relatively congenial relations with rural workers to prevent the latter from leaving and working for someone offering better working conditions (Gudmundson 1989a:231; Stone 1983:462; Samper 1990:65). Edelman (1992:4, 16), discussing the latifundios of Guanacaste, notes that prior to the 1930s rural workers could ask for wage advances as a condition of employment. These wage advances were different from the system of debt peonage that existed in Guatemala; he contends that in Costa Rica the ability to secure advance wages indicated rural labor's strength, an argument impossible to sustain in Guatemala. Moreover, ethnic homogeneity prevented large landowners from taking refuge in racist excuses for employing harsher forms of labor control such as debt peonage. Indeed, labor relations were left largely unregulated and would remain so until the 1940s (Vega Carballo 1981:297–98).

The development of a coffee-based, agro-export economy in Costa Rica, therefore, had a dividing effect on the rural work force, which prior to coffee had primarily engaged in subsistence agriculture or bartering for its livelihood. Part of the peasantry developed successful small farms, where it grew coffee for export; the remainder found itself no longer capable of sustaining itself on the land and, therefore, became seasonal or full-time wage labor. This process of differentiation, which occurred throughout the last two-thirds of the nineteenth century, gave way in the twentieth to a secular decline in standards of living (Hall 1982; Gudmundson 1986a:74–77). By the end of the nineteenth century, 70 percent of Costa Ricans were landless laborers (Dunkerley 1988:20). Decreasing size of landholdings, increasing landlessness, and increasing impoverishment constituted secular and interrelated trends. Yet, whereas in Guatemala the primary source of conflict occurred between the landholders and those who worked the land, in Costa Rica this landowner-worker conflict was muted. The primary source of rural conflict in Costa Rica developed during the Liberal period between processors and financiers versus small producers (Acuña Ortega 1986 and 1987; Gudmundson 1989a:231–32).

THE DEPRESSION: ADDRESSING RURAL CONFLICT

As it did elsewhere, the Great Depression's dramatic impact on financial markets struck the Costa Rican economy hard, intensifying the primary rural conflict between Costa Rica's coffee elite and smallholders. Costa Rican Liberals responded by increasing reliance on fraud and violence and creating new economic institutions to channel and divert the conflict that developed between smallholders and the coffee elite.

Following the Depression, electoral fraud and manipulation continued, although in a more visible and centralized manner. The main difference between fraud in the early years of the Liberal period and that practiced in the 1920s and 1930s was the direct participation of the executive in this process. The 1930s culminated in the major party consolidating an electoral machine, which organized at the national, regional, and local level, capable of mobilizing the rural vote with the help of patronage. Executive influence over this electoral machine facilitated control over electoral outcomes and essentially maintained elite unity in the 1930s behind the National Republican Party (Creedman 1971; Samper 1988:201).

Manipulation of state institutions and officials culminated during the presidency of León Cortés Castro (1936–40). He regularly used state employees as part of his political machine to carry out tasks and to spy on the opposition. He fired all officials loyal to others and, consequently, sought to place individuals loyal only to him in state positions. Like Ubico, he sought to increase his control over the state and its resources. Also like Ubico, he sought to diminish the idea of the state as an arena of accommodation. Cortés's control of society, however, was not as penetrating, pervasive, coercive, or absolute as that of Ubico in Guatemala.

The rise of parties with more radical agendas—the Partido Reformista in the 1920s and the Communist Party in the 1930s—challenged the nominal respect held for the electoral process by elite political parties. These new, nonoligarchic parties benefited from the expansion of the electorate in the twentieth century and the rise in the numbers of urban and rural workers. However, elections remained fraudulent, and the results announced were not always respected.

The regime, therefore, generally confined nonoligarchic participation to the electoral stage. In 1931, Congress prevented the recently formed Communist Party from running in national elections. In 1934, communists were allowed to run, but there was widespread fraud (Samper 1988:170). The regime denied the right to assume office to those communists elected in legislative races (Bulmer-Thomas 1987:68; Samper 1988:170; Cerdas Cruz 1991:68). Overall, elite machine politics maintained a measure of formal respect for the electoral political process. Nonoligarchic parties gained the right to enter elections, and workers gained the right to vote. But the oligarchy essentially maintained veto power over who had the right to assume office and whose vote mattered. Politics in the 1930s institutionalized formal participation but denied voice.

State efforts during the 1930s to impede substantive political participation along class lines coincided with private efforts by international and national capital to undermine social organizing. The rise in unemployment, coupled with the decline in real wages, sparked nonelectoral organizing, worker demonstrations, and riots in Costa Rica, as in the rest of the Americas. In 1932, the state responded to social protest by suppressing civil guarantees (Woodward 1985:216). Private companies, in turn, monitored extra-electoral organizing efforts. The U.S.-owned banana companies on the Atlantic Coast developed a "systematic network of surveillance against 'labor agitators' in the second and third decade of this century to prevent labor organizing. The company headquarters also called for the creation of formal political blacklists in the 1940s" (Bourgois 1989:11). In 1934 the Costa Rican state repressed workers striking the U.S.-owned banana company.[41]

If the oligarchy confronted an increase in urban opposition in the political arena, so too did it confront increased rural opposition in the economic arena from smallholders.[42] The rapid decline in value of agricultural products, in particular the secular decline in coffee values following the coffee boom of the second half of the 1920s, had a dramatic impact on the Costa Rican economy; coffee and bananas accounted for close to 90 percent of export earnings (Bulmer-Thomas 1987:33). Between 1929 and 1932 the market value of Costa Rica's coffee declined from a base value of 100 to 43 (Cerdas Cruz 1991:279–80). Despite an increase in levels of coffee production and export, the value of coffee exports dropped from $9.78 million in 1929 to $4.92 million in 1935; it further declined to $3.98 million in 1940 (Vega Carballo 1986:316; Dunkerley 1988:91). Costa Rican processors, exporters, and financiers displaced their costs to the smaller producers in the form of higher processing and exporting prices. As in the past, when international coffee values declined, processors frequently delayed payment for coffee they had purchased from smallholders. Delayed payment increased the margin of profit for the processors while decreasing that of the small and medium producers. Consequently, these producers often found themselves without enough capital to cultivate their land. These problems intensified during the mid-1930s with the dramatic decline in world coffee prices (C. Hall 1982:48; Acuña Ortega 1985:188, and 1987:2).

During the Depression, producers formed associations to combat the decline in market values. This pattern occurred throughout the Central American region except for Guatemala, where Ubico had banned these associations. In 1930, Costa Rican coffee producers founded the Asociación Nacional de Productores de Café to regulate the relationship between themselves and exporters (Bulmer-Thomas 1987:59). Bulmer-Thomas (1987:72) implies that this association had some influence over the government decision to depreciate the currency; Guatemala's currency, by contrast, maintained parity with the dollar. Depreciation in Costa Rica favored the traditional oligarchy and its production, financing, and commerce of coffee.

The small and medium producers confronted what they considered unfair economic relations. When they appealed to the state, President Ricardo Jiménez, in his third term (1932–36), created the Institute for the Defense of Coffee (IDECAFE) in order to regulate the relationship between smaller producers and processors of the crop (C. Hall 1982:48–49; Stone 1982:132–33; Bulmer-Thomas 1987). IDECAFE ensured that processors paid the smaller producers on time and also established set prices to ensure that the processors did not acquire a net gain of more than 12 percent. IDECAFE assumed the right to establish the different processing prices to be paid for coffee, depending on the region and the quality of the coffee cultivated (C. Hall 1982:49).

The creation of IDECAFE suggests at first glance that the state provided an institutional arena for accommodation between different classes in the 1930s. IDECAFE, however, did not function in the way small producers had hoped. Initially, processors disregarded its regulation, incurring minimal or no sanctions. Later, the oligarchy managed to appropriate influence within IDECAFE, turning it away from a potential arena for accommodation to a platform for the oligarchy to reassert domestic economic power and gain international influence. After IDECAFE's founding, the legislature subsequently modified the law so that processors could draw a higher profit, diminishing the gains ostensibly achieved by smallholders. The producers called this action the *rebelión de los beneficiadores,* or the processors' rebellion (Acuña Ortega 1985:191). Moreover, IDECAFE assumed a role on the international market, on behalf of the exporters, to protect their prices and markets, particularly in the late 1930s.[43]

Small and medium producers came to identify IDECAFE as a state institution working in favor of elite processors and exporters. In 1936, however, IDECAFE once again adopted measures that regulated prices and, for the first time, sanctioned the exporters who did not respect its regulations. The following year the conflict subsided, at least temporarily, as the producers and processors-exporters respected, if begrudgingly, the regulations (Acuña Ortega 1985:192–93, 199).

IDECAFE exemplified the role of state intervention in accommodating and assuaging the basic rural class conflict while simultaneously maintaining the existing economic conditions. IDECAFE and its role as price regulator, particularly after 1936, demonstrated the success of the small producers; they convinced the state to intervene on their behalf and to create an institution designed to set more equitable economic relations. But small producers did not achieve a sustained or influential voice in the organization and policy process that they had helped to create (Acuña Ortega 1985). Their victory in fact highlighted the smallholders' limited influence and the preponderant power of the oligarchy, as a class and as individuals, to determine state policy in the 1930s. Although the processors, financiers, and exporters were to submit to new regulations, which they did unevenly in the first years of IDECAFE, they ultimately gained an additional institutional voice. Their representatives came to dominate IDECAFE, which not only served to regulate domestic squabbles but also to represent the exporters on the international market (Acuña Ortega 1985).

Overall, the Liberal regime's institutional response to the economic crisis paralleled that in the political arena. It increased the space for formal participation by nonoligarchic sectors—extending the suffrage and creating IDECAFE—but subverted the latter's political influence through oligarchic control of state institutions and resources. In the final analysis, the Costa Rican Liberal regime created a state institution to incorporate the *voices* of both national capital and the smallholders. The institutions mediated conflict through the state and thereby defused class conflict between these two sectors. The new state role led the smallholders to perceive that they had a stake in supporting the existing regime. The smallholders, however, did not gain notable *influence* in the state. Ironically, the state institution created to improve the bargaining position of the smallholders vis-à-vis the oligarchy in fact resulted in improving the Costa Rican oligarchy's ability to maneuver on the international market. Ultimately, the Liberal regime in Costa Rica, as in Guatemala, did not attempt to diversify the export economy or transform the relations therein.

Coda

The Guatemalan and Costa Rican regimes of the 1930s adopted harsher forms of rule within the context of Guatemala's dictatorial and Costa Rica's oligarchic authoritarianism. Similarly, they enacted economic policies that upheld the regimes of accumulation in the coffee (and banana) economies and muted the primary rural class conflict associated with it. In both cases, the state assumed an active role.

The Depression was important, therefore, insofar as it reinforced rather than modified the political and economic institutions consolidated with the Liberal reforms of the 1870s. The state responses to the Depression, however, contributed to the subsequent overthrow of Liberal rule and consequently affected the reform agenda and coalitional options for the reform movement. In both Costa Rica and Guatemala, the Depression and World War II coincided with the emergence of new urban social sectors among the urban working and middle classes, which experienced restrictive political environments and a decline in living standards. (As the Depression had negatively affected the price of coffee, World War II negatively affected the countries' market shares.)

The popular social sectors, disadvantaged and controlled, articulated and pushed for a reform platform that would characterize the subsequent reform period of the 1940s. Given the space for expression in Costa Rica, these sectors began to organize and voice their concerns in the 1930s; however, their actual political influence was obstructed by the state. By contrast, in Guatemala, discontented sectors were closely watched and heavily repressed. The government restricted the development of civil society, thereby limiting not only political influence but also political organizing.[44] In both cases, the Liberal state resisted effective democratization, although it did so through different means.

Part II analyzes the democratizing coalitions that emerged in the 1940s to challenge Guatemala's and Costa Rica's authoritarian regimes. In both countries, these coalitions would initiate a cycle of reform and reaction, underscoring the significant parallels in Guatemala and Costa Rica's political trajectories—from authoritarianism to democracy—despite different markets and states.

Yet, if we cannot derive regime outcomes from economic structures, neither can we make sense of the foundation and durability of regimes without reference to these same economic structures. Indeed, inherited institutions—in the economy as well as the polity and society—informed social interests, the types of conflicts, and constellation of coalitions that emerged with democratization. The markets and states that the Liberal reforms institutionalized foreshadowed the strategies, development agendas, and coalition politics that polarized the mid-twentieth-century democratic periods and precipitated their overthrow.

The Democratic and Social Reform Period, 1940s–1950s

CHAPTER 3

Demanding Democracy

Allied propaganda during World War II championed the defense of democracy, the pursuit of freedom, and the fight against fascism. These goals galvanized support among incipient labor groups and the middle classes throughout Latin America. With the attack on Pearl Harbor and the entry of the United States into the war, many Latin American countries joined the Allied cause—even if they remained lukewarm about the Allies and their ends. This international fight to defend democracy rang hollow when measured against authoritarianism in Latin America. The distance between international democratic rhetoric and domestic authoritarian practices collapsed, however, in the "interwar period" following World War II and prior to the Cold War. In the years 1944 to 1947, most countries in the region experienced a political opening in which organized labor and leftist parties gained ephemeral political influence in governing circles and in the workplace. The striking parallels from country to country in political opening and closure between the years 1944 and 1947 have led many recent studies to highlight the role of international factors in creating a mid-twentieth-century window of opportunity for a transition to democracy. This opportunity was subsequently forsaken in the fight against the presumed global communist threat.[1]

In line with a trend throughout Latin America, Costa Rica and Guatemala initiated short-lived periods of political reform in the 1940s. The mid-twentieth-century reform coalitions that emerged in Costa Rica and Guatemala transformed state-society relations. They challenged the exclusionary basis of oligarchic politics associated with the Liberal period, opened up spaces for working- and middle-class participation in governing circles, created spaces for the growth of civil society, and legislated entitlement, regulatory, and redistributive policies. Reforms included constitutional chapters on social guarantees, social security reforms, labor codes, tax reforms, and land reforms. In the process, they redefined the appropriate spaces, form, and content of political participation and the role of the state in redefining the boundaries of capital accumulation, labor markets, and social policy.

International ideas and conflicts no doubt influenced the rise of democratic aspirations and ideals in the 1940s. Yet they cannot on their own explain the rise and decline of democratic movements in Latin America in general and Costa Rica and Guatemala in particular. The Costa Rican reform movement began at least two years prior to the democratic wave, and the counterreform movement ended with the founding of democracy rather than authoritarian rule, in contrast to the rest of Latin America. The Guatemalan reform period began at the moment of democratization in the rest of the region, but ended only at the height of the Cold War in 1954; if international and Cold War politics alone could explain political outcomes, Guatemala would have experienced a crackdown on labor movements, a reversal of social reforms, and a return to authoritarian rule at the end of the 1940s, along with the rest of the region.

This chapter explains the domestic origins, strategies, and evolution of the mid-twentieth-century democratizing reform coalitions that emerged in Costa Rica and Guatemala. The argument is threefold. First, a publicly expressed division within the elite in the context of rising popular demands for political and economic inclusion precipitated the formation of democratizing reform alliances. Second, the Liberal period shaped the reform strategies deployed and the alliances formed. Third, the balance of power within the reform coalition determined the stability of the reform coalition itself. Overall, these arguments illustrate the largely domestic factors that set in motion the dynamic of reform and reaction that redefined political alliances, identities, and political trajectories in Costa Rica and Guatemala.[2]

Let me briefly elaborate on these arguments. A publicly salient division within both countries' elite, at a moment of rising popular and middle-class organizing, largely created the "window of opportunity"— the conditions for the formation of the multiclass coalitions that would oversee the democratic and social reform periods of the mid-twentieth century. While ideas from the international arena surely shaped the discourse and aspirations of key social actors, domestic factors largely explained the emergence of these crucial coalitions—both the reform coalition discussed here and the counterreform coalitions discussed in Chapter 6. In both Costa Rica and Guatemala, a part of the oligarchy voiced its opposition to the existing regime; elite divisions became salient when they were expressed publicly, as with the the formation of new opposition parties or the publication of an open letter. This public opposition represented a declining social base for the Liberal regimes and a decline in oligarchic solidarity, thereby posing a new set of possibilities for coalition politics to undermine authoritarianism and construct democratic rule. Attempting to strengthen its political position vis-à-vis the existing regime and the faithful oligarchic faction, the opposition oligarchy appealed to previously excluded or underrepresented sectors. Indeed, the economic crisis and political constraints of the 1930s had generated a disenfranchised but vocal urban sector maneuvering for reform. Multiclass reform coalitions emerged in Costa Rica in 1942 and in Guatemala in 1944.

These possibilities for new alliances, however, unfolded in different contexts. The strategies available to initiate the reform period and the sectors open to mobilization once the initial reform coalition had been formed were largely shaped by the conditions each country inherited from the Liberal period.* On the one hand, the type of states that had developed alongside the authoritarian regimes shaped the range of strategies available to the reform coalition. In Costa Rica, where civilian institutions had largely dominated authoritarian politics, it was possible to initiate reform through the institutions that had previously been used to sustain Liberal rule. What proved consequential was whether the reform coalition included an oligarchic faction that was in or out of power. In the former circumstance, legislative means to reform were possible; in the latter, resorting to force seemed a greater likelihood. In Guatemala, the dictatorial basis of authoritarian rule—which had politically marginalized the oligarchy as well as other sectors—precluded possibilities for democratic reform within existing institutions. Rather, an emerging reform coalition tended toward violent means to overthrow the regime, to assume a position of political power, and to reconstruct democratic institutions.

On the other hand, the varied ways in which the Liberal regimes had institutionalized civic organizing and mediated primary rural conflicts

---

*The scope and depth of the emergent civil society and the targets of reforms during mid-twentieth-century reform periods also reflected conditions inherited from the Liberal period, points discussed in later chapters.

shaped the range of available allies and the policy agenda of the ensuing reform coalitions; in particular, this institutionalization determined whether that country's rural sector was available for mobilization by reformers. In Costa Rica, where the state had attempted to mediate rural conflict through governmental institutions, the rural sector was largely disinterested in mobilizing alongside the reform alliance that emerged. Without political pressure from the rural sector, the Costa Rican reformers developed a largely urban-biased agenda. In Guatemala the rural sector, which had been repressed in prior years, was available for mobilization by the reform coalition, which in turn placed rural reform on its policy agenda.

The ensuing stability of the reform coalition, however, was more historically contingent—as much a result of the oligarchy's relative power in the initial reform coalition as a legacy of the Liberal period.[3] In Costa Rica, part of the oligarchy came to assume the preeminent political role in the reform coalition—dominating the presidency and the legislature—thereby diminishing the likelihood that anything but a moderate reform agenda would emerge. With the oligarchy dominating electoral politics in both the reform and the counterreform movements, the constellation of coalition partners remained relatively stable, especially given that the rural sector was not available for mobilization. In Guatemala, the oligarchy did not establish this preeminent position; a weak civil society prior to the reform period and the absence of oligarchic participation in electoral politics made it difficult for any particular sector to assume and maintain a dominant position in the reform coalition. With the rapid emergence of new political parties and of civil society, urban and rural popular social sectors came to dominate the reform coalition and to pursue a more radical reform agenda than their Costa Rican counterparts. In the process, they alienated the part of the oligarchy that had previously supported them. With the exit of the oligarchy and the need to address its increasingly rural-based constituency, the reform coalition pursued changes that directly challenged the oligarchy's basis of capital accumulation.

Costa Rica

The 1940 election of Doctor Rafael Angel Calderón Guardia of the Partido Republicano Nacional (PRN) with 85 percent of the vote seemed a continuation of the oligarchic politics that had characterized 70 years of Liberal rule. Handpicked by the outgoing PRN president, León Cortés

Castro (1936–40), Calderón appeared as a respected and trustworthy representative of the Costa Rican oligarchy (Salazar 1980: 141; Oconitrillo 1981; Stone 1982; Rojas Bolaños 1986: 43). Fernando Soto Harrison, Secretary of the Interior during Calderón's presidency, states in his memoirs:

> To arrive at the presidency, Rafael Angel Calderón counted on the support of the powerful capitalist class, owner of the country, because he was a very attractive figure for them due to his public persona, because he was the son of Dr. Calderón Muñoz, because he was a descendent of President Mora and a great nephew of General Guardia, because he was the Doctor of the Giustinianis and of many of Costa Rica's important families. . . . The rich assumed that Dr. Calderón Guardia was going to be the Costa Rican oligarchy's big representative. (Soto Harrison 1991: 32–33)

Calderón's administration, however, witnessed the demise of the oligarchy's largely uncontested control over state resources and policies. In the first years of his presidency, the elite divided as the popular classes started to organize more vigorously. This division within the oligarchy precipitated a scramble for political allies that ultimately pitted a reform movement spearheaded by President Calderón, the communists, and the Archbishop of San José against an opposition alliance composed of the conservative faction of the oligarchy and middle- and upper-middle-class members of the Social Democratic Party. The striking multiclass coalitions that distinguished this decade formed on the basis of commonly identified enemies rather than programmatic sociopolitical and economic objectives. Consequently, they temporarily overlooked their internal conflicting political projects.

The reform coalition governed Costa Rica from 1942 to 1948.* It challenged the Liberal oligarchic basis of politics, incorporating the urban working class into the governing coalition and legislating social reforms that targeted the popular classes. Significantly, and in contrast to Gua-

---

*The beginning dates for the *reform period* (1941 to 1948) and the *reform coalition* (1942 to 1948) do not coincide. In 1941, President Calderón legislated social security as a paternalistic and isolated effort to extend social services to the poor; while he had no intention at this stage of challenging oligarchic politics by initiating a more sustained and democratic reform period, his social security legislation nevertheless came to represent the beginning of a reform period that extended through 1948. The nature, intent, and impact of the reform period, however, changed with the formation of the democratizing reform coalition in 1942. The reform coalition initiated legislation and programs that created avenues for popular participation in political circles, formalized economic and social rights in the workplace, and encouraged organizing among workers. I argue, therefore, that the reform coalition that governed from 1942 to 1948 was responsible for democratizing political, economic, and social relations in Costa Rica.

temala, the oligarchic reformers dominated the reform coalition, controlling both the executive and legislative branches. The coalition altered the political system from within and, ultimately, oversaw a period of moderate reform. The alliances and legislation of the 1940s challenged the political structures of the 1870s Liberal reforms and shaped political identities that have left an abiding political and institutional legacy.

OLIGARCHY DIVIDES

The Costa Rican oligarchy, which had united around Calderón for the 1940s elections, divided within the first two years of his term, apparently over three issues: selection of the president of the national legislature; adoption of an anti-Axis position that cut off German markets as well as persecuted German nationals and Costa Ricans of German descent; and legislation of social security. Calderón's position on these three issues, elaborated below, precipitated a division within the oligarchy, part of which began to fear that the Calderón administration would prove detrimental both to the oligarchy's continued political hegemony and its ability to accumulate capital through the control over finance, coffee processing, and commerce. These fears created a fissure within the electoral apparatus that the PRN had crafted during the 1930s.

Elections for the president of the national legislature created the first important controversy. Ex-president Cortés, in exchange for supporting Calderón's 1940 candidacy, had assumed that Calderón would support Cortés's son, Otto, as president of the national legislature. Instead, Calderón chose to support the candidacy of Teodoro Picado Michalski.[4] Cortés had not expected such independence. He and those personally loyal to him distanced themselves from Calderón, the man whom they had actively supported (Rodríguez 1980: 39–42; Oconitrillo 1981: 135; Rojas Bolaños 1986: 61; Contreras and Cerdas 1988; Interview with Eugenio Rodríguez, July 27, 1990; Lehoucq 1992: 165–66).

The Calderón administration's wartime persecution of German nationals and descendants living in Costa Rica exacerbated the personal divisions between Calderón and Cortés.[5] Part of the oligarchy perceived Calderón's actions as an attack on oligarchic solidarity and private property, given that the Germans had formed an integral part of the Costa Rican agro-export elite. German nationals had attained influential positions within coffee production, processing, financing, and commerce. And, in the 1930s, Costa Rica increased its trade dependence on Germany. By the end of that decade Germany purchased around 25 percent of Costa Rican exports, including an estimated 18.9 percent of coffee exports and 80 percent of cocoa exports (Bulmer-Thomas 1987: 78–79; Cerdas Cruz 1991: 281–82): "The political sympathies of important national leaders for the political experience of Italy and Germany strengthened traditional family and financial ties that already existed between those countries and the coffee growers and exporters" (Cerdas Cruz 1991: 281–82). Despite the prominent role of Germans within Costa Rica's economy, the Costa Rican government declared war on Germany on December 11, 1941.[6]

Part of the Costa Rican oligarchy reacted against the government's new hostility toward Germans. An executive decree in December 1941 stated that Germans, Italians, and Japanese had to apply for the right to move about the country. That same month, the government forbade commercial relations with Axis countries, and the military occupied the buildings that housed the German Club, the Italian House, and the electric plant owned by German nationals. In January 1942, Germans, Italians, and Japanese officially had to declare their goods and property; the government had already started making a list of these properties. At the end of February, an executive decree published a list of names and properties that the Office of Coordination subsequently controlled. And a month later, an executive decree founded the Junta de Custodia de la Propiedad de los Nacionales de los Países en Guerra con Costa Rica (Junta for the Custodianship of Property of Those Nationals from Countries at War with Costa Rica). In May, the junta began closing down German-owned coffee processing plants. In June, the executive published a blacklist of 200 names and gained the right to expropriate the property of Axis-country nationals (Schifter 1986: 144–45). Many, although certainly not all, of those on the list participated in or were sympathetic to fascist organizations.[7] The government then used these blacklists to take land and goods held by Costa Ricans of German and Italian descent and to place these citizens in internment camps in Costa Rica and Texas. Costa Rica eventually deported over 200 Germans and placed German-owned businesses under Costa Rican administrators (Bell 1971: 109–12; Rodríguez 1980: 52–58; Schifter 1983: 180 and 1986: 136–49; Rojas Bolaños 1986: 55–57).[8]

Costa Rican elites also bristled at popular-sector attacks on the Costa Rican population of German descent. With the sinking of a ship docked in Costa Rican waters, allegedly by a German submarine, protests and attacks on German- and Italian-owned businesses occurred, without control or reproach by the police. Jacobo Schifter argues that, in fact,

Calderón sought to create an image of popular pressure for action against (potential) Axis sympathizers. Less than a week after the boat was torpedoed, the administration detained 350 Axis nationals; it deported 100 of the detainees and placed 75 under house arrest. Ultimately, the detention camps held around 300 Germans living in Costa Rica (Schifter 1986: 147–48).

The Costa Rican government's anti-German policy followed U.S. directives, but it simultaneously provided Calderón with an excuse to dismiss state officials whose loyalty he questioned. Calderón fired a number of alleged Nazi officials beginning in April 1941, apparently abusing the campaign against fascism to target political enemies and weaken Cortés's position (Schifter 1986: 136–37). He fired pro-Cortés officials and replaced them with more loyal cadre. Germans, those in and out of the country, allied with or bolstered their ties to Cortés, who had already begun to distance himself from Calderón.

Many within the oligarchy, sympathetic to the Axis, reacted strongly against Calderón's anti-Axis policies, which directly attacked some of the most influential and affluent individuals in Costa Rica. Given the Germans' integral role in the economy and politics, many non-German oligarchs perceived Calderón's anti-German policy and his distancing of himself from Cortés as a weakening of oligarchic political hegemony and solidarity. However, Calderón's economic policies, broadly speaking, did not negatively affect the coffee elite as a whole. To the contrary, at the same time that he undermined the Germans' ability to conduct business, Calderón promoted coffee production and export by doing away with national and municipal taxes on them (Rojas Bolaños 1986: 49–51; Bulmer-Thomas 1987: 91). Agricultural exports did not decrease during the war, even if they switched their market destination from Germany to the United States. In fact, the state offered these economic exemptions at the expense of an important source of state revenues, leading to a substantial growth in the fiscal deficit (Schifter 1986: 32, 107–8).

The third point of contention, the creation of new social legislation, further divided the elite. On October 31, 1941, the administration passed a social security law designed to cover costs incurred for sickness, maternity, old age, and death for all workers below a certain income. This program required the state, owners, and workers to contribute to the fund designated to cover these costs. The social security law, however, did not affect all sectors equally; workers in urban industry or commerce gained more benefits than rural workers. Eligibility requirements stipulated that workers had to log a certain number of days per year to earn coverage; workers on coffee plantations did not meet this requirement, given the short duration of the harvest, and, therefore, did not gain this coverage.

Despite this varied impact and implementation, much of the oligarchy, including the industrial, commercial, as well as landed sectors, opposed the social security legislation (Rojas Bolaños 1986: 55). However, the cortesistas in congress were careful not to denounce the social legislation. Concerned with sustaining mass support, they remained noticeably silent on the issue. The Catholic Church, by contrast, came out in favor of the reform. Archbishop Sanabria in fact had called for action to redress the social question in his pastoral letter "Sobre el Justo Salario," delivered shortly before the social security legislation was presented to the legislature (Rosenberg 1983: 53; Aguilar 1989: 31).

State regulation of capital-labor relations did not necessarily represent a threat to the Costa Rican oligarchy. This social security legislation could have become an institutional arena to mediate urban class conflicts, ostensibly on behalf of the popular classes, just as the state had mediated rural class conflict with the institutionalization of IDECAFE in the 1930s (as discussed in Chapter 2). The social security legislation occurred, however, within a context of an already-divided elite, which had begun to question Calderón's political motives. This legislation, therefore, served to raise doubts about the administration's goals for regulating the economy.

In short, in the first two years of Calderón's administration, the choice of the president of the legislature, the treatment of German nationals, and social security legislation created politically latent divisions within an oligarchy, some members of which perceived these developments as a threat to their political hegemony and basis of capital accumulation. As the reform period progressed, the first two causes subsided in importance. The elite opposition focused increasingly on the composition of the reform coalition that developed, legislation of additional social reforms, and popular mobilization.

RISE IN URBAN POPULAR ORGANIZING

The division within the elite occurred at a time of rising urban working- as well as middle- and upper-middle-class organizing and demands.* The 1930s had witnessed the simultaneous growth of urban working

*Future references to the "(upper) middle class" refer to both the middle and the upper-middle classes.

and middle classes, the rise in alternative forms of political organizing, and the continued exclusion of these groups from assuming an active political role (Cerdas Cruz 1991: 278). At the same time, these sectors confronted high inflation, a high deficit, and a decline in agricultural production. Consequently, their respective living standards declined, particularly during the first couple of years of Calderón's administration.[9] In fact, during the first four years of the 1940s, real per capita gross domestic product (GDP) fell in Costa Rica, as it did in Guatemala and Honduras. Moreover, the internal debt doubled in the first five years of the 1940s, and the fiscal deficit increased to 42 percent of revenue in 1943. Rumors of corruption by state officials and a campaign to encourage tax evasion were a political response to the economic situation (Bulmer-Thomas 1987: 97, 101).

Two alternative, class-based movements emerged to challenge the existing Liberal regime: the communist party (CP),* which primarily mobilized urban and banana plantation workers, and the Centro para el Estudio de los Problemas Nacionales (the Centro), a political study group of (upper-) middle-class intellectuals. These organizations shared a commitment to broaden political and economic participation for underrepresented sectors. However, the manner in which they sought to challenge the Liberal regime varied, primarily in terms of whom they mobilized.

Calderon's administration offered the politically marginalized working- and middle-class sectors the opportunity to gain political influence as opposing factions of the divided elite attempted to cultivate popular support in order to bolster their weakened political positions. In the early 1940s the communist party was a more established force that could mobilize organized labor. The Centro remained a weak political force, although it was subsequently an important intellectual movement. It appears, therefore, that the CP became the numerically most attractive alliance partner. (I discuss the CP, insofar as it became part of the reform coalition, below; the Centro, which joined the opposition movement, I discuss in Chapter 6.) The ensuing oligarchic alliances with the communist party created the conditions for both the initiation and the overthrow of the reform coalition.

---

*Before 1943, the Costa Rican communist party's official name was Bloque de Obreros y Campesinos, which changed in June 1943 to Partido Vanguardia Popular (PVP). To demonstrate organizational and ideological continuity between these political party formations, despite name changes, I refer throughout this book to both the Bloque and the Partido Vanguardia Popular as the communist party (CP), as was common practice among party members and the opposition.

The communist party was one of the first in Costa Rica to organize around a programmatic platform. It advocated socialist reforms, antifascism, and nationalism.[10] Founded by a group of intellectuals, artisans, and workers, it primarily mobilized artisans in the capital and banana-plantation workers on the coast. It claimed as members a small number of industrial workers—unsurprising given the limited degree of industrialization in Costa Rica.

From its inception, the CP articulated a commitment to struggle for socialism. The party had always argued, however, that socialism was a long-term goal for Costa Rica, given its backward stage of development. It maintained that Costa Rica needed to complete its capitalist stage of development before it could actively pursue socialism.

While advocating a militant position in the first half of the 1930s, the CP after 1935 let this militant rhetoric subside (Rojas Bolaños 1986: 72–73). The Costa Rican communist party largely repudiated violence and advocated an electoral strategy. Manuel Mora Valverde, the founder and then secretary general of the Costa Rican communist party, repeatedly stated that revolution could come about through nonviolent means (Mora 1980: 95–97). Rather than revolution, the CP advocated reforms. For example, it called in 1938 for an increase in the minimum salary, an eight-hour work day in the city and the countryside, protection for female workers, accident laws that would apply in urban as well as rural areas, an increase in agricultural diversification and production to provide for domestic consumption without overproduction, and an agrarian reform law and the provision of credit in order to benefit small owners (Mora 1980: 102–7; Edelman and Kenen 1989: 74–76). The Costa Rica Liberal regime encouraged this strategy. The evolving space for forming a party, running campaigns, and voting enhanced the possibilities to participate in the system to which reformers like the communists believed they might have access.

In line with popular front strategies adopted throughout Latin America, the Costa Rican communists proclaimed a prodemocracy platform in 1936 as part of the fight against fascism (Contreras and Cerdas 1988: 37–38). Antifascist struggles, particularly in Spain, mobilized and shaped the identities of many Costa Rican communist leaders and rank and file, who played a central role in the subsequent reform period. In 1938, Mora Valverde declared, "Given that fascism is our number one enemy, and given our struggle to defend democracy, our primordial duty will be logical. . . . We must unite efforts."[11] The salience of this antifascist battle emerged in one of many interviews with Arnoldo Ferreto, a party militant for 60 years. In a discussion about the initial years of the party, he unexpectedly went into his study to retrieve a book of poems by Carlos Luís Sáenz. He read out loud a poem to evoke the passion and significance of the antifascist struggle that characterized the Costa Rican communist party's work during the late 1930s. Similarly, party militant Alicia Cerdas explained that she became interested in and ultimately joined the Costa Rican CP because of its active role against the fascists in the Spanish Civil War:

> When I was young, I was not very serious; I would go out to parties, and I had a lot of boyfriends. But when the Spanish Civil War began, I began to work with those who were trying to help the Republicans. I began to think about many things, especially given that the communist party played a very important role in this antifascist effort. As a result, I decided to attend a course on Marxism offered by the [communist] party so that I could know what it was. Moreover, given that I was a librarian, I began to read everything that I could. I joined the communist party around 1938. I was active in the Communist Youth, which at that time had around three women. The communist party at that time did not struggle for women's rights; rather, they emphasized socioeconomic demands with an emphasis on electoral struggles.[12]

Finally, the Costa Rican communist party advanced a nationalist position. It downplayed the internationalist image often identified with communism and denied allegiance to the Soviet Union over that to Costa Rica. Although the Costa Rican CP did not operate according to instructions or directives originating from the Soviet Union, it did follow broad international positions such as the call for a popular front strategy.[13]

The communist party had committed to an electoral strategy that by the end of the 1930s stressed nonviolence, reform, antifascism, and nationalism. Yet, while the Costa Rican Liberal regime permitted electoral participation, it often denied those communists who had won elections the right to assume legislative seats. Of the 1938 elections, Arnoldo Ferreto of the communist party wrote, "During the campaign, we were objects of all forms of limitation and abuse. We were denied permission to hold meetings; other meetings were arbitrarily dissolved. Our militants were beaten and imprisoned by public force. As is expected, we did not receive representation in the electoral boards, or even in the boards for the polling stations. And when the time arrived, they also prevented us from placing public prosecutors at the polling stations" (Ferreto 1984: 66).[14]

The communist party had maintained a critical oppositional stance toward Calderón's presidential candidacy. It argued that he was a product of the coffee oligarchy and that he had received support from pro-fascist individuals such as Cortés (who had attempted to prevent the CP from assuming political offices). The communist party maintained its anti-Calderón position during the first year and a half of Calderón's government.

Calderón's popularity declined after the 1940 election. The popular sectors that had originally voted for him increasingly withdrew support as the economy weakened and inflation increased in 1941 (Rojas Bolaños 1986: 60–61). Calderón then suspended individual guarantees in conjunction with the declaration of war against the Axis powers, further increasing popular anger. Rumors of rampant corruption contributed to a general distrust of the administration. These developments created the possibility of increasing the ranks of the communist party. It is within this context, one in which urban popular support for Calderón plummeted and the communist party provided a politically organized alternative to the oligarchy, that the oligarchy divided.

THE REFORM COALITION: EXPANDING ELECTORAL POLITICS

The division of the elite within the context of the mobilized popular sectors demanding economic and political reforms precipitated a scramble for political allies. Coalition building was attractive because no single group had a large enough electoral constituency to advance its agenda or achieve political viability independently. The logic of electoral competition led factions of the elite to court multiclass alliances to bolster their respective strength in the political arena. This period of alliance building led to ideologically opposed political bedfellows.

If a changed domestic situation—division of elites and increasing popular organization—created the space and incentive for multiclass alliances, the changing international conditions made it ideologically feasible to do so. Wartime allies, following the collapse of the German-Soviet pact, rekindled the alliance between the capitalist and communist countries. They also resuscitated the popular front strategy, which encouraged the creation of antifascist alliances, regardless of conflicting political ideologies.[15] This international context expanded the space in Costa Rica (and throughout much of Latin America, including Cuba, Chile, and Venezuela) in which unusual reform coalitions could arise (Bethell and Roxborough 1988; R. Collier 1993; Rock 1994).

These changed domestic and international conditions precipitated a reconfiguration of the Costa Rican ruling political coalition and the formation of distinctive multiclass reform alliances that governed from 1942 to 1948. Opposition within the agro-export and industrial sectors resulting from the failure to elect Otto Cortés as president of the Congress, the treatment of German nationals and their descendants living in Costa Rica, and the recent promulgation of a social security law all allegedly prompted arrangements for a coup d'état.[16] Manuel Mora has stated on several occasions that Jorge Hine—representative of the anti-Calderón faction, director of the Bank of Costa Rica, prominent member within the economic elite, and a presidential hopeful for the 1944 elections—invited the communist party to join the anti-Calderón alliance. Hine presumably sought to garner a larger constituency for both future elections and the alleged coup. The communist party was numerically appealing because it had grown in strength and had garnered 16 percent of the votes in the 1942 legislative elections (Carvajal Herrera 1978: 40). Mora claims that he declined to participate in the coup because the oligarchic opposition's motivation for organizing it stemmed from opposition to Calderón's anti-Nazi policies, the one area in which the communist party agreed with Calderón. Moreover, Mora argued that a successful coup would create an even less-propitious political environment for labor. A coup never materialized.

Mora states that the Costa Rican communist party rejected this alliance with the opposition oligarchy only to form one with President Calderón, who came to symbolize the more reform-oriented oligarchic faction. The CP decided, at Mora's suggestion, to approach Calderón to form an alliance. This decision contradicted the party's previous criticism of Calderón during both the 1940 election and Calderón's first two years as president. Nonetheless, the party decided that its dual imperative, to decrease the likelihood of a conservative coup and to advance a project of additional reforms, compelled it to suggest and promote an alliance with Calderón's government. Calderón's declining popularity and his espousal of social security suggested that he both needed new support and might be open to promoting additional reforms. Consequently, on the night that Hine approached Mora, Mora called a communist party meeting, after which he approached Calderón and made an informal alliance.

Mora's lively, and largely unsubstantiated, story of a proposed coup is countered by those who argue that Calderón pursued the communist party to form an alliance when confronted by his declining support.

Whether the CP approached Calderón or Calderón pursued the CP, the overall argument remains the same. The division within the oligarchy created the political opportunity and political imperative for the different factions of the oligarchy to make alliances with the popular sectors. The new multiclass coalitions would oversee future reforms.

It is not clear what Calderón's agenda for his presidential term would have been had he not needed to create an alliance with the communists. Some argue that Calderón had developed a social Christian consciousness when exposed to Cardinal Mercier's writings as a medical student in Belgium, which informed his political desire to enact social reforms. Others argue that the tactical need to form an alliance with the communist party led to the legislation of additional reforms. A more realistic explanation identifies the interaction of these two factors as the impetus for the social reforms that ensued. Calderón had not voiced concern about social conditions during his terms as legislative deputy nor had he emphasized the need for social reforms during his presidential campaign. However, on the eve of his inauguration, he did refer to the need for social reforms and, independent of pressure from the communist party or the working class, initiated social security legislation. The more comprehensive democratic and social reforms that followed, however, were initiated in response to communist party pressures and the related desire to rally working-class support. The unlikely reform alliance would not have been viable had the two parties not been able to converge around reform legislation.

This alliance was announced symbolically on May 1, 1942, with the labor day march and the president's speech. Calderón arrived with Mora at the march. Workers carried banners announcing "national unity for the defense of the country" and "against fifth columns." The president's message on this day reiterated his support for social security (which had already been passed) but also announced his support for an increase in salaries, recognition of the right to strike, and the need to provide land and economic support to *campesinos*. He proposed a new chapter on social guarantees for the constitution. These two events—the two previously antagonistic leaders marching together and a presidential message that committed to additional social reforms—opened a new chapter in Costa Rican politics, one characterized by increased political participation and social change (Rojas Bolaños 1986: 82; Contreras and Cerdas 1988: 86–87).

The PRN and communist party alliance bolstered Calderón's political situation following the previous dramatic decrease in elite and popular support.[17] In particular, Calderón appeared to gain support among the lower classes in San José and in the banana plantations, the two sectors where the CP was especially strong. The communist party in turn was able to increase substantially its influence in official political circles beyond its actual numbers as well as gain space for energetic labor organizing. Wary of criticism, Manuel Mora declared in a 1942 radio message:

> Some people have objected to the plan of my party and consider it not at all revolutionary. And they add, that this is not a socialist plan but a bourgeois one. To this I must respond categorically that these people are right: that we are not trying to make a socialist revolution at this moment, but to find a practical form to put a brake on the economic crisis. . . . We have an emergency plan. . . . For the moment, what matters is to combat nazism-fascism and to combat hunger. (Mora 1980: 163–64)

Calderón sought to increase support for the official party's alliance with the communist party by acquiring the blessing of the Catholic Church. Calderón had already established good relations with the Church. In November 1940 the Congress had passed a law that permitted religious education in the schools; the 1940 decree had legalized an executive decree passed in 1929, which had already authorized the right to offer religious education in schools (Rodríguez 1980: 35). Moreover, Calderón had attempted to legitimate the legislation of social reforms by referring to their basis in Christian doctrine, as illustrated by this excerpt from a 1942 statement by the president:

> I had before me this alternative: either I could govern attending to vested interests and representing the perpetuation of privilege and domination based on the unjust treatment of the working classes, or I could prepare myself to fulfill my duties as Head of State to govern the people in an eminently Catholic tradition. Either I tolerated my own cowardice, renouncing the right—or perhaps duty—that my people had placed in my hands, to intervene with my authority, to search for a remedy for the undeserved poverty of the proletariat and in order to procure the arrival of norms and institutions that would better the economic, moral, and social conditions of our peasants and workers, or I was going directly to fulfill my ideals of better justice in national life. For this, I indicated in my 1940 message that my government would sustain in politics, the social christian doctrine, as disclosed in the admirable Encyclicals of Leon XIII and Pius XI, and as synthesized by the Cardinal Mercier in the Malinas Code of which I have spoken.[18]

But the Catholic Church would not sanction an alliance that included a self-proclaimed communist party.

Unexpectedly, Mora and Archbishop Sanabria exchanged letters dated June 14, 1943, and made public concessions to facilitate an alliance between the National Republican Party and the communist party.[19] As noted earlier, on June 13, 1943, the communist party, known officially as the Bloque de Obreros y Campesinos, dissolved itself. The "ex-communists" replaced the Bloque with Partido Vanguardia Popular (PVP). The "new" party, however, did not really change its program or membership. The archbishop, in turn, declared that Catholics could adhere to the program of Vanguardia Popular. He justified this declaration by appealing to the papal encyclicals *Rerum Novarum* and *Quadregessimo Anno*; in particular, he highlighted Catholic Action's role in sponsoring the latter encyclical. Moreover, he emphasized Vanguardia Popular's plans to work with Calderón, whose reforms he claimed were informed by the papal encyclicals. The archbishop emphasized that the principles stated by Vanguardia Popular did not "pervert or impair" the Church's doctrines.

These formal changes cleared the way for a historic democratizing alliance sanctioned by the Church. Archbishop Sanabria's decision to accept the alliance distinguished this already unlikely populist coalition even further, as it garnered popular support within parts of Costa Rica's Catholic community. Sanabria declared that one could not condemn the PVP's platform because "it does not seek to impose the dictatorship of the proletariat, nor is it an enemy of property, nor does it promote class struggle, nor does it persecute religion, the Church or the family."[20] Sanabria's position, however, broke with a hemispheric tradition of antagonism between the Catholic Church and communist parties. Indeed, its only precedent appears to have been the worker priests in France.

The PRN and PVP formalized their rapprochement on September 22, 1943, with the electoral alliance Bloque de la Victoria. On that date Calderón's Republican Party and Mora's Vanguardia Popular signed a seven-point accord: (1) to work together to elect Teodoro Picado Michalski as president;[21] (2) to struggle to decrease the cost of living; (3) to root out political corruption; (4) to fight against totalitarianism and to collaborate with democratic countries in the war; (5) to increase democratic guarantees and to support worker and *campesino* movements; (6) to respect religion, family, and property; and (7) to ensure that each party retained its independence and right to criticize.[22] Calderón had opened up the regime to a nonoligarchic party in exchange for increased political support. The PVP, in turn, traded its right to run a presidential candidate in the 1944 elections for the opportunity to define the electoral platform.

Indeed, Bloque de la Victoria's platform coincided with that of the communist party. The communists did not ask for any formal position in the upcoming government. Rather, they reserved the right to demand the fulfillment of the pact and, therefore, to promote social reforms (Rojas Bolaños 1986: 94; Contreras and Cerdas 1988: 103).

This historic union of the National Republican Party, the communist PVP, and the Catholic Church shocked many and instilled fear in others. The presidential candidate for the Bloque de la Victoria, Teodoro Picado Michalski, won the elections with about 60 percent of the vote.[23] For the PRN, 60 percent represented a substantial decrease from the 1940 elections, in which Calderón had secured 85 percent of the vote. Calderón, however, had run in an essentially uncontested race supported by a united oligarchy.

It would be foolhardy to conclude that these elections were suddenly free and fair, but they were significant for having crystallized divisions within the oligarchy, as opposing factions backed competing political parties, and for having incorporated nonoligarchic parties into electoral alliances. The subsequent formation of the multiclass reform coalition created an unprecedented opportunity to democratize access to state institutions, to increase the political influence of previously marginalized popular sectors, to legislate social and redistributive reforms, and thus to challenge the oligarchy's prior monopoly over political decision making. These developments further polarized politics and defined political camps through the 1948 elections.

Guatemala

Two successive multiclass movements emerged to challenge Guatemala's authoritarian regime of the Liberal period. The first movement began with the organization of university students for peaceful urban protests in June 1944. The Ubico dictatorship (1931–44) responded with force and thus provoked a public statement of reproach by the part of the Guatemalan elite that had become disaffected from the dictator. The multiclass movement that eventually emerged forced Ubico to resign. Ubico's resignation, however, did not signal an end to the military authoritarian regime, and a second multiclass reform coalition emerged. Unable to negotiate a peaceful democratic transition, this coalition organized for the regime's overthrow. It conspired with dissident military officers whose disaffection from the authoritarian regime weakened the dictatorship's coercive capabilities. The second multiclass, civilian-military movement overthrew the Liberal dictatorship in October 1944 and replaced it with a democratic regime. Thus the overthrow of Guatemala's military-authoritarian rule resulted from the confluence of a rise in urban popular organizing in the context of a group of disaffected elites and dissident military officers.

The multiclass reform coalition that oversaw the ensuing reform period was less institutionalized and stable than the Costa Rican reform coalition. On the one hand, the Guatemalan reformers had to build new political organizations. The reform parties maintained a loose alliance but were often beset by internal disputes that weakened the individual parties as well as the reform alliance. Moreover, the reform faction of the oligarchy did not dominate electoral politics and was unable to moderate social and economic legislation designed to address inequalities rooted in the Liberal period. The increasingly radical content of the reforms mobilized popular support but also alienated the parts of the oligarchy and military that had supported the original reform coalition. Consequently, the Guatemalan reform coalition assumed an increasingly popular cast, particularly with the final mobilization of the indigenous peasantry. Overall, the reform coalition followed a cycle of cooperation and conflict that ultimately founded a broadly based political front in the context of extreme political polarization.

RISE IN URBAN POPULAR ORGANIZING

General Jorge Ubico, dictator from 1931 to 1944, pursued political and economic policies to overcome the Great Depression and to promote economic stability. These policies were adopted at the expense of the popular classes. As discussed in Chapter 2, Ubico implemented new forms of repressive labor control over the indigenous and the poor and heavily repressed efforts to organize the incipient working class—most notably in 1932 and again in 1934, when he imprisoned and killed communist and union organizers. Economic policies during the 1930s and early 1940s resulted in frozen salaries, a decline in the standard of living, and a resort to forced labor through the public-works programs (Villamar Contreras 1960; Solórzano 1974: 78; Monteforte Toledo 1975: 11–12). The cost of living in Guatemala City rose approximately 30 percent between 1937 and 1944; food prices alone increased by 40 percent while per capita GDP decreased by about 21 percent for the same period (Bulmer-Thomas 1987: 100, 312).

The middle class, in contrast to the urban and rural lower classes, initially benefited economically from the Ubico dictatorship. Economic expansion and commerce led to a rise in small industry and the service professions. Moreover, the number of teachers in Guatemala City quintupled between 1920 and 1940. These developments contributed to an increase in the number of middle-level management, lawyers, and businessmen (Monteforte Toledo 1975: 11–12; Grieb 1976: 525, and 1979: 34–35, 271; Bulmer-Thomas 1987: 101). By the mid-1930s, however, the middle class began to share the fate of the urban working class confronted with declining economic opportunities and a reduction in the number of jobs. Handy (1985: 89–90) argues that two developments, in particular, adversely affected the middle and working classes and their opportunities for economic and social mobility. On the one hand, an industrial slowdown limited the number of jobs for both sectors: "Industrial production grew hardly at all in Guatemala during the depression and the percentage of gross domestic product coming from industry actually declined dramatically beginning in 1935." On the other hand, strict implementation of anti-inflationary policies coincided with a decline in public-sector spending, which decreased the number of private- and public-sector jobs. By 1940, public-sector spending had only regained two-thirds of the level achieved by 1929, before the Depression. This public cutback particularly affected university graduates who had traditionally found employment with the state (Handy 1986: 90).

Ultimately, the Liberal regime denied middle and working classes economic opportunities for social mobility and political opportunities for participation. By the mid-1930s, an increase in repression targeted not only the working class but also members of the middle classes. Guatemalan exiles in Mexico, in turn, organized against the Guatemalan regime. These efforts in fact contributed to the increased repression in the late 1930s directed against anyone suspected of subversion. To control society Ubico even required the registration of equipment and facilities used for printing (Grieb 1979: 266).

In the early 1940s, students at the University of San Carlos (USAC), primarily from middle-class families, organized a student association in defiance of state efforts to restrict freedom of expression and organization. Organizing occurred first among the thirteen law students at USAC who founded the Students' Law Association on October 20, 1942 (Petersen 1969: 63). Within a year students revived a university-wide association, Asociación de Estudiantes Universitarios (AEU), composed of student representatives from the different academic departments.

Two factors facilitated the emergence of this civic group. First, students carefully crafted their public discourse and activities to belie their political intentions and avoid political repression.[24] They organized ostensibly apolitical sociocultural events, such as beauty contests, which nonetheless often became forums for politically informed activities. As stated by Manuel Galich, an important student leader noted for his brilliant if sometimes paternalistic oratory, student leaders owed much to "the gentle university queen, under whose protective mantle the student conspiracy thrived" (Petersen 1969: 62, cited in Galich 1977: 91).

World War II constituted the second factor that provided a meager measure of protection for student organizing. Ubico had no ideological affinity with the Allies and indeed admired the administrative efficiency of Italy's Benito Mussolini. Nonetheless, for geostrategic reasons, he positioned himself on the side of the Allies. The U.S. embassy actively distributed Allied propaganda, including Franklin D. Roosevelt's Four Freedoms—freedom from fear, freedom of thought, freedom of conscience, freedom from misery. The Allied propaganda contrasted with Ubico's antidemocratic practices. Ubico said, "While I am president I will not grant liberty of the press nor of association because the people of Guatemala are not prepared for democracy and need a firm hand."[25] The outbreak of World War II and Ubico's alleged support for the Allied fight to defend democracy against fascism made it patently more difficult for Ubico to attack civic groups. Indeed, the rhetoric of World War II highlighted the clear contradiction between support for the Allied struggle to defend democracy and the Guatemalan regime's denial of simple democratic rights.

The emergence of these student associations signified a startling challenge to state control over society and, in particular, the weakening of the absolute control that the Liberal dictatorship of the 1930s had held over society. Galich, who became a reform politician, wrote, "But if [organizing the AEU] was the first defeat inflicted on the immovable and relentless Guatemalan totalitarian dictator, it also constituted triumph over the complex of fear, over the apathy . . . over the loss of the citizen's dignity" (Galich 1977: 232).

The Salvadoran uprising against Maximiliano Hernández Martínez in 1944 inspired the Guatemalan students. Indeed, Guatemala's most widely read daily newspaper reported that a Salvadoran student group had organized a demonstration that became an avenue to protest against Martínez. In April, more organized opposition occurred, including a strike by doctors. Women distributed propaganda in the streets, went from store to store to urge the shopkeepers to close their doors, and stood in front of theater entrances so that no one could enter. When a mass commemorating the uprising was banned, five thousand women dressed in black paraded through the streets of San Salvador in protest. In many ways, these events foreshadowed events in Guatemala in May and June of 1944.[26] The Guatemalan students invited a Salvadoran student revolutionary, Rogelio Herrera, to talk at Guatemala's University of San Carlos, where he delivered a fiery speech. Ubico responded by forcing Herrera to leave the country and dismissing the university's dean and his secretary, actions which outraged the students (Galich 1977: 244–59).

This confluence of events—international propaganda about the Four Freedoms, the overthrow of Martínez in El Salvador, and the dismissal of the university administration—inspired a group of Guatemalan students to stand up to the military regime. The students demanded the dismissal of university officials recently appointed by Ubico and the right to elect their replacements. Ubico agreed. This unexpected victory surprised the students, accustomed to coercive attempts to restrict freedom of expression and organizing, and they began to consider a call for broader and more radical political changes (Morales de la Cruz 1944: 29–30; Galich 1977: 309–11).

On June 21, 1944, the AEU called a general meeting in which members decided to deliver an ultimatum calling for university-wide changes. The ultimatum gave Ubico 24 hours to respond to the demands, after which students threatened with a general strike. Given that students held jobs in key areas of the country, including primary and secondary schools and state offices, their actions credibly threatened to generate wider disturbances (Palacios 1950: 11–12; Petersen 1969: 78–79). The ultimatum called for university autonomy, reform of the university's authoritarian rules and regulations, creation of departments such as humanities and education, founding an Institute of Indian Studies, freedom of the university press, and the right to student participation in university issues (Morales de la Cruz 1944: 30; Petersen 1969: 78, 95; Galich 1977).

Ubico responded by suspending constitutional guarantees on June 22, after which most of the student leaders took refuge in the Mexican embassy. Ubico issued two documents. The first document restricted articles 25, 26, 30, 37, and 38 of the constitution, thereby retracting the right of association, freedom of the press, protection from detention or imprisonment without legal cause, the inviolability of private property, including books, paper, and correspondence, and the inviolability of one's dwelling. In the second document, he claimed that agitators threatened the country and that their actions compelled him to reinstate order.

Ubico never explicitly identified the students as agitators, although the inference was unmistakable. He argued that a suspension of constitutional guarantees would restore order, peace, and "the defense of democratic institutions and liberty of nations" from the alleged nazi-fascist tendencies (*El Imparcial*, June 22, 1944). He claimed that he would reinstate the constitutional guarantees when the agitators stopped their provocations.

The stated suspension of constitutional guarantees was nothing new. The dictator had not respected constitutional guarantees throughout his thirteen-year rule. Nonetheless, the suspension presented a clear threat to the students and simultaneously transformed student demands from a primarily university struggle to a political one of national scope (Grieb 1976: 529; Galich 1977: 326). Persecution targeted the students of the AEU and teachers in the Asociación Nacional de Maestros. This repressive policy did not differ from that of the previous thirteen years; however, the extent of public and organized opposition within the university, which then spread to the urban popular sectors and parts of the oligarchy, did.

OLIGARCHY DIVIDES

The suspension of constitutional guarantees exacerbated latent opposition within parts of the oligarchy to the Ubico dictatorship. One part of the oligarchy organized a public response to protest the symbolic suspension of constitutional guarantees and treatment of the university students. This response marked a weakening of the Ubico dictatorship, which had ostensibly defended the oligarchy's economic interests during the Depression. With a declining economy, much of the oligarchy decreased its support for Ubico, and, with the restrictions placed on political organizing, part of the oligarchy came to oppose the authoritarian regime itself.

Ubico had eradicated governmental corruption, provided increased infrastructure (which was beneficial for coffee transport and exports), and balanced the budget to achieve a more financially stable environment by the mid-1930s. Despite Ubico's ability to restore Guatemala's financial standing, the policies did not develop an internal market or boost the industrial, commercial, and financial sectors. Indeed, Ubico had drastically restrained production and commerce in order to maintain the deflationary situation (Solórzano 1974). By the early 1940s, the economy had stagnated, showing a decline in foreign exchange and monetary circulation that simultaneously reduced the cost of living, froze economic ac-

TABLE 8

Gross Domestic Product in Guatemala, 1930–44

Year	GDP	Year	GDP
1930	449,595	1938	670,863
1931	419,222	1939	754,982
1932	366,919	1940	862,410
1933	370,676	1941	908,491
1934	419,296	1942	920,326
1935	484,637	1943	613,709
1936	665,639	1944	594,863
1937	652,826		

SOURCE: Bulmer-Thomas 1987:308.
NOTE: 1970 prices (thousand dollars calculated at purchasing-power parity exchange rates). Net factor cost.

tivity, and increased poverty (Solórzano 1974: 78). Ubico's orthodox economic policies no longer seemed golden. As Table 8 indicates, following a steady increase in GDP from 1932 to 1942, Guatemala experienced a rapid drop, of approximately 35 percent, between 1942 and 1944 (Bulmer-Thomas 1987: 308). Consequently, the oligarchy began to voice support for the development of a more diverse and developed economy.

Some of these disaffected elites began to organize a new party, called El Partido Social Democrático, between May and June of 1944 (Morales de la Cruz 1944: 29–30). They organized clandestinely because Ubico had also closed the space for elites to organize either political or economic organizations. With the declared suspension of social guarantees, these reform oligarchs decided to ally with the students and, for the first time during the thirteen-year-old dictatorship, they declared their opposition to a public decree that encroached on civil guarantees (Petersen 1969: 78–79).

Disaffection culminated on June 24, 1944, in the publication of a document called *Memorial de los 311*, which denounced the suspension of social guarantees. According to a former student leader, Marco Antonio Villamar Contreras, among the 311 signatories were many prominent members of Guatemalan high society, many of whom Ubico considered to be his close friends and supporters (Interview with Villamar Conteras, Oct. 27, 1989). The *Memorial de los 311* did not really protest the *suspension* of constitutional guarantees, since there had been an absolute disrespect of these rights for thirteen years. Rather, it reflected disaffection by part of the oligarchy from the authoritarian regime. Economic policies no longer benefited the oligarchy, and, in the absence of advantageous economic policies, part of the oligarchy appeared less willing to tolerate or support the control and repression of civil society.

Ubico tried to regain elite support by attacking the Germans who had established a strong economic base in coffee, banking, and marketing (by 1940 they owned 109 plantations) but had not sought to assimilate, maintaining dual citizenship and geographic isolation (Handy 1984: 97; Woodward 1985).[27] By the end of June, Ubico passed Decree 3115, which expropriated the coffee farms belonging to German nationals (*El Imparcial*, June 23, 1944; Galich 1977: 351). Ubico calculated that these decrees would stir up economic nationalism among the national oligarchy, who did not maintain strong ties with the powerful German elite and, therefore, would not perceive confiscation of German property as an attack on private property or their oligarchic position and privilege. Simultaneously, these actions would place Guatemala on the Allies' side.[28]

These measures did not increase the Guatemalan oligarchy's support for Ubico, as he had hoped (Grieb 1979: 249–63; Handy 1984: 97–98; Gleijeses 1989a: 44). Nor did they inhibit the elite from publicly expressing its disaffection from the regime. Indeed, with the publication of the *Memorial de los 311*, middle-class and elite opposition joined forces to oppose the regime. This multiclass alliance challenged Ubico and eventually oversaw the overthrow of the dictatorship (Morales de la Cruz 1944: 28–39; Petersen 1969: 78–79; Galich 1977: 334–36; García Añoveros 1978: 136; Herrera 1986: 64).

THE REFORM COALITIONS: OVERTHROWING THE REGIME

The written challenges to Ubico from the university students and the 311 members of the elite developed into a broader political movement by June 24, 1944. University students and teachers led a silent march through the streets, which mobilized not only the middle classes but also the urban poor and working class. In a public display of pride and anger that contrasted markedly with the thirteen years of fear and silence, the marchers broke the silence with their presence rather than with words to demand that Ubico step down (Grieb 1976: 529; Galich 1977; Gleijeses 1989a: 51). On the following day, another demonstration took place that mobilized vocal and even larger crowds; that afternoon the first martyr, teacher María Chinchilla Recinos, was killed by Ubico's forces. On the third day of demonstrations, offices, shops, and transportation services closed in protest.

Commercial participation in the general strike clearly strengthened the students' demands and highlighted the degree of societal opposition to the dictatorship. The regime passed a law threatening to punish those businesses that closed their doors in deference to the general strike. To avoid a total standstill, the government militarized transportation services. Women in the opposition traveled from house to house to discuss the importance of the general strike and to convince people to close shop, despite the newly declared penalties. This communication link recalled the role played by Salvadoran women in the 1944 spring uprising against the Salvadoran dictator. The Guatemalan government called these demonstrations communist and fascist, but few believed these charges (Morales de la Cruz 1944: 51–56; Galich 1977). Individuals and groups from all classes—workers, professionals, merchants, and others—drew up petitions that they sent to Ubico. An army general assessing the situation concluded that Ubico would most likely not be able to control the popular mobilization. He suggested to Ubico that he resign (Morales de la Cruz 1944: 90–94).

These audacious developments—a rise in popular organizing, opposition to the regime within the oligarchy, and the spontaneous multiclass protest movement—challenged Ubico's stated worldview. He had declared that authoritarian rule was not only necessary but also desirable. He is reported to have believed that the Guatemalan people admired and supported him. Ubico therefore thought that the protests would subside and Guatemalans would rally together to request his continued rule. The institutions that he had constructed reinforced this perception, because they limited the space to voice opposition.[29] According to U.S. ambassador Boaz Long, the dictator became disillusioned and embittered as the protests continued.[30] Ubico resigned on July 1, 1944. Those who had mobilized against him thought that they had opened the doors for democratic rule.

Ubico's resignation removed the dictator physically from the National Palace but did not excise his power base. Ubico appointed a triumvirate of military officials to replace him without replacing the state institutions that had sustained authoritarian rule. Without any particular regard for their political or military merit, he chose three officers— Federico Ponce Vaides, Eduardo Villagrán Ariza, and Buenaventura Pineda—who happened to have been waiting in the hall. Given the disproportionately high number of generals in the army and the limited duties for all of them, military officers had had a habit of waiting in the National Palace to receive their daily assignments (Grieb 1976: 532).

Ponce eventually muscled his way into the position of provisional president. He passed progressive legislation that restored constitutional guarantees, extended amnesty to those who had become political prisoners during the last period of Ubico's rule, and provided space for the organization of political parties and unions. He also increased salaries for public workers, conceded to student demands, abolished Ubico's monopolies in the sugar, meat, and tobacco industries as well as other government controls of the economy, and publicly declared that he would hand over power to the winner of elections to be held from November 17 through 19 (Grieb 1976: 536; Herrera 1986: 65). With this perceived opening, urban activists quickly organized political parties, unions, and social clubs.

Following this brief political opening, Ponce oversaw an increase in repression in the fall of 1944. Efforts to control or suppress civic organizing, however, often had the opposite effect, as Guatemalans realized that political change would not occur without further organization against the regime. For example, on September 23, 1944, the Ponce government replaced Dr. Arriola, director of the Escuela Central para Varones. A number of students left the school in protest. As September progressed, one subdirector and a number of inspectors resigned in protest. The students of the secondary schools declared a strike, with the support of the AEU, many of whom were teachers at the school. Along with the strike, the students sent a manifesto to the palace in which they demanded Arriola's reinstatement. Ponce responded by closing the school, canceling fellowships, and arresting Arriola (Palacios 1950: 34–42; Petersen 1969: 85). This series of events actually fueled opposition to Ponce as his initial respect for civil rights gave way to coercive efforts to control civic organizing.

Government repression increased in scope in October 1944, targeting not only popular sectors but also influential members of society. The October assassination of Alejandro Córdova, the prominent owner and editor of *El Imparcial*, the most widely read newspaper in Guatemala, was a watershed. Córdova's paper had not denounced Ubico's dictatorship. However, during the apparent opening under Ponce, *El Imparcial* more openly criticized the regime. It was commonly assumed that the government had ordered the killing. The murder boldly demonstrated that Ponce was willing and capable, like Ubico, to target all members of society. It also highlighted that freedom of expression did not exist. Indeed, Córdova's murder led many to confirm beliefs for the need to overthrow a regime which would continue to resort to violence against critics, regardless of their social standing.

With the rise in popular organizing and the increasing electoral support for presidential candidate Juan José Arévalo Bermejo and the reform parties, Ponce made it clear that he would not pass on the executive mantle. Following the example of Ubico, he rigged the congressional elections in October 1944, in which the official slate won, literally, 48,530 votes out of a total of 44,571 ballots. On October 16, the non-government parties agreed that it was impossible to continue with their campaigns in this repressive environment. On October 18, students and teachers initiated another strike (El Imparcial, Oct. 24, 1944).

Corruption, disrespect for the constitution they had been trained to uphold, and disparities in pay scale exacerbated divisions within the military (Grieb 1976: 539–40), which occurred primarily along rank lines. Junior officers became disaffected by the existing military organization. During the 1930s, professionalization of the military constituted one of the important objectives outlined by the dictator. The military academy inculcated cadets in the 1930s with a new set of principles and curricula, presumably based on the merit system.[31] Nonetheless, the Guatemalan military had become a travesty of professionalism, and training contrasted markedly with the practices of the army itself. By 1944, the military had over 80 generals for a force of some 15,000 men (Grieb 1976: 526; Interview with Paz Tejada, Aug. 11, 18, 1990). Many of these generals had been promoted for political reasons without any regard for their merit. Rumor had it that some were illiterate. Ponce's mediocre record embodied the contradiction between the professionalization of the military that had occurred under Ubico's dictatorship and the unprofessional nature of those who held the highest positions in the military. Junior officers saw little room for advancement, given the top-heavy structure of the military and the top brass's lack of respect for the military principles that they had learned. As a final insult, senior officers made five times more money than the junior officers who were often more competent and skilled.

With the failure of a student plan to overthrow the regime, parts of the military joined forces with the students and dissident oligarchy to re-craft and implement a plan to overthrow Ponce.[32] Representatives from the student movement, professionals, and the military held a meeting in mid-October, 1944. Jacobo Arbenz Guzmán, who in July 1944 had resigned from the military, and Major Carlos Aldana Sandoval plotted much of the military strategy. They emerged with a plan that outlined an attack on the Guardia de Honor, where the tanks and other heavy armament were held. Sandoval went to El Salvador before the planned attack, but the conspirators invited Major Francisco Arana, commander of the Guardia de Honor, to lead the rebellion at his own post. Joined by an estimated two to three thousand civilians who had received arms the night of October 19, the conspirators successfully overthrew Ponce on October 20, 1944.[33]

The resort to arms and successful overthrow of Ponce marked the end of the Liberal authoritarian regime and is referred to colloquially as the October Revolution.[34] The composition of the following revolutionary junta demonstrated the multiclass nature of the revolt: it was headed by two military officers, Jacobo Arbenz Guzmán (who had helped to plan the uprising) and Francisco Arana (who had helped in the last stages of planning the military success at the *Guardia de Honor*), and a wealthy business professional, Jorge Toriello. The successful uprising created the space for the political and social reform period. The revolutionary junta prepared the way for elections, respect for civil rights, and a constituent assembly to institutionalize democratic rules.

After thirteen years of Ubico's tight control over the state and society, the elections created a general excitement and disarray. Political parties formed, campaigns were launched, and support committees emerged. Most prominent among the reform parties were the Frente Popular Libertador (FPL) and Renovación Nacional (RN), which included members from the student movement and teachers who had played key roles in the two coalitions that had overthrown the regime.

Juan José Arévalo Bermejo won the presidential election and mobilized majority support. Arévalo had been living in Argentina as a teacher and philosopher. His distance from the authoritarian regime symbolized a political purity that others who had lived in Guatemala could rarely claim.[35] Arévalo won the 1945 elections with 85 percent of the vote. The students who had mobilized the reform movement and engineered Arévalo's candidacy also won overwhelming support. In the first Congress of the Republic, 46 out of 50, or 92 percent, of the deputies were university students who were under 35 years of age (Silvert 1969: 35). The electoral support for Arévalo and the university students signaled the popular mandate for reform. In this electoral context, the reform faction of the oligarchy was less successful. Unlike its Costa Rican counterpart, it did not dominate the reform coalition that governed Guatemala between 1944 and 1954.

EVOLUTION OF THE GOVERNING REFORM COALITION

A multiclass coalition initiated the reform period in the absence of well-defined political parties and civic associations. This poorly organized political and civil society was a legacy of the Liberal period in Guatemala. Although the electorate gave widespread support to the students of the AEU and their candidate Arévalo in the 1945 elections, the progression of the reform period in the absence of well-formed associations saw politicians and activists scrambling to create political institutions and to forge political platforms. In some cases, these activists formed new parties on the basis of ideological concerns; in others they formed them on the basis of political ambitions. In this context of political flux, 24 parties emerged during the ten-year Guatemalan reform period (Silvert 1969: 162), but the newly formed parties generally lacked a well-defined political apparatus.

The first student-organized political parties, Frente Popular Libertador and Renovación Nacional, would change once the initial euphoria of toppling Ubico and Ponce had subsided. As the new politicians refined political platforms and became better acquainted with their colleagues as political players, new political parties emerged while other short-lived ones passed away. As Figure 3 illustrates, a series of reform parties emerged from 1944 to 1954. The fluid reform alliance found its most coherent institutional expression in electoral fronts during the 1944 and 1950 presidential elections.[36] With support from urban and rural popular sectors, these fronts were able to sustain their legislative majority and, therefore, to increase their political independence from the reform faction of the oligarchy, which often objected to significant reform bills but was unable to prevent their legislation.

But despite these electoral coalitions the reform parties themselves engaged in cycles of cooperation, factionalization, and fusion, as illustrated by Figure 3. Divisions occurred both within parties and between them. The Guatemala reform parties splintered first around the radical-versus-moderate nature of the reforms passed and later around affiliation with the Communist Party (founded in 1950 and renamed the Partido Guatemalteco del Trabajo [PGT] in 1952).[37] Moreover, with increasingly radical reforms and the identification of the PGT with the reform coalition, the reform alliance alienated its erstwhile oligarchic and middle-class allies from 1944. As discussed in Chapter 6, the opposition that followed failed to organize electorally and resorted to violence to combat the reforms and mobilization overseen by the reform alliance.

By the presidential administration of Jacobo Arbenz Guzmán (1951–54), the reform alliance included middle- and working-class-based parties and relied heavily on popular organizations for their support. Although the reformers created a front to combat increasing coup threats from the opposition, they did not create or sustain an institutional front.

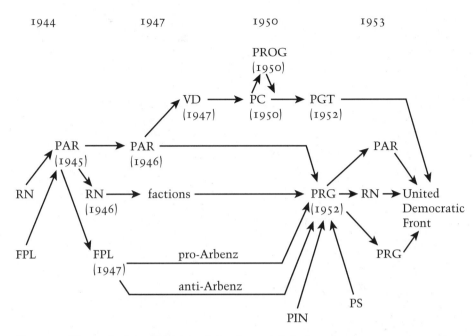

1944   1947   1950   1953

Figure 3. The evolution of Guatemala's reform political parties from 1944 to 1954. RN stands for Renovación Nacional, FPL for Frente Popular Libertador, PAR for Partido de Acción Revolucionaria, VD for Vanguardia Democrática, PC for Partido Comunista, PROG for Partido Revolucionario Obrero de Guatemala, PGT for Partido Guatemalteco del Trabajo, PRG for Partido de la Revolución Guatemalteca, PIN for Partido de Integridad Nacional, and PS for Partido Socialista. Members of VD, the majority of whom were also in the PAR, met clandestinely after 1947, and formed the Partido Comunista in 1950. Following conflict within the PC, labor leader Víctor Manuel Gutiérrez left the party in 1949, formed the PROG in 1950, but rejoined the PC in 1952. The PC became the Partido Guatemalteco de Trabajo in December 1952 (see Gleijeses 1991:78–79).

By the end of the reform period, the reform parties formed a loose political alliance that generally voted together on reform legislation and sought to defend the democratic regime from the rising counterreform opposition. When threats of a coup became palpable in 1953, these parties joined forces once again, including the PGT, to form the United Democratic Front.

The mid-twentieth-century coalitions that emerged from a division within the oligarchy and the rising organization of popular sectors created a democratic opening in Costa Rica and Guatemala. The 1940s and

1950s witnessed a striking rise in labor organizing and the increased influence of these sectors within the governing reform coalition. These governing coalitions, in turn, institutionalized a new set of state-society relations with the legislation of labor codes, social security, and redistributive reforms. The reforms targeted the concentration of economic power associated with the respective regimes of accumulation inherited from the nineteenth century. Chapters 4 and 5 explore the mobilization and reform that distinguished this mid-twentieth-century democratic opening and generated the counterreform movements responsible for its overthrow.

CHAPTER 4

Addressing the Social Question

The mid-twentieth-century reform coalitions confronted the historic task of addressing the social question in Costa Rica and Guatemala.* They codified civic rights, constructed democratic institutions, and enacted social welfare policies. These legal, institutional, and social reforms expanded individual and collective rights, increased popular and middle-class access to the state, and resulted in the popular sectors' increasing influence in politics. Organized labor, in particular, increased its clout in political circles as it engaged in more effective organizing in the workplace. In the process, the governing reform coalition redirected the state's mandate to oversee reforms and attempted to strengthen state capacity to protect these newly acquired rights. For this reason, this complex of democratic reforms and social welfare policies has variously been referred to as the beginning of mass politics, the period of initial labor incorporation, and the expansion of citizenship rights.

The expansion of popular-sector participation and representation in governing circles culminated in demands to reform the concentration of economic power that had developed with the commercialization of agriculture. In both cases, reform coalitions that had initially focused on legislating entitlement and regulatory measures for labor-capital

---

*The *social question* refers to elite and middle-class fear and/or concern about how to address the growing poverty and conflict generated by capital-labor relations in order to alleviate social misery and stave off a social uprising.

relations in the city began to formulate policies to redistribute property and wealth. These pressures became particularly salient as the coalitions found themselves increasingly dependent on organized popular sectors in civil society and increasingly the target of an ever-more-hostile opposition.

This chapter focuses on the parallel forging of democratic institutions, social welfare policies, and redistributive reforms that were designed to address the social question and expand citizenship rights in Costa Rica and Guatemala. In both cases, these reforms polarized society between proreform sectors and an opposition that ultimately would overthrow the reform coalitions. While examining the parallel construction of these institutions and reforms, this chapter underscores important differences in their scope and targets.

The scope of institutional changes and social reforms proved more comprehensive in Guatemala than in Costa Rica, in large part because of combined differences in the balance of power within the respective reform coalitions, the availability of the rural sector for mobilization, and the strategies deployed to initiate the reform period. In Costa Rica, where the reform coalition initiated a gradual transition and where the elite dominated this move with little support from rural sectors, the reforms assumed a moderate, urban character. By contrast, the abrupt transition to democratic politics in Guatemala created the political opportunity to dismantle repressive institutions and to redesign the political constitution along more inclusive and democratic lines. The subordinate role assumed by the Guatemalan oligarchy created political spaces for the popular and ultimately for the rural electoral basis of the reform coalition to push for more comprehensive reforms and access to the state.

In their efforts to democratize the political system, the Costa Rican and Guatemalan reformers targeted the institutional mechanisms used during the Liberal period to bypass popular input into the political process. In Costa Rica, these institutional changes included the creation of more transparent institutional mechanisms to oversee an electoral system previously characterized by fraud and corruption. In Guatemala, institutional changes included the restructuring of the military and rewriting of the constitution that Guatemalan dictators had used to sustain their authoritarian power. The Costa Rican and Guatemalan reform coalitions also launched significant socioeconomic reforms. In the initial stages, the reform coalitions in both Costa Rica and Guatemala focused on entitlement and regulatory policies that largely affected urban areas; organized labor increased its political influence in elections while

TABLE 9

*Scope and Target of Democratic and Social Reforms in
Costa Rica (1941–48) and Guatemala (1944–54)*

	Costa Rica (Moderate reforms)	Guatemala (Radical reforms)
Democratic institutions	Electoral reform law (1946) limits fraudulent practices typical of Liberal period	New constitution (1945) extends suffrage; demilitarization and decentralization of politics counteract dictatorial and coercive practices from Liberal period
Entitlement and regulatory policies	Social insurance (1941), chapter on social guarantees (1943), and labor code (1943) codify, uphold, and extend ad hoc rights from the Liberal period	New constitution grants freedom of association and expression that had been denied during Liberal period; labor code (1947) grants rights to labor organizations that are eventually extended to rural areas
Redistributive policies	Tax reform (1946); state effort to redistribute capital challenges oligarchy's prior control over finance and, therefore, the regime of accumulation	Land reform (1952) challenges oligarchy's concentrated control over productive lands; coupled with labor reform, land reform challenges the regime of accumulation

it engaged in more effective organizing in the workplace. In the later stage, the reform coalitions focused on redistributive reforms. The target of these reforms varied according to differences in regimes of accumulation originally established with the commercialization of agriculture in the nineteenth century. In Costa Rica, a taxation reform attempted to regulate capital and to finance the urban social reforms already legislated. In Guatemala, land reform attempted to regulate access to land (see Table 9).

As with any significant political initiative, these institutional changes generated heated debates and heightened opposition to the reform coalitions—particularly within oligarchic circles. During the reform periods these conflicts tended to revolve around access to and influence over the state. Opposition circles decried their waning influence over policy making, the assumed communist influence over decision making, and the alleged communist penetration of state offices. This opposition became particularly vehement as the reform coalitions moved from legislating entitlement and regulatory policies to redistributive reforms that were perceived by many oligarchs as a threat to property, wealth, and the existing regime of accumulation. These reforms also alienated many sectors of the middle class, which questioned the consequences of these policies and were persuaded by arguments that communists would increase their control. In both Costa Rica and Guatemala, in the face of rising doubts about the ability to assume state office through elections, rising fears of communist influence over decision making and penetration of state offices, the perception of redistributive reforms as an attack on property relations, and speculation that the reform coalition could continue to rely on democratic procedures to advance additional economic and political reforms, the opposition eventually turned to arms.

The historical reform sequences discussed below raise the question of the relationship between private property, broadly defined, and democracy. This chapter and the ones that follow emphasize that the governing coalitions overseeing the mid-twentieth-century democratic reforms politicized economic relations in a polarizing fashion. Enfranchised groups began to pressure for redistributive reforms. These redistributive reforms in turn generated the opposition that overthrew the democracy itself. What can one infer from this? Can new democracies ever implement redistributive reforms without precipitating an oligarchic reaction to overthrow the regime? Otherwise stated, what are the conditions under which an oligarchy will accept reforms that directly challenge the terms of capital accumulation and, hence, the basis of its economic power?

This chapter analyzes two cases in which redistributive reforms generated an oligarchic opposition that organized against the reforms. Chapter 6 presents a case in which an oligarchy did not overthrow the regime following redistributive reforms. A comparison of these two failed and one successful case suggests that sequencing matters. When reform coalitions implemented redistributive reforms after democratic institutions were set up, they generated an oligarchic opposition to democracy, which turned to arms when two conditions were met: the oligarchy had lost consecutive elections and, therefore, doubted that it could affect policy making or have access to state resources; and the oligarchy could envision a better and viable alternative to the one being offered by the governing coalition. Without the hope of putting up a good fight within the democratic system, the oligarchy turned to the overthrow of the system it held responsible for the challenge to property relations. These conditions describe Costa Rica and Guatemala during their respective reform periods and led the oligarchic opposition to turn to arms to overthrow the governing coalitions. Conversely, as explored in Chapter 6, the ability to reform property relations without undermining democracy was viable precisely at the moment a democratic regime was founded—when the oligarchy was politically divided (i.e., weakened) and reluctantly forced to conclude (and hope) that the redistributive reforms initiated were the unexpected and one-time price it had to pay for a new regime that would be better than the last; the oligarchy accepted these reforms so long as it expected that the new system would not exclude its members politically but would create the institutional space for their participation.

In short, the mid-twentieth-century reform coalition reacted against the Liberal period and promoted a policy agenda to create democratic institutions and to address the social question. The balance of power within these coalitions would influence the scope of these reforms and the unity of oligarchic opposition.* Comprehensive reforms generated unified oligarchic opposition in Guatemala; moderate reforms resulted in continued elite division in Costa Rica. In both countries, the opposition would overthrow the democratic regimes, shortly after redistributive reforms had been passed. As it did in the reform coalitions, the unity or division of the oligarchy within the counterreform coalition would prove significant. In the aftermath of the overthrow, Guatemala's unified elite closed the doors on democracy while Costa Rica's divided elite kept those doors partially open.

Costa Rica: Moderate Reforms

The Costa Rican reform coalition legislated moderate reforms during the administrations of Presidents Calderón (1940–44) and Picado (1944–48) as part of a politically expedient exchange with the communist party and Archbishop Sanabria. Following the initial social security measure passed by Calderón in 1941, the reform coalition passed a labor code, a constitutional chapter on social guarantees, and eventually an income tax law. The reform politicians extended individual and collective rights, particularly to labor, increased the state's role in administer-

---

*This chapter does not include documentation regarding the increase in popular organization and the political opposition that ensued. Refer to Chapters 5 and 6 regarding the increasing polarization that surrounded and resulted from these actions.

ing these rights, and increased organized labor's access to government through the participation of the communist party in the reform coalition. In the end, the reforms simultaneously mobilized labor support for, and further alienated part of the oligarchy from, the Calderón and Picado reform administrations.

In the absence of any coherent ideology shared by the reform coalition, the Costa Rican communist party's platform influenced the political tone of the social policies between 1942 and 1948. The party's impact on social policy represented the first time that nonoligarchic organizations had acquired a consequential and sustained role in executive circles. Through its discourse and politicking the CP pushed for reforms that primarily advanced urban labor interests.[1] Although most of the social legislation adopted language that applied to all sectors, a graduated implementation in effect gave priority to urban, male labor over other sectors. The reform coalition limited popular participation, however, in making or implementing the social reforms themselves (Rosenberg 1983; Dunkerley 1988; Edelman and Kenen 1989:83).

Yet, as the communist party increased its political influence, it remained overshadowed by Calderón's executive power. Appealing to the ideals of social Christian thought contained in the papal encyclicals *Rerum Novarum* of Leo XIII and *Quadregessimo Anno* of Pius XI and reinterpreted by Cardinal Mercier of Belgium, President Calderón and Archbishop Sanabria set out to address the social question with the goal of pursuing "the harmony of classes" (Salazar 1981:88–89). Given Calderón's relative power, the reform coalition did not seek to transform property relations or to redress rural class relations. So long as the oligarchic faction within the reform coalition dominated both the executive and the legislature, it was able to temper pressures for reforms in the economic and political realms. Hence, while the reform coalition oversaw the increased power of incipient organized urban labor, it also minimized the state's role in defining economic development issues, which remained the preserve of the private sector. In fact, Calderón promised that the government would not become involved in areas where Costa Rica's elite could adequately promote economic development. In this spirit, his administration supported new private initiatives by providing tax credit and foreign-exchange privileges (Bell 1971:27–28). Presidents Calderón and Picado, however, were identified more clearly with reforms that benefited the popular sectors over the oligarchy.

Costa Rica's reforms from 1941 to 1948 were of three types: electoral, entitlement, and redistributive. Together, these reforms advanced citizenship rights but stimulated opposition. Entitlement and associated regulatory policies alienated a fraction of the elite and part of the organized middle and upper-middle class, which mobilized behind Cortés and later Ulate, as discussed in Chapter 6. The rising opposition within oligarchic circles compelled the administration to generate additional political support among the popular sectors, upon which they had come to depend.

A subsequent tax reform during the Picado administration sought to increase state revenues, in large part to support the increase in state spending for social services. Elites perceived the redistributive legislation as a threat to their control over capital and as a symbol of a state role increasingly antagonistic to oligarchic interests. The tax legislation, more redistributive in cast than the prior legislation, created a more active opposition among Costa Rica's elite, which combined its opposition to the tax with demands to control the newly created electoral tribunal. Ultimately, the elite lent its support to the armed opposition.

ENTITLEMENT AND REGULATORY POLICIES

President Calderón's administration codified and regulated social programs that largely targeted urban labor. The social insurance Calderón announced in 1941, before the formation of the reform coalition, sought to systematize and extend an earlier social insurance policy. State workers had received a modicum of social security coverage for accident insurance as well as old age and disability pensions prior to 1940. The state had assigned pensions on an ad hoc basis and generally responded to individual petitions rather than to collectivities; in contrast to most other Latin American countries, the state had not tended to provide concessions in response to pressure from organized popular sectors—except in the case of railroad workers (Rosenberg 1983:42–49). The social insurance program began operation in November 1942, although the government still had to fix rates of contribution and benefit and outline administrative procedures (ILO May 1942:575–76).

The social insurance legislation created a Social Insurance Fund to provide coverage for maternity, sickness, disability, and old age, and insurance for widows, orphans, and survivors. The reform made insurance compulsory for industrial or agricultural workers, self-employed artisans, and domestic employees who made a monthly salary of 300 colones or less and were younger than 60; the administration later raised this wage limit to 400 colones.[2]

With the Social Insurance Act, Costa Rica became the first Central

American country to legislate such a reform. The comparatively impressive coverage, however, was not automatically extended. The reformers gave priority to the low-income sectors in the urban areas, and, in November 1943, the Costa Rican Insurance Fund issued a regulation clarifying that coverage would remain limited. Until further notice, the fund would only cover sickness and maternity in the country's six largest cities, thereby postponing both the coverage for all services in the rural areas and the full coverage in the cities that were stipulated by the original act.

The Social Insurance Act also created state institutions to educate the population and to enforce compliance. The Caja de Seguridad Social established an office to perform outreach; it distributed propaganda to educate the targeted population and those who might attempt to resist the program. Additionally, the fund created a body of inspectors who possessed the legal right to investigate the number of workers employed at a particular establishment and whether employers were paying adequate wages and contributing appropriate amounts to the fund. In cases where employers made it difficult for inspectors to carry out their work, a fine could be levied. Those employers found guilty of sidestepping the Social Insurance Act were to have their names printed and publicized (ILO Jan. 1942, May 1942, Apr. 1943, Aug. 1944; Bell 1971:30; Rosenberg 1983:60–73).

With the formation of the reform coalition in 1942, the legislature became a site of more active debate over how to extend social services and codify labor rights. Rather than legislating measures in purely top-down fashion, the reform coalition responded to organized social pressures and created new avenues for political participation and union activity by Costa Rica's popular classes. The new reform coalition sent a series of proposals to the Congress in 1942 that included a constitutional chapter on social guarantees, a commission to draw up a labor code, a proposal to freeze rents and to create housing cooperatives, and the proposal to allow rural laborers to work uncultivated and untitled land. On December 23, 1942, Congress made arbitration compulsory between workers and employers in industry and commerce (ILO June 1943; Bell 1971:28; Rojas Bolaños 1978:20, and 1986:82; Dunkerley 1988:126; Ministerio de Educación Pública 1994).

Even though President Calderón had suspended individual guarantees for security reasons related to World War II, the Congress approved the proposal to add a chapter on social guarantees to the constitution. Calderón signed the proposal in July 1943. The final version created the constitutional parameters and legal framework to pursue a number of subsequent social reforms and legitimated an increased role for the state to advance those reforms. The International Labour Office reported, "The proposed amendment states that the social aim of the State shall be to provide a minimum of welfare for every inhabitant of the country by the rationalisation of the production, distribution, and consumption of wealth, by giving the worker the special protection to which he is entitled, by protecting mothers, children, and the aged and disabled, and by adopting all other measures for ensuring collective progress and concord" (ILO Nov. 1942:588).

The chapter created the conditions to legislate labor rights. It declared that work was a social duty but also stipulated individual and collective rights, including the right to association, the right to strike, a minimum wage that would periodically be adjusted, an eight-hour workday, overtime pay, a weekly rest day, and annual vacations. To protect these rights, the chapter sanctioned the formation of trade unions, the right to collective bargaining and to strike, and the creation of work tribunals. The chapter also privileged hiring Costa Rican workers over workers from other countries. Furthermore, it highlighted the need to protect the family, stipulated conditions under which Congress could expropriate private property to serve "the social interest," and supported the formation of cooperatives (ILO Nov. 1943:587–88; Bell 1971:30–31; Rodríguez 1980:79; Rojas Bolaños 1978:20, and 1986:82; Salazar 1981:84–85; Aguilar 1989:20; P. Williams 1989:109). Although the chapter advanced a constitutional and philosophical commitment to social rights, it did not carry legal weight. Rather, it provided an opening from which subsequent social legislation could be passed (Bell 1971:30–31).

The constitutional chapter on social guarantees provided the legal mandate to legislate a labor code, which the Congress approved on August 26, 1943, two months after it had approved the chapter. The first article stated that the code was written in accord with social Christian thought. According to Oscar Barahona Streber, who wrote the code,[3] the draft was originally sent to Archbishop Sanabria for his comments and approval:

> Archbishop Sanabria received me and said to me, "Look Don Oscar . . . there is a big difference between the social guarantees and the labor code." And I said to him, "Monsignor, what difference? They have been written by the same hand." He said, "In the social guarantees, you explained very clearly that they were based in Christian principles of social justice. But one does not find [this explanation] in the draft for the labor code." I said, "Monsignor, it is because the labor code is derivative of the constitutional

reform." . . . "Okay," he said, "but one has to prepare this code to avoid any doubts." Already, the Monsignor feared that the communists were going to claim this legislation as their own. Therefore, I said to him, "Monsignor, we are going to arrange this in a very simple manner. The first article of the labor code that you have in your hands says that the present code regulates the rights and obligations of patrons and workers with respect to work, period. Monsignor, instead of placing a period, we will put a comma and add, in accord with the Christian principles of social justice." He remained watching me, stood up, embraced me, and said, "Everything is taken care of. With this change, the Catholic Church fully supports this legislation." (Interview with Barahona Streber, Aug. 23, 1994)

The code systematized state policy on labor issues and created a Labor Ministry and labor courts to carry forth this policy. Like the constitutional chapter on social guarantees, the code sanctioned the right to organize labor unions. However, the code went beyond the constitutional chapter by making collective bargaining compulsory in labor-capital disputes (Bell 1971:31). Two years later, on June 20, 1945, the reformers passed Decree 20, which created regional commissions to address minimum wages in agriculture, industry, and commerce. While the labor code had called for annual assessments to establish the minimum wage, Decree 20 called for biannual assessments.

The creation of the state institutions as well as the obligation to engage in collective bargaining made the labor code distinct from previous legislation in Costa Rica. During his administration, Calderón also created the Secretary of Labor and Social Security. These changes gave an institutional voice to labor as a corporate unit. However, the labor code as a document was not a dramatic departure for Costa Rican workers, who had already experienced de facto and de jure rights to association as well as a number of measures to protect work conditions. Between 1920 and 1937, workers had benefited from legislation that mandated a maximum workday (1920), accident insurance (1925), a minimum wage (1933), protection of mothers and children (1933), a commission to establish salaries (1934), and industrial hygiene (1937) (Facio 1943:7; Salazar 1981:78; Ministerio de Educación Pública 1994). Consequently, the labor code, like the chapter on social guarantees, realistically provided the constitutional and institutional basis for labor representation in the political arena and workplace as well as the codification of already-existing labor legislation. Moreover, it suggested an increased political influence of the Costa Rican communist party while creating an auspicious political environment for workers to organize. With a supportive governing coalition, the code increased compliance with reforms that had largely been ignored in the 1920s and 1930s (Interview with Azofeifa, Aug. 25, 1994; Interview with Soto Harrison, Aug. 25, 1994).

Under the labor code the number of officially reported labor disputes increased. According to figures from the executive office, three strikes and nineteen collective labor conflicts occurred in 1944 over salary and demands to meet the established minimum wage (Picado 1945:25). In 1945, a total of 2,119 individual conflicts occurred over a wider range of issues covered by the labor code; in that same year, the number of collective conflicts went down, but the number of collective contracts increased (Picado 1946:26). In 1946, there were 2,941 conflicts reported (Picado 1947b:29). Overall, the labor code sanctioned an increase in labor activity and organizing, as discussed in Chapter 5.

Although the labor code encouraged labor organizing and codified workers' rights, these reforms should be placed in context. As in Argentina, for example, the code prohibited unions from forming closed shops and maintained that all workers, regardless of union status, should reap the benefits of any collective contracts that were negotiated. These provisions created the classic conditions for collective-action problems. The increase in organized labor's rights provided a clear incentive to join a union; this incentive, however, was tempered by the fact that benefits negotiated by the union accrued to union and nonunion members alike. In other words, workers in a union shop benefited from union activity, regardless of whether they were union members. Moreover, the labor code allowed owners to dismiss workers without giving formal justification as long as they provided indemnification to the dismissed worker.[4] Finally, the labor code had limited application to the rural areas. It was less comprehensive than the original plan proposed and ultimately exempted coffee workers, prohibited strikes in rural areas, and excluded coverage for rural workers employed on farms of five or fewer workers.

While the reform coalition codified urban labor rights, it took limited steps to advance rural labor organizing.[5] The coalition's urban focus reflected the communist party's ideological focus on organizing labor in the cities and the banana plantations.[6] And, perhaps more important, it reflected the dominant role played by a part of the oligarchy in the reform coalition; neither Calderón nor Picado articulated a desire to transform agricultural production relations.

The code finally barred unions from engaging in explicitly political activity. As President Picado (1944–48) said in 1947,

The Labor Code limits the functions of unions when it says in Article 280 that "the unions are to be sanctioned if it is proven that they are intervening in politico-electoral affairs, that they are initiating or developing religious struggles, that they are engaging in activities which are antidemocratic . . . or that in some form or another they are infringing on Article 263." What this article says is that it is absolutely prohibited for all social organizations to engage in any activity that is not rooted in developing socioeconomic interests. (Picado 1947b:9)

Given that the communist party dominated the largest labor federation, as discussed in Chapter 5, and given that communists had important political influence, formally in the legislature and informally at the presidential level, this restriction was pro forma.

This collection of entitlement and regulatory reforms was a response to increasing pressures to respond to the social question in the urban areas and a response to the politically expedient exchange by Calderón, Mora, and Sanabria. The reforms created the political context for increasing labor organization in the workplace, but they also seemed to reinforce the political divisions that had already taken place within the oligarchy. Many refused to adhere to the new labor code. While a number of prominent men in the economic elite who identified with the president's party, PRN, published a letter supporting the labor code,[7] members of the banking community and coffee-export elite, who identified with Cortés's Partido Demócrata (PD), attacked Calderón's reformist tendencies, the CP's political influence, corruption, fiscal problems, and the rising cost of living (Salazar 1981:81; Lehoucq 1992; Interview with Azofeifa, Aug. 19, 1994; Interview with Soto Harrison, Aug. 25, 1994). The Calderón administration, however, also passed a fair number of measures to overcome economic difficulties precipitated by World War II and to support the oligarchy, of which, after all, Calderón remained a part. It would be overblown to claim that Calderón attempted to transform fundamentally the pyramid of economic control in which coffee elites dominated small and medium-sized coffee producers. Indeed, the Calderón administration expressed the need to protect the banks, industry, commerce, and agriculture. His administration guaranteed the domestic financing of coffee, and the government negotiated guaranteed access to markets and prices. Legislation eliminated a majority of export taxes, established a minimum price for coffee, and allowed for the free export of agricultural products (Salazar 1981:79, 93–97).

Moderate opposition to the reforms also developed among (upper-)

middle-class intellectuals organized in the Centro. While stating their support for social reforms in general, they argued correctly in the pages of their newspaper, *Surco*, that the reform coalition had passed this legislation as a form of political opportunism without providing a developmental ideology and/or adequate solutions based in thorough and scientific analysis. In particular, they argued that the chapter on social guarantees contradicted Calderón's decree to suspend individual guarantees as a national security measure for World War II. In this manner, they supported reform, in contrast to the oligarchic opposition, but argued against the ad hoc manner in which the reform coalition had pursued the legislation. Salazar (1981:91) reasonably claims, although does not demonstrate, that the middle-class and rich peasants also joined in this opposition, highlighting the failure of the reform coalition' to win support within this sector.

If the oligarchy and the Centro differed in their evaluation of the reforms, they coincided in their opposition to the role of the communist party in the policy-making process and its access to state institutions. This anticommunist sentiment shared by the oligarchic faction and the Centro was not strong enough to push the two factions to coalesce into an oppositional alliance in the first administration of the reform period, suggesting both that they were unprepared politically to respond to these developments and that the entitlement and regulatory policies were only mildly inflammatory. Indeed, the first round of reforms elicited substantial although ineffective rhetorical opposition. The two poles of dissent organized separate spheres of action.

BUILDING DEMOCRATIC INSTITUTIONS

The reformers claimed that the activities and practices sanctioned by the labor code would promote democratic practices and popular culture among workers through the creation of industrial associations and cooperative organizations: "We declare that the legal constellation of social organizations, be they unions or cooperatives, are in the public interest, as one of the most effective means to contribute to the maintenance and development of popular culture and of Costa Rican democracy" (*Costa Rican Labor Code* 1943, Title 5, Article 262). However, claims about workplace democracy and ideals of fostering a democratic culture proved limited in application and reach without a reform of the political system that had been marred by electoral fraud and manipulation during the Liberal period.

The legislature passed an electoral reform law during the Picado administration. The scope of this law was considerably more moderate, however, than attempts at democratic institution building in Guatemala. At one level, this is not surprising, given that Costa Rica had fewer institutional barriers to democracy than did Guatemala. In effect, the institutional culprit had been electoral fraud and corruption. Hence, there was less pressure to overhaul the entire political system. This was particularly so given that the Costa Rican oligarchy, which had benefited from the political system, continued to dominate the governing coalition and, so, could benefit in future elections from an unreformed electoral apparatus. During the first reform administration, Calderón did not oversee electoral reforms and remained lukewarm toward these debates as they emerged during the subsequent administration. Indeed, common knowledge assumed that Calderón would resort to fraud in upcoming presidential elections should he fail to generate sufficient electoral support in clean elections. Finally, the gradual transition to the reform period had provided less political space to introduce abrupt and comprehensive institutional changes, as would take place in Guatemala.

During the Costa Rican debates over electoral reform, the two oligarchic parties, the Partido Republicano Nacional and the opposition Partido Demócrata, remained ambivalent about the reform. The only party that voiced unambiguous support for the reform was the communist Partido Vanguardia Popular; the communists had been calling for electoral reforms since the 1930s, particularly because fraud had been used against them in previous legislative elections. Picado's proposal to implement a least-remainder electoral system was likely to increase communist representation in the legislature, given that the prior system of calculating votes into seats had disadvantaged smaller parties. While Picado was unable to command total PRN support, he did rely on part of the PRN along with the PVP to push this reform through. His administration oversaw the drafting of an electoral reform law by two PRN legislators and one PVP legislator (Lehoucq 1992:228–29).

The proposed amendments and debates that followed illustrated the politically complicated nature of this proposal. A PRN amendment to extend female suffrage, for example, was seen both as a more democratic move and a ploy by part of the PRN to discredit or sink the electoral reform bill—because the extension of the suffrage was a constitutional rather than a legislative matter.[8]

The electoral law, passed in January 1946 after extensive and often vitriolic debates and postponements, ostensibly sought to combat the fraud characteristic of Costa Rican elections. The law created an Electoral Tribunal with three members who were to be nonpartisan. It had the power and responsibility to oversee elections, to count ballots, and to declare provisional electoral results; the legislature assumed the role of declaring official results. The law also created new conditions for the Electoral Registry and voting booths designed to minimize electoral fraud.

The 1946 law constituted the one conscious effort to reform the political system in a democratic direction. It sought to transcend machine politics to ensure an honest electoral process and to limit the power that the executive had developed in this process. With the legislation of redistributive reforms, discussed next, the opposition concluded that it would need to gain control over the Electoral Tribunal and Registry. For, indeed, the second administration of the reform period highlighted that legal means could be used to redistribute wealth. With the communists in the governing coalition, this was not a reassuring fact for the opposition.

REDISTRIBUTING WEALTH

Failed efforts at political reconciliation with the oligarchic opposition compelled Picado to rely on the reform coalition originally formed during the Calderón administration. While he did not advance additional social reforms, he did legislate moderate redistributive reforms. Mild redistributive land measures were passed with little fanfare and little opposition, in large part because the politics of economic control in Costa Rica had resided with the coffee processors, financiers, and exporters who had accumulated capital through their control over capital-intensive processes and over international market access.[9] Indeed, these laws seem to have targeted producers for the domestic rather than export market. Picado made it clear that the government had established these laws to help urban workers achieve a higher standard of living (Picado 1947b, and 1945). These economic measures collectively sought to increase productivity for the domestic market without disrupting practices and the politics of economic control in the coffee sector.

The reform coalition did not seek, therefore, to transform fundamentally the power of coffee elites over small and medium-sized coffee producers. On the one hand, a part of the oligarchy was the senior partner in the coalition and as such did not want to overhaul an economic system in which it dominated the financial and processing markets. On the other hand, the 1930s state creation of IDECAFE had mediated and muted the conflictual relationship between the small producers and the financial and processing oligarchy. Consequently, the small produc-

TABLE 10

Customs Revenue in Costa Rica, 1934–45

(in colones)

Year	Amount	Percentage of total public revenues
1934	13,012,340.67	48
1938	11,127,602.31	40
1939	20,298,716.86	47
1940	17,881,420.32	42
1945	22,318,353.10	36

SOURCE: Picado (1947a:30).

ers did not voice a challenge to the existing economic system nor were they wide open for mobilization. Given that the reform coalition as a whole had not placed much emphasis on economic development and transformation, the organization of the economy remained relatively unchanged.

Nonetheless, the second Costa Rican reform administration confronted a dilemma. To sustain its popular support, it had to maintain the new social programs and state institutions. Rising state expenditure coincided, however, with declining state revenues. With a decrease in world market prices for coffee, exports stagnated between 1941 and 1946, while imports rose. Consequently, Costa Rica's balance-of-trade deficit was larger than total exports in 1945, and the budget deficit rose almost fifteenfold between 1940 and 1943. This trade imbalance also produced a severe foreign-exchange crisis and fiscal deficit exacerbated by the lowering of export taxes in a primarily agro-export economy (Salazar 1981; Dunkerley 1988:156, n. 33; Lehoucq 1992:128–30).

With the 1931 law *impuesto cedular de ingresos*, only 800 individuals and corporations (*individuos naturales y jurídicos*) paid the existing tax. The expansion of social services and growth in the bureaucracy, coupled with the declining revenue collected from tariffs and insufficient revenue generated from the 1931 law, led to increasing budget deficits (Picado 1947a:16–17, citing *La Tribuna*, Jan. 23, 1947). In addition to the poor rate of income tax payment, the percentage of rent collected for customs taxation vis-à-vis public expenses had also declined, further exacerbating the budgetary crisis of a state increasingly committed to supporting entitlement and regulatory social services (see Table 10).

The reform administrations of Calderón and Picado, therefore, confronted a rise in state expenditures that the existing budget could not

cover. In addition to loan requests, the Picado administration decided
to adopt a two-pronged approach, one administrative and the other legal, to generate badly needed state funds (Bell 1971). The administrative
changes set out to increase state capacity to improve fiscal management
and revenue collection; prior to the reform period, the state had not
made any real effort to collect tax payments from an elite that had assiduously avoided paying them. The reform coalition's commitment to
exact tax payments through these administrative changes signaled a substantive change in state-society relations. At least legally and discur-
sively, the state distanced itself from the oligarchy and committed itself
to supporting programs favoring the popular sectors. Changes included
the creation of a comptroller's office intended to oversee fiscal matters
(the newly created office replaced a less-competent administrative office), legislating the outline for drafting and implementing the budget,
and increasing the supervisory power of the National Treasury to oversee
revenue-receiving operations of the different governmental offices. In
short, these administrative changes provided the basis for a "more efficient collection and allocation of resources" (Bell 1971:75).

Administrative reorganization coincided with the legislation of taxation law 837, *impuesto sobre la renta*, on December 20, 1946. The Finance Committee of Congress—chaired by Manuel Mora and with the
active participation of two PRN legislators, Francisco Quesada Smith
and Antonio Rigioni Rubillo—drafted the bill for income and territorial
taxes (Schifter 1986:193; Lehoucq 1992:132).[10] Building on recommendations from U.S. technicians, the administration argued that individuals should pay according to their ability (based on income and property
values). Indeed, the administration had rejected a proposal to generate
additional income through indirect taxation, a regressive measure that
would have hit the poorest sectors hardest. The proposed indirect taxation would neither have generated adequate funds, given the inelasticity
of lower-class incomes, nor have generated additional support for the
regime (Picado 1947a:30).

According to President Picado, taxation law 837 did not seek to im-
poverish the rich nor to enrich the state, but "to put a little bit of equity
in the distribution of fiscal charges" (Picado 1947a:10–11). The 1946
tax law increased the property tax (*impuesto territorial*) for large landholders with property valued at more than 250,000 colones. Similarly, it
exempted those with property valued at less than 10,000 colones. De-
duction was permissible for indispensable family as well as business-
related expenses. Those with incomes between 6,000 and 25,000 colones

would pay a 2 percent tax. Those with incomes over 500,000 colones would pay a 20 percent tax. Those with middle-range incomes paid a tax between 2 and 20 percent. In short, the tax law sought to amend indirect taxation, disproportionately paid by the poor, with the legislation of progressive and direct taxation, paid by all citizens in accordance with their income:

> No one doubts that direct taxes are the most scientific and fair. . . . The most famous economists and most highly considered statisticians, as well as the conscience of all honest men, are all in agreement that these tributes—in which the rich pay as a rich person and the poor pay as a poor person—are the most logical; this is in contrast to what has been happening in our country where the rich pay very little or nothing and in which the poor have to carry public expenses on their backs. We have already calculated that in Costa Rica a poor family supports the national budget with 15 percent of its scarce income whereas the truly rich, if they pay taxes, pay in inverse proportion to their income. (Picado 1947a: 5–6)

This redistributive tax law primarily affected elite landowners and wealthy processors, financiers, exporters, and industrialists. Yet, whereas the moderate entitlement legislation of the early 1940s had caught the conservative elite off guard and politically unorganized, by 1946 the elite opposition was better organized—although it still focused on political figures rather than platforms. The 1946 taxation law engendered further opposition and wrath within elite circles, which noted that the only other income tax proposal in Costa Rica's history, during Alfredo González Flores's administration (1914–17), had precipitated a coup in 1917. Economic associations, including the Agricultural Chamber of Costa Rica, the Chamber of Commerce of Costa Rica, the Syndical Association of Import Merchants and Retailers, the Syndicate of Coffee Growers and Employers, and the Syndicate of Sugar Producers and Employers, initially levied harsh criticism against arguments supporting the need for the tax (Lehoucq 1992: 133–35). Bell (1971: 76) has suggested that this opposition to the tax law led national capitalists to finance the opposition campaign.

Those opposed to the tax law organized a demonstration in July 1947, which turned into a capital strike in which supporters of the opposition closed their shops and banks. This action foreshadowed the capacity and willingness of the opposition to employ nonelectoral tactics and strategies to bring the opposition into the streets. In response to opposition challenges that the law was communist, Picado defended the tax and its benefits in a series published in the Costa Rican newspaper *Tribuna* (Schifter 1986:193–94).

In an effort to quell the civil unrest associated with the 1947 capital strike organized by the opposition (discussed further in Chapter 6), Picado conceded to the opposition's demands: the right to equal representation in the Electoral Tribunal and the right to appoint the president of the Electoral Registry. In essence, the opposition gained the power to oversee the electoral process and related reformed institutions. The opposition, however, was not entirely mollified by this significant concession, which preempted the governing parties' ability to manipulate elections in their favor but did not assuage the opposition's distrust of the governing reform coalition. Indeed, oligarchic and middle-class opposition shared an antipathy for the rising influence of the communists and popular sectors in the state, and to the rising strength of a "civil oligarchy" that ostensibly controlled the state and had gained autonomy from civil society.[11] Both opposition sectors resented their perceived inability to influence the policy process or gain access to state institutions and resources, particularly as they saw their chances of winning electoral office dwindle. It is within this context that part of the opposition prepared an armed response.

Guatemala: From Moderate to Radical Reforms

The violent overthrow of Guatemala's authoritarian regime in 1944 created the possibility and necessity to reconstruct new political institutions. In the euphoria that emerged with the October Revolution, people rallied in the streets of Guatemala City for democratic reforms and demanded the rights that the discourse of World War II had proclaimed. As in Costa Rica, the Guatemalan reformers oversaw the creation of more participatory and civic political institutions, the extension of individual and collective rights, and the development of a state mandate dedicated to social welfare ideas and practices. Yet the creation of democratic institutions and the legislation of social reforms were individually and cumulatively more comprehensive and radical in Guatemala than in Costa Rica. As the Guatemalan reform coalition increased its support among urban and then rural workers, it set out to legislate entitlement, regulatory, and redistributive reforms in response to newly organized popular demands. In the process, the reform coalition alienated the part of the oligarchy that had initially supported the multiclass reform government. With the legislation of labor and then land reform, the oligarchy united in its opposition and joined forces with a multiclass opposition that became increasingly wary of what it perceived as rising communist control of the state and society.

Guatemala's democratic reform period oversaw three phases: the increase of civic rights, the undermining of the oligarchic state, and the promotion of capitalist developmental policies. In the first phase, the revolutionary junta and multiclass Constituent Assembly dissolved the authoritarian political and military structures and created new governing institutions and practices designed to create a functioning democracy. In the second phase, coterminous with President Juan José Arévalo Bermejo's term (1945–51), the reformers legislated entitlement and regulatory polices to address the social question that extended individual and collective rights, particularly to the urban areas. From a comparative perspective, therefore, the social policies passed in this second phase were most similar to those passed in Costa Rica's reform period. Focusing on urban labor, the reform coalition sought to provide basic collective rights in the workplace and in the communities, providing labor codes, social security, and housing. In contrast to Costa Rica, however, this stage of Guatemala's reform period was more inclusive insofar as democratic and social policies targeted women—extending qualified terms of suffrage, creating day-care centers, and legalizing common-law marriage—to make them economically more secure and independent. This round of social reforms increasingly alienated the elite from the reform coalition. The elite united as a class in its opposition to the social legislation and to the role that the state had come to assume vis-à-vis these social sectors. The elite opposition further increased the reform coalition's political dependence on the popular sectors, the mobilization of which in turn further alienated parts of the middle class.

The third phase, coterminous with President Jacobo Arbenz Guzmán's term (1951–54), legislated redistributive policies. The reformers sought to redress the central conflict embedded in the existent political economy—the issue of control over and ownership of land—in order to transform it and promote a capitalist, nationalist, and developmental economic program. The Arbenz administration implemented reform that redistributed land largely to the rural, indigenous, peasant population. The labor code and land reform challenged the oligarchy's access to cheap labor and control over land. The land reform, which increased the access of indigenous peasants to the state, brought together and cemented a multiclass opposition to the regime.

BUILDING DEMOCRATIC INSTITUTIONS

The revolutionary junta composed of Jacobo Arbenz, Francisco Arana, and Jorge Toriello oversaw the transition from authoritarian to democratic rule between October 20, 1944, and March 15, 1945. The junta had the unique opportunity to overhaul the institutional framework that had undergirded authoritarian rule and to create a democratic constitution and set of political institutions. The junta dissolved the legislature and held presidential elections. It issued 67 decrees to undermine coercive state practices and to extend individual and collective rights (Silvert 1969:29; Handy 1985:94). Most dramatically, it called for a Constituent Assembly with popularly selected representatives to reconstruct a democratic framework and initiated a substantial demilitarization process that undermined the coercive and centralized control characteristic of the Liberal period.[12]

The Constituent Assembly set the legal parameters by March 1945 for the political and social reform period in Guatemala. Representatives drew from the constitutions of the United States, Mexico, Cuba, Costa Rica, and the Soviet Union, and created a presidential system that ostensibly had a strong congress with 50 to 54 elected deputies representing around 3 million people (Silvert 1969). The 1945 constitution also extended suffrage rights to all men and literate women on the basis of their status as citizens. In practice, the constitutional provisions meant that indigenous men and wealthy, ladina women acquired the right to vote. The debate registered in the minutes of the Constituent Assembly and the pages of the press, however, revealed at least a modicum of discomfort in the process of making this decision.[13] Political representatives and commentators voiced concerns about the potential for nondemocratic forces to manipulate Indian men and women of all ethnic backgrounds as well as the potential that this manipulation would and had led to authoritarian rule; some deputies blamed Indians for the recurrence of authoritarianism in Guatemala. In a typical quote, Reyes Cardona stated, "I am not in agreement with the anticipated extension of the suffrage to the illiterate masses for the following reasons: the illiterate masses and the indigenous masses have effectively been the most ominous for sustaining dictatorships as a result of their lack of civic consciousness, which many women do possess."[14]

Following this debate, the deputies in the Constituent Assembly granted citizenship rights and, therefore, extended the suffrage to all men and literate women.[15] The terms for practicing male suffrage, however, were distinguished along ethnic and class lines. The constitution stipulated that voting was obligatory and secret for all literate men. For illiterate men, it was optional and public for all except municipal elections, in which case voting was obligatory. The majority of the male Indian population and impoverished ladinos was largely illiterate; a 1940 census found that 65.36 percent of the Guatemalan population over 7 years of age was illiterate (*Diario de Centro América*, Oct. 10, 1944:1).

With the 1945 Constituent Assembly, literate women also acquired suffrage rights. In practice, this provision guaranteed that only (upper-) middle-class ladina women could vote, given limited educational possibilities for both poor and indigenous women. In essence, the male, ladino reformers in the Constituent Assembly feared that these illiterate women would not vote responsibly and would easily be manipulated by conservative forces such as the Catholic Church. As a result, they restricted female suffrage, in effect, along ethnic and class lines. The conditions under which literate women could vote also suggested ambivalence on the part of the deputies in the Constituent Assembly. Suffrage for literate women was optional and secret; the optional nature of this right suggested the belief that women—along with illiterate and indigenous men—were not full or necessary citizens; yet the secret nature of the female vote suggested that ladina women were trusted more than indigenous men, whose vote was optional. In short, the extension of the suffrage provided literate women with an important opportunity to participate in politics; yet, the optional nature of this participation suggested that the reformers considered them optional citizens as well.

The multiple layers of meaning contained in these provisions—about who was a citizen, who could vote, and under which conditions, optional or secret—highlighted the fear and distrust within conservative and reform circles of Indians, the poor, and women. The fact that illiterate—understood as indigenous and poor—men were compelled to vote publicly, should they choose to exercise their right to vote at all, contrasted with the secret vote extended to literate women—understood as ladina and wealthier. Yet, despite these significant ethnic and gendered limitations to the practice of citizenship, it is also important to put these changes in comparative perspective; illiterates did not gain suffrage rights until 1970 in Chile, 1979 in Ecuador, 1980 in Peru, and 1985 in Brazil (Lapp 1994:3).

The extension of the suffrage, however partial, increased political participation at the national level and was comparatively impressive in its scope. With the legislation of a 1946 municipal law, local communities also gained an important degree of autonomy. The law provided for local elections and indirectly sanctioned local autonomy within indigenous communities (García Bauer 1948:61; Silvert 1969:183–95; Cruz Salazar 1987:9–10; Dunkerley 1988:139).[16] The Instituto Indigenista found in a study of 45 predominantly indigenous municipalities that 27 had elected indigenous mayors (Silvert 1969:188). Two important facts contravened this extension of local autonomy. First, the executive maintained substantial discretion and control over the municipalities:

> Apart from the constitutional requirements that the municipal governments be autonomous and popularly elected, that each municipality have its own political power under the exclusive jurisdiction of the mayor, and that the municipalities can impose taxes for their own expenses with the approval of the Executive, all other questions concerning the organization and functioning of the local government are under the discretion of either the Executive (through the Ministry of Gobernación) or Congressional legislation. (Silvert 1969:189)

Second, the vagrancy laws, which the 1945 constitution did not really challenge, impeded participation by rural community members in local decisions. The economic imperative to gain a substantive livelihood, given the lack of sufficient and productive land surrounding them, still compelled indigenous men to travel far distances for seasonal work on plantations. Their absence from the community made it difficult to engage in local politics for much of the year (Dunkerley 1988:139, citing Falla 1978).

The initiation of democratic rule, however, entailed more than the creation of a presidential system and improved conditions for political participation. Indeed, the junta and the Constituent Assembly understood that democratic rule required restructuring the military that Liberal predecessors had used to maintain rule and contain society. They renamed the military El Ejército Nacional de la Revolución, the National Military of the Revolution, in Article 3 of the Constitutive Law of the Military. In line with this new image, the written and visual propaganda from this era projected a military of and for the people—helping the nation in a series of projects including literacy campaigns, highway construction, and agricultural training programs.[17]

Effectively creating a new military entailed demilitarizing political rule and reorganizing internal military structure along apolitical and

meritocratic lines. The transition government, therefore, committed itself to these tasks.[18] Ubico, in particular, had increased his local control
in the 1930s by appointing military officers as *comandantes políticos*
and *comandantes de armas* in each department. He also had placed military and police forces in all of the local areas. For all intents and purposes, Ubico had merged military and civilian positions by assigning
military officials to political posts and by making politically based regions coexistent with military ones.

To reverse military control in the regions and over political offices, the
social reformers attempted to disentangle military and civilian responsibilities and to undermine centralized military control by changing the
administrative organization of the country. First, the municipal law
just mentioned undermined military control over local communities
and delegated that authority to the communities and to the national
civilian political administration. At the regional level, the reformers
also created gubernatorial provinces to substitute civilians for the *comandantes políticos* and *comandantes de armas* (Cruz Salazar 1987:9).
The president had the responsibility of nominating these governors and
could remove them at any time; they in turn were responsible to the
minister of the interior. The appointed civilian governors, therefore,
were effectively administrators for the nationally elected civilian government rather than direct representatives of the populace that did not
elect them (Silvert 1969:198–99).

A demilitarization of local and regional governing institutions coincided with the re-creation of military zones that were independent of the
gubernatorial provinces. Theoretically, the reform coalition demarcated
the political mandate of the gubernatorial provinces from the military
mandate of the military zones. A chief of military reserves assumed control over the military zones. The reformers considerably restricted the
chief's power compared to that of the local commanders during the
Ubico dictatorship. In the new military zones, the military chiefs assumed responsibility for military operations, including recruitment efforts, executing orders and mobilizations, and premilitary instruction
(Cruz Salazar 1987:10; Interview with Enríquez Morales, Feb. 27, 1990).[19]

The effort to disentangle military and civilian political institutions
coincided with a call to depoliticize a corrupt and unprofessional military. Civilians and military men alike called for internal military reform.
They hoped to create a meritocratic military committed to upholding
the 1945 constitution and to defending the country against foreign aggression. They also sought to institutionalize an apolitical military,

meaning that members of the military would not meddle in political decision making or pursue elected political offices in their capacity as military men. To this end, the revolutionary junta issued Decrees 17 through 19, and the Constituent Assembly legislated reforms that restructured the military and its relationship to the state.

Article 1 of the Constitutive Law of the Military underlined that the military was an apolitical body. To create this more professional and nonpartisan military, the transition junta reformed the curriculum at the Escuela Politécnica[20] and dismissed corrupt generals from the Liberal period.[21] Those military officers who had risen through the ranks without professional training had to attend the Escuela Politécnica for a brief period; failure to do so would foreclose future promotions (Cruz Salazar 1972:80). Moreover, the reformers constituted a new military command structure independent of the civilian government. The president was technically the supreme chief of the armed forces; nonetheless, he did not exercise power over the military. The reformers hoped to limit executive control over the military, which during the Liberal period had been used to centralize power and control in the hands of dictators. The reformers hoped that this institutional change would limit political efforts to manipulate the army as well as inhibit the army from participating in political decision making.

To this end, two positions with different lines of military purview were created: the minister of defense, who participated in the executive cabinet but had limited input into internal military affairs, and the chief of the armed forces, who assumed judicial and administrative purview over the military as an institution.[22] The chief of the armed forces was selected in a process that took place within the military and with limited participation by the executive and legislative bodies. Neither the executive nor the legislature could appoint officials in the armed forces. The legislature could dismiss the chief of the armed forces under extremely restricted conditions, as stipulated in the constitution.

The newly constituted Superior Council of National Defense played the central role both in selecting the virtual head of the armed forces as well as overseeing internal military affairs. Its operations were largely independent from the executive and legislative branches. It was composed of the chief of the armed forces, the minister of defense, the seven chiefs of the military zones, and thirteen chiefs and high officials in the permanent force, elected by secret vote by all the chiefs and high officials of the permanent forces. The council selected the future chief of the armed forces from a list, subject to legislative approval (1945 *Ley Consti-*

tutiva del Ejército, Article 13; Cruz Salazar 1987:11; Handy 1994:181).

These administrative and institutional reforms were intended to de-politicize the military apparatus by preventing arbitrary and political control by the executive. However, as discussed in Chapter 6, they actually created an institutional arena for the chief of the armed forces to cultivate an autonomous power base within the military institution—independent of civilian control—which, in fact, reflected partisan affiliations and experience.[23] The reforms unintentionally created an unmediated political dependence of the junior officers on the chief of the armed forces and the Superior Council of National Defense. The new institutions also contributed to the executive's ignorance of political dynamics, sympathies, and concerns within the military.

This conglomeration of institutional changes in military-state relations—the demilitarization of civilian political rule, the professionalization of the military, the armed forces' autonomy from civilian control—created a type of corporate commitment within the armed forces. Common training, common experiences, common dependence, and political savvy instructed the military officers to maintain their loyalty to the military structure. They acquired, along with their troops, an esprit de corps, loyalty, ideology, and internal power hierarchy within the military that was largely autonomous from civilian rule but presumably dedicated to upholding the democratic institutions outlined by the 1945 constitution.

As discussed in Chapter 6, the conscious effort to build autonomy within the military would prove detrimental to the stability of the democratic regime. While the reforms inhibited manipulation by elected politicians, they also had two unintended consequences. First, the military became internally politicized as military officials created their own power bases autonomous from and, at times, in opposition to the regime. This autonomy within the military institution would become particularly clear when a significant portion of the military rallied around the unsuccessful 1949 Arana uprising and later around the successful 1954 counterreform movement. Second, the autonomy of the military from civilian rule meant that not all officers actually respected or supported the reform coalition's increasing commitment to comprehensive reforms and popular organizing. This would be the case especially because the military never fully rid itself of the antipopular and anti-communist ideology with which it had been inculcated during the Ubico period. Parts of the military, therefore, would become receptive to the opposition.

ENTITLEMENT, REGULATORY, AND
DEVELOPMENTAL POLICIES

The 1945 constitution, which outlined the institutions for democracy in Guatemala, also provided the legal parameters for legislating policies to address the social question. With the election of Juan José Arévalo Bermejo, Guatemala's first democratically elected president, the first reform administration focused on extending entitlement and regulatory codes to enhance social rights and the role of the state in defending them. Arévalo explained his social commitment as part of a philosophy that he entitled "spiritual socialism." Inspired by the United States' New Deal and wary of Marxism, he emphasized the right to association, to participation, and to basic social services as essential to a strong mind, soul, and dignity. However, it is generally acknowledged that his efforts to integrate and transcend liberalism and socialism resulted in a confused philosophy that overlooked the obstacles to and conflicts over development in the countryside (Dion 1958; Melville and Melville 1971, ch. 3; Handy 1985:100). During the Arévalo administration, the governing reform coalition that had mobilized support in the urban areas focused on the urban social question and ad hoc development measures.

As in Costa Rica, the reformers enacted early on a national, unitary, and obligatory social security based on Article 63 of the constitution (García Bauer 1948:65). Social security operated on the principle of minimum provision, which contended that basic health services were a right of all individuals regardless of economic background. The reformers created a state institution, Guatemalan Institute of Social Security (IGSS), to meet the services outlined in the reform legislation. IGSS provided health services and coverage for accident insurance, maternity, orphans, invalids, widows, expenses associated with death, and work-related sickness. As in Costa Rica, the reformers stipulated a graduated implementation schedule. IGSS would provide services first to working people and their families in urban areas, and would later extend these services to workers in rural areas; all workers would receive coverage before IGSS extended coverage to other sectors in society (García Bauer 1948:67, 171–80).

The legislation of social security and creation of IGSS highlighted an expanded vision of individual rights in Guatemala. Moreover, the legislation formalized a new set of social norms that dictated the financial responsibility of the state and capital to provide for the health of workers. IGSS's operating budget drew from required contributions from workers (25 percent), employers (50 percent), and the state (25 percent). When the plan had ultimately been extended everywhere, working individuals were to contribute sums proportional to their incomes and supplemented by the state where necessary. By the end of Arévalo's presidency, IGSS had extended coverage to "several tens of thousands of blue and white collar urban workers." The program, however, had postponed coverage of rural workers. Financial problems experienced by the agency minimized the possibility of extending coverage to this sector, particularly because rural workers and employers alike failed to contribute accordingly (Gleijeses 1991:42).

The 1945 contitution also foreshadowed Guatemala's 1947 labor code, which was drafted by Oscar Barahona Streber, the same man who drafted Costa Rica's. This code was a significant departure from the Ubico dictatorship, during which time the state asserted strict control over the incipient labor force. The labor code established collective bargaining rights, minimum wages, compensation for industrial accidents, and regulation of work hours. It also outlined the right to an eight-hour day,[24] to unionize, to bargain collectively, and to strike. It protected against unlawful termination by requiring employers to provide financial compensation to workers summarily dismissed. The code identified and regulated rights for women as workers and mothers.[25] According to the law, employers could no longer discriminate against women workers on the basis of their marital status, nor could they demand heavy work from pregnant women in the last trimester of their pregnancy (Bishop 1959: 44–45; García Bauer 1948:97). The labor code also stipulated provisions protecting child labor. Due to budget considerations, maternity care and child care were not provided until 1953 (Handy 1985:105).

In practice, the labor code legalized and sanctioned union organizing and activity. With the overthrow of Ubico, workers started to organize, particularly in the cities, banana plantations, and railway companies. The code also increased the role of the state in mediating capital-labor relations and, for the first time, highlighted areas for which the state would protect labor. State mediation occurred through the newly created labor arbitration council, mandated by the 1945 constitution. The creation of these councils and the code encouraged workers to file with the state an increasing number of labor disputes. Most of the disputes were individual rather than collective complaints. The inspector general of labor reported in 1951 that 8,703 disputes had been registered (Bishop 1959:55, 59, 74–75).[26] These labor tribunals adopted decisions that predominantly favored workers on the basis of the labor code clause stating that "private interests must yield to the social or collective interests" (Woodward 1985:234). "The alliance of the labor movement with the revolutionary parties . . . breathed into the implementation of the labor code a spirit of militant action in favor of the worker's interests" (Bishop 1959:75).

If the labor code legalized and sanctioned urban union activity and provided urban labor with important access to state institutions and resources, it had limited practical implications for the rural areas. Significantly, the labor code overturned the vagrancy laws employed during the Liberal period.[27] Estate owners, however, often did not comply and, in fact, often engaged in debt peonage. The code theoretically provided labor rights to the rural areas, but the conditions under which these rights were extended were highly restrictive. The code stipulated that peasants could form unions only where plantations employed at least 500 people, a condition that excluded the vast majority of rural workers. In 1948 the legislature amended the code to allow peasants to unionize, provided that they organized at least 50 members, of which two-thirds had to be literate. Given that an estimated 98 percent of the peasantry was illiterate at the time, rural unionization remained an extremely arduous task.[28] Finally, peasant organizers who succeeded in forming rural unions did not have the right to strike (Cambranes 1984:138, 350). Handy (1988b: 705) notes that "even after the prohibition of rural organizations was lifted in 1948, strikes during the harvest were still forbidden. Almost until the end of the Arévalo administration the army intervened readily against striking rural workers, often employing significant violence."

Overall, the social policies legislated in the first years of the reform period focused on urban workers. The reform coalition graduated its implementation of social security and passed measures in the labor code that restricted the rural population—measures it considered necessary to sustain national production of coffee and to restrain a population the reformers initially distrusted. This set of urban-biased policies encouraged urban support and created the legal impetus for organizing unions as well as other urban sectors. The policies, however, increasingly alienated the elite and weakened the faction of elite support for the reform coalition that had formed in 1944. While the labor code was being discussed in the Congress, elites voiced their opposition to it in a series of paid advertisements in the newspapers, which came out before the Congress passed the code. It was clear that elites liked neither the political voice nor the economic power gained by organized labor and that they suspected that labor organizing was a sign of increased communist infiltration. Moreover, it became clear that organized labor had gained an increased voice and sympathetic representatives in the Congress, a development perceived by elite organizations as changing the nature of the state itself.

The urban bias of the social policies paralleled the urban bias of the Arévalo administration's development policies, which reflected a nonintegrated set of ideas regarding how to spur national development.[29] The most articulate policies targeted and had the largest impact in the urban areas. By contrast, this initial period legislated ad hoc development measures for the rural areas. Arévalo announced boldly at the beginning of his administration that Guatemala did not have an agrarian problem. In this oft-quoted phrase he remarked, "In Guatemala, what one can properly call an agrarian problem does not exist because our countrymen have lived in a psychological and political climate that has impeded them from expressing their yearning to work the land to benefit the family and the nation; this is the reason why the government must create within the Guatemalan peasantry the necessity to work the land in a more effective manner than they have done up to now."[30]

The Arévalo administration's entitlement and regulatory reforms created a political, social, and economic space for urban labor organizing that was initially exuberant but frenetic and divided. It also increased opposition within the landed elite and parts of the military and middle classes, which suspected communist organizing and questioned the impact of these changes on political stability and economic growth. Yet these reforms were to foreshadow even greater redistributive reforms in the rural areas as the reform coalition turned to the peasantry for political support. By the end of this moderate stage of reform, the governing coalition began to identify the need to promote rural development as part of an industrialization program.[31]

REDISTRIBUTING THE LAND

Jacobo Arbenz Guzmán won the 1951 presidential elections after a bitter race that highlighted the polarization that had taken place during the Arévalo administration. Arbenz's platform explicitly championed a nationalist, capitalist, and developmental ideology. In a message as president-elect he stated, "When we refer to agrarian reform, to industrial development, to an increase in production in all sectors, when we speak of liquidating latifundios and feudal serfdom, in reality we are speaking of promoting capitalist production and of developing capitalism in Guatemala" (*El Imparcial*, Jan. 18, 1950). In office, the Arbenz administration initiated economic projects that included plans for a national highway, a hydroelectric plant, and a national port, all of which challenged the monopoly of U.S. subsidiaries affiliated with the United Fruit Company. These projects were designed to increase domestic control of and benefits from the country's key infrastructure and reverse a pattern in which profits from these monopolies had accrued abroad.

The governing reform coalition in this second administration argued that real capitalist and industrial development required a change in access to land and redistribution of landholdings. The publication of the 1950 national census had indicated that an estimated 2 percent of the agricultural units claimed 72 percent of the arable land. Moreover, much of this land remained idle or cultivated by sharecroppers. In contrast, 76 percent of the peasants owned only 9 percent of the land. Overall, land use suffered from concentration, lack of diversification, and undercultivation. These findings were all the more pressing given that an estimated two-thirds of Guatemala's population depended on agriculture (Handy 1988a:677, and 1994:78). The reform coalition argued that land distribution to the rural poor would lead to the cultivation of previously unproductive lands. Access to land, they further declared, would increase household revenues, raise standards of living, and, consequently, create an internal market. Hence, land reform became a necessary step to initiate national, capitalist, and industrial development. But the commitment to land reform also followed a political imperative. With the increasing organization of urban and rural popular sectors, and the increasing polarization of society, the reform parties sought to strengthen their appeal to a newly mobilized rural constituency, which was calling for land reform.

The governing reform coalition came to champion land reform as a necessary measure and part of a larger development ideology. Indeed, reform legislators and labor leaders had been calling for land reform since shortly after the fall of Ubico. At least six land-reform proposals came before the legislature between 1949 and 1952.[32] The debates around the terms and scope of the land reform were rather vitriolic, with heated exchanges and counterattacks printed in the daily newspapers. Arbenz and his close advisors worked on a bill that drew from recommendations made by the International Bank for Reconstruction and Development survey. But his close advisors included prominent communists— including José Manuel Fortuny (secretary general of the recently formed Communist Party) and Víctor Manuel Gutiérrez (a prominent teacher and labor leader who had headed various national labor confederations over the course of the reform period)—who heavily influenced the bill that was finally proposed by Gutiérrez and Ignacio Humberto Ortiz. This agrarian reform bill did argue for capitalist development and production in Guatemala, an objective shared by Arbenz and his advisors, and while it envisioned substantial changes in the countryside, it was hardly revolutionary from a comparative perspective. The communists' role in formulating proposals and the accompanying increase in indigenous peasant mobilization, however, heightened opposition within many circles—particularly among the landed elite, which had been accustomed to the Liberal state's protection of its lands. Despite opposition, the legislature passed the agrarian reform law, Decree 900, on June 17, 1952 (Gleijeses 1991; Handy 1994:86–87).

The constitution had provided the legal basis for the land reform. Private property was to serve a social function. Accordingly, the state had the constitutional right to expropriate land where it would advance the needs or interests of the general community (Handy 1988a:679). The agrarian reform law outlined the procedures and requirements for expropriating idle lands on large landholdings but did not allow for expropriation of cultivated lands, regardless of how large the actual plantation was.

What then could be expropriated? The law targeted state-owned lands, uncultivated plantations, and some municipal lands. During the reform period, the government held 68 percent of all Guatemalan territory. Included within this figure were the *fincas nacionales* (national farms), which covered an estimated 8.45 percent of the total agricultural area (García Añoveros 1987:101, 123). The agrarian reform stipulated that the *fincas nacionales*, which had largely been expropriated from the Germans during World War II, would be distributed. It also allowed for the expropriation of idle land previously rented in exchange for labor services on private plantations of more than six *caballerías*.* Moreover, uncultivated lands on plantations of two to six *caballerías*, where at least one-third of the plantation was idle, were also subject to expropriation. Farms of less than 2 *caballerías*, regardless of whether or not they were cultivated, could not be expropriated. Finally, the law allowed for the expropriation and distribution of municipal lands to legal indigenous and peasant communities. The state compensated for expropriated lands with agrarian bonds.[33]

Expropriation between January 1953 and June 1954 was extensive and

*One *caballería* equals 109.8 acres. One *manzana* equals 1.7 acres.

expeditious, leading to a substantial change in Guatemala's land tenure in a relatively short period of time. Exact figures on the amount of land expropriated differ, ranging from 765,233 *manzanas* to 866,344 *manzanas*.[34] These figures do not include the lands that had been identified but not ruled on for expropriation prior to the 1954 coup. Nor do they include land invasions, which increased with the announcement of the land reform. Conflicts and land invasions were reported not only in the opposition press but also in the pages of the communist newspaper.[35] The agrarian reform institution, Departamento Agrario Nacional (DAN), also expropriated over two-thirds of the United Fruit Company lands at a cost of $1,185,000, the declared tax value made by UFCO.[36] This expropriation caused UFCO to increase its opposition to the regime and align itself with Guatemala's opposition elite.

About 100,000 peasant families benefited from the short 18-month tenure of this law. Handy (1988a:688; 1988b:723) calculates that 500,000 people, or one-sixth of the population, benefited from the land reform. The agrarian reform law stipulated that beneficiaries could acquire land as private property, lifetime usufruct, or cooperatives.[37] Most beneficiaries took land in usufruct. In general, those who worked on the *fincas nacionales* and large tracts of privately owned land, either as day or resident laborers, had first priority in the distribution of these lands. Beneficiaries could receive between 5 and 10 *manzanas* of cultivated land or 15 to 25 *manzanas* of uncultivated land. Any land remaining after all the previous workers of a given plantation had received their portion could be distributed in usufruct among individuals from other places (García Añoveros 1987:173; Handy 1988a:685; Gleijeses 1989b:460).

The reform law also created national institutions to provide support services to the beneficiaries of land distribution. The latter had access to state-provided technical assistance and credit with low interest loans through the National Production and Programs Office and the National Credit Association, respectively. The National Credit Association oversaw 17,843 loans related to the reform law totaling 3,371,185 quetzales.[38] On July 7, 1953, a year after legislating Decree 900, the reformers founded the National Agrarian Bank, to finance activities related to agrarian reform.[39] The bank established an office in the capital and in six different regions in the country, increasing the capacity of individuals living in rural communities to request loans and of the banks to assess, process, and make loans. Between March 1953 and June 1954, these two agencies distributed loans, worth some $9 million out of a total of $11,881,432 that had been approved, to 53,829 people. Loans averaged about two and one-half times per capita rural income (Gleijeses 1989b:466–67). The creation of these state institutions highlighted the changes in the state from the nineteenth-century Liberal reforms to the twentieth-century social reforms. Whereas Liberal leaders had employed the state to coerce indigenous peasants to work on coffee plantations, mid-twentieth-century reform leaders refashioned the state to respond, at least partially, to demands and needs of these same people. Ironically, the appointed head of the DAN was a military man, Alfonso Martínez, who was promoted from captain to major in September 1952 (*El Imparcial*, Sept. 16, 1952).

Not only did passage of the law increase the state's role in rural areas, but implementation of the law also increased the power of local communities and organizations.[40] Decree 900 created local agrarian councils composed of five local representatives: one from the municipality, one appointed by the department's governor, and three from the *campesino* or rural workers' union; where unions did not exist, the community elected three representatives. Petitions for land were made at the local council, which then investigated the petitions and made a recommendation to the regional departmental agrarian committee. The regional organization, like the local ones, included representatives from various organizations: one each from the two national labor federations, one from the landowners' association (which vehemently opposed the reform), one appointed by the governor of the given province, and one from the National Agrarian Department. The regional committee oversaw the work of the local level and then made a recommendation to the National Agrarian Department, which made the final recommendation. As stated, the president had the final word in this process and the final authority to adjudicate agrarian reform disputes (Paredes 1964:24–29; Handy 1988b: 709; Gleijeses 1989b:460–61).

The implementation process, therefore, simultaneously increased the power of the president and of the local communities. The centralization of power cut short avenues to challenge the agrarian reform law. A number of landowners did attempt to challenge the law in court. In one case, the Supreme Court ruled in February 1953 that the agrarian reform was unconstitutional because it did not allow for judicial review. This ruling opened the door to overthrow the law or to slow its implementation seriously. In a special session of Congress, the deputies voted 41 to 9 to dismiss the judges and replace them with others more sympathetic to the agrarian reform.

The reform coalition essentially sidestepped and overrode the courts'

TABLE II

Selected Trade Figures for Guatemala, 1946–54

(in U.S. dollars)

Year	Value of coffee exports	Balance of trade
1946	—	+ 475,000
1947	—	− 5,286,000
1948	—	− 18,184,000
1949	33,670,000	− 15,757,000
1950	—	− 3,616,000
1951	—	− 4,761,000
1952	—	+ 11,741,000
1953	68,229,000	+ 9,384,000
1954	71,380,000	—

SOURCE: Gleijeses (1989b:477). Also see García Añoveros (1987:79).

jurisdiction in order to expedite implementation of the agrarian reform. Given Arbenz's commitment to the reform, landholders recognized that they had no legal recourse to dispute the land reform as a whole or its particular implementation, especially because the landowners had decided earlier not to send representatives to the agrarian reform councils responsible for making the local and regional decisions (Handy 1988a: 692–93; Gleijeses 1989b:464–65).

In short, the change in land tenure and the creation of state institutions posed a challenge to a landed elite whose primary basis of capital accumulation had grown out of control over land and over the laborers who had tended their plantations; the elite had depended on the state during the preceding Liberal period to bolster this process of debt peonage and agrarian capitalism. Yet these dramatic changes to previous regimes of accumulation did not trigger an initial drop in production, in contrast to agrarian-reform experiences in Bolivia, Cuba, Peru, and Nicaragua. With the implementation of the Guatemalan agrarian reform, there was an increase in agricultural output for many crops, including corn, wheat, and rice. Moreover, as shown in Table 11, Guatemala achieved the second largest coffee crop in its export history after 1953, more than doubling the value of coffee exports from 1949 until then (García Añoveros 1987:183; Bulmer-Thomas 1987:111, 308; Gleijeses 1989b:468; Interview with Capuano, Aug. 1990; Handy 1994:95).[41] Gleijeses states that

In August 1953, the [U.S.] Embassy reported a 15% increase in the production of corn—corn, it added, "is the chief crop of small landholders in Guatemala and is cultivated by the majority of persons who have received land under the Agrarian Reform Law". Almost a year later, the Embassy concluded that "production of food crops in 1953 was satisfactory". The corn harvest was "about 10 percent higher than 1952", rice and wheat production had increased by 74 and 21% respectively over 1952, and bean production had remained the same. In 1953 coffee production did decrease slightly, but this was "due principally to weather conditions". Furthermore, recovery was swift: the 1953–4 coffee crop was the second highest in Guatemala's history. (Gleijeses 1989b:468)

If the land reform proved beneficial for the majority of the rural population, the urban population during this time did not experience similar economic improvements. An increase in prices for basic goods, indirect taxes, and inflation counteracted wage increases in the urban areas. With the rise in social spending, the government also experienced a cash-flow problem leading to late payments and a reduced budget for low-priority state offices (Handy 1985:153, n. 16; García Añoveros 1987:80; Gleijeses 1989b:478).

Faced with reforms that gave the masses increased access to land and government, and its inability to gain anywhere near a majority in the legislature, the oligarchy reunited and sealed its opposition to the governing reform coalition and the democratic regime that had created this situation.[42] In addition, the middle classes began to align themselves with the oligarchy, in part as a result of their opposition to the Arbenz administration's disregard for the autonomy of the Supreme Court. Finally, parts of the military began to bristle at the increased independence and organization of the rural indigenous communities (Handy 1994). What united these opposition forces was a common fear of rising communist influence:

> It appeared to many that Arbenz had lost control of the situation and was prepared to allow the peasant league and labour federation free reign in the countryside. Much of the urban middle class that had supported the revolution through more than eight years of struggle now deserted it. As more and more of the moderate political sectors abandoned the revolution, Arbenz needed to rely more heavily on peasant and labour organizations, adding weight to the claims that communists were in danger of taking over the government. (Handy 1985:277)

These trends did not bode well for the survival of democracy in Guatemala.

In many ways the Guatemalan reform period paralleled that in Costa Rica, insofar as both coalitions democratized political institutions and passed entitlement, regulatory, and redistributive policies. However, reforms were more comprehensive in Guatemala, where reformers dismantled authoritarian institutions and replaced them with democratic ones. Moreover, the regime extended the reforms to rural as well as urban areas. The institutional reforms went so much further in Guatemala in large part because the oligarchy had assumed a subordinate role in the initial reform coalition, in contrast to Costa Rica. Not able to call on a prior legacy of political organizations, the Guatemalan oligarchy remained politically weak in numbers and in ideological appeal. Simultaneously, the middle-class and popular sectors were able to assume the dominant political role within the governing reform coalition. Their platforms for greater democratic and social reforms garnered political appeal and in turn generated new demands for democratic and social changes in the rural areas.

Despite these significant differences in the scope and target of reforms, redistribution and perceived communist hegemony polarized politics in both Costa Rica and Guatemala. Chapter 5 discusses the popular organizing engendered by the reform period, while Chapter 6 discusses the opposition that ensued.

CHAPTER 5

Organizing Labor

Organized labor developed an unparalleled political strength by the middle of the twentieth century in Costa Rica and Guatemala. With the codification of the right to association, collective bargaining, and social welfare benefits, the respective governing coalitions created auspicious political conditions for labor union activity and influence. As newly organized workers articulated collective demands both in the workplace and the political sphere, they created pressure for and defended the legislation of the entitlement and redistributive reforms that were passed. Unions were able to mobilize votes and marches to demonstrate this support both in the electoral arena and in the streets. In this sense, a strong symbiotic relationship developed between the governing reform coalitions and the dominant labor movement, whose respective strength and standing rested on their mutual support for one another.[1]

This chapter and Chapter 4 serve as stepping stones to explain the rise of parallel opposition movements that would ultimately take up arms to overthrow the governing reform coalitions, to rupture the influence achieved by the labor movement, and to reverse many of the social reforms. In Costa Rica and Guatemala, opposition movements reacted against the rising influence of the communist party within these movements. The latter's influence would prove all the more salient with the legislation of redistributive reforms and more pressing as a result of the opposition's failure to compete successfully for political dominance either in the labor movements or in electoral politics. In this context, the labor movement became a contested site for political control and ultimately a target of the opposition. Analyzing the labor movement in Costa Rica and Guatemala, therefore, provides insight into the political pressure for reforms and political reaction that ultimately challenged democracy in both countries.

Parallel reform and reaction also coincided with significant differences in the scope and political unity of the labor movements in Costa Rica and Guatemala. The Costa Rican labor movement proved weaker and more politically divided than its Guatemalan counterpart. Three legacies of the Liberal period explain these differences: the presence or absence of an organized civil society during the Liberal period, the role of a communist party in founding the labor movement, and state responses to the primary rural conflict. In Costa Rica, the reform period inherited an existent, if weak, civic tradition of organizing, a state that had created an institutional space to address, if not redress, the rural conflict, and a communist party that had founded an incipient labor organization. By contrast, in Guatemala, the reform period inherited a weak civil society with little tradition of organizing, a state that had repressed rural conflict, and a communist party that emerged only halfway through the period. These two different complexes led ultimately to an institutionally more developed but politically divided labor movement in Costa Rica and a larger and politically more united labor movement in Guatemala. Let me elaborate on these three points of divergence.

First, Liberal leaders had overseen civil society's development in Costa Rica and its suppression in Guatemala. Consequently, the implications of the reform period were subject to a much greater range of interpretations in Costa Rica than in Guatemala. In Costa Rica, twentieth-century Liberals had tolerated the incipient labor movement. The 1940s reform coalition, therefore, could not depict their Liberal predecessors as repressive autocrats but, rather, faced the challenge of claiming responsibility for advancing democracy by advancing labor's interests, rights, and influence—a more ambiguous claim that the opposition contested with partial success. In Guatemala, by contrast, the emerging labor movement did not question the relationship between the reform coalition and democratic transition, for it suddenly gained the right to association, expression, and participation. Infighting did not give way to sustained political polarization within the Guatamalan labor movement; nor was it open to persuasion by opposition groups committed to limiting the space for popular organizing and expression. By the end of the reform periods, the Costa Rican opposition had captured the political support of part of the labor movement, while the Guatemalan governing coalition maintained the loyalty of a labor movement that had united politically to defend the regime.

Second, the Costa Rican reform period inherited a political society that had allowed for the founding of a communist party—even if prior governments had short-circuited communist efforts to assume legitimately elected political office. In Guatemala, by contrast, the reformers inherited no political parties or society of note. The Costa Rican and Guatemalan communist parties during the reform period, therefore, had different relationships with their respective labor movements. Where the communist party founded and dominated the labor movement, as in Costa Rica, the opposition found it easier to divide the movement. The undisputed communist influence over Costa Rica's labor federation served as a lightning rod for other established associations and led the Catholic Church to create a parallel anticommunist labor federation. In light of the clear role of the communist party in Costa Rica's labor movement and in the initial reform coalition, the opposition laid claim to the Catholic labor movement and attempted to equate the reform coalition with communism, thus countering the coalition's claims of democratic and social advances. The Costa Rican labor movement divided in the second half of the reform period, despite the Archbishop's ties to the reform coalition as a whole. By contrast, the popular movement in the beginning of Guatemala's reform period was more heterogenous and lacked the political institutionalization and communist identification of its Costa Rican counterpart. Conservative efforts (for example, by the Catholic Church) to create an anticommunist labor federation were less successful in this multipolar and less-institutionalized political environment. When the Guatemalan communist party later did assume leadership positions, the labor movement had already developed a political affiliation with the reform coalition, which it credited for creating and advancing democracy. With the rise of a perceived united opposition and threat to democracy, the Guatemalan labor and popular movements joined forces, which in turn alienated part of the middle class. A united popular movement, subsequently, contributed to political polarization and elite opposition.

Finally, the scope of these labor movements rested on the availability of the rural sectors for mobilization, also a legacy of the Liberal period, coupled with the composition of the reform coalitions. Organized labor in both countries targeted urban and banana plantation workers. However, Guatemalan unions organized more energetically along urban and rural as well as ethnic lines. The Costa Rican rural sectors were largely unavailable for mobilization by the labor movement; the Liberal government of the 1930s had assuaged smallholder demands with the creation of the state's *Instituto de Defensa del Café* (IDECAFE); moreover, the reform coalition, dominated by the oligarchic reform president, was not interested in reforming rural relations and did not implement its new social reforms in the countryside. In Guatemala, by contrast, the rural sectors had been repressed and excluded in the 1930s. Once the oligarchic faction and parts of the middle class distanced themselves from the reform coalition, it turned increasingly to the popular sectors for support and encouraged organizing in the Guatemalan countryside. Popular support remained dispersed between the various parties that composed the reform coalition but was unambiguously supportive of the reform coalition as a whole.

The rest of this chapter analyzes the parallel rise of labor movements in Costa Rica and Guatemala that challenged the restrictive boundaries of civil society from the Liberal period and attempted to redefine those boundaries along class lines. These popular movements both supported the reform coalitions (discussed in Chapter 3) and pressured them for social reforms (highlighted in Chapter 4). The popular mobilization, however, was more comprehensive, inclusive, and ultimately more united (although not institutionalized in one party) in Guatemala than in Costa Rica. As Chapter 6 explains, the organization of labor helped to generate in Guatemala an ideologically more cohesive and hostile counterreform movement than that in Costa Rica, one that equated the rise of civil society with communism.

Costa Rica

Labor leaders began to organize more vigorously and with greater success following the political alliance of President Calderón, Manuel Mora, and Archbishop Sanabria. Social legislation between 1942 and 1943, which included a labor code and social guarantees, created a legal framework for union organizing. Union registration increased substantially in 1943 (85 unions) and 1944 (115 unions) and tapered off to between 15 and 25 unions between 1945 and 1948. With the codified labor legislation, union efforts to redress grievances increased as well.[2] Underscoring these more auspicious political conditions for labor organizing, Arnoldo Ferreto, a communist leader of the time, noted:

Before this [the social legislation], unions existed de facto. However, the legal mechanisms provided by the labor code—such as the creation of the Ministry of Labor (before there had been an Office of Labor in the Ministry of the Interior), the provision of legal mechanisms to inscribe unions, the ability to make collective contracts, to strike . . . etc.—allowed the [communist] party to take advantage of this new situation to increase the [size and influence] of the labor movement. (Interview with Ferreto, July 10, 1990)

The communist party continued to dominate labor organizing during the reform period.

Despite the infamous exchange of letters between Archbishop Sanabria and the communist party's Manuel Mora, the archbishop was ambivalent toward communist hegemony over the labor movement. But he was committed to organizing labor and selected a Costa Rican priest to found a Catholic labor movement as an alternative to the communist-affiliated labor movement. Both the communist- and Church-inspired labor federations sought to address the social question and fought to support the entitlement and regulatory social reforms passed in this period. They demanded better salaries and fought against the rising costs of living. Both federations sought to work within the existing system and called for a working political alliance with national capital. Although each was organizationally affiliated (in contrast to the Guatemalan unions, which developed originally in an organizational vacuum), these two labor federations also shared a common genesis, insofar as both the CP and Church had been effectively marginalized, and at times excluded, from political participation during the Liberal period. The communist and Catholic labor federations differed, however, in their analysis of capital-labor relations. The communist union relied on a rhetoric of class conflict. Conversely, the Catholic union argued for class collaboration. Moreover, where the communist labor federation more successfully organized in urban areas, the Catholic federation was more successful in rural areas.

The two Costa Rican labor federations cooperated with one another in the initial years to organize workers and to defend their rights in accord with the newly legislated labor laws; this period of cooperation coincided domestically with the initial alliance between President Calderón, Manuel Mora, and Archbishop Sanabria and internationally with the popular fronts that developed during the Second World War.

In the postwar period, cooperation gave way to confrontation. Political polarization increased both between the governing and opposition coalitions as well as between the communist and Catholic labor federations. Faced with this divided labor movement, the largely urban-based communist movement supported a comparatively moderate governing reform coalition and demanded less comprehensive reforms than its Guatemalan counterpart. The Catholic federation, on the other hand, adopted an increasingly hostile position toward the communist-dominated labor federation and, consequently, the governing reform coalition. This would become particularly apparent after the redistributive tax reform of 1946 and the capital strike that ensued. The Catholic labor federation joined the opposition as it rallied against the communist party's influence in the governing reform coalition, over policy, and in the workplace.

DEVELOPMENT OF THE COMMUNIST LABOR MOVEMENT

The communist party's ability to mobilize part of the labor force predated the reform period. In the 1930s it focused its organizing energies on urban workers and artisans as well as banana workers on the coast. The CP won its first major victory in the 1934 banana strike, and it created the Comité Sindical de Enlace in 1938, a liaison labor committee that pressured Congress to pass a labor code. Not until the oligarchy divided politically and the communist party became part of the governing reform coalition in the 1940s, however, did organized labor become a political constituency with influence in policy making circles.

On October 4, 1943, shortly after the Costa Rican labor code was passed, the communist party created the Confederación de Trabajadores de Costa Rica (CTCR) to replace the Comité Sindical de Enlace. While the CTCR did not achieve juridical standing until June 1946, within a week of its founding, the federation claimed 96 unions and 30,000 members (Aguilar 1989), and by 1945 it embraced 125 unions (Rojas Bolaños 1978:23).[3] The federation mobilized workers from all sectors of production, including construction, metallurgy, lumber, shoemaking, banana, and sugar cane (Interview with Efraín Rodríguez, July 3, 1990). Like the labor organizers of the 1930s, the new federation focused on urban and banana-plantation workers, although the CTCR did organize a few *campesino* leagues concerned with access to land and credit.

Despite a weak organizational presence in the rural areas, the CTCR became the largest and most professional labor organization in Costa Rica. It adopted the political line of the international Latin American labor federation Confederación de Trabajadores de América Latina (CTAL), to which it belonged.[4] And following suggestions made by the head of CTAL, Lombardo Toledano, the CTCR created a full-time executive committee to provide a more coherent national organization; previously, the Comité Sindical had depended on workers to assume leadership positions during their nonworking hours (Rojas Bolaños 1978:22–23; Salazar 1981:89; Aguilar 1989:25–26).

The rise in labor organizing and influence in political circles coincided with educational efforts to foster a "proletariat consciousness." The communist party and its affiliated labor federation organized educational projects to disseminate theoretical information and news on workers' struggles—for example, in its weekly newspaper, *Trabajo*. It offered a new framework with which to examine Costa Rica's political economy and government as well as provided analytical and organizing skills to increase the ranks of the union.[5] In essence, the CP sought to develop a new analytical discourse to highlight the importance of organizing along class lines and struggling collectively in the workplace and in politics. While nonviolent in its methods, the CP was confrontational in its rhetoric.

By the middle of the reform period, the CTCR had increased its ranks, its influence in ruling political circles, and its efforts to create a new social discourse of struggle and workers' rights. The organized labor movement increased pressure on congressional deputies to enact social reforms, to rally around candidates at election time, and to defend the regime (Creedman 1971:215, 223–24; Rojas Bolaños 1986; Interview with M. Mora, July 12, 25, 28, 1990; Interview with Ferreto, July 8, 10, 1990). In a 1943 strike on the United Fruit Company's banana plantations, for example, the government forced UFCO, for the first time ever, to negotiate with the union (Backer 1978:132). Furthermore, in the 1944 presidential elections, the CTCR supported the reform coalition's Bloque de la Victoria, even though the CTCR claimed autonomy and neutrality (Aguilar 1989:30). In short, the government and the communist-dominated labor federation provided each other with needed political resources. Calderón received political support; the labor movement gained access to the ruling coalition and the ability to exercise new rights in the workplace and in the streets.

This mutual political support rested, however, on an uneasy alliance. The CTCR voiced occasional frustration with the government, as illustrated by a March 1947 march calling the government to lower its level of corruption, commercial speculation, and the cost of living, while also asking for general wage increases (Rojas Bolaños 1978:23). In turn, Calderón stated that while he had fought to promote workers' rights, he had never intended for the labor movement, particularly the communist labor movement, to become a political player. So long as the elite remained divided, this uneasy alliance between government and labor would prove mutually beneficial. And, so long as Calderón remained in the dominant position, the government's reforms and labor mobilization would retain a moderate cast. Calderón stated in 1942, "Spontaneously, without state control, the union movement is growing in proportions which, if it is not regulated, can be dangerous. One must avoid, at all costs, a development in which unions assume political characteristics which are contrary to their real purpose, which is to defend economic interests" (Salazar 1981:90).

CATHOLIC INFLUENCE IN THE LABOR MOVEMENT

Archbishop Sanabria had voiced the Catholic Church's concern for addressing the social question. In this spirit, he issued a pastoral letter calling for just wages for workers and supported the reform coalition and its policies. The archbishop, however, did not wholeheartedly embrace the emerging labor movement dominated by the communist party (even after the CP changed its name to Partido Vanguardia Popular). Indeed, he believed that the Church was better suited to organize workers and address their concerns. He set out to create a Catholic alternative to the communist-identified labor federation. On June 14, 1943, the archbishop wrote to Manuel Mora, "I have to take advantage of this opportunity to say that the ecclesiastical authority is and will be obliged to form Catholic workers' groups and to amplify those that already exist, not to weaken the cohesion of the working class, but to direct this movement, in the manner that is best suited and in line with the broad paths delineated by papal teachings" (Soto Harrison 1991:90). Consequently, he promoted three organizations rooted in social Christian doctrine: la Liga Espiritual Obrera (Liga, Workers' Spiritual League), la Juventud Obrera Católica (JOC, Catholic Workers' Youth), and la Confederación Costarricense de Trabajadores Rerum Novarum (CCTRN, Rerum Novarum).* CCTRN had greater success and significance for labor organizing than the Liga or the JOC.[6]

Sanabria had sent Father Benjamín Núñez to the United States in 1940

*The Church first founded the Central de Sindicatos Costarricenses Rerum Novarum (CSCRN). On May 1, 1945, it renamed the CSCRN the Confederación Costarricense de Trabajadores Rerum Novarum (CCTRN). To highlight the institutional continuity shared by these labor organizations, and despite the name change, I refer to both as CCTRN.

to receive training in union organizing and development. Before Núñez had completed his studies, Sanabria requested his return to Costa Rica to form this alternative labor movement. Thus Núñez announced the creation of a new Catholic union movement on August 2, 1943, the day of the Virgin of Los Angeles, Costa Rica's patron.[7] Núñez's goal was to compete with the communist-dominated labor movement, a mandate he made explicit on the day he announced the Catholic alternative: "It is the aspiration of Rerum Novarum to finish with communism in Costa Rica" (Aguilar 1989:32)—a point that he repeated in a 1994 interview. Núñez developed contacts with the AFL CIO and Confederación Interamericana de Trabajadores (CIT), which had a clear interest in promoting noncommunist unions in Latin America in opposition to the more radical CTAL, to which the communist union belonged (Cooperative Oral History Project 1970b; Interview with Núñez, Aug. 17, 1994). Father Núñez, as president, and his brother Presbyter Santiago Núñez, as treasurer, formed the federation on September 15, 1943, with 15 unions.[8] Núñez said in a 1970 interview, "My historical function was to offer the workers a noncommunist, democratic type of organization where they could organize themselves" (Cooperative Oral History Project 1970b:1). Almost 25 years later he stated, "We proposed to organize our union movement in a spirit of cooperation in the interests of the working class. We, as Christians, wanted to weaken the communist labor movement. We wanted to offer the workers a new form of struggling for their interests" (Interview with Núñez, Aug. 17, 1994).

The Catholic labor federation targeted urban areas but also began organizing in the rural areas, where its efforts outpaced those of the communist labor federation. Indeed, the communists never developed a strong rural base, despite occasional efforts to organize rural workers and smallholders (Interview with Ferreto, July 8, 10, 1990; Interview with M. Mora, July 12, 25, 28, 1990; Interview with Efraín Rodríguez, July 3, 1990). The Liberal government had already involved smallholders in negotiating with the state and exporters through IDECAFE (see Chapter 2); they were, therefore, largely unavailable for political mobilization. Moreover, the social reforms had had limited application in the countryside and, therefore, the governing reform coalition did not develop a strong rural constituency. Finally, the rural elite, on which rural workers and smallholders depended financially, had propagated a strong anticommunist message in the 1930s, reinforced by former president Cortés, who became a leader of the opposition from the early 1940s until his sudden death in 1946. Speaking of this anticommunist and pro-Cortés position in the countryside, former president Monge, who supported the Catholic CCTRN, stated, "In the rural areas, Cortés was very important, he was an idol. Everyone was a cortesista. Cortés [in the mid-1940s] symbolized the struggle against arbitrariness and against the alliance with the communist party" (Interview with Monge, Aug. 26, 1994). Against this backdrop, the CCTRN proved comparatively more successful than the CTCR in organizing rural sectors, which remained allegiant to the traditional political leaders of the Liberal period and, consequently, espoused a virulent anticommunism.[9]

Overall, the Catholic union did succeed in creating a parallel labor movement that downplayed the role of class struggle and promulgated social Christian doctrine. By 1945, Rerum Novarum claimed about 5,000 members and 102 unions (of which only 85 were apparently active) in the urban and rural areas. By 1947 it claimed 15,000 members. It did not, however, outdistance the communist federation in terms of either membership or political influence in the ruling reform coalition. Rerum Novarum remained between one-sixth to one-half the size of the CTCR— if we take each group's self-proclaimed, and most likely inflated, statements about union membership as the basis for this calculation.

LABOR MOVEMENT: FROM INTERNAL COOPERATION (1943–45) TO CONFRONTATION (1945–48)

The communist and Catholic federations developed a relationship of cooperation from 1943 to 1945. In these years Mora apparently supported Archbishop Sanabria in the latter's effort to organize agricultural, clerical, and municipal workers, sectors that had proven resistant to communist labor organizing (Miller 1993:521–22). Both labor federations demanded better salaries and fought against the rising cost of living.[10] On occasion the two federations jointly mobilized workers for the social reforms (Backer 1978:133, citing Núñez). Days before the legislature signed the labor code, for example, the Comité Sindical de Enlace (which later became the CTCR) and the CCTRN both provided support in the streets and in the congressional galleries to pressure the deputies to vote for the reforms:

> The bill came up for final approval on August 20, 1943 in a raucous atmosphere, with the public galleries packed with sympathizers from both Communist and Catholic organizations. Father Núñez had sent out a call to the unions affiliated with *Rerum Novarum* to come to the assembly to demonstrate for the labor laws. . . . The leftist *Comité de Enlace*

(Liaison Committee) called a general work stoppage so workers could come to the Assembly and demonstrate for the bill's final passage. (Creedman 1971:224)

In the initial two years of coexistence, the two federations signed a pact stipulating that workers had a right to vote in elections at each factory to decide which federation to join; following an election, the losing federation was to step aside. Further, the two labor federations formed a Committee of Intelligence, comprising two representatives from each. The impetus to sign this agreement reflected the close working relationship established by Mora and Sanabria. CCTRN's small size and inexperience presumably also contributed to its tactical decision to collaborate with rather than confront the larger, stronger, and more experienced labor organization (Backer 1978:133–34; Aguilar 1989:35; P. J. Williams 1989:115).

The cooperative working relationship gave way to one of hostility after 1945. Shortly after the defeat of fascism, the West eschewed its alliance with the Soviets and adopted anticommunist rhetoric to replace that of antifascism, presaging the beginning of the Cold War. Under these new international conditions, both Costa Rican labor movements began to question collaboration with one another, particularly Rerum Novarum, which had grown in strength and had become more independent (Aguilar 1989:35; P. J. Williams 1989:115). The ensuing competition and tension between the two labor federations arguably contributed to the rise in union membership itself (Rojas Bolaños 1978:23). By 1947, the CTCR and CCTRN jointly claimed 228 labor unions, 46 employer unions, 18 federations, 2 confederations, and 23 cooperatives (Picado 1947b:31).

The division within the labor movement did not indicate a parallel division between Archbishop Sanabria and the communist party in the reform coalition. Rather, the Catholic CCTRN's increasingly vitriolic position toward the communist CTCR and the reform coalition indicated the Catholic federation's increasing autonomy from Archbishop Sanabria, who still sanctioned the reform administration. The Catholic labor movement distanced itself from Sanabria's position and actions even though the archbishop had both proposed the creation of the parallel labor movement and had chosen Núñez to carry out this task.

The increasingly independent leadership and membership of the organizations created by Archbishop Sanabria were unwilling to support or affiliate with a reform coalition that included communists, no matter what the archbishop wanted. Some members of the clergy even denounced Sanabria as a communist (Backer 1978:114; Rodríguez 1980: 80; P. J. Williams 1989:114–15, 120).[11] With time, the CCTRN members followed Father Núñez and sided with the counterreform movement that had developed against the reform coalition. While their refusal to follow the leadership of Archbishop Sanabria was a subversion of Church hierarchy, it should be made clear that Sanabria's position, not the Catholic labor movement's, appeared anomalous. Indeed, Sanabria's inability to carry the labor movement with him suggests the strength of prior institutions that had pitted the Catholic Church and rural areas against the communist party (Backer 1978:103–55; Rodríguez 1980: 80; Fernández Vásquez 1982:224; Booth 1987:221; P. J. Williams 1989: 114–15; Aguilar 1989:32–34; Miller 1993:522–23).

As the CCTRN's connections to the opposition became clearer, Sanabria in turn began to distance himself from the federation (P. J. Williams 1989:115–16). Former president Luis Alberto Monge stated:

> The archbishop became the object of attacks that he was favoring communism. The leaders [of the opposition] attacked him. . . . Sanabria, however, was sincere. He was committed to addressing the social question as a Catholic. But, he had very strong feelings against the coffee oligarchy and for this reason he supported the governing alliance. . . . He supported the unions. But he did not want there to be too much conflict. . . . But Núñez was uncomfortable with his [Sanabria's] position. (Interview with Monge, Aug. 26, 1994)

Under Father Núñez's leadership, the CCTRN associated itself with the opposition coalition. In the second half of the reform period, Núñez and the CCTRN developed an increasingly intimate financial relationship with important coffee elites participating in the opposition and with the U.S. government. According to Father Núñez, a member of the U.S. embassy, who played golf with members of the Costa Rican elite, convinced ten of the wealthiest Costa Rican capitalists to make monthly contributions to the CCTRN (Cooperative Oral History Project 1970b: 1–4; Interview with Núñez, Aug. 17, 1994). The financial contributions made by coffee elites to the Catholic labor movement did not suggest a new oligarchic support for labor rights or the Church as much as a strategy to weaken both the potential for a united labor movement and the role of communists therein. The U.S. embassy encouraged this policy, although according to Núñez the embassy itself did not assume an instrumental role in promoting it (Cooperative Oral History Project 1970b:1–2). The AFL also fostered divisions in the labor movements of Venezuela and Mexico against their respective communist unions.

Núñez stated that the Catholic labor movement would maintain its apolitical position despite the origins of this financial support. Through these financial contributions, however, the Costa Rican oligarchy in the opposition assumed greater power over the Catholic federation than Núñez's statement would suggest. The opposition elites donated money to the CCTRN to encourage a demonstration independent of the May Day celebration dominated by the CTCR. According to newspapers, the CCTRN march held later in the year highlighted the anticommunist sentiment shared by both the CCTRN and the elite and middle-class opposition (Schifter 1986:201–2).

The Catholic federation leadership's decision to adopt a more anti-communist position found favor with those workers who opposed the communists' rising influence both in the government and within the labor movement. They joined the CCTRN as a statement of opposition to the government as much as a commitment to Catholic labor organizing: "As a reaction, a large sector of workers took recourse to Rerum Novarum, worried not only about their labor problems but also for their political-partisan issues, in order to defend their interests and, at the same time, to consolidate this union organization in front of those they called communists, hoping to weaken the forces of support for the regime, which they opposed" (statement by Núñez, cited in Aguilar 1989: 35). The two labor movements assumed opposing sides in the momentous capital strike of 1947 and the civil war, discussed in Chapter 6.

The communist-dominated labor movement achieved significant gains for Costa Rican workers during the reform period. In a context characterized by a supportive reform coalition and "pro-labor" social legislation, organized labor increased in numbers. Consequently, the communist-dominated labor federation gained the ability to mobilize popular sectors in the streets, to bargain for economic rights in the workplace, and to influence policy decisions in the ruling coalition. With the rising polarization in society, this movement acted, sometimes violently, to defend the regime.

Conversely, the opposition perceived this organization of civil society along class lines as potential chaos in society, a threat to its property and wealth, and the precursor to a communist-dominated state. In other words, all segments of the opposition feared that the communists had mobilized labor to reshape civil society, to transform the economy, and to dominate the state, foreclosing in the process participation by those hostile to the governing coalition and to its reform agenda. The opposition, therefore, sought to diminish the communists' influence in the emerging labor movement. Rather than working through political means to do so, the oligarchic opposition supported social efforts by parts of the Catholic Church to strengthen a parallel and alternative labor movement. The Catholic labor federation did achieve important levels of societal support, but never surpassed the ranks or the influence of the communist-based labor federation, which continued to dominate the labor movement.

This rise in class-based organizing mirrored and fueled the political polarization that had developed between the governing reform coalition and the opposition, a point developed in Chapter 6. The inability of the opposition to develop a successful alternative to the communist-dominated labor federation, along with its inability to reshape the ruling coalition or its policies, contributed to the opposition's decision to take up arms. However, the divided nature of the labor movement generated a less cohesive and homogeneous counterreform response in Costa Rica than the opposition that developed in Guatemala, where the labor movement ultimately presented a united front of urban and rural workers in support of the reform government.

Guatemala

The democratic reform period in Guatemala constituted a "triumph of civic consciousness."[12] In interviews with the period's leaders, articles in newspapers, and autobiographies, participants in the October Revolution of 1944 emphasized the spontaneous mobilization that preceded the overthrow of the thirteen-year dictatorship and the ongoing organizing that followed in the ensuing decade. In the absence of established political parties and civic associations, urban Guatemala experienced an initial flourishing of public activity, from children helping to direct traffic, to students preparing for upcoming elections, to teachers traveling to the countryside to promote the ideals of democratic citizenship. Against the backdrop of thirteen years of repression, this public activity was striking in fact and in scope.

Class-based labor organizations came to play a central role in mobilizing Guatemalan society over the next decade.[13] In the initial years, labor organizers primarily focused on urban areas and pressured the government for urban-based reforms, as discussed in Chapter 5. These efforts were somewhat fragmented during the Arévalo administration, given that the new unions lacked any prior institutional history, party affiliation, or clearly defined goals. Indeed, the 1940s unions engaged in a cycle of splintering and fusion, as did Guatemalan political parties. Division often resulted from the suspicion of communist influence in the labor movement, even though the Communist Party was not officially founded until the 1950s. Despite these divisions, the labor movement as a whole largely presented unified political support for President Arévalo and the governing reform coalition. The course of the Guatemalan labor movement, therefore, contrasted with that of Costa Rica, which became politically divided between the reform and counterreform movements.

Guatemala's organized labor movement provided both pressure for social reforms and legitimacy for the government. This political dynamic alienated the reform faction of the Guatemalan elite and, therefore, increased the governing reform coalition's dependence on the newly organized popular sectors. During the administration of Jacobo Arbenz Guzmán, labor leaders organized more energetically, with a particular focus on rural areas. In conjunction with the agrarian reform law, the oligarchy saw this rural organizing as a threat to traditional regimes of accumulation for coffee production; it also reacted against the increasing organization of indigenous communities, which the reform coalition in fact attempted to incorporate and assimilate into the polity that had previously excluded them. If the redistributive reforms largely alienated the Guatemalan oligarchy, the popular mobilization alienated both the oligarchy and parts of the middle class and military.

The increasing political polarization and threat of a coup led the various popular organizations to overcome institutional fragmentation and to unite to defend the democratic regime against threats of an overthrow. At this point, when the popular organizations started to join efforts, members of the newly founded Guatemalan communist party, Partido Guatemalteco del Trabajo (PGT), assumed important leadership roles in the labor movement, which many reform leaders opposed. However, the reform parties as a whole depended on the organized popular sectors for their own political survival and that of the democratic reforms and institutions. According to Alfredo Guerra Borges, who was the editor of the communist newspaper *Tribuna Popular* in the 1950s, the reform parties had relatively little choice: "Political parties could not break with the PGT because they did not want to risk rupturing their relationship to the popular movement" (Interview with Guerra Borges, on Aug. 8, 1990). Moreover, the late emergence of the communist party relative to the development of the reform coalition and labor movement in turn made it more difficult for other parties to create a viable, anticommunist labor movement.

This section, therefore, seeks to analyze the development of Guatemalan civil society between 1944 and 1954, which included the organization of popular sectors primarily along class lines and secondarily along ethnic lines. This decade constitutes the only time in Guatemala's history that popular sectors have had the freedom to organize, make demands, and influence policy without fear of political retaliation by the state. By the end of the reform period, these organizations had created a united front to defend the regime against the rising opposition. This section serves as a backdrop for analyzing the development of the counter-reform movement, which reacted against the increasing organization of urban and rural labor and the increasing local power of organized indigenous communities. The opposition would eventually view the growth of civil society as a communist threat.

URBAN LABOR MOVEMENT: FROM INTERNAL CONFRONTATION TO COOPERATION, 1945–51

Workers did not play a particularly active role in overthrowing the Liberal dictator Ubico. During the reform period, however, they assumed a crucial role in defining the emergent civil society, as labor unions formed and oversaw political and civic organizing.

Between the July 1944 overthrow of Ubico and the October 1944 overthrow of Ponce, two unions assumed a particularly important role in mobilizing Guatemala's workers. The Sindicato de Trabajadores de Educación de Guatemala (the teachers' union, or STEG) and Sociedad de Auxilio Mutuo Ferrocarrilero (the railroad workers' union, or SAMF) organized members throughout the country in the cities and countryside.[14] The teachers, in particular, organized in outlying areas of the country and, therefore, acquired an influence that surpassed that of any other union, particularly with the later implementation of the 1952 agrarian reform. Educators active in the STEG hoped to cultivate democratic citizens for the post-Liberal period: "To divulge democratic ideas and spread a new political culture in order to arrive at a new democratic culture which would really give Guatemala a notion of her political, social, and economic rights, as well as allow for the exercise of these rights" (Interview with Anonymous A, Jan. 31, 1990). With this mission, teachers and students traveled throughout the countryside to inform the population about democratic ideals, constitutional rights, labor codes, and land reform legislation. They encouraged active participation in unions, political parties, and agrarian reform committees. In essence, these educators sought to articulate and disseminate a new cultural hegemony infused with the "spirit and ideals of the October Revolution."[15]

Throughout the reform period, STEG and SAMF came to embody the radical and moderate wings, respectively, of the labor movement. SAMF often charged that reforms or other labor leaders were communist, charges that, in general, replicated the anticommunist language and fears that Ubico had reinforced. In the initial years, these charges undermined efforts to form a single, unified labor force. For example, the new unions attempted to form a single labor organization, Confederación de Trabajadores Guatemaltecos (CTG), but their efforts gave way shortly thereafter to internal union fears of suspected communist organizing in their school, the Escuela de Capacitación Sindical Claridad (Escuela Claridad) (Schneider 1958; Bishop 1959; López Larrave 1976:28; García Añoveros 1987).[16] Internal dissent among labor organizations over Escuela Claridad coincided with the government's opposition to the school. President Arévalo decreed in January 1945 that the school be closed because it ostensibly violated Article 32 of the 1945 constitution, which prohibited political movements with international ties.[17]

The fallout over Escuela Claridad precipitated divisions within the labor movement. Between 1946 and 1951, three labor centrals existed: the CTG, the Federación Sindical de Guatemala (FSG), and the Federación Regional Central de Trabajadores (FRCT) (*El Imparcial*, Jan. 28, 1946; López Larrave 1976:32–33; Cardoza y Aragón 1955a:97; Handy 1985: 107–17).[18] In contrast to Costa Rica, however, these divisions did not reflect a decision by the more moderate part of the organized labor movement to affiliate with the political opposition—even though both the FSG and the Guatemalan opposition voiced an explicit fear of communism.[19] Rather, the various Guatemalan labor centrals remained committed to the reform coalition as a whole, which they identified as the bearer and protector of democratic politics. However, the different labor organizations did identify with different parties, which at times were at odds with one another, within the reform coalition.[20]

Institutional divisions within the labor movement were balanced, therefore, by general political support for the reform coalition parties as a whole. In December 1946, a year after the CTG had splintered into the CTG, FSG, and FRCT, the three centrals formed a coordinating organization called the Comité Nacional de Unidad Sindical (CNUS), which sought to provide a stable base of political support for the reform coalitions and regime. The CNUS formed political committees, such as the Comité de Acción Política de la Clase Trabajadora, and urged the reform parties to form a united political front in elections against the opposition, which in 1947 had already started to focus on anticommunism (*El Imparcial*, July 14, Aug. 4, 1948). Labor leaders had formed the CNUS to achieve organizational unity, and they attempted to avoid formal political affiliation with any of the reform parties. They neither achieved institutional or ideological unity nor successfully maintained autonomy from the political parties and reform coalition. Víctor Manuel Gutiérrez, a well-respected labor leader and politician of the time, criticized the CNUS because it did not maintain a position that was independent of the government (Gutiérrez G. 1964:44). In addition to this political support role for the reform coalition, the CNUS became a mechanism to pressure for improved legal and living conditions for urban and rural labor (*El Imparcial*, Aug. 4, 1947; Bishop 1959:26–27, 41, 99, 102).[21]

Organized labor's support for the reform coalition increased during the Arbenz administration. In his position as minister of defense (1945–51), Arbenz had cultivated close relations with organized labor and with PAR, the more radical reform party. In fact, labor supported Arbenz before any of the significant reform parties did by forming the Comité Político Nacional de Trabajadores to support his candidacy (Handy 1985: 142–43).

Immediately after his election there was an increase in labor militancy in the form of strikes in such key areas as railways, education, and the national plantations (*El Imparcial*, June 9, 1951; Handy 1985: 165). Nonetheless, during the Arbenz administration, labor organizations moved toward increased cooperation and centralization. In October 1951, the fragmented labor movement reorganized into a single confederation, the Confederación General de Trabajadores de Guatemala (CGTG), with an estimated membership of around 50,000 members in 285 unions. The new federation claimed membership of all unions except the peasants' union, discussed below.[22] At its height in 1954, before the counterreform, CGTG claimed an estimated 100,000 members in 500 unions, highlighting not only the institutional national unity achieved by the labor movement but also an increase in labor organizing both in the city and in the countryside (Cardoza y Aragón 1955a:98; Bishop 1959:137–48).[23]

The labor movement united and grew stronger to confront the rise of an antireform, antiregime, and antipopular opposition under increasingly polarized political circumstances.[24] The gap between the governing reform coalition, backed by the labor movement, and the anticommunist opposition increased with the actual foundation of the Communist

Party in 1950, which became the Partido Guatemalteco del Trabajo
(PGT) in 1952. Although the Guatemalan communist party had not
founded the labor movement, its leaders assumed prominent positions
in the new federation, including secretary general, first and second vice
president, and two seats on the executive committee (Bishop 1959:
142). In some cases, labor leaders and/or legislative deputies split from
other parties to join the PGT. Speaking about the relationship between
the labor movement and the communist party leaders, José Manuel Fortuny, the secretary general of the PGT at the time, said that "Víctor Manuel Gutiérrez [a well-respected labor leader] was not elected to the CGT
for his communist ideas, because he rose to prominence prior to the
founding of the PGT. He was considered dedicated, hard-working, and
very honest. And the same thing happened with the others [the communist leaders]. . . . If it had been otherwise (that is to say, to elect labor
leaders on the basis of communist ideas), things would have turned out
otherwise. What mattered was what they [the labor leaders] did" (Interview with Fortuny, Aug. 3, 1990).

Thus, although communist leaders assumed key positions in the unified labor federation that developed in the early 1950s, the labor movement as an institution did not assume or demand PGT affiliation of the
rank and file. Indeed, as Fortuny noted, it realized that the Guatemalan
labor movement had not embraced this ideology.

With the development of this vital labor movement, the reform faction of the oligarchy defected from the governing coalition, as did some
members of the middle class. With their defection, the governing coalition increased its dependence on the rising labor movement and turned
to its rural sectors for support. By the early 1950s, the governing coalition came to include a mobilized rural work force and peasantry, which
organized in tandem and ultimately in coordination with the urban labor
movement.

MOBILIZING AND INCORPORATING
RURAL SECTORS

If the social reform legislation during Arévalo's term opened up the
arena for urban labor organizing, it was both prohibitive and, at times,
repressive toward the rural sector. The first reform administration occasionally adopted coercive measures against rural organizing, and the
army often used violence to put down strikes in rural areas (Gutiérrez
Alvarez 1985:98–101; Handy 1985:214).

Although President Arévalo did not encourage and, at times, did not tolerate rural organizing, parts of the urban labor movement dedicated important resources to organizing rural workers. In particular, members of the labor organization CTG and some members of the PAR recruited rural labor into unions and sought to create support for the reform coalition as a whole. By the end of the first reform administration, efforts to establish a rural labor movement autonomous from those based in the urban areas resulted in a distinct organization.

The labor organizers responsible at the national level for rural mobilization were urban ladinos, who viewed the individuals and communities they wished to incorporate into their movement along class lines. They did not adequately acknowledge the ways in which rural class differences overlapped with ethnic differences in Guatemala. Indeed, the majority of Guatemalan *campesinos* were (and are) indigenous. The ladino labor organizers assumed that increased integration into society along class lines would eventually lead to a desired assimilation of the indigenous communities. This assumption was made explicit by artists and politicians of the period.

During the Arévalo presidency, the primarily urban CTG devoted some resources to organizing in the rural areas, despite restrictions imposed by the labor code. The CTG, and the CGTG after it, believed that peasants were the working class's natural ally; consequently, organized labor needed to join with peasants in a common struggle. And while Arévalo occasionally responded to rural militancy with coercion, according to Bishop (1959:78) the CTG executive committee claimed that Arévalo had santioned its work with rural members (Handy 1985:215). Throughout the Arévalo period, members of the CTG and its member union STEG traveled throughout the countryside to organize *campesinos* and rural workers. The first *campesino* organization joined the CTG in 1945 (Gutiérrez Alvarez 1985:87). The CTG demanded two changes to improve rural conditions. First, it pressured the government to overturn restrictions on rural organizing included in the 1947 labor code. Second, it called for land reform, which the urban labor movement (CTG and later CGTG) saw as a prerequisite for the development of a national, capitalist economy (Figueroa Ibarra 1980:118; Gutiérrez Alvarez 1985:85–86).

Some reformers in the predominantly urban labor movement put forth the idea that an autonomous *campesino* movement should develop and coexist with the urban labor movement (although this did not mean that the urban workers saw the peasants and rural workers, largely indigenous, as their equals). Under the direction of Leonardo Castillo Flores, who had been part of the CTG, the reformers created the Confederación

Nacional Campesina de Guatemala (CNCG) in May 1950. According to Fortuny, the former secretary general of the PGT, "The peasant union emerged at the margins of the communist party and of Marxist ideas" (Interview with Fortuny, Aug. 10, 1990).

The move to create an autonomous *campesino* organization initially fostered hostility and suspicion on the part of the CTG, which had been organizing in the rural areas since 1945.[25] Initial hostility gave way to a fairly cooperative and competitive relationship at the national level, with both organizations agreeing not to organize in areas in which the other federation was already present (Handy 1985:344).[26] The two federations issued fraternal statements 1952 through 1954. However, fraternal statements issued at the national level did not always translate into fraternal and harmonious actions at the local level. Conflicts emerged particularly around the implementation of land reform and access to land. To minimize conflict, the two sister federations created a liaison committee after the land reform decree (Interview with Guerra Borges, Aug. 8, 1990). Despite these national efforts, tensions between the CNCG and CTG at the local level remained.[27]

The CNCG, with eventual help from the CGTG, organized at the heart of the economy to improve *rural* working conditions and to increase access to land and credit. The CNCG, along with the CGTG and the teachers union therein, also tried to invoke a new spirit within the countryside. It promoted literacy programs and with the help of teachers and students organized chats and conferences to teach these communities about reform legislation and to create a new "revolutionary culture" (Interview with Anonymous A, Jan. 31, 1990; Interview with Anonymous B, May 19, 1990; Interview with Fortuny, Aug. 3, 1990). For example, it supported the Alianza Femenina Guatemalteca (AFG) when it held its first congress in November 1953, which, in part, discussed women and agrarian reform.[28] Bishop (1959:150) found that the CNCG even received 25,000 quetzals from the president's office to distribute materials to infuse the rural population with a revolutionary spirit and culture in defense of the social reforms and governing reform coalition. The reformers participated in this effort to create a revolutionary and Western ethic among the *campesinos* by distributing the monthly *El Campesino*, which had an estimated circulation of 50,000 (Gutiérrez Alvarez 1985:76).

The CNCG's influence over local and regional politics increased with the institutional arrangements created by the 1952 agrarian reform. As discussed in Chapter 4, the implementation of the law integrated organized rural workers at the local and regional level. This increased the formal political influence of the CNCG and its local members in the political decision making necessary to implement the redistributive agrarian reform. With the rise in rural organizing and increased incorporation of rural labor organizations into local and regional political decision making came isolated cases of land invasions, which a few communist party leaders, most notably Carlos Manuel Pellecer, apparently encouraged.[29] The national press covered the land invasions and exaggerated the degree to which they occurred (Gleijeses 1991:162).

By the end of the reform period, the CNCG developed into the largest popular organization. The federation had mobilized unions throughout most of the country and claimed six large regional federations that included 2,500 *campesino* and 300 agrarian unions. The CNCG had organized between 200,000 and 240,000 *campesinos,* 37 percent of the economically active rural population, twice as many people as the CGTG in half the time (Cardoza y Aragón 1955a; Schneider 1958; López Larrave 1976; Figueroa Ibarra 1976; Handy 1985:229; García Añoveros 1987:139).

By the final days of the revolution, the CGTG and the CNCG recruited and organized around 100,000 and 240,000 members respectively. The urban and rural workers and *campesinos* joined forces to strengthen their position and to defend the political, economic, and social rights achieved during the reform period. To this end, they successfully organized local unions and affiliates throughout the country and transformed the nature of civil society. In the process, they gained a significant degree of autonomy and influence in the implementation of the agrarian reform law and a mutually supportive relationship with the Arbenz administration.

The CNCG's Third Congress illustrates the ties of the *campesino* movement, the labor movement, and the governing coalition of reform parties. The Congress gathered together in 1954 some 7,000 delegates from around the country. Present were President Arbenz, the president of the legislature, the secretary generals from the main reform parties— PAR, PRG, PGT, RN—the secretary general from the CGTG, and leaders from the CTAL. Supported by the reform coalition and popular organizations, this Congress resolved among other things to support the Arbenz government against the rising opposition, to fight against the sectarian application of the agrarian reform law, and to sustain the alliance of *campesinos* and workers in the Frente Unico de Masas (Gutiérrez Alvarez 1985:294–95).

THE LEITMOTIF OF INDIGENOUS
INCORPORATION

This effort to organize peasants and rural workers unwittingly raised questions about ethnic relations and politics. Indigenous communities constituted the majority of the rural population. The labor organizers, therefore, organized and mobilized indigenous communities, even though their point was to strengthen the class basis of political identity and action. This rural organizing in indigenous communities coincided with ambivalent efforts by politicians and intellectuals to assimilate Mayans. Reformers orchestrated this paternalistic effort from above, including the extension of partial citizenship to all men. Their long-term goals were to undermine indigenous identity and practices; in the short term these ideological and educational efforts reinforced oligarchic and middle-class fears of an indigenous uprising—one in which class and ethnic conflict would prevail. Yet the reformers were themselves ambivalent about incorporating indigenous rural communities into the newly democratic polity.

Guatemalan reformers simultaneously sought to appropriate Mayan heritage as the essence of the Guatemalan nation and to assimilate Indians into ladino culture.[30] These reformers assumed that through assimilation Indians would lose their public and private identity as Indians. Many Guatemalan intellectuals and artists during the reform period, influenced both by the Mexican revolution and Peru's Alianza Popular Revolucionaria Americana (APRA), wrote about the noble Mayan origins of Guatemala and of the Guatemalan nation. This movement, led by ladinos, generally articulated a mythical conception of ancient Mayan culture and practices, which ostensibly infused the very blood and lifeline of a presumed nation. Many of the student and artistic movements, such as Saker-Ti (a group of young ladino artists and writers committed to redefining a revolutionary and national culture) and those who produced the *Revista de Guatemala*, dedicated poems, printed pictures, and cited the *Popul Vuj* (the Mayan book of creation) in their efforts to create the new Guatemalan nation and culture, one with Mayan roots. A member of Saker-Ti wrote, "We [the intellectuals and artists in Saker-Ti] were trying to find the totality of our national expression in our Mayan ancestry" (Alvarado 1953:11). He concluded with a call to create a new nation, democratic and revolutionary, rooted in the Maya.[31] However, while the reformers highlighted the historical Mayan roots of the Guatemalan nation, they also sought to destroy the existing Mayan people, which many, including reform politicians, feared and which ladinos admittedly did not understand.[32]

The reform politicians held a widespread belief in Western notions of unilinear evolution. They believed that Western culture, political organization, and economic development foreshadowed the preferred and inevitable path of other non-Western people. From this perspective, Indian culture was not only anachronistic, but also an obstacle to cultural, political, and economic development. Liberals and Marxists in the reform coalition shared this set of beliefs about development.

The reform coalition responded to its "Indian problem" by creating a new state institution, the Instituto Indigenista Nacional (IIN) in 1945. The IIN had the mandate to investigate and to learn about the Maya in order to resolve the Indian problem (Galich 1945:83–84).[33] The first director of the IIN, Antonio Goubaud Carrera, stated that he sought to create a "homogenous nationality"—read ladino nationality—and opposed the creation of a new culture and set of values that would be multidimensional (Goubaud 1945:88).[34]

While IIN investigated indigenous communities, the state promoted educational and cultural campaigns that sought, but failed, to acculturate Mayans into Western culture. President Arévalo, for example, organized Misiones Ambulantes de Cultura (Traveling Cultural Missions). The Misiones Ambulantes were both educational and moral campaigns. They taught literacy skills, talked about the rights and responsibilities of citizens, and provided ideas about how to improve community hygiene. The Misiones Ambulantes also sought to "bring culture" to communities as a means to facilitate acculturation. A teacher who participated in these efforts remarked that some Misiones, for example, traveled to indigenous communities with phonographs to play Mozart and Beethoven (Interview with Meléndez de León, Jan. 5, 1990).

The state also sought to increase education with a much-touted literacy campaign and efforts to train bilingual indigenous teachers.[35] These campaigns, which did improve literacy and increase access to schooling, clearly operated with a vision of providing indigenous communities with a Western civic consciousness in order to assimilate them into an ill-defined ladino culture and, consequently, make them "good citizens." With literacy came the obligation to vote in elections with a secret ballot. Hence, state-sponsored education was designed to create a responsive and responsible citizenry among indigenous men.

These ambivalent efforts to incorporate indigenous men into the regime and into ladino culture coincided with efforts to ensure that Indian *campesinos* would have increased economic opportunities and the hope that they would stay on the land rather than move to the city. A state sponsored journal, *El Campesino*, targeted indigenous communities and disseminated the aforementioned political, social, and economic messages. *El Campesino* provided information to improve farming techniques and agricultural yields. It also disseminated information to improve community sanitation and health. And it propagated an explicit moral message through stories about "Juan Chapín," ostensibly included in the journal to promote literacy. *Chapín* is colloquial for *Guatemalan*. On the one hand, the stories encouraged *campesinos* to go to school as a means to improve their productivity and that of the country. The stories, however, also encouraged the adoption of non-Indian practices to replace Mayan culture. One story about Juan Chapín states, "One of Juan's three children is an agronomist, another is dedicated to commerce in woodworking, installing in the capital a well-furnished carpenter's shop. The youngest is studying abroad to become an agricultural engineer. María, his wife, still wears her traditional indigenous clothing, but her children are now ladinos, without embarrassment of their parents who are Indians" (*El Campesino* 21, 22 [Jan.–Feb. 1947]). The stories, therefore, encouraged Indian *campesinos* to adopt Western practices and allegiance to the Guatemalan state.[36] However, while these stories encouraged indigenous *campesinos* to westernize, they also encouraged them to stay on the land rather than come to the city, which was characterized by sin:

> Man of the countryside! . . . Man of peace and of work! Always remain on your farm, on your land, cultivate your land with love! Don't allow yourself to be seduced by the city, do not allow yourself to be deceived by appearances. . . . If you abandon the farm and the solitary life of the countryside, in the end it will be an irreversible catastrophe for your well being and that of your nation. . . . The property of the country rests on the shoulders of its *campesinos*, in the workers who sow seeds, who use science in their harvest, and fulfill their duties with humility and honor. (*El Campesino* 32, 33 [Jan.–Feb. 1948]: 11–12)[37]

These vignettes capture the ambivalence of ladino reformers in Guatemala between 1944 and 1954. On the one hand, they wanted to assimilate Indians and to improve their standards of living. On the other hand, they wanted to keep Indians on the land to sustain production for the domestic market and to provide labor for export markets. By encouraging Indians to stay away from the evils of the cities, they implicitly attempted to keep the ladino and indigenous communities separate.

In short, the reformers developed ambivalent ideas and practices in their efforts to incorporate the indigenous communities. They provided the legal conditions for political participation by Indians as citizens. They expanded the cultural idea of the nation rooted in Mayan tradition and history. They sought to improve indigenous standards of living. All of these efforts, however, were mediated by ladino suspicion of the indigenous community: fear of its inability to participate responsibly in politics, desire to assimilate Indians into ladino culture, and hopes that Indians would maintain their class position as *campesinos* in agricultural professions and away from the cities.

Yet, if the reformers were ambivalent about their efforts to organize within indigenous communities, the counterreform opposition was not. The latter reacted against changes in political participation, construction of the nation, and changes in economic practices. According to the opposition, with the land reform, Indians, *campesinos*, and communists had come to dominate rural civil society in a way that threatened traditional regimes of accumulation and ideas about political order.

During the Guatemalan reform period, therefore, the governing coalitions oversaw the unprecedented rise in popular organizing, particularly among urban ladino and rural indigenous workers. The various reform parties competed for popular-sector support. No particular party, however, entirely dominated either the urban or rural sectors—despite widespread fear of communist control of each. With the reform coalition's increasing electoral dependence on the popular sectors, the latter gained influence within the government and, indirectly, over policy. In the absence of ties to one reform party alone, the organized popular sectors maintained a certain degree of autonomy from the reform coalition. So too, in the absence of a more established organizational tradition, the regional and local organizations also maintained a certain degree of autonomy from the national ones to which they belonged. Hence, for example, with the 1952 land reform, the organized labor and peasant organizations gained influence in the implementation of the reform but also occasionally mobilized outside of it—as witnessed by the brief but noted rise in land occupations and rural conflicts in some regions of Guatemala.

Yet, if popular-sector support was fragmented between reform parties, it remained solidly behind the reform coalition as a whole. As the threat of an invasion from the United States appeared imminent, the different popular sectors united under the banner of the Frente Unico de Masas to defend the democratic regime.[38] The presumed unity of an urban and rural popular movement that unambiguously supported the governing coalition heightened fear within a growing opposition movement that tended to equate the growth of civil society with communism. Opposition increased all the more so as mobilization and reforms occurred at the rural heart of the economy. In the absence of a viable political party legally able to challenge these redistributive reforms and mobilization, the opposition turned to arms.

PART III

From Reform to Reaction: Democracy versus Authoritarianism

CHAPTER 6

From Opposition to Regime-Founding Coalitions

The reform coalitions in Costa Rica and Guatemala had championed the cause of democracy to legitimate the social reforms and popular mobilization that they had overseen. They would not remain unopposed. Movements in both countries challenged the democratic rhetoric of the reform coalitions. The opposition denounced the influence of communists in the respective governments, warned of their rising influence over state agencies and civic associations, decried the challenge to property relations, and instigated fear of an impending communist dictatorship. By shifting the debate from democracy against authoritarianism to democracy against communism, the opposition in both countries echoed the anticommunism of the 1930s. It also drew on the ideological language of the Cold War.

Confronted with a material challenge to property relations, an ideational and political fear of communism, and an electoral loss at the polls, the Costa Rican and Guatemalan opposition movements took up arms. With the threat of force, the opposition movements overthrew the democratically elected governments of President Teodoro Picado Michalski in Costa Rica in 1948 and President Jacobo Arbenz Guzmán in Guatemala in 1954. The counterreform coalitions that took power in Costa Rica in 1948 and Guatemala in 1954 sent into exile the prior political officials, banned communist or suspected communist parties, and demobilized much of the labor movement.

Despite similar actions to overthrow the reform governments, the Costa Rican and Guatemalan opposition founded different political regimes. The Costa Rican opposition movement installed political democracy while the Guatemalan opposition installed military rule. This chapter addresses this dual dynamic of parallel overthrows and divergent political outcomes. With a common set of motives for overthrowing the reform governments, why did the Costa Rican and Guatemalan opposition movements found political democracy and military rule, respectively? This chapter develops the argument that variations in Costa Rica's and Guatemala's counterreform coalitions (the unity of elites, institutional organization, and ideological cohesion) explain the foundation of political democracy in Costa Rica following the 1948 civil war and authoritarianism in Guatemala following the 1954 coup.

A political division within the elite community provided a necessary, although not sufficient, condition for the formation of democratizing multiclass coalitions; these coalitions emerged in Costa Rica in 1942 and in 1948, and in Guatemala in 1944, and engendered processes of democratization. By contrast, a united oligarchy had little incentive to consent to political democracy, particularly when it feared that democracy itself had unleashed communist influence; in the aftermath of Guatemala's 1954 coup, elite unity in the opposition movement foreclosed the possibility of a democratic outcome in that country.

The unity versus division of the elites by the end of the reform period derived from the position first assumed by the oligarchy in the reform coalition. Where part of the oligarchy dominated the reform coalition, as in Costa Rica, it limited the transformational aspects of reform and popular mobilization and remained divided, with only part of its members participating in the counterreform coalition. Conversely, in Guatemala, the oligarchy had assumed a subordinate, even peripheral, role in the reform movement and, subsequently, became alienated from the initial reform coalition, which had legislated increasingly more comprehensive reforms alongside increased popular mobilization; in this context, the Guatemalan oligarchy as a whole supported the counterreform movement.

Once the reform governments had been overthrown, the future of democracy depended on the existence of institutionally competitive political organizations within the counterreform coalition. The Costa Rican counterreform coalition included competing political organizations with conflicting ideological visions. With the overthrow of the reform coalition, the counterreform coalition engaged in a process of internal political struggle. Stalemate ensued and was resolved in a democratic compromise allowing for an alternation in power. In Guatemala, the counterreform coalition included a multiplicity of closely tied civic opposition groups that shared a common ideological preference for authoritarian rule over fear of communism under democracy. Yet this Guatemalan opposition lacked any semblance of institutionalized political parties or any viable political organizations capable of governing or self-consciously designed to govern. In the absence of viable political parties or leaders, the Guatemalan opposition deferred to the military as the strongest institution within the coalition.

This pattern of competitive civic and political organizations in Costa Rica and their absence in Guatemala was an inherited legacy of the Liberal period. The longer historical trajectory of civic organizing in Costa Rica facilitated the development of already-formed political positions and parties that could lock horns in the post–civil war period. Conversely, in Guatemala, Liberal attempts to limit, and in the 1930s to negate, the growth of civil society and political parties therein led to a dramatic growth during the reform period of fairly large but shallow organizations in the reform and counterreform movements; the Guatemalan opposition, therefore, depended on protest and, ultimately, the military to carry out its actions. In this sense, the opposition in each case relied on an institutional legacy and replicated an institutional repertoire that had been developed in the Liberal period.

Following each overthrow, the best-armed sectors in the counterreform coalition assumed office first and came to dominate political institutions thereafter. In Costa Rica, the (upper-) middle-class sectors organized in the Partido Social Demócrata (PSD) developed political hegemony in a democratic regime that endured. In Guatemala, the military assumed the executive mantle of an authoritarian regime that similarly endured.

This chapter stresses, therefore, the role of domestic factors to explain the overthrow of democracy in the middle of the twentieth century and coalitional analysis to explain the founding of democracy versus authoritarianism. This argument parts company with prevailing analyses about these two countries, which tend to focus on leadership for Costa Rica and international factors for Guatemala. While José Figueres Ferrer is generally touted for his political prowess, charismatic leadership, and visionary role in defending and founding political democracy in Costa Rica, the United States is generally held responsible for founding military rule in Guatemala. As the ensuing narrative highlights, the roles of Figueres and the United States are apparent and noted. Yet these arguments are particularistic and do not provide ample explanation across cases. In the absence of a Figueres, Guatemala experienced the overthrow of its reform government. In the presence of U.S. involvement, the Costa Rican opposition founded political democracy. What the comparison of these two cases highlights is that we need to assess the rise of the domestic opposition and coalition politics. This chapter puts forth the argument that variations in the unity of elites, institutional organization, and ideological cohesion are more important than international influence or individual actions in explaining the divergent regimes founded by each country's counterreform coalition.

Costa Rica

THE ELECTORAL OPPOSITION:
DIVIDED ELITE AND COMPETITIVE
POLITICAL ORGANIZATIONS

Opposition to Costa Rica's reform coalition first developed within elite circles, building on the opposition that had originally developed against then President Rafael Calderón. Elite opposition rallied against communist influence in governing circles, changes in social policy (particularly the tax reform), and increases in labor organizing (see Chapter 3). In contrast to the Guatemalan oligarchic opposition, the Costa Rican opposition dedicated significant resources to organizing an electoral alternative to the reform coalition, drawing on the pattern of oligarchic competition that had developed with the Costa Rican Liberal period. Traditional politics had been based on institutionalized and privileged access to state mechanisms that had enabled political officials to distribute resources and manipulate votes; the opposition, therefore, attempted to create a new electoral machine by building on personal loyalties established during the Liberal period. Yet the oligarchic opposition no longer marshaled the same resources it had in the prior decades. For the 1944, 1946, and 1948 elections, the opposition rallied around two key opposition leaders: former president León Cortés and Otilio Ulate Blanco.

Cortés emerged as the voice and candidate of the opposition that developed in these years. Prior to the division within the oligarchy, it had been assumed, if not decided in back-room negotiations, that Cortés would run for the presidency following the end of President Calderón's term in 1944; Costa Rican law prohibited two successive terms in office. By the early 1940s, it became apparent that Calderón had no intention of handing power back to Cortés. Cortés, in turn, had become alienated from Calderón for sidestepping Cortés's son as president of the national legislature, initiating social reforms, and allying himself with the communists. Given his national stature as a firm, efficient president with anticommunist credentials from the 1930s, Cortés became the oligarchic opposition's natural presidential candidate for the 1944 elections. Cortés ran as the candidate for the Partido Demócrata (PD). He campaigned against the politically influential role assumed by the communist party and the mobilization of cadre and union members in the streets and workplace. Moreover, he tried to discredit Calderón by pinpointing the rise in administrative corruption that had taken place during the latter's government, in contrast to Cortés's much-heralded legacy as an honest and efficient administrator. Cortés was a foreboding figure whose message of honesty and efficiency resonated not only with the oligarchic opposition but with entrepreneurs, some intellectuals, and much of the countryside.[1] Former president Luis Alberto Monge, who was then part of the opposition, said,

> *Monge*: All the Costa Rican peasants were cortesistas. . . . Because he came to symbolize the struggle against arbitrariness that had developed during the government, against the alliance between the government's party and the communist party. . . .
> *Author*: What did he do to develop this support?
> *Monge*: He was minister of development and had a lot of contact with the interior of the republic. He had a lot of contact with the rural areas and did a lot of work with very few resources. . . . He was remembered in many areas for having built bridges, roads, schools, and all of these things. . . . Second, his presidential administration was considered an honest administration and one responsible for a lot of material works. (Interview with Monge, Aug. 26, 1994)

Cortés lost the 1944 presidential elections to President Calderón's handpicked successor, Teodoro Picado Michalski. The opposition protested that the administration had stolen the elections and had broken with the democratic tradition of Costa Rican politics. It is undeniable that fraud and violence took place. However, it remains uncertain that Cortés would have won had the elections been clean, particularly given his ambiguous position on the social reforms.[2] Moreover, denunciations of fraud as much as fraud itself were characteristic of Costa Rican elections. Despite this electoral defeat, Cortés continued to carry out a two-pronged opposition strategy. On the one hand, he was committed to organizing through and for elections, no matter how fraudulent. He sustained a personal following rather than creating an institutional and programmatic one. On the other hand, he hoped to negotiate the political reunification of the divided elite, which was contingent on the expulsion of the Partido Vanguardia Popular and its communist leaders from the reform coalition.

Without access to state resources, the opposition was particularly dependent on the media to divulge its message. Otilio Ulate Blanco played a significant role in this regard. He had experience as a legislator who had fought in nationalist struggles in the 1930s, and as leader of the Partido Unión Nacional (PUN), he had mobilized support among Costa Rica's urban entrepreneurs. In the 1944 elections, Ulate did not play a prominent role, as the majority of the opposition rallied around Cortés. However, he did play an important role in opposing the regime in his capacity as a newspaper publisher, using this medium to voice his opposition to the reform coalition and to undermine the latter's legitimacy. He referred, for example, to social reforms in the media as "the opiate of the social guarantees," implying both that Calderón was a Marxist and that he was duping the working class. He stated that "these socialistic reforms are excellent, but when we have the economic wherewithal." Ulate essentially criticized the social reforms by arguing that Costa Rica did not have a developed economy and that the reforms, in the context of a largely agricultural economy, were "luxuries and stupidities." He further attacked the reform coalition by arguing that the labor code included antidemocratic practices and would evolve into obligatory unionism, while other legislation had opened the doors for the government to challenge private property. Rather than fighting for social reforms, he argued that Costa Rica needed better administration, and planned production, education, and social hygiene (Creedman 1971:184, 217, 218; Torres 1986:140–51). As a prominent newspaper owner, Ulate helped to shape political discourse against President Calderón and later President Picado. He also backed Cortés in the 1944 presidential election.

The agro-business and entrepreneurial elites that supported Cortés in the PD and Ulate in the PUN organized as traditional politicians. It would be misleading, however, to argue that opposition only developed within oligarchic circles. In the early 1940s, two groups of young intellectuals developed in opposition to Calderón: the Centro para el Estudio de los Problemas Nacionales (Centro) and Acción Demócrata (AD). While these two groups started off as small opposition currents, they came to assume an essential role in the opposition.

The Centro started off as a small study group on April 3, 1940, formed by students and professors of law, some of whom had been active in education campaigns in the 1930s.[3] They developed an intellectual framework and national critique that challenged the political and economic underpinnings of the Liberal regime and existing agrarian capitalism. Prior to 1948, the members of the Centro wielded minimal political influence. As Isaac Felipe Azofeifa, one of the founders of the Centro, said, "No one was listening to the Centro" (Interview with Azofeifa, June 13, 1990). Nonetheless, the intellectual framework and personal ties developed in the years of the Centro provided the ideological and institutional foundation for politics and political affinities after the 1948 civil war. Moreover, the Centro organized a generation of politicians and intellectuals who have shaped Costa Rican political discourse and public policy since 1948.[4]

The members of the Centro had three main objectives.[5] First, they denounced the Liberal project and wanted to modernize the political system. They denounced the personal, nonideological party system that emerged and disappeared with each cycle of fraudulent and corrupt elections. They argued that these practices, in conjunction with the complete lack of political education of the society as a whole, prevented the growth of a politically aware and active populace. In response, the Centro called for permanent political parties with a clear ideological orientation and a commitment to economic and social reforms in Costa Rica. While the Costa Rican communist party was the only party of the time that met these criteria, the Centro attacked the party for its Leninist orientation and political opportunism.[6] Like most of the noncommunist Latin American left, the members of the Centro supported the formation of "modern" but noncommunist political parties.

Second, the Centro analyzed and denounced the social inequities produced by an unregulated free-market economy. Influenced by APRA of Peru, the Liberal Party of Colombia, Keynes, and Roosevelt, this group argued that the Smithian/Liberal conception of the advantages of laissez-faire economies failed to predict and account for the disadvantages of the lower and middle sectors.[7] In the case of Costa Rica, it announced the need for the growth of a technocratic state bureaucracy, state intervention, and state regulation in order to modernize the economy and to mitigate the poverty produced by the system. It also stressed the need for a more reliable bureaucracy that would not fall prey to corruption and rent seeking as it argued had happened during the Calderón administration.

Third, the Centro advocated a new model of economic development to include agricultural diversification, industrialization, increased access to credit, and the establishment of cooperatives. It argued that this model should replace the exhausted oligarchic model of growth and rule. In contrast to the Latin American national, populist movements and the European social democratic parties that influenced them, the Centro did not actively mobilize labor as part of its strategy or vision.[8] Throughout the early 1940s, the Centro remained weak, claiming no more than 200 members, although it did have chapters in all but one province.[9]

Ironically, the Centro ostensibly shared a commitment to the *content* of the reforms passed by the reform coalition. Nonetheless, it attacked Calderón as a politician who opportunistically promoted these reforms, without careful analysis or planning, in order to increase badly needed public support. The Centro's opposition to the reform coalition and subsequent alliance with the oligarchic opposition has led many to question whether it, in fact, really supported the reform legislation at all.[10] Based on its subsequent actions, the Centro did support developmental and social reforms, but not under the guidance of a reform coalition that included a Liberal oligarch and the communist party.

Acción Demócrata, the other opposition group of young intellectuals, had developed as an opposition within the structure of traditional oligarchic parties. According to Alberto Martén, one of the founders of AD, a number of young men active in León Cortés's party decided to form a political tendency within the party. The political tendency extended strong support for Cortés but opposed the closed political process by which the party selected the electoral list of deputies. Voicing their opposition to a politics of personality and electoral machines, the members of AD campaigned within the party for more open procedures. The most visible members of AD, José Figueres Ferrer, Francisco Orlich, and Alberto Martén, first gained notoriety, however, not for their party reforms but for a 1942 radio speech by Figueres in which the latter attacked the government of Calderón. Government forces cut the speech short and expelled Figueres.[11] The government never suspected that this single action would not only help make Figueres a political martyr and provide him with political cachet within the country but would also provide him with the opportunity to make preparations for an armed overthrow of the government; it was in exile that he began considering an armed response. Nonetheless, during these initial years, from 1942 to 1944, AD expressed its commitment to party building. The members of AD decided that the best means to establish a permanent political party was to work within Cortés's already-established personalistic party.

The Centro and AD merged and founded a political party, the Partido Social Demócrata (PSD), in March 1945. It is commonly asserted that whereas AD provided the political brashness of the PSD, the Centro provided the intellectual framework. Against the intellectual principles elaborated by the Centro, Alberto Martén stated:

> The PSD at this moment was not a party characterized by discipline and doctrine. But it was the result of a rebellious and idealistic movement of young students. We were against the domination of the old personalistic politicians, more or less corrupt, and we wanted a change.
>
> The Social Democratic Party [PSD] was not the social democracy that we think of today. What's more, I proposed the name and I did not propose it in reference to European social democracy but as an artificial thing, a type of terminology that sounded good. (Interview with Martén, Aug. 17, 22, 1994)

While the Centro and AD merged with two different sets of intellectual principles, they shared a commitment to change and suspicion that the Partido Vanguardia Popular harbored intentions to impose a communist dictatorship. They became a vocal opposition in the newspapers and radio, but the PSD lacked votes (Gardner 1971:51).

The opposition, therefore, coalesced into three parties: the Partido Demócrata (former president Cortés's party), the Partido Unión Nacional (Ulate's party) and the Partido Social Demócrata (the fusion of the Centro and AD). In each case, the parties drew a significant number of political actors who had been active before the reform period began and, therefore, had experience and commitment to party politics and campaigning. Drawing on this institutional legacy, these three parties opposed the reform coalition initially by separately running for office against the reform parties, which had not secured a formal national alliance, for the 1946 midterm elections.[12] During this campaign, the opposition warned of the dangers of "caldero-comunismo," while the reform alliance touted the social reforms of the past few years. The outcome of the 1946 elections favored the government parties (57,154 votes), followed by the opposition parties (41,821 votes) and independent parties (3,000 votes) (Aguilar Bulgarelli 1983:179, 185).

The electoral results compelled the opposition to confront two political realities. First, the government party had experienced a secular decline in its electoral base, but the communist party had experienced a secular increase, from 4 to 6 deputies out of a total of 46 (Mora 1980: 196). In other words, the communists had increased their power within a still-dominant reform coalition. Second, the opposition, even if united, would not have been able to defeat the reform coalition in legislative elections.

Under these conditions, Cortés tried to effect a rapprochement between the two sides of the divided elite. He approached President Picado after the 1946 midterm elections, proposing that the opposition provide electoral and financial support to Picado and Calderón in exchange for the PRN's break with the communist party. Picado requested a week's time to think the proposal over (Acuña 1974; Aguilar Bulgarelli 1983: 192–193; Rojas Bolaños 1986:132). The potential exchange never came to fruition, because Cortés died unexpectedly before Picado had come to a decision. It is not unreasonable to believe, however, that Picado would have accepted Cortés's offer. Picado had been lukewarm toward the communists before he was elected and, therefore, might have agreed to Cortés's plan, which would have reunified the elite, decreased the political influence of the communists, halted the social programs, and brought an end to the social reform period. Cortés's diplomatic gesture, therefore, might have reversed the direction of the reform period and the particular circumstances surrounding the outbreak of the 1948 civil war. However, given the historical turn of events, we will never know whether this exchange would have taken place or what the reaction of the communist party or the PSD members would have been. By 1946, Figueres of the PSD had already been planning an armed overthrow of the government; it is not evident that a negotiated reunification of the elite would have prevented Figueres and his cohort from beginning a civil war. But it would have changed the configuration of allies—most likely leading to an alliance between the Centro and the communist party, both of which would have been excluded from an oligarchic political decision-making process.

Instead, Cortés's death precipitated the formal political alliance of the three heterogeneous opposition parties, although each maintained its organizational and ideological autonomy (Gardner 1971:52). In the opposition convention for the 1948 elections, the various parties elected Ulate as presidential candidate.[13] He was a more acceptable figure to PSD members than Cortés had been.

The opposition's electoral alliance coincided with its efforts to undermine the reform coalition's legitimacy. Ulate's newspaper continued as a mouthpiece to voice opposition to the existing regime. The paper and various radio stations promoted an anticommunist discourse and attacked Archbishop Sanabria for having sanctioned membership in the communist Partido Vanguardia Popular (Torres 1986:136, 144–45, 149). The opposition also organized to combat the popular and more militant labor organizing by the communists. As discussed in Chapter 5, the opposition financed the Church-affiliated labor movement Rerum Novarum as an alternative to the communist-affiliated one. Rerum Novarum, in turn, supported the opposition as the latter prepared for the presidential election and then the civil war.

The opposition mobilized its most defiant protest in 1947, shortly after the legislation of the redistributive tax reform and before the 1948 presidential elections. It began as a demonstration in July 1947 and turned into a commercial strike, commonly referred to as the *huelga de los brazos caídos*.[14] The opposition claimed that the strike was designed to achieve broader electoral guarantees against fraud and to defend democracy. The governing coalition concluded that it was a protest against the 1947 tax reform. Luis Alberto Monge, whose party (PSD) had supported the *huelga*, stated in an interview 46 years later that the government was partially correct:

> Behind the *huelga de los brazos caídos* were the most conservative groups in the country. Definitely. It is true. But they built on the indignation and protest of the popular sectors because of the abuse against the government and the people. . . . [Those who supported Ulate] supported the *huelga de los brazos caídos*, including giving resources and funds for the strike. . . . In this grand opposition, provoked by arbitrariness, the presence of the communists, the co-government with communism, there was a very powerful economic wing, very influential over the means of communication. . . . They would say that they were struggling for liberty, but in essence they were struggling for other things. Apart from all this, I admit that sincerely, in essence, they were fighting against the social reforms and other things. (Interview with Monge, Aug. 26, 1994)

The *huelga* heightened the already-existing political polarization and became a testing ground for both sides. The opposition used the strike to voice its disapproval of the redistributive reforms and to try to gain control of the recently reformed electoral apparatus. Under the auspices of the *huelga*, commercial shops and banks closed down, and were joined by the electric company and Northern Railways. Strikers distributed mimeographed information in the streets and attempted to increase the ranks of the strike by boycotting those businesses that stayed open. The strike gained momentum on August 2, when thousands of women demonstrated in the capital of San José to demand guarantees to prevent fraud in the next election. The march ended only when government troops fired shots into the air.

Faced with the strike, the Catholic and communist labor federations took opposing sides, with the Catholic Rerum Novarum (CCTRN) supporting the strike and the communist CTCR supporting the government. The CCTRN officially adopted a neutral position, offering to provide food throughout the city to whoever needed it, helping an estimated 8,000 families. Former president Monge, who supported Rerum Novarum, confirmed that the Catholic confederation distributed food because it could not participate directly in politics. Presbyter Santiago Núñez, Benjamín Núñez's brother, took charge of this distribution effort. In fact, according to Santiago Núñez, his brother and other CCTRN members did actively take part in promoting the strike, including the distribution of propaganda. These actions heightened the Catholic union's support for the opposition and increased its distance from Archbishop Sanabria, who, on the other hand, played an active role in trying to bring an end to the strike (Backer 1978:146–47; Aguilar 1989:35).[15]

The communist CTCR, on the other hand, supported the governing reform coalition and mobilized on its behalf; banana workers even traveled from the coast to support the government against the *huelga de los brazos caídos*.[16] Some workers helped police forces control the city. The reform coalition hoped that this demonstration of support for the regime would undermine the legitimacy of the strikers and place pressure on the opposition to end the strike. Schifter (1986:217–21) suggests that the reform coalition also sought to take advantage of the opposition's anticommunism; by consciously instilling fear that the continuation of the strike would lead to increasing communist presence in the streets and a possible communist takeover, the reform coalition hoped that the opposition would back down.

Indeed, the progovernment demonstrations became confrontational. Some ended in the pillage of stores that had closed down in deference to the capital strike. Moreover, the communists called in their *brigadas de choque* (shock brigades), which had been created to defend themselves from attacks, including efforts to disrupt their meetings and attempts to bomb Mora's car and house (Mora 1980:269–70). The brigades admittedly engaged in arbitrary violence that further polarized the political situation.[17] The communist labor federation also demonstrated on behalf of the government and called for additional reforms to extend the labor code to all industrial workers, to include a greater role for the labor courts, and to enforce government wage and price controls.[18] The communists' proreform demonstrations increased the opposition's fear. It also served to heighten the U.S. government's suspicions that Picado could not control the communists (Schifter 1986, ch. 7).

The reform coalition coupled these popular demonstrations with efforts to minimize the financial consequences of the strike. It militarized banking establishments and created the Institute for the Mobilization of Credit, which was designed to cash checks for those unable to access money deposited in banks participating in the capital strike. The opposition claimed that the institute would seize bank deposits. The police also tried to force some shops to open and increased its presence at opposition events (Aguilar Bulgarelli 1969:219; Rojas Bolaños 1986:141). These sanctions penalized those who acted in the capital strike but also tried to allay the fears of those who had money deposited in the striking establishments.

The strike ended on August 4, 1947, with the administration providing the electoral guarantees that the strikers had been demanding. The reform coalition had lost the upper hand to an opposition that had appropriated the language of democracy even while many of its members had subverted democratic procedures in the 1930s and even though the reform coalition had passed a new electoral code in January 1946. President Picado agreed that Ulate, as the opposition's presidential candidate, could decide the composition of the new Electoral Tribunal, the final arbiter in the electoral process. With this concession, the opposition gained control over the electoral process, which had historically provided the opportunity to oversee and commit fraud. Twenty-seven calderonistas supported this concession. The communists refused to sign, because they had played an active role in drafting and fighting for an electoral code that would prevent electoral fraud, and especially because they did not trust the opposition to ensure the honesty of the upcoming elections. Indeed they suspected the opposition of seeking only to ensure its dominant position within the electoral apparatus (Aguilar Bulgarelli 1983:223–26; Interview with Mora, July 25, 1990; Interview with F. Cerdas, July 7, 1990). Nonetheless, united opposition at the polls and an increasingly public and aggressive opposition in the media and streets succeeded in dominating the Electoral Tribunal and selecting the president of the Electoral Registry.

FROM ELECTIONS TO ARMS

National elections took place on February 8, 1948, in a context of political polarization, violence, and, ultimately, intrigue. The reform coalition campaigned on the merits of its social and democratic reforms. Calderón's PRN and the communist PVP had put forth separate legislative candidates, but they united behind Calderón as presidential candidate. The opposition alliance championed the cause of free and honest elections; it more fervently promoted an anticommunist line and gained political capital from the fact that the PVP had recently joined the Comintern (Rojas Bolaños 1986:139–40). Consequently, the opposition sought to identify Calderón with international communism (Bell 1971:61; Schifter 1986:219–20).

The shady process of counting votes and ratifying the winner sparked the civil war. The opposition-appointed Electoral Tribunal announced a split victory: it declared Ulate the presidential winner, with 54,931 votes to Calderón's 44,438, but announced that the reform coalition had won a majority of the legislative seats; the number of PVP seats increased to 12 out of 45 (Aguilar Bulgarelli 1983:248–52; Cerdas Cruz 1991:290). Prior to the announcement of these results, the president of the three-person Electoral Tribunal left to join the opposition forces in the hills, which had started to organize an armed response. Another member of the tribunal voiced his lack of confidence in the results because of time constraints placed on recounting the ballots, which was required by law, and because a suspicious fire destroyed approximately two-thirds of the ballots before they could be recounted. Under such conditions, the Electoral Tribunal had in fact dissolved. Both the reform and counterreform coalitions cried fraud. The reform coalition denounced the fact that the registry had not processed all of the applicants for electoral registration and had changed some photographs used for identification purposes. The opposition in turn charged the reform coalition with sending in photographs that did not correspond to the registered name (Aguilar Bulgarelli 1983:260–265; Dunkerley 1988:130).

The legislature, however, had the final responsibility to ratify the Electoral Tribunal's politically charged and contested declaration. The communists and the archbishop argued that the legislature should accept Ulate's declared victory, even if there was fraud, but Calderón demanded another election. After much debate, the reform coalition, and delegates in the legislature, decided to annul the presidential electoral results but to accept the legislative results. In essence, the legislature denied the opposition the right to assume the executive office while granting the right of the reform coalition to assume the majority of seats in the legislature.

With the decision to annul the presidential elections, the opposition as a whole concluded that it could not effect change through the democratic process. Ulate took refuge in the U.S. embassy, while other opposition members joined the army that was forming under Figueres's leadership.[19] The results of the 1948 elections led the opposition to doubt whether the existing regime would have allowed it to assume office even had there been clean and undisputed elections. Moreover, the gains made by the communists in the 1948 legislative elections suggested rising popular support for the more radical part of the reform coalition, raising doubts about the ability of the executive branch to overturn reform legislation and to limit popular mobilization. In other words, the opposition faced obstacles in terms of both perceived opposition from within the regime and ambivalent popular support from without. Whether the elections were fraudulent or not, it is doubtful that the opposition would have been able to reverse the legislative power wielded by the reform coalition; in the opposition's best-case scenario, it would have been able to stall the reform coalition's agenda.

With the breakdown of electoral procedures, José Figueres Ferrer and his army initiated the civil war in March 1948, a little over a month after the voting and less than two weeks after the legislature voided the presidential elections. This armed movement contrasted markedly with the dominant electoral strategy of the opposition in the prior years. Figueres declared that he resorted to arms because the reform coalition had demonstrated complete disrespect for the electoral processes and Costa Rica's much discussed historical democracy. There is little doubt that most Costa Ricans were outraged by the decision to void the elections. However, focusing on abuses in the 1948 elections as the cause of war overlooks the fact that Figueres had been contemplating an armed response since 1943. Alberto Martén, who worked closely with Figueres in the 1940s, highlighted Figueres's commitment to armed struggle early on, before the elections: "While Figueres was more preoccupied with figuring out an armed response, I [Martén] had always been more interested in thinking about a concrete economic program, which was vague in Figueres's plans" (Interview with Martén, July 13, 1990). Figueres also notes that he was organizing an armed response while politicians, who probably thought he was crazy, pursued diplomatic venues to resolve the conflict (Figueres 1987:147). He had organized the opposition army without revealing to most leaders in the opposition his intentions to take up arms. According to Figueres, "the main Opposition leaders did not know anything about my activities, except for don Otilio Ulate, who suspected something about my actions" (Figueres 1987:134). Some of Figueres's closest confidants in the PSD knew that he was organizing an armed opposition but did not know about his ties with the Caribbean Legion, which had helped Figueres to acquire both arms and people to fight the civil war.[20] When knowledge of Figueres's army began to spread, some opposition members and many Costa Rican peasants took to the hills to join the fight against the regime.

Figueres and his army started to fight on March 12. The junior members of both the reform and counterreform coalitions, the communist

PVP and opposition PSD, fought primarily against one another. It appears that the armed opposition was one-fifth the size of proreform forces. Interviews with members of both sides of the war corroborate estimates of 600 men in the opposition and 3,000, mostly communists, for the reform coalition (Interview with Martén, July 13, 1990; Interview with Mora, June 25, 1990). The government, ill-prepared despite knowledge of Figueres's intentions, relied primarily on the communist party's *brigadas de choque*, mobile units under Picado's command, and the police, largely responsible to Calderón and his party (Schifter 1986:277). The Costa Rican military played a minimal role in defending the regime. Fernando Soto Harrison, who had been secretary of the interior in the first part of the Picado administration, stated that "the army practically did not participate [in the fighting]. Only the army's mobile unit and the police remained in San José to fight" (Interview with Soto Harrison, Aug. 26, 1994). The opposition for its part relied on men from the Caribbean Legion, members from the PSD, and rural workers and peasants who mobilized in support of the opposition.[21] What is clear from this brief discussion is that neither side of the divided elite took up arms, but relied on the communist PVP and the opposition PSD to fight the civil war. In this fight, the better armed and trained opposition outmaneuvered the communists in battles over the key cities of San José and Cartago. As Schifter (1986:286–88) has noted, the failure of the Picado government to prepare for the civil war remains unexplained, given that the government knew of Figueres's plans. Picado had expected, however, that Nicaragua's dictator, Anastasio Somoza García, would intervene militarily in his defense.

POLITICAL STALEMATE
AND DEMOCRATIC COMPROMISE

The 1948 civil war ended with the victory of the opposition alliance composed of the PSD and the PUN. Competition between opposition organizations and other political agendas within the counterreform movement quickly became apparent. During negotiations with the government, Ulate and Figueres disagreed over how to resolve the war: Ulate agreed to an arrangement with the government whereby an interim president would take office and new elections would be held; with this agreement, Ulate effectively resigned as president elect (Rojas Bolaños 1986:152; Figueres 1987:188); Figueres rejected this possibility and continued fighting, unwilling to compromise with the reform coalition that had flouted the 1948 elections.

Figueres, as chief of the opposition armed forces, subsequently displaced Ulate as the key power broker for the opposition movement in the negotiations. He, not Ulate, set the terms for the end of the civil war. Benjamin Núñez, who had initiated and overseen the Catholic-affiliated labor movement, was the opposition's chief negotiator and became chaplain for its armed forces; he did not represent the official Church position. The negotiations took place at the Mexican embassy in the presence of U.S. negotiators. During the course of the negotiations Nicaragua invaded Costa Rica, at the likely request of Picado. The invasion angered not only the opposition, but also the communists and the U.S. army. President Picado denounced the invasion that he had probably known about and sanctioned in advance. Somoza's troops retreated. Schifter (1986) convincingly argues that, despite U.S. reactions and pressures in support of the opposition once the war began, the United States was not responsible for initiating the civil war, forcing the overthrow of the government, or for determining the important role that Figueres came to play. The war ended on April 19, after an estimated 1,000 to 1,300 people had died (Gardner 1971:54–55; Schifter 1986, ch. 8).

President Picado and Father Núñez agreed to end the war on the following terms: Santos León Herrera would assume the interim presidency until May 8, 1948; distinguished members of the outgoing government would be given safe exit from the country; all those involved in the government and war would receive guarantees of life and property; the new government would compensate the victims of the war regardless of their partisan affiliation; and the new government would protect the social reforms and advances made by labor. In the eighteen months following the peace pact, the counterreform movement reneged on many of these agreements.

Immediately following the civil war the opposition coalition collapsed; having overturned the reform coalition, it lost its raison d'être. Fundamental differences in economic, political, and social objectives emerged among its members and came into sharp relief in discussions over who would assume executive power immediately after the war, the type of constitution to write, and the direction of socioeconomic policy. Conflict over these three areas both shattered the counterreform coalition and led to political stalemate, as neither the PSD nor the PUN could impose its vision.

The two factions of the erstwhile counterreform coalition first reached loggerheads over who would assume political power and under what conditions. For those who claimed that the war had been fought to defend political democracy and for those who sought to reverse the reforms, Ulate, representing the oligarchy and entrepreneurs, stood as the natural and undisputed person to assume the presidency in the post-reform period. The 1948 presidential elections had conferred legitimacy on him as the next president. With the collapse of the reform coalition and the end of the civil war, Ulate began to voice doubts that Figueres would in fact permit him to take office. Indeed, Figueres (1987:295) notes in his autobiography that people rallied in the streets to pressure him to hand over power to Ulate rather than form a de facto government. Ulate and the oligarchy, however, lacked arms or access to any army. Also, they had to contend with Figueres's military legitimacy as chief of self-proclaimed liberation army that had defended Costa Rica's democracy.

Figueres and his cohort did not want to hand power over to Ulate. Indeed, many of the PSD's political and economic plans, as developed by the Centro, conflicted with beliefs held by Ulate and others in the PUN. Many argued that Ulate's resignation during the civil war meant that he no longer had a claim on the presidency. Yet Figueres could not impose a de facto government because he had neither the financial resources nor the electoral legitimacy and support necessary to stabilize the postwar situation and to advance the PSD's political project.

Neither leader could set the terms in the immediate postwar period: Figueres had the arms and had created a reputation of having defended democracy; Ulate and the PUN claimed electoral legitimacy deriving from the preceding presidential elections. As such, the two leaders agreed on a democratic compromise.

Figueres and Ulate resolved their competing claims to executive power with the Figueres-Ulate pact, signed in 1948. The agreement appointed Figueres to head the revolutionary junta for eighteen months, confirmed Ulate's presidency, provided that the latter would assume office following the revolutionary junta, and called for a Constituent Assembly. In short, the leaders of the PSD and PUN adopted a compromise that enabled both of them to rule in the immediate postwar period. After Figueres's direction of the revolutionary junta for eighteen months, Ulate assumed the presidential office for a full four-year term.

The revolutionary junta took power on May 8, 1948. To institutionalize the new democratic compromise and reconfigure bases of social power, the junta began by annulling the 1871 Liberal constitution, suspending the Congress, calling for a new Constituent Assembly (see Table 12 for the strength of each party in the new assembly), and declaring the founding of the "Second Republic." With this declaration, Figue-

TABLE 12

Party Strength in the 1948 Costa Rican Constituent Assembly

Parties	Votes	Deputies
Partido Unión Nacional	62,300	34
Partido Constitucional[a]	10,815	6
Partido Social Demócrata	6,415	4
Partido Confraternidad Nacional	2,439	1

SOURCE: Aguilar Bulgarelli (1983:459).

[a] The PRN (Calderón and Picado) and communist PVP (Mora) were not allowed to run for the Constituent Assembly. These parties, however, supported the recently formed Partido Constitucional.

res also propounded four pillars of post-1948 politics: reestablishment of morality; introduction of technical rather than political means in administration; social progress without communism; and a higher level of solidarity with people in other parts of the world (Figueres 1986:207–17). The radically divergent political projects of the PUN and the PSD became even more apparent in debates held by the Constituent Assembly on the new constitution. Whereas the PSD wanted to work with an entirely new proposal as the basis of discussion, the oligarchic elements wanted to work with the previous 1871 constitution, demonstrating its unambiguous affinity for the status quo ante. In the end, the Constituent Assembly did in fact reject the junta's draft proposal and work from the 1871 constitution. Whereas the PSD deputies promoted state intervention in social and economic areas, the oligarchic representatives promoted the benefits of laissez-faire policies. The deputies compromised, ending with an interesting mix of welfare state and classical liberal policies. Moreover, they extended the suffrage to women and blacks in 1949 and eliminated property and literacy requirements, increasing the scope of individual participation. Finally, whereas the majority of the PUN leaders sought to ban communist parties, some of the PSD representatives, in opposition to voices emerging from the Constituent Assembly and within the revolutionary junta, argued in vain that this position was antidemocratic and, therefore, dangerous (Costa Rica 1951).

DEMOBILIZATION AND REDISTRIBUTIVE REFORMS: BEGINNING OF PSD HEGEMONY

Yet, while the PSD-dominated junta's electoral support base was remarkably weak in both the pre–civil war 1948 elections and the post-1948 Constituent Assembly, the PSD succeeded in establishing its political hegemony in the post-1948 period at the expense of older political groups. It did so by simultaneously persecuting those against whom it had fought and weakening those with whom it had allied. At the end of the junta's rule, the communist party and labor movement had been marginalized and the oligarchy had lost its historic financial monopoly. The junta's decision to act during the transition against both the reformers and financial monopolies left the oligarchy with few alternatives but to support the junta. The oligarchy had no arms and had depended on the PSD to fight against the even greater perceived evil of impending communist rule and an ensuing threat to private property in general. By weakening the oligarchy financially and incorporating it politically, the PSD reconfigured the space for democratic politics. In the end, the PSD would become the dominant political actor.

In its eighteen months of rule, the PSD-dominated revolutionary junta persecuted those affiliated with the outgoing regime, including the political reformers and the supporting labor movement. It forced many of them into exile, jailed others, and submitted many to undemocratic court hearings. These measures particularly affected the communists. The junta and Constituent Assembly banned the Partido Vanguardia Popular, imprisoning its members and exiling others. The post-1948 government sent about 1 percent of the population into exile and jailed 3,000 people (Dunkerley 1988:131). It also prosecuted reformers through two newly formed tribunals, the Tribunal de Sanciones Inmediatas and the Tribunal de Probidad.

The Tribunal de Sanciones Inmediatas, founded a month after the peace pact, on May 19, assessed criminal charges against individuals associated with the Calderón and Picado governments, but neither Calderón nor Picado was tried. The tribunal judged the accused without jury, without the right to appeal, and even at times in absentia. Contrary to expectations, the Tribunal de Sanciones Inmediatas did not find all those brought before it guilty (Gardner 1971:393–403; Aguilar Bulgarelli 1983:439). By contrast, the Tribunal de Probidad, founded on June 2, 1948, adopted a guilty-by-declaration approach. This tribunal charged those who had allegedly profited at the expense of the state. Without any trial, the tribunal published lists of people it considered guilty, after which the state confiscated the accused's property. Trials took place only if the accused initiated them to prove their innocence; the tribunal falsely charged a number of families (Gardner 1971:406–20; Aguilar Bulgarelli 1983:440).

Along with delegitimating and persecuting members of the reform coalition, the junta initiated a campaign to weaken the communist-dominated organized labor movement, CTCR, in defiance of the terms of the 1948 peace pact; it did not initiate antilabor actions against the Catholic CCTRN, which never acquired the membership of the CTCR.[22] On May 11, 1948, the junta laid off all public employees without compensation or the right to appeal. Moreover, it authorized private firms to lay off all workers identified with the previous administrations or perceived as politically dangerous (Gardner 1971; Schifter 1981:112; Aguilar Bulgarelli 1983:439; Dunkerley 1988:131). By the end of 1948, 163 of 204 labor unions, primarily those affiliated with the communist-dominated CTCR, became inactive. In 1949 alone, the Ministry of Labor dissolved 51 unions. And, in June 1949, the minister of labor called for the dissolution of the CTCR itself, as well as its affiliated unions. From 1948 to 1953, the number of unions registered with the Ministry of Labor declined from 204 to 74.[23]

Since the immediate post–civil war repression, labor in Costa Rica has been regulated by the courts, the Ministry of Labor, and the Ministry of Public Security. Restrictive labor laws include the prohibition of political activity by labor unions (a charge of which can lead to the dissolution of the union), the failure to provide legal protection for union leaders, the possibility of laying off workers who try to organize unions, and the ability to lay off workers without providing justification. Moreover, workers on coffee, sugar, or African palm farms do not have the right to strike (Aguilar 1989:73–78). Since 1948 organized labor, particularly that affiliated with the communist party, has diminished considerably in numerical, organizational, and political strength, for the unions have not been able to reorganize effective economic or political institutions in the face of stringent state laws and *solidarismo*, a nonunion form of capital-labor relations.[24]

Destruction of the reform coalition and the communist-dominated labor movement created the space for the PSD to appropriate the role of reformer. Since 1948, the PSD, which became the Partido Liberación Nacional (PLN) in 1951, has taken credit for many of the reforms legislated between 1941 and 1948, before it came to power.

This support for the reforms surprised the PSD's former allies within the oligarchy; the latter had believed that the PSD also opposed the social reforms. Figueres (1987: 288) confides that with the end of the civil war he was approached by a group from the elite opposition that proposed that he annul the social guarantees, the labor code, and the social security law; this group thought that Figueres was only spouting populist rhetoric when he stated earlier his support for the reforms.

To the surprise of its erstwhile oligarchic allies, the junta passed Decrees 70 and 71 on June 21, 1948, which challenged the oligarchy's property rights and traditional monopoly over finance. Decree 70 mandated a onetime, 10 percent tax on capital of more than 50,000 colones. Decree 71 nationalized banks that received deposits (Gardner 1971:293–96, 304–5, 359–61). Alberto Martén, who proposed and wrote Decree 71 as minister of the economy and finance, explained:

> When I arrived at the ministry, I asked for the director of the system of direct taxation, who is the person who collects taxes. They said to me, "There is no such office. . . . The national bank took charge of the collection of taxes." What an outrage. . . . Since the government did not have a dime, the banks authorized an overdraft in order to pay the workers at the end of the month. Who administered the treasury? The Bank of Costa Rica. In other words, the government's payments passed through the [private] bank, which charged a commission. Then, the banks used the people's money. They charged commissions in exchange for authorizing overdrafts. How outrageous! The government had neither a director of taxation nor money to pay. What a scandal! And a few private bankers used the public deposits and the flow of payments from the government itself— well, they robbed this money—to later lend it. And all this was going to make me sick. Therefore, at that moment I proposed that we nationalize the bank deposits. I did not propose that we expropriate the banks, but Figueres said it was better that we expropriate the banks because nationalizing deposits would ruin us. . . . [He said, therefore, that] it was better to buy the banks at a good price. (Interview with Martén, Aug. 17, 1994)

On June 21, 1948, the junta nationalized three banks—Banco de Costa Rica, Banco Anglo-Costarricense, and the Banco Crédito Agrícola de Cartago—using Decree 71. The nationalization of the banks was intended to increase the state's control over the oligarchic-dominated financial institutions.[25] In line with positions advocated by the Centro, the junta sought to promote both agricultural and industrial development but with decreased dependence on privately financed capital and increased dependence on state-supervised financial institutions.[26] The decrees facilitated the growth of a new urban entrepreneurial class, albeit still in a primarily agro-export economy.

Yet it would be mistaken to conclude that the junta set out to antagonize the oligarchy as a whole. To the contrary, the junta's conscious political aim was partially to accommodate the elites whom it had financially challenged. To appease the oligarchy, the government paid a high price for the bank and bank shares. It initially also sought to create avenues for oligarchic influence over the banks. Martén's initial proposal, in fact, increased the power of the economic chambers of agriculture, commerce, and industry, but this process of financial corporatism was never formalized as law. In the short term, however, this process served to increase elite participation and potentially to divide the oligarchy further between the financial sectors that had lost power and other economic associations with increased influence.[27] In this sense, the radical reforms could be seen as onetime events rather than precursors of more to come.

While balancing between decrees that challenged property rights of the elites and measures to appease the same group, the PSD-dominated junta took one significant precaution to decrease the Costa Rican elites' ability to overthrow the transition government: Article 12 of the 1949 constitution officially dissolved the Costa Rican army. The oligarchy protested loudly, but with no army could provide no credible threat to force the junta to reverse the decision. On April 2, 1949, Colonel Edgar Cardona, who had actually participated in the opposition army and the junta, plotted an uprising (known as the *Cardonazo*) against the junta. In a radio speech, the rebels said, "We are not making a coup d'état. We demand that the Junta de Gobierno modify its decree laws relating to economic policy, referring to the nationalization of the banks, and the ten per cent tax" (Gardner 1971:156). Cardona also feared that the junta would not transfer power to Ulate (Gardner 1971:164–65). After the failed *Cardonazo*, the junta purged the military's high command.

The junta, however, did not leave Costa Rica or the PSD defenseless. The post-1948 Civil Guard assumed the army's responsibility, and Figueres maintained his extralegal army (English 1971; Gardner 1971:232; Edelman and Kenen 1989).[28] Figueres transformed San José's military barracks, Bella Vista, into the national museum. The abolition of the Costa Rican military became one of the most important symbols of Figueres's contribution to Costa Rican political democracy. At his public funeral in 1990, one of the commemorative pictures distributed was of him at the Bella Vista barracks, smashing a wall with a sledgehammer.

The 1940s closed with a politically weakened oligarchy and labor movement. The PSD intellectuals and politicians consolidated and appropriated the social reforms of the 1940s while simultaneously transforming the political system. Through official discourse they advanced the myth of Costa Rica's pre-1940 democracy and stripped Calderón of the role that he had played in promoting fundamental social reforms in

Costa Rica. Moreover, they succeeded in replacing rural-sector loyalty to oligarchic patrons with support for the PLN. Indeed, following the civil war, the PLN became the party to which the rural sectors delivered the majority of their votes, as discussed in Chapter 7. Ultimately, therefore, the members of the PSD succeeded in legitimating the civil war as a restoration of democracy and in labeling themselves literally as liberators of the Costa Rican people. Although the PSD had a weak showing in the 1948 Constituent Assembly elections, from 1951, when it changed its name to the Partido Liberación Nacional, through the 1980s, it has dominated Costa Rican electoral politics.

The redefinition of politics that occurred after the Costa Rican civil war, therefore, recalls Przeworski's (1980) discussion of class compromise, but with a twist. Przeworski argues that we can understand the stability of Western European capitalist countries as rooted in a compromise between capital and labor, in which capital agrees to provide a decent wage for labor in exchange for labor's agreement not to engage in struggles against the system. In Costa Rica, the decision to institutionalize a political democracy led to the reconfiguration of a new dominant political coalition. But whereas Przeworski highlights a compromise between labor and capital, in Costa Rica, as throughout much of Latin America, a class compromise was established between the rising middle class and the divided oligarchy.

The compromise included the commitment to political democracy and economic opportunities for the middle class with the commitment to maintain the oligarchy's political and economic position. Figueres partially betrayed this compromise with the rapid nationalization of banks, but coffee land, processing, and commerce were not altered, and new channels for influence by the elite were created. The compromise was also predicated on the political exclusion of the communists and those organizations perceived as being affiliated with them. To sustain popular exclusion without creating worker radicalization or social polarization, the Costa Rican regime after 1948 consolidated the welfare state created during the reform period with the intention of providing social services for and preempting demands by urban and rural popular classes. In the end, the oligarchy had to operate in a new political and economic system. It had lost its monopoly over finance and the allegiance of rural sectors. It now had to compete with organized (upper-) middle-class sectors for access to and influence over the state. This weakened position seemed preferable, however, to the communist threat that it had perceived in 1948.

Guatemala

The Guatemalan reform period began in 1944 with a groundswell of support in the capital as men and women of all social sectors celebrated the overthrow of the dictator with spontaneous demonstrations and a dramatic growth in civic associations. A decade later, people were still demonstrating in the streets. However, the mobilization included efforts by small but powerful sectors within society to oppose the governing reform coalition. Despite a diverse class background, these groups shared a set of common fears and opposition to the regime. As did their counterparts in Costa Rica, they denounced communist control of the governing reform coalition, the direction of social policy, and the rise in popular mobilization. With the legislation of developmental reforms challenging traditional property relations and with increasing political organization along class and ethnic lines, the various opposition sectors strengthened their commitment to challenge the governing reform coalition and replace it with a government of order. The loosely coordinated opposition movement, however, did not have the institutional capacity to do so through elections. It depended on dissident military officers, both those ousted by the reformers and those acting in the armed forces, to betray the regime. In the absence of strong political organizations of its own, the opposition movement turned to the military to assume political leadership in a post-reform authoritarian regime. Its support for an armed overthrow created a polarized political situation within which the U.S. government acted as a catalyst to overthrow the Arbenz government.

THE PROTEST OPPOSITION: UNITED ELITE AND WEAK POLITICAL ORGANIZATIONS

Divisions within the oligarchy originally contributed to the overthrow of Ubico and the installation of political democracy in Guatemala in 1944. In the initial years following the overthrow, part of the oligarchy was active in the formal political institutions of the new democracy. It participated in the 1944–45 Constituent Assembly, ran for legislative seats, and contributed to political exchange in the media. The Guatemalan oligarchy, however, never assumed a dominant political or moral position in these forums but, rather, a subordinate position in the country's newly constituted political democracy. Unlike its Costa Rican counterparts, it did not enter the reform period with a tradition of even personalistic or ephemeral political parties, experience, or competition. Instead, the Guatemalan oligarchy entered the reform period with a fairly limited historical tradition of political participation and narrow repertoire of representative political institutions or practices. In the reform period, it replicated prior modes of political action and placed little emphasis on party building and more on rebuilding economic associations. In the absence of a viable political party, the Guatemalan oligarchy did not have the legal means to inhibit popular-class organizations in urban and rural areas or to prevent the legislation of labor and land reforms that ultimately challenged rural property relations. As the governing reform coalition increased its electoral support within popular sectors, the majority of the oligarchic faction that had supported the overthrow of Ubico began to distance itself from the regime and to join the oligarchic opposition.

The oligarchy coalesced in the Asociación General de Agricultores (AGA), which Ubico had banned in the 1930s. With his overthrow, the Guatemalan oligarchy reconstituted AGA on July 13, 1944 (*El Imparcial* July 14, 1944).[29] AGA appeared to reserve final judgment regarding the reform coalition in the initial years of the reform period. Mild condemnation was voiced in the editorials of the weekly *Boletín de la AGA* from 1945 to 1947. With the 1947 labor code legislation, however, AGA began to lambaste the government, and its opposition grew more hostile and violent with the 1952 land reform.

To voice its opposition, AGA organized campaigns against the 1947 labor code and 1952 agrarian reform. Editorials criticizing these reforms consistently appeared in the pages of the *Boletín de la AGA* and the daily newspapers. In both cases, AGA protested that it had been excluded from the process of drafting reform policy. For example, AGA denounced the congressional commission that drafted the labor code for not addressing or integrating its positions (*Boletín de la AGA*, Aug. 8, 1945, June 29, July 6, 13, 20, 27, Aug. 3, 10, 1946; also see *El Imparcial*, Sept. 18, 1947). In a document coauthored with one of the industrial associations, Comité de Comerciantes e Industriales de Guatemala (CCIG), it complained that not only was it excluded from determining policy, but that the labor federations had increased their ability to influence the state at the cost of the elite and the future of democracy:

> Reforms of this nature [to the labor code proposed by the labor federation] make us think that they [the labor federation] are trying to distance the patronal sectors from electoral struggles and to intervene substantially in politics, and in this form the labor organization can demand, from one

moment to the next, the intervention of State forces to oblige the patronal class to remain at the margin of all political content and discussion and to facilitate the establishment of a totalitarian regime that will destroy the democratic institutions of all citizens. (AGA and CCIG 1948:5)

In a similar manner, the reformers did not integrate the landlords' concerns or analysis into the land reform legislation. AGA representatives had met with President Arbenz to discuss agricultural policy; they argued that productivity rather than land distribution was the crux of Guatemala's agrarian problem. Disregarding AGA's analysis, the 1952 land reform sought to redress land concentration and distribution. AGA denounced the land reform in the pages of the *Boletín de la AGA* and the national newspaper.

If the oligarchy protested its own limited access to the policy-making process and to state institutions, it also argued that the reforms were inimical to national development (*Boletín de la AGA*, July 29, 1946). Members of the oligarchy argued that national development depended on their ability to accumulate capital through traditional regimes of accumulation. They argued that the reforms should not challenge rural property or labor relations. The 1947 labor code and 1952 agrarian reform law, designed to ensure liberal rights and promote national capitalist development, simultaneously challenged the historic patterns of development and capital accumulation established during the Liberal period, characterized by coercive labor practices and concentrated landholdings.[30]

The 1947 labor code, preceded by the overturn of the vagrancy law, created state institutions to consider the demands of organized labor and to protect newly extended labor rights. As a result, the oligarchy could no longer depend on a coercive state apparatus to exploit labor for the coffee harvest. Although the labor code placed stringent restrictions on rural labor organizing, AGA protested the code vociferously, arguing that it would ruin the national economy. When possible, the landed elite disregarded labor rights stipulated in the code and continued to coerce workers to prevent unionization.[31]

The 1952 land reform, in combination with the repeal of the laws of forced rental, further eroded historic forms of capital accumulation by challenging property rights over land ownership and use. Furthermore, the regime denied the oligarchy any means to challenge land reform implementation; the land reform decree placed the final decision-making powers with the president. When the Supreme Court challenged one of these rulings, Arbenz dismissed four of the judges who had challenged the implementation of the land reform, creating an uproar within the oligarchy and middle class. The oligarchy concluded that together the labor code and land reform threatened its economic well-being as well as further highlighted an antioligarchic stance of the regime and state, leaving little space for elite participation or influence in government.

The oligarchy argued that the labor code and land reform engendered popular organizing that was increasingly characterized by instability and chaos, opening the doors for communist and Soviet control of the state, economy, and society. In a 1948 discussion of the labor code, members of AGA and CCIG wrote that the code provided the labor movement with an ability to create economic instability, to call for the abolition of private property, and, ultimately, to found a dictatorship of the proletariat, controlled from abroad:

> The only reason that exists for which the CNUS [labor federation] is asking for the [labor] code . . . is the union leaders' necessity to provoke total economic disequilibrium in order to demand and to justify nationalization of land and the expropriation of the means of production, an extreme tendency which detracts from the good faith that one must suppose in those who are presenting themselves as leaders of the vindictive movement of the working class; and as such it is to fear that, as it is understood, they are not concerned about general well being, insofar as they succeed in the ultimate goal, which is the abolition of private property.

> Today we feel that we are in a position to affirm that we are certain in having identified the existence of a ploy to paralyze the country's agrarian production; that will force private property and the very State, through strikes at harvest time, to accede to all types of pretension which occur to the union leaders; that they are trying to achieve total disequilibrium and complete insecurity for people and for goods in order to easily impose a dictatorship of the masses led and sustained by professional leaders. (AGA and CCIG 1948:28, 114)

In an attempt to discredit popular organizing even further, the oligarchy and industrialists argued that unions, particularly those calling for reforms, did not truly form part of the nation and acted against the interests of Guatemala. AGA and CCIG suggested that only agriculturalists, merchants, industrialists, and nonorganized workers could be considered part of the nation. Starting August 18, 1948, the bulletin began printing on its masthead "At the service of agriculture and the nation United we will forge the motherland." AGA and CCIG also proclaimed in a joint publication,

> We must say that the Nation is not constituted by the persons who have been demanding the reforms. The Nation is integrated by fundamentally

free workers, who are actually in the immense majority throughout the country and the rest of the social classes; the productive forces of agriculture and of industry, as well as of commerce, which in this instance are united, constitute fundamental elements of the Nation. The Nation is not composed of those who are asking for the reform to the [labor] code, but the union leaders of the Republic, who before the failure of voluntary union organizing, are trying to make obligatory organizing. (AGA and CCIG 1948:9)

The oligarchy also feared Indians, particularly as they joined rural organizations, supported the governing reform coalition, and gained access to the state through the regional and local agrarian committees created by the 1952 agrarian reform law. The oligarchy claimed that labor organizing within indigenous communities would initiate race wars which in turn would exacerbate class conflict. The rise in rural organizing in time would threaten national production, lead to civil war, and allow the agrarian committees to become "an unlimited, dictatorial, and absorbing power," all of which was part of a communist plan (*El Imparcial*, June 3, 1952).[32]

By 1952, the opposition's anticommunist discourse had become hostile and pervasive. Editorials and paid advertisements in the weekly *Boletín de la AGA* and in the daily newspapers from 1952 to 1954 consistently warned of communist influence against the popular will. AGA undertook a survey in June 1952 to demonstrate popular opposition to the land reform and printed the results in the most widely read daily newspaper, *El Imparcial*. In the reporting, it was unclear who was surveyed and what the methodology was. Drawing from this survey, AGA claimed that 98 percent of those surveyed thought that the agrarian reform project was "bad." Ninety-eight percent also did not think the agrarian reform would benefit the *campesinos*. When asked how they thought the agrarian reform would affect the national economy, 89 percent said it would provoke a crisis, 8 percent said that it would diminish production, and 1 percent said that it would lower state revenues. In short, AGA's survey said that only 2 percent had a positive assessment of the original project (*El Imparcial*, June 1952, especially June 5).

AGA also decried what it saw as the attack on private property, the rise in totalitarian state socialism, an envisioned decrease in productivity, and an increase in conflict between labor and capital leading to anarchy (*El Imparcial*, May 15–17, 19, June 2, 4, 5, 11, 14, 1952).[33]

The first step is about to be taken: the expropriation of land. It will be followed by the nationalization of industry, and commerce. The totalitarian State. It is evident that the country is in a state of shock since the

executive sent to the Congress of the republic its project for the promulgation of a Marxist agrarian law. . . . Are we going towards a socialist State?
How far will the State go in its march towards socialism? What will be the
next national sector that will suffer the aggression of the State? (*Boletín
de la AGA,* June 30, 1952)

The oligarchy's opposition, through the media and social forums, promoted a national discourse of communism versus anticommunism. The
oligarchy referred to the reform leaders, the policies enacted, and the ongoing popular mobilization as "communist," "communistic," or "com-
munistoid." It argued that the Soviets orchestrated this communist control; by implication, foreign agents in control of the reform coalition and
leadership positions orchestrated the inclusive and comprehensive reforms and popular mobilization. The actors of the reform period, who
had tried to expand the idea of the nation along class and ethnic lines,
had provoked an oligarchic opposition that considered these very developments a threat to the Guatemalan nation.

AGA tried to foster hysteria among various social sectors through propaganda, particularly following the legislation of increasingly more radical reforms. AGA, however, did not have the capacity or experience to
reverse the reforms or influence the direction of politics in its capacity
as an economic association; rather, it constituted a pressure group with
no constitutional influence over policy. During the reform period the
failure to develop a viable and institutionalized party or electoral coalition left the oligarchic opposition operating outside of a political system
that it concluded was adversely reshaping property relations. Unable to
influence the policy process, the oligarchic opposition channeled its protest through the media. With limited ability to influence politics and
without the ability to compete in the electoral arena, the Guatemalan
oligarchy eventually supported and helped to finance a violent response.

The Guatemalan Catholic Church joined the oligarchy in its vehement opposition to the governments of Arévalo and Arbenz.[34] Despite an
easing of Church-state relations during the reform period, in marked
contrast to the anticlericalism of the Liberal period, Archbishop Rossell
y Arellano aggressively criticized the government beginning in the first
few months of the reform period. In contrast to Costa Rica's Archbishop
Sanabria, Rossell y Arellano sharply distanced himself from the reformers and, by mid-1945, warned of communism in Guatemala and Mexico
(*Acción Social Cristiana,* Feb. 8, 1945, Feb. 28, 1946).

The archbishop was particularly troubled by the organization of a labor movement that talked about class conflict and demanded rights for

labor. The archbishop argued that elites should address the social question through charity and individual efforts to improve working conditions. Elites should improve capital-labor relations, but labor should not
organize to achieve better working conditions. Indeed, the archbishop
suspected all labor organizing, including that in other Latin American
countries, as communist agitation. Editorials in the Catholic publication argued that international communists directed the unions:

> Before everyone, it is appropriate to make them see, that the contempo-
> rary social movement in Latin America is not spontaneous; it does not
> obey impulses born from the masses themselves, but is the fruit of con-
> stant agitation, the work of irresponsible leaders. . . . Impudent participa-
> tion by worker and peasant unions in public life is the best demonstration
> of what we are talking about. . . . Unfortunately in Guatemala the Com-
> munists have won ample territory to the point where many are Commu-
> nists without even knowing it; they profess Communist ideas; they go
> against capital; they are procuring its destruction; they desire general so-
> cialization; they abdicated all spiritual conceptions and are looking only
> for material satisfaction; they are participating in and fomenting a class
> struggle. (*Acción Social Cristiana,* Jan. 1, 1947)[35]

The archbishop argued that communism would lead to atheism and a
rise in anti-Church sentiment. It viewed support for the reform coalition
as an attack on religion and the Church, and, therefore, supported short-
lived efforts to compete electorally with the reformers. The Partido
Anticomunista Demócrata Cristiano and the Partido de Unificación
Anticomunista (PUA) called for anticommunist street demonstrations
sanctioned by the Church.[36] A 1948 flyer announcing an anticommunist
demonstration organized by the PUA said, for example, "He who does
not attend is a traitor to his country and to his religion" (AGCA, Hermeroteca, *Hojas Sueltas*, 1948). The initial efforts to discredit the regime
through party politics and the Church newspaper were only mildly
effective.

Archbishop Rossell y Arellano therefore turned to the pulpit to lambaste the reformers. In late 1953, he traveled throughout the country to
mobilize anticommunist opposition to the regime, carrying with him a
replica of one of Guatemala's most revered Catholic icons, the Black
Christ of Esquipulas.[37] The archbishop hoped to generate fear of communism and belief in increasing communist control in Guatemala.

The archbishop also issued a pastoral letter in April 1954, just months
before the June 1954 overthrow of the Arbenz government. Clergy or the
equivalent read the letter in every church throughout the country. The

letter equated communism with atheism and antipatriotism. As many
have noted, it legitimated rising against the regime:

> We again raise our voice to alert Catholics that anti-Christian commu-
> nism—the worst atheist doctrine of all time—is stalking our country
> under the cloaks of social justice. We warn you that those whom the com-
> munists help today, they will condemn to forced labor and terrible suffer-
> ing tomorrow. Everyone who loves his country must fight against those
> who—loyal to no country, the scum of the earth—have repaid Guatemala's
> generous hospitality by fomenting class hatred, in preparation for the day of
> destruction and slaughter which they anticipate with such enthusiasm....
> Guatemala must rise as one against this enemy of God and country.[38]

The archbishop supported and advocated public protest against the regime and developed close ties with the former military officer Castillo
Armas, who ultimately led the mercenary army that overthrew Arbenz.
It is virtually impossible to estimate the impact of these campaigns.
What is certain, however, is that the archbishop set out to discredit the
reform movement in its incipient stages and that the ensuing opposition
movement employed religious rhetoric to legitimate the counterreform
movement.

Rising opposition within parts of the middle class echoed the fears
expressed by the Church and the oligarchy. Middle-class sectors had unambiguously supported the overthrow of Ubico in 1944 and the election
of Arévalo. This unanimity broke down as leadership struggles and ideological differences emerged in the reform coalition, often resulting in
party factionalization (as mentioned in Chapter 3). These differences became particularly acute with the emergence of the Communist Party in
1950 and the Partido Guatemalteco del Trabajo in 1952. Many within
the ruling reform coalition bristled at the suggestion of allying with the
PGT in elections or in the legislature. This opposition to the PGT did
not push all middle-class politicians into the opposition; however, it did
increase ambivalence to the reform coalition on the part of many of these
politicians.

A small but active middle-class group outside the legislature also began to distance itself from the reform coalition. Members of this group
had gained basic political and civic rights as well as social services such
as health insurance. Nonetheless, some of them became anxious about
the role of the PGT in the governing coalition. This anxiety developed
amongst professionals, teachers, students, state workers, and property
owners (Torres Rivas 1977:81; Jonas and Tobis 1976:106–7). In a few
cases, some individuals from these sectors sided with the oligarchy and
the Church in the campaign to discredit the regime.

For example, while the University of San Carlos had generated in 1944 some of the governing reform coalition's most esteemed politicians, by the early 1950s the university community had become the site of militant organizing by both radical and anticommunist students (García Añoveros 1978). A combative opposition movement formed the Comité de Estudiantes Universitarios Anticomunistas (CEUA), founded January 1952. García Añoveros (1978:174) estimates that 500 students out of a population of 8,000 became involved in this movement; by no means did they (or their radical student counterparts) represent a majority or plurality of the students. However, in conjunction with the other anticommunist movements, they became quite vocal and combative, receiving steady press coverage of their activities. They opposed the popular organizations as well as the reform policies. They actively organized anticommunist activities in the city. They often made excursions on the weekend to the rural areas to try to convince *campesinos* of the negative impact of the agrarian reform (García Añoveros 1978). The CEUA also coordinated with a group of anticommunist Guatemalan exiles that published scathing and insurrectionary literature.

The market women worked with the students and the Church to launch some of the most aggressive and visible campaigns against the regime.[39] According to Concha Estévez, a leader among the market women, communism was evident in the rising chaos engendered by the organized popular sectors.[40] Believing that communists had infiltrated the government, these women feared that the Arbenz administration would expropriate all private property, including their market stalls. To defend their interests, they formed an anticommunist association, actively participated in opposition demonstrations, accompanied the students in their anticommunist activities, and gained a reputation for their militance and commitment to organize against the regime. Following a rumor that the government was going to expel the archbishop, the market women gathered in front of the National Cathedral, across from the National Palace, to protect him. The archbishop did nothing to dispel this unfounded rumor and permitted the women to sleep on the patio outside of the cathedral, armed with covered baskets filled with stones.[41]

The anticommunist movement, as a whole, played off the middle class's and oligarchy's fear that increased organization of the working-class and indigenous groups would threaten not only the national economy but also basic property rights, religious ideals, and family practices. They saw popular organizing as an indicator of the popular sector's desires to impose a dictatorship of the proletariat. Arbenz's dismissal of the four Supreme Court judges who had challenged the implementation of the land reform further reinforced fear that the governing coalition would sidestep the law to advance the popular sector's agenda. While the democratic and capitalist reforms had sought to improve political and economic opportunities for both the popular and middle classes, many within the middle class feared that democracy itself had opened up the doors to communism.

The opposition movement, therefore, developed in Guatemala City with active participation from a united oligarchy, the Catholic Church, and parts of the middle class. This opposition by no means represented the majority of Guatemalans, but it did represent a majority of the most financially powerful and articulate sectors within Guatemalan society, which could rely on a religious morality to sanction their position. These heterogeneous groups shared a homogenous opposition to alleged communist control and a commitment to overthrow the democratic regime, reverse much of the reform legislation, and demobilize the popular sectors. During the first reform administration, the opposition sought to overcome fragmented counterreform efforts and formed in 1948 the Partido de Unificación Anticomunista (PUA). The opposition party had its greatest success in the cities, particularly Guatemala City, where it won almost all elections. Nonetheless, it did not generate substantial national electoral support; indeed, the conservatives lost support as the reform period progressed. Opposition parties held only 25 percent of the mayoral offices nationwide in 1953, compared to 35 percent in 1947 and 30 percent in 1950. By 1951, the opposition held only 19 percent of the seats in the legislature, a drop from 26 percent in 1947 (Monteforte Toledo 1965:317). In the January 1953 elections, the opposition won only 5 out of 56 congressional seats.[42] In short, the opposition both placed limited emphasis on party building and, where it did run, fared poorly, suffering a secular decline in representation over the ten years of reform.

By the time of the Arbenz administration, the opposition tried consciously to create a polarized political climate. It organized protests in the streets, published scathing editorials, and called on people to take up arms. Sociologist Monteforte Toledo (1965:317), a moderate reform politician of the period, argued that the opposition had committed to organizing in accord with the following principles: "a) to operate through civic, Catholic, regional and trade unions; b) to reduce their definition exclusively to 'anti-communism'; c) to discredit and negate constructive programs advanced by the government; d) to incite military coups; and e) to consume the left's power in unimportant skirmishes." In this destabilizing campaign, the oligarchy in AGA wrote provocative editorials and provided financial support to the opposition's domestic protests and its armed movement developing abroad.[43] The Church took advantage of its moral social status to legitimate the opposition movement and spur an uprising. Middle-class opposition sectors pursued their agendas at the street level, organizing demonstrations and traveling to rural communities to discredit the regime, the reform parties, popular organizations, and the labor and land reforms. Much of the press provided a communication link to advance anticommunist propaganda.[44] The loosely coordinated opposition movement, however, did not have either the political capital, institutional capacity, or will to overturn the coalition through legal electoral means. It depended on dissident military officers, both those ousted and those acting in the armed forces, to betray the regime.

The revolutionary public image the military cultivated during the reform period belied its conservative institutional setting, in which military officials also questioned the direction taken by the governing reform coalition. The revolutionary junta of 1944, which included two military officers, renamed the armed forces El Ejército Nacional de la Revolución, the National Military of the Revolution. Government propaganda continually highlighted the military's new revolutionary mandate. The official military journal, the *Revista Militar*, stressed the new revolutionary era in its first issue after Ubico's overthrow.[45] The newspapers occasionally printed photographs depicting the harmonious relationship between the military and the Guatemalan people. Following the land reform legislation, one of the government advertisements pictured a military man seated next to a *campesino*, suggesting the army's commitment to the peasants and their new future.[46] The official propaganda also suggested that the National Military of the Revolution was apolitical.[47]

The military's public image, however, belied conflicting and antisystemic movements behind the scenes. The institutions created in 1944 to depoliticize the military actually had the opposite effect. While autonomy from civilian rule did inhibit manipulation by elected politicians, it also meant that officers developed ideological and institutional loyalties independent of the civilian administration. In turn, the civilian government did not have institutional mechanisms to monitor whether officers respected or supported the reform coalition, more comprehensive reforms, and the rise in popular organizing. The institutional makeover of the Guatemalan armed forces, therefore, contributed to a corporate mentality that, unbeknownst to some leaders like President Arbenz, had sustained a commitment to prereform ideas over defense of the civilian regime. Despite public statements supporting the new democratic ideals and goals, many within the military continued to question the formation of civic organizations and the legislation of reforms.

The military, in fact, never fully accepted the reforms between 1944 and 1954, nor did it fully reject the ideological training inculcated during the Ubico years, when it learned to equate popular organization with subversion and communism.[48] "Ubico was a good ruler from that period. . . . After 1944, Dr. Arévalo appeared. He brought us communism," stated one military officer (Interview with Anonymous C, Mar. 29, 1994). With this set of ideas, military officers were receptive to anticommunist cries voiced by AGA, the archbishop, and the middle-class opposition movement. Opposition within *parts* of the military led to an estimated 30 coup attempts during Arévalo's reform administration. Paz Tejada, who became chief of the armed forces from 1949 to 1951, has emphasized the anticommunist and antisystemic tendency within the military that motivated coup efforts.[49]

The military also became internally politicized, as conservative military officials created their own power bases autonomous from and, at times, in opposition to the democratic regime. This autonomy within the military threatened the regime at two points: the unsuccessful 1949 Arana uprising (discussed below) and the successful 1954 counterreform coup (discussed in a later section). Colonel Francisco Arana, as chief of the armed forces, had cultivated a following within the military independent of and in opposition to the reform coalition. During the Arévalo administration, counterreform forces turned to Arana as a conservative presidential candidate. He died at the hands of government forces in 1949, and the events surrounding his death are still disputed. President Arévalo claimed that Arana had presented him with an ultimatum backed by the threat of a coup. The government stated that, in an attempt to prevent the coup, Arana was killed in crossfire. Conservative forces retorted that the reform government killed Arana in cold blood in order to destroy his power within the military and the potential for his election. Arana's death provoked an uprising by those in the military who had developed a personal loyalty to him. The government turned to the few loyalist military officers and policemen as well as to civilian volunteers, particularly workers and students, to whom it issued arms, to defend the regime. Together, the military loyalists and civilians defeated the aranista rebels. The government's success at putting down the 1949 uprising enabled the reform coalition to purge the opposition from the military, creating an ostensibly proreform and prodemocratic armed forces. Thereafter the reform coalition assumed that it could depend on the military, as well as the popular organizations, to defend the regime.

With Arana's death, opposition forces concluded that they could not reverse the direction of the reform period through legal means. Bereft of a viable presidential candidate, without an institutionalized opposition party, and without popular support, the conservative forces, within the military and without, could not win the elections. The opposition movement argued further that the reform movement would employ all measures—including murder—to prevent the election of a conservative candidate. Arana's death, therefore, further polarized society because the opposition not only did not believe the administration's account of the death but felt robbed of the presidential candidate it believed might have reversed the direction of the reform period (Petersen 1969:107–10; Cáceres 1980:42–48; Handy 1985; Guerra Borges 1988:111–12; Dunkerley 1988:143–44; Gleijeses 1991:64–71).[50]

When Jacobo Arbenz assumed the presidency two years after Arana's death, he believed that he commanded respect and loyalty from the military high command as well as military officers who had taken civilian positions. Arbenz had been, after all, a military man. He had distinguished himself as a student and later as an instructor in charge of all the cadets at the military academy prior to Ubico's overthrow. And, of course, he had participated in the 1944 revolutionary junta alongside Arana and Toriello. Assuming office in 1951, he seems to have believed that he sustained support from the military as a whole, particularly with the purge of military dissidents following Arana's death. He tried to maintain good graces within the armed forces by treating military officers particularly well and offering them substantial financial benefits (Silvert 1969:95).

Despite this, however, many within the military reacted against Arbenz as a result of what they perceived as a rise in communist influence in four areas. Many feared Arbenz's working relationship with communists, even if they did not believe that Arbenz himself was a communist. Others feared that Arbenz's wife and her assistants were communists. Fear also followed from conjectures that the peasant union was indoctrinating the indigenous peasantry with communist doctrine. Finally, many disagreed with the land reform.[51] On these last two points, Handy (1994, ch. 7) has convincingly demonstrated that the military reacted against its loss of control in the countryside as peasants organized in rural unions, participated in the implementation of the land reform, and, in some cases, initiated land invasions. Following the land reform, conflicts also emerged between military commissioners and guard commanders versus the labor and peasant organizations in the countryside, conflicts in which some military commissioners sided, at times violently, with

elites in land disputes. Labor and peasant organizations, however, increased their political influence following the land reform and were able
to influence the posting and dismissal of officers according to the latter's
support of or antagonism toward land reform. Rumors of arming a popular militia to defend the Arbenz government, at a moment when the
United States had effectively launched an arms embargo against Guatemala, also increased opposition within military circles:

> The military command became increasingly concerned about its loss of
> control in rural areas. There were rumors that the military planned to
> move on its own in defiance of the president against those who were be-
> lieved responsible for land invasions. In 1954, the Superior Council of Na-
> tional Defense appointed a commission to study the situation in the coun-
> tryside, with a special emphasis on re-forming the local militias. The
> report of the commission was alarming; it stated, "We encounter at this
> date the following panorama: TOTAL LACK OF CONTROL AND ABSOLUTE
> MILITARY DISORGANIZATION of the militias." The commission went on to
> suggest that the military would be unable to mobilize effectively in the
> face of attack. While the report focused on assessing the possible response
> to outside aggression, it was also obviously partly concerned about the
> military's rapidly diminishing control over rural communities. (Handy
> 1994:186–87, emphasis in original)

Military officers hinted at their contingent loyalty to the president and
the democratic regime shortly before the June 1954 invasion in a rare
meeting called by Arbenz to address a drop in military morale. Arbenz
invited the officers to submit a list of questions outlining their concerns.
All the questions focused on communist influence in Guatemala, asking
whether or not Arbenz would diminish communist influence in his government. Arbenz assured the officers that the communists were not a
threat, and thought that this exchange had mollified concerns. He assumed that the military high command still supported the reform coalition (Schlesinger and Kinzer 1982:164–65; Blasier 1985:173–74; Gleijeses 1991:305; Villagrán Kramer 1993:130–34; Interview with Paz
Tejada, Aug. 11, 18, 1990; Interview with Anonymous C, Aug. 29, 1994).

It is within this context of heightened political polarization, opposition to the regime, and fervent anticommunism that the United States
government acted as a catalyst to overthrow the Arbenz government.[52]
Individuals within the Guatemalan opposition had approached the U.S.
government seeking money to finance an armed uprising. The opposition had clearly voiced its commitment to toppling the regime but had
not demonstrated the armed capacity to do so against a Guatemalan
military that, despite increasing ambivalence, had thus far supported

first Arévalo and later Arbenz against various coup attempts and invasions. Miguel Ydígoras Fuentes and Carlos Castillo Armas both sought U.S. support; both had been trained as military men during the Ubico period and had originally supported the democratic opening ushered in with the 1944 overthrow of the dictator. Castillo Armas, for example, had written the first article in the *Revista Militar* following Ubico's overthrow, praising the ideals of the 1944 October Revolution. Castillo Armas later participated, however, in the uprising following Arana's death in 1949, was imprisoned, and later escaped. Ydígoras Fuentes, by contrast, remained in the country to run as a presidential candidate against Arbenz in the 1950 elections, which took place amidst street violence and an unsuccessful coup attempt. Following the failed coup, Arbenz maintained low visibility and the government issued a warrant for Ydígoras Fuentes's arrest, based on the charge (never substantiated) that he had played a role in the coup attempt. Ydígoras Fuentes conducted the rest of his presidential campaign in hiding and, with the announcement of his defeat, left the country crying fraud (Handy 1994:37). In exile, both Castillo Armas and Ydígoras Fuentes tried to organize an opposition army.

In 1952, Ydígoras Fuentes and Castillo Armas signed the *Pacto de Caballeros*, or gentlemen's agreement, that outlined the process by which they would advance the counterreform offensive.[53] This agreement masked the real competition that existed between the two. Ydígoras Fuentes and Castillo Armas approached the United States individually to finance an invasion. The United States dismissed Ydígoras's advances but decided to back Castillo Armas in a plan entitled "Operation Success."

U.S. government leaders in the Central Intelligence Agency (CIA) and State Department sought to destroy what they perceived as the communist menace on Guatemala's shores; in 1954, Guatemala was the only country in the hemisphere that had not experienced a conservative reaction and a limitation on political participation (Bethell and Roxborough 1988; R. Collier 1993). The United States employed two types of destabilizing measures. On the one hand, it engaged in combative diplomacy. The U.S. government pressured the Guatemalan government to pay the United Fruit Company almost ten times the sum stipulated by the 1952 land reform decree. UFCO in turn initiated a public-relations disinformation campaign in Washington policy circles and in the U.S. press decrying the rise of communism in Guatemala. UFCO also helped finance such armed opposition as the failed effort to rise up against the regime in Salamá (Handy 1984:143). The U.S. government itself initiated a de facto ban on arm exports to Guatemala and effectively pressured other countries to do the same.[54] Finally, the United States pressured the other countries in the hemisphere to sign an anticommunist resolution at the Tenth Interamerican Conference of the Organization of American States in March 1954. Guatemala alone voted against the resolution, fearing that the United States would use it as an excuse to legitimate armed intervention. Seventeen countries supported the resolution; Argentina and Mexico abstained. All this combative diplomacy, however, was a smoke screen for the decision taken in the summer of 1953 to help Castillo Armas engineer the overthrow of the Arbenz regime, which Castillo Armas had made up his mind to do prior to the U.S. decision to back him.

FROM PROTEST TO ARMS

Colonel Carlos Castillo Armas launched the invasion of Guatemala from his base in Honduras on June 17, 1954. His small, inadequately armed force included mercenaries from other countries and had received financial aid and military support from the United States. As had been the case in Costa Rica, the opposition army called itself "the liberation army." This poorly organized military effort composed but one part of a counterreform offensive. The U.S. Central Intelligence Agency and State Department organized sporadic and chronic bombings to exaggerate the military strength of the invasion army and thereby decrease morale in the country. The counterreformers, aided by the CIA, also started operating a clandestine radio right before the outbreak of the civil war; they exaggerated the successes of the "liberation" forces and the defeats of the army. They also distributed flyers to incite insurrection. One flyer, for example, depicted two scrolls placed in front of the Guardia de Honor: one scroll said, "Fight for God, Your Country, Liberty, Work, Truth, and Justice"; the other said, "Fight against Communist Atheism, Communist Intervention, Communist Oppression, Communist Poverty, Communist Lies, Communist Police." The flyer called for Guatemalans to "Fight with your patriotic brothers. Fight with Castillo Armas" (AGCA, Hermeroteca, *Hojas Sueltas*, 1954). Despite radio broadcasts heralding the successes of the mercenaries, Castillo Armas and his small army did not advance far beyond the Guatemala/Honduras border. Indeed, given the limited training and skill of the army, the United States questioned whether the effort would even be successful.

Throughout the invasion, Arbenz believed that the military would defend the administration and regime, as it had in 1949 (Guerra Borges

1988:111–19). With a purged army and popular sectors on their side, the reformers believed that the military would overpower this invasion, as it had done others. The army had not taken any recent actions to suggest otherwise. Colonel Carlos Enrique Díaz, the chief of the armed forces, had gone before the Congress to swear the military's loyalty to the country, the people, and the constitution (*Tribuna Popular*, May 14, 1954). Colonel Enrique Parinello de León, chief of staff of the Guatemalan army, had stated on a radio show to the Guatemalan people that the army supported peace and would support the country against foreign aggression (*Tribuna Popular*, May 27, 1954). And in June an official military bulletin stated that "more than ever, the patriotic National Military of the Revolution provides all support for the citizen, President Jacobo Arbenz" (*Tribuna Popular*, June 16, 1954).

This time, however, the Guatemalan military failed to defend Arbenz and refused to deliver arms to the progovernment organizations, despite popular calls to do so and Arbenz's orders to this effect. The Guatemalan military put up little defense against the ragtag operation led by Castillo Armas. Despite the Guatemalan high command's disdain for Castillo Armas, it was not willing to defend a president whom it feared had provided too much leverage to communist organizers, particularly following the land reform. Indeed, the military high command concluded that it was time to replace Arbenz and put an end not only to the invasion, but to the direction taken by the government.[55] Colonel Díaz, Colonel Parinello, and Colonel Carlos Sartí (president of the Superior Council of National Defense) approached President Arbenz and demanded his resignation, threatening to surround the National Palace if he did not do so.

Arbenz resigned on June 27, 1954. Díaz assumed executive power and assured Arbenz that he would defend the reforms, expel Castillo Armas's army, and protect the lives of political and popular leaders. Without Arbenz's knowledge, the high command had already initiated a dialogue with the United States to end the invasion. Its members had no intention of turning power over to Castillo Armas, for whom they had the greatest disdain. Indeed, each member had ambitions of assuming leadership in the days following Arbenz's forced resignation.

What remained at issue was who within the military would oversee the counterreform authoritarian regime. It is at this juncture that the United States played the key decision-making role. Díaz had already discussed Arbenz's resignation with the U.S. ambassador; Díaz believed that if he assumed power and demobilized the popular sectors, the war would end. Thus he banned the communist PGT. He refused, however, to execute alleged communist leaders and continued the war against Castillo Armas. In this context, the United States first forced Díaz to resign in favor of Colonel Elfego Monzón, whom it then forced to resign in favor of Castillo Armas (Jonas and Tobis 1976:136; Torres Rivas 1977: 68; Blasier 1985:174). The Liberation Army entered Guatemala City on July 3, 1954, embraced by the domestic opposition.

In the aftermath of the invasion, the Guatemalan counterreform movement did not divide into competitive organizations vying for political power, as had Costa Rica's. Indeed, the Guatemalan opposition's civic associations had not developed the institutional capacity or experience to govern or to carry out the counterreform goals that had motivated their actions. Rather, they remained united in their support for the military as the institution most capable of fulfilling the task of demobilizing the popular sectors and reversing many of the reforms. With the Liberal period offering them the only alternative experience of how to reinstate order, they relied on the military to carry out this task. And despite the initial confusion over which military leader would initialize the post-reform period, the opposition appears never to have questioned that the military—via either invasion or coup—would govern following Arbenz's overthrow.

DEMOBILIZATION AND REPRESSION: RISE OF MILITARY HEGEMONY

The military established political hegemony in the post-reform, authoritarian regime. With Castillo Armas at the helm, the counterreform movement suspended the 1945 constitution, which had provided the democratic framework for the reform period. It changed suffrage laws for illiterates, preventing the majority of the indigenous and rural population from voting. It purged state institutions, arguing that communists held key positions in the Presidential Palace, Ministry of Foreign Affairs, the Labor Department, Social Security office, and congressional commissions. It closed down many state institutions, including those responsible for land reform, labor inspection, education, indigenous studies, and even cultural forums such as the symphony. It challenged many important social reforms. The post-reform labor code reestablished restrictions on rural organizing. Like the original 1947 labor code, the post-reform labor code stipulated that rural unions needed at least 50 members, of which 60 percent had to be literate. Given the high level of illiteracy, this greatly diminished possibilities for rural organizing. The 1956 constitution later made vagrancy punishable (Bishop 1959:170–

71). The counterreform coalition also passed Decrees 31 (in 1954) and 559 (in 1956). These two decrees did not disagree ostensibly with the 1952 agrarian reform law but did stress the need to decrease unrest in the rural areas and to take away power previously delegated to peasants in the form of local and regional agrarian reform committees. The counter-reformers therefore stopped the redistribution of land and returned the greatest majority—603,775 out of 765,233 *manzanas*—to the original landowners (Handy 1994:197). These changes were dramatic and created a tenuous environment for those who had supported the reform govern-ment, unions, and reforms.[56]

The counterreform administration coupled these attacks on the re-form institutions and legislation with direct repression of politicians and organized popular groups. The counterreform repression began immedi-ately after the coup and assumed largely familiar forms: short-term im-prisonments, political exile, and an estimated 300 killings of popular leaders and activists—a number which most likely underestimates the repression in the rural areas (McClintock 1985:29–30; Dunkerley 1988: 435, and 1991:136; Handy 1994:194–95). Decree 59 of August 1954 banned communist organizations and created a register of alleged com-munist members and of those who had participated in communist events (Bishop 1959:173). The newly created National Defense Committee Against Communism had the right to operate outside of constitutional jurisdiction to investigate and arrest communist suspects. The govern-ment identified 72,000 people as communists or communist sympathiz-ers within four months—17,000 of whom were imprisoned; the PGT had only claimed a membership of 5,000 to 6,000 (Jamail 1972:30–31; Schles-inger and Kinzer 1982:221; Dunkerley 1988:435; Gleijeses 1991:195). A study sponsored by the U.S. government indicated that many of the 9,000 jailed within the first year had no idea what communism was (Newbold 1957). The counterreformers also issued Decrees 21 and 48, which dissolved the 533 labor organizations that had existed. The gov-ernment seized organizational resources and funds belonging to these unions.[57] By the end of the Castillo Armas administration, union mem-bership had dropped from 100,000 to 27,000 (Schlesinger and Kinzer 1982:219).[58]

The reversal of many of the reforms and the demobilization of labor and peasant movements created a space for the Guatemalan oligarchy to resume practices reminiscent of the Liberal period.[59] It was, therefore, able to recapture land and reinstate coercive labor practices, reestablish-ing its traditional regime of accumulation in the counterreform period.

This differs from the case of its Costa Rican counterpart, which lost control over the national banks; where the Guatemalan military attempted to control the countryside, in part to help Guatemala's elite, the Costa Rican state nationalized the banks and strengthened the economic maneuverability of the Costa Rican peasant vis-à-vis the elite financiers. However, the Guatemalan elite remained a weak electoral force with no representative political party in the regime. In the absence of a strong political party, the Guatemalan elite influenced politics through its economic associations and has relied on the military to govern. In this context, the Guatemalan military became the dominant political force in post-reform Guatemala.

The redefinition of politics in post-reform Guatemala, therefore, did not rest on a compromise between the middle class and oligarchy, as in Costa Rica, but on a political understanding between the Guatemalan military and oligarchy. The Guatemalan military assumed the right to govern in exchange for maintaining political order—particularly in the countryside. The Guatemalan elite regained the right to accumulate capital through traditional regimes of accumulation and did not attempt seriously to develop an institutionalized political presence in public affairs. Jointly, the military and oligarchy regained a sense of political order. To contain the emergence of civil society, the military deployed increasingly more systematic and brutal forms of repression to strengthen its own political hegemony and existing property relations—defined by the military as national security. The post-1954 era, therefore, developed an enduring authoritarian regime marked by polarizing cycles of protest and repression.

The 1948 civil war in Cost Rica and the 1954 coup in Guatemala marked an end to a decade of popular-sector mobilization, social reforms, and democratic participation. Opposition coalitions in Costa Rica and Guatemala had failed to win elections. Motivated by similar fears of growing communist political power, redistributive reform agendas, and increased popular organizing, these opposition coalitions successfully overthrew the mid-twentieth-century governing reform coalitions. In the aftermath of these overthrows, the opposition banned reform parties, exiled reform leaders, persecuted sympathizers, and demobilized more radical labor organizations.

Yet the opposition movements founded divergent political regimes. Costa Rica's multiclass opposition founded political democracy in 1948. With an elite divided between support for the reform coalition and the opposition, and competing organizations with divergent political ideologies, the Costa Rican regime-founding coalition became stalemated. It resolved competition among all these groups in a democratic compromise between the middle class and the elite political parties. The Guatemalan multiclass opposition, by contrast, founded authoritarian rule in 1954. With a united elite committed to authoritarian rule, the possibilities to found democracy were slim. Yet neither the Guatemalan elite nor its middle-class allies had the organizational capacity to govern; without well-formed political organizations, the Guatemalan opposition turned to the military. It did so on the basis of an evolving political accommodation between the military and a united elite.

This chapter has demonstrated that while the Liberal reforms of the nineteenth century foreshadowed the strength of political organizations in each coalition, the unity or disunity of each country's oligarchy could not be explained by historical factors alone; rather, they depended on the position first assumed by the oligarchies in the initial reform coalitions and the ensuing scope of reforms and mobilization. The coalitional analysis, therefore, provides the mechanism to analyze how historical and conjunctural factors interacted to found political democracy in Costa Rica in 1948 and authoritarian rule in Guatemala in 1954.

The coalitions that founded political democracy in Costa Rica and authoritarian rule in Guatemala proved powerful enough to sustain each regime. They derived that power not only from the institutions and compromises forged when each regime was founded, but from the social bases that they subsequently cultivated. This question of endurance is the focus of the last chapter.

CHAPTER 7

Enduring Regimes

The endurance of Costa Rica's and Guatemala's respective political regimes in the second half of the twentieth century is puzzling. Costa Rica and Guatemala, like the rest of Latin America, experienced political closure in the decade following World War II. Antidemocratic and/or conservative coalitions toppled or constrained Latin America's populist coalitions. Labor movements were repressed. Political parties on the left were banned. And military coups often toppled democratic regimes and replaced them with authoritarian ones. This pattern of democratic breakdowns and political closures foreshadowed the cycle of regime change that came to characterize much of post–World War II Latin America (Bethell and Roxborough 1988, and 1992; R. Collier 1993; Rock 1994).

Yet if Costa Rica and Guatemala experienced political closure at midcentury, they did not experience the subsequent rounds of regime change so common throughout the region. Indeed, the political regimes founded in the aftermath of Costa Rica's 1948 civil war and Guatemala's 1954 coup endured despite radically different types of regimes. Costa Rica established a durable democracy. With the overthrow of democratic regimes in Chile and Uruguay in 1973, Costa Rica's became the longest-lasting and most respected form of political democracy in the region. The abolition of the Costa Rican military reinforced civilian control over politics. With the extension of social welfare programs, Costa Rica developed one of Latin America's more generous welfare states. Guatemala, on the other hand, developed an entrenched authoritarian regime.

The military essentially governed the country after 1954—with military officers directly assuming the presidency, creating coup coalitions, and unleashing repression globally recognized for its brutality. In the 1980s, when most of the region moved away from military authoritarian regimes, the Guatemalan military maneuvered a transition in which it sustained ultimate authority. The Guatemalan military maintained effective veto power over electoral outcomes and policy processes. To date, it has not been held accountable for the ongoing human rights abuses for which it is responsible.

The endurance of Costa Rican democracy and Guatemalan authoritarian rule is curious when compared to the pattern of regime change in the rest of the region. This book has largely focused on the origins of democracy and authoritarianism. This chapter explores the question of endurance. Why have Costa Rica's and Guatemala's contemporary political regimes endured when the democratic regimes immediately preceding them did not? Can these cases provide insight into varied patterns of regime endurance in Latin America and beyond? This chapter draws out the implications of the argument developed earlier to address these questions. It emphasizes the need for comparative research on the coalitional politics of the countryside. Accordingly, it explores the argument that in an age of mass politics, regime endurance depends on the regime-founding coalitions' capacity to "control" the countryside. While the politics of the countryside cannot be the sole explanation of regime endurance, this chapter concludes that it is paramount.

Regime Endurance and the Countryside

In a discussion of regime endurance, why return to the politics of the countryside? Indeed, the contemporary theoretical literature on democratic transitions and consolidation would not have us do so. "Transitologists" and "consolidologists," as Schmitter and Karl (1994) call them, have largely analyzed urban, elite, and institutional transactions, including elite accommodations, pact making, institution building, agenda setting, and party systems (for examples, see O'Donnell, Schmitter, and Whitehead 1986; Malloy and Seligson 1987; Przeworski 1988; Di Palma 1990; Higley and Gunther 1992; Mainwaring, O'Donnell, and Valenzuela 1992; Linz and Valenzuela 1994; Mainwaring and Scully 1995). By focusing on national political institutions, forms of representation, and agenda setting, these scholars have underscored the different types of democracy that urban politicians can construct. These newly constructed institutions matter not least because they provide a clear set of rules and regulations for ordering political interaction and making politics more transparent and predictable; freeze power relations and institutionalize compromise; and create a new set of vested interests. Institutions matter, therefore, for the locus and direction of political interaction.

The comparative historical analysis of Costa Rica and Guatemala reminds us, however, that democratic institutions are not always so strong. They can be quite fragile in the absence of organized social support. The contemporary democratization literature, however, neglects to analyze if and how these institutions incorporate and sustain social support—focusing as it does so closely on the institutions that are constructed and pacts that are made and so little on whether these institutions and pacts will be respected or upheld by social actors and groups outside of the state. The Costa Rican and Guatemalan cases suggest that we need to analyze why powerful social sectors tolerate democracy when it can threaten their control over valuable political and economic resources. In other words, we need to look more closely at the social forces that can destroy or disrupt democracy and the conditions under which they are willing to accept it.[1]

In developing countries, this power of disruption often lies in the countryside, a fact not addressed in the contemporary democratization literature but central to an older literature on regimes and revolution. From Moore (1966) to Huntington (1968) to Paige (1975) to Skocpol (1979), earlier scholars recognized that power in developing countries lay, almost by definition, in the countryside and that traditional elites and the rural poor had the potential to destabilize politics. Accordingly, these scholars analyzed the distribution of resources, the organization of power, the capacity to mobilize, and the related coalitions that took countries down one path or another. Chapter 1 outlined why the historical determinism of the earlier studies of regimes provided only partial insight into political trajectories of regime change, but the narratives in Costa Rica and Guatemala remind us that we should not, therefore, just dismiss the countryside as irrelevant to national politics.

To the contrary, the countryside matters. It often hosts the country's potentially most disruptive social sectors: agrarian elites and the rural poor.* Agrarian elites tend to maintain a disproportionate control over

---

*Rural poor refers here to both smallholding peasants and rural workers; these categories assume different meanings in different countries and often blend into one another as individuals move between cultivating their own land and working on that of others.

economic resources and influence over political governance—if not at the national level then quite commonly at the local level—and tend to view politics as a set of zero-sum conflicts. Agrarian elites often have the power to uphold and subvert any central state. They have the economic resources and political ties to subvert democratic decisions about property relations, taxation, labor regulations, and the like. And they are rarely held accountable for their actions.

But agrarian elites, no matter how powerful, do not have the power of numbers. The rural poor, by contrast, perhaps have only that. Despite significant collective action problems, political parties and movements have often attempted to secure their allegiance, attempting to mobilize the rural poor on their behalf. The rural poor, therefore, possess both electoral allure and revolutionary potential. Their numbers can break elections and make revolutions. Not all regimes with the support of the rural poor have endured. However, it seems that no electoral regime in the age of mass politics has endured in the absence of institutionalized rural support; similarly, no authoritarian regime has survived if it could not secure rural support or repress the threat of rural opposition. As Huntington (1968) and Mao both argued, he who controls the countryside, controls the country.

Given elite power over resources and rural poor power in numbers, governing coalitions in an age of mass politics have had to contend with the countryside, particularly if they intended to endure. Governing coalitions have succeeded in establishing rural control only insofar as they have met three conditions: they have inherited or established the state's autonomy from the traditional elites while delineating the latter's political stake in the existing political regime; they have cultivated and sustained control over the rural poor through some combination of electoral incorporation (for example, in exchange for social services or subsidies) and repression; and they have developed the organizational capacity to govern by developing political party discipline and outreach and/ or strengthening state bureaucracies.

Costa Rica's contemporary political democracy and Guatemala's authoritarian rule endured because their governing coalitions asserted control over the countryside in this way. This pattern is not unique, however, to these two cases. Countries as diverse as Mexico, Venezuela, Japan, and India have all replicated this pattern.

For those who have studied the political economy of development or Central American politics, this argument will appear commonsensical.[2] It is a point that has eluded most of the contemporary literature on Latin American regime politics, however.[3] Two notable and excellent exceptions include the comparative work by Evelyne Huber Stephens (1989) and Ruth Berins Collier and David Collier (1991).[4] This book draws heavily on their arguments and methodologies. However, both of these studies relegate the countryside to historical discussions rather than looking at how it figures into the working and maintenance of contemporary political regimes. This book ends, therefore, with an injunction to bring the countryside back into studies of democracy and authoritarianism. Stated more boldly: no rural control, no endurance.

The Cases

The cases of Costa Rica and Guatemala bear this argument out. Below I analyze the regime trajectories of Costa Rica and Guatemala in the age of mass politics through the lens of the politics of the countryside. Drawing in a stylized way from the narrative developed in Part II, I reassess how the overthrown mid-twentieth-century democratic regimes failed to control the countryside. I then explore at greater length how Costa Rica's and Guatemala's regime endurance in the second half of the twentieth century has depended on the governing coalition's capacity to control the rural poor at the political expense of traditional elites.

FAILED EFFORTS TO CONTROL THE COUNTRYSIDE

In Costa Rica (1942–48) and Guatemala (1944–54), midcentury reform coalitions neither secured a commitment by the traditional elite to participate in democratic politics nor successfully weakened the elite's capacity to challenge democracy itself. In both cases, an elite opposition fared poorly in elections. In both cases, these elites felt excluded from policy debates. And in both cases, they feared the capacity of democratic institutions to challenge traditional regimes of accumulation in the countryside. Faced with popular pressures to redistribute property, reformers implemented changes that further alienated these elites from the governing coalition and cemented their opposition to the regime. In this sense, traditional elites felt neither politically incorporated nor economically protected by Costa Rican and Guatemalan midcentury democracy. To the elites, democracy appeared unbounded and their property unprotected.

If the Costa Rican and Guatemalan reformers failed to institutionalize traditional elite participation, so too they failed to institutionalize participation by the rural poor. In Costa Rica, reformers made an extremely limited effort to cultivate an electoral constituency among the peasantry. Drawing on the sectoral strengths of the communist party, the reformers focused largely on the urban areas and coastal regions but did not reach out to the rural areas, making only limited efforts to extend social services to the countryside and to organize the peasantry. Indeed, the peasantry and rural workers remained most clearly allied to their agrarian elite patrons. In Guatemala, reformers did successfully bring change to the rural areas. A quickly mobilized rural constituency did vote for the reform parties. But the reform parties themselves were so fragmented that rural support was not institutionalized in any given party, even though the rural poor remained broadly sympathetic to the reformers and their political project. Moreover, while peasant organizations did participate directly in the legal implementation of the land reform, the governing coalition was unable to control the significant but isolated cases of land invasion that occurred against the wishes of the reform parties and outside of the letter of the law. The Guatemalan opposition interpreted this overall situation as one of chaos in the countryside.

Within a decade in both cases, agrarian elites mobilized against the democratic regime while the rural poor largely failed to mobilize to defend it. These opposition movements became violent shortly following the legislation of redistributive reforms that challenged the elites' control over resources tied to agricultural production. Armed oppositions toppled the democratic reform governments in Costa Rica in 1948 and Guatemala in 1954.

SUCCESSFUL EFFORTS TO ASSERT CONTROL OVER THE COUNTRYSIDE

The regime-founding coalitions that installed political democracy in Costa Rica in 1948 and authoritarianism in Guatemala in 1954, however, endured. In contrast to their regional counterparts, they successfully thwarted later efforts to found different regimes. In each case, these regime-founding coalitions came to dominate the countryside. In each case, the dominant governing coalition governed at the political expense of traditional elites. In Costa Rica the post-1948 reformers would do so through a combination of rapid redistributive reforms, social welfare policies, and electoral incorporation, while in Guatemala the post-1954 rulers would do so by military repression. Strikingly, the reassertion of electoral and military control over the countryside would facilitate the endurance of two very different sorts of regimes, as the following stylized sketch of each illustrates.[5]

Costa Rica. The regime-founding coalition of 1948 included two very different factions: the middle-class opposition of the Partido Social Demócrata (PSD) and the oligarchic opposition of the Partido Unión Nacional (PUN). As the last chapter laid out, leaders of the PSD headed the revolutionary junta. During that eighteen-month period, the PSD succeeded not only in demobilizing the communist party and labor movement, against which they had fought, but also in outflanking the divided elite, with which they had allied. The PSD weakened the elite economically while gaining the political support of the countryside.

By rapidly nationalizing the banks, imposing a one-time tax, and dismantling the Costa Rican army, the PSD succeeded in diminishing a central basis of the elite's economic and political power. In contrast to earlier efforts during the reform period, the PSD successfully challenged property rights precisely because it initiated these redistributive reforms in tandem with the transition from the prior regime. The one-time tax and bank nationalization appeared more palatable to the elites (bitter though it must have seemed) than the earlier reform coalition's unbounded project. More fearful of the past than the present, Costa Rica's elites largely concluded that they had few options but to accept bank and tax reforms.

In the postwar period, Costa Rica's elites, therefore, lost an economic monopoly over finance. They never regained a dominant political position. While the elites reunited into various political parties, they remained a poorly institutionalized political force until the early 1980s.[6] As Table 13 depicts, the elite-dominated, conservative-party coalitions rarely assumed a controlling position in the legislature. Given the centrality of the Costa Rican legislature, this lack of control circumscribed conservative projects even when the same coalition assumed the presidency.[7] The Costa Rican elite, however, did not lose all political influence, as noted in Table 14. The 1948 junta agreed that the elite's candidate, Ulate, could assume the presidency in 1949. Moreover, conservative party coalitions did win four out of eleven presidential elections between 1953 and 1994.[8] They also assumed positions in the so-called Autonomous Institutes, which play a significant role in important economic arenas such as banking, commerce, development, and public health. But the Costa Rican elite never regained the dominant political influence that it had had in the state during the Liberal period.

A weakened but politically incorporated elite proved auspicious for democracy. The junta achieved this balance in the context of factional divisions within the elite, rapid but bounded redistributive reforms, and

TABLE 13

Percentage of Vote Won by Party or Bloc in
Costa Rican Legislative Elections, 1953–90

Year	PLN[a]	Conservative (alliances)	Left
1953	64.8	21.2	—
1958	41.7	22.4 (PRNI)	—
		21.4 (PUN)	
1962[b]	48.9	33.5 (PR)	2.4
1966	48.9	43.2 (PUnN)	—
1970	50.7	35.9 (PUnN)	5.5
1974	40.9	24.7 (PUnN)	4.4
1978	38.9	43.4 (CU)	7.7
1982	50.5	33.8 (CU)	7.2
1986	47.8	41.4 (PUSC)	5.1
1990	41.9	46.2 (PUSC)	< 2

sources: *Inforpress Centroamericana; Keesings Record of World Events;* Ruddle and Gilette (1972); Seligson (1987); Seligson and Gómez B. (1989); Jiménez Castro (1977, 1981, and 1986). Table 13 was first printed in Yashar (1995).

note: The sources listed above sometimes conflict with each other. Figures do not always total to 100 percent due to a combination of abstentions, invalid ballots, incomplete data, and votes cast for smaller parties not included here.

[a] The PSD changed its name to the Partido Liberación Nacional (PLN) in 1951.

[b] Voting was made mandatory beginning with this election.

TABLE 14

Percentage of Vote Won by Party or Bloc in
Costa Rican Presidential Elections, 1953–90

Year	PLN	Conservative (alliances)	Left
1953	64.7	35.3	—
1958	42.8	46.4	—
1962	50.3	35.3	0.9
1966	49.5	50.5	—
1970	54.8	41.2	1.3
1974	43.4	30.4	2.9
1978	43.8	50.5	2.9
1982	58.8	37.5	3.3
1986	52.3	45.8	1.3
1990	47.3	51.4	0.9

sources: *Inforpress Centroamericana; Keesings Record of World Events;* Ruddle and Gilette (1972); Seligson (1987); Seligson and Gómez B. (1989); Jiménez Castro (1977, 1981, and 1986). Table 14 was first printed in Yashar (1995).

note: The sources listed sometimes conflict with each other. Figures do not always total to 100 percent due to a combination of invalid ballots, incomplete data, and votes cast for smaller parties not included here.

signals that the elite would be allowed to assume political office and participate in policy debates. These last two elements were lacking when the prior reform coalition governed from 1942 to 1948.

In this context, the PSD developed a formidable political party in the post-1948 period. Building on the ideological foundations established by the members of the Centro, the PSD actively set out to construct a national, competitive, and permanent political party. In 1951 it renamed itself the Partido Liberación Nacional (PLN). Because it had lacked electoral support in the 1948 Constituent Assembly, it subsequently organized a rural constituency; unlike the previous oligarchic parties, it could not rely on established patronage ties from the Liberal period. The PSD did not establish a peasant branch within the party but did promise, and delivered, state services to cultivate and sustain peasant support.

By late 1952, the PLN had established itself in all of Costa Rica's cantons as well as 82 percent of all the districts (English 1971:53). Studies of Costa Rican elections have all concluded that the PLN has traditionally been strongest in the rural areas (Jiménez Castro 1977:12; Monge 1976a, and 1976b; Denton 1971:70; Martz 1967). This is particularly so in the central valley, where the majority of Costa Ricans live. Writing two decades after the civil war, Martz (1967:906) observed that "of the four provinces centering on the meseta central, all but one [Cartago] has consistently shown the party to be stronger outside the urban areas. . . . This clearly indicates that the party strength has come from the rural rather than the urban areas in the provinces. . . . In the two coastal provinces the pattern is different. Liberación Nacional has run stronger in the city than in the province in three of the four elections in Puntarenas and in all four contests in Limon." The PLN, therefore, penetrated the countryside electorally at a moment in which traditional elites were politically divided.

The PLN cultivated this rural support in exchange for the growth of a regionally impressive welfare state. Drawing on the studies of the Centro in the 1940s, the PLN built upon the incipient welfare programs and institutions first constructed by the 1940s reformers. Through the 1970s, this system provided excellent heath care, social security, and guaranteed prices for rural producers.[9] The post-reform regime nationalized the Instituto de Defensa del Café (IDECAFE) (which had incorporated the peasantry in the 1930s, as discussed in Chapter 2) and renamed it the Oficina del Café. Following the original intent of IDECAFE, the new office set out to regulate the prices and credits that the *beneficio* paid small producers. Moreover, the junta transformed the Consejo Nacional de Producción (CNP) into a semiautonomous institution to promote agricultural output for domestic consumption. Via agricultural subsidies, credit programs, price-stabilization policies, provision of high-quality seeds, and state stores guaranteeing prices on basic goods, the state substantially increased its regulation of the rural sector. Price-stabilization programs, for example, encouraged production of agricultural staples by guaranteeing small producers a minimum price and purchase by the CNP of any quality of output at that price. This amounted to an effective subsidy to the producers and protected them against the drop in prices that often accompanied the harvest. The state would then sell the products later in the year after prices had risen. The economic boom of the postwar decade sustained a distributive social welfare system that provided tangible, if not equitable, benefits.[10]

Drawing on this rural support, the PLN has dominated Costa Rican politics since 1953. It has held a majority in the Congress, except for two periods: 1978–82 and 1990–94. Given the primary role of the Costa Rican legislature, the PLN has asserted tremendous leverage over the direction of state policies. Moreover, it has won the majority of presidential terms: José Figueres Ferrer (1953–57); Francisco Orlich (1962–66); José Figueres Ferrer (1970–74); Daniel Oduber (1974–78); Luis Alberto Monge (1982–86); Oscar Arias Sánchez (1986–90); and José María Figueres (1994–98). The primary figures in the PLN who have fundamentally directed the party, as well as shaped policy, participated in the AD, Centro, and the PSD. Their political power was secured with rural support in exchange for social services and subsidies.[11]

In short, the electoral basis of the PLN has been rooted in the countryside. It was able to cultivate this support initially because it organized the 1948 civil war and later because it extended state programs to the rural sectors. Against the backdrop of a weakened traditional elite, the PLN emerged in the four decades following the 1948 civil war as the dominant and stabilizing political force in Costa Rican politics. This control over the countryside was a political objective that Costa Rica's failed social reformers of the 1940s never pursued.

Guatemala. The politics of the countryside also proved central to the endurance of Guatemala's post-reform regime. In the immediate aftermath of the 1954 invasion, the Guatemalan military repressed the urban and rural unions, persecuted political leaders, banned reform parties, and reversed much of the previous social legislation, including the land reform of 1952. As in Costa Rica, the victorious sector in Guatemala marginalized those against whom they had fought; unlike the Costa Rican case, however, the ensuing Guatemalan governing coalition sustained the rule of arms to enforce and institutionalize its position. Over the years the Guatemalan military deployed increasingly brutal forms of repression that militarized state and society. This repression has occurred throughout the country, but nowhere has it been more apparent than in the countryside.

In this repressive context, it has often been assumed that traditional elites reclaimed a powerful position in post-1954 Guatemalan society, with a deferential military operating at its behest. Yet, if the Guatemalan elite has reclaimed its control over a countryside that had been subject to land reform and peasant organization, to date it has not developed the political capacity to govern commensurate with its economic capacity to profit.

Traditional elites have maintained highly concentrated landholdings, despite the legislation of showcase land reforms. The Inter-American Committee of Agricultural Development reported in 1965 that 2.1 percent of farm units claimed 72.2 percent of all land, while 88.4 percent of farm units claimed 14.3 percent (Handy 1984:208–9). While exact figures have varied over time, they have all indicated extreme inequality in land tenure in contemporary Guatemala. The U.S. Agency for International Development, for example, reported in the late 1970s that an estimated 90 percent of the population living in the Guatemalan highlands had too little land to meet basic needs (Dunkerley 1988:473). In addition, traditional elites have rarely provided decent wages (whether defined as a minimum or a living wage) or living conditions to rural workers. Moreover, they have continued to resort to repressive labor practices, with paltry state provisions and protection for rural workers. Indeed, Guatemala's landholders commonly have relied on local military and police forces even as the former resort to violence against rural workers on their plantations. These patterns of land concentration and repressive labor practices have constituted the backbone of Guatemala's economy. In the late 1970s, agriculture's percentage of GDP was among the highest in the region, and 53.7 percent of the population depended on agriculture for their livelihood (Handy 1984:209; Grindle 1986:49–50).[12]

With the central role assumed by agriculture, elite economic associations have clearly played a role in shaping economic policies, the terms of state extraction, and general state finances. In the decades following the 1954 coup, economic interest associations increased quite significantly in number (Adams 1970:195–96, 351–52). Asociación General de Agricultores (AGA), the older economic association that supported the

1954 coup, has remained particularly important among them. With the post–World War II diversification of the economy, other types of associations emerged as well. In 1957, the elites formed a confederation of these associations, Comité Coordinador de Asociaciones Agrícolas, Industriales y Financieras (CACIF), to articulate a uniform public position for agricultural, commercial, industrial, and financial elites. As military men began to become landlords themselves, it becomes difficult to disentangle the interests of landlords from governing military officers with large agricultural properties.

If the Guatemalan elite has developed powerful economic organizations, it has not developed the political counterpart. It has lacked an independent, organized political force within the government itself. Harkening back to practices during the Liberal period, the Guatemalan elite has made little effort to develop independent political parties or to represent its own interests (competing though those interests surely are) in a broader political realm. The failure to develop viable political parties, in particular, has left the traditional elites with no sustained capacity to participate via legal and open political channels. Consequently they have not been able to participate democratically or to govern effectively. Poor elite organization bodes poorly for democracy, but well for authoritarian endurance. Guatemalan elites have largely relied on the military to govern the countryside and, therefore, the country as a whole.

In this context, the military institutionalized its position through a combination of fraudulent elections and coercion. It also relied on U.S. military aid and training to develop a more professionalized military.[13] In its initial years in power, the military was clearly divided among itself, as different officers vied for political power at the same time that they tried to clamp down on political expression and the population as a whole. As Table 15 summarizes, the military oversaw a series of fraudulent elections and coups, which not only were used to control popular input to the political process but also to subvert or decide competition between military officers. With the 1963 coup ending Ydígoras Fuentes's corrupt and incompetent administration, the military began to rule Guatemala more consciously as an institution than it had previously, systematically subordinating civilian rule. Having failed to construct a hegemonic party system and confronted with the emergence of guerrilla movements based in the countryside, the military began to rely more actively on coercion than on elections to assert political control.[14] Even during the administration of Julio César Méndez Montenegro (1966–70), the only civilian president from 1954 to 1985, repression increased—re-

TABLE 15

Presidents and Governing Juntas in Guatemala, 1954–85

	Means of assuming power	Complete term?
Carlos Castillo Armas (1954–57) MDN (becomes MLN)	Invasion "legitimated" by plebiscite	No: killed in 1957
Miguel Ydígoras Fuentes (1957–63) Redención	Claimed fraud, forced MDN to step down and hold another round of elections	No: coup in 1963
Enrique Peralta Azurdia (1963–66)	Coup; forms PID	Not a term
Julio César Méndez Montenegro[a] (1966–70) PR	Elections; allowed to take office only after agreeing not to interfere in military affairs; assumed presidency under state of siege	Yes
Carlos Arana Osorio (1970–74) PID, MLN	Elections in the context of political violence	Yes
Kjell Laugerud (1974–1978) PID, MLN, and CAO[b]	Electoral fraud against Ríos Montt	Yes
Benedicto Lucas García (1978–82) PID, CAN, and PR	Fraudulent election	Yes
Efraín Ríos Montt (1982–83)	Coup to protest electoral fraud; heads junta, March 1982; declares himself president, June 9	Not a term
Humberto Mejía Víctores (1983–85)	Coup; oversees constitutional assembly to return to civilian rule	Not a term

[a] The only civilian president between 1954 and 1985.
[b] Central Aranista Organizada (CAO), which later becomes Central Auténtica Nacionalista (CAN).

. sulting in the death of an estimated 10,000 people, the rise of paramilitary forces, and the development of a more pervasive military presence throughout the countryside (Cáceres 1980:24; Handy 1984:157–63; Dunkerley 1991:139–42; Rosada Granados 1992:96; Trudeau 1993).[15]

The professionalization of the military after 1963 increased both the state's capacity to penetrate rural (and urban) areas and the military's capacity to dominate the state political apparatus itself. By the mid-1980s, military officers had assumed prominent decision-making powers in most if not all branches of the government. In the process, they developed professional and economic interests that became integral to the maintenance of a state that employs violence to restrict civil and political society and to foster the politics of public silence. Given the increasingly more brutal cycles of repression, few civilian politicians left of center had the courage or the faith to run; in the few cases where they did, they were often gunned down, disappeared, or forced into exile whenever military or paramilitary forces saw them as viable alternatives. Political society had effectively been reduced to the politics of military men. As depicted in Table 15, between 1954 and 1985, military officials assumed executive powers in Guatemala, and in the decade following Méndez Montenegro's administration, even opposition parties began to field military presidential candidates (Rosada Granados 1992:97).

Against military rule, protest movements emerged. Popular organizations and guerrilla movements began to organize—most actively in the countryside. The Comité de Unidad Campesina, for example, emerged in the 1970s to demand basic labor and land rights. Communities organized cooperatives to develop their economic independence from traditional elites. Guerrilla forces demanded the overthrow of the state. Faced with such protests, both inside and outside the existing legal framework, traditional elites supported the military as it organized to reestablish control over rural areas.

In this struggle over the countryside, the military eventually proved more powerful. While mobilizing against guerrilla forces, it targeted the countryside as a whole. This campaign against the countryside reached its apex during the administration of General Efraín Ríos Montt (1982–83), who initiated a program of "beans and bullets"—seeking to build support among peasants with food programs while repressing them with arms. In his eighteen months of rule, "the military was able to complete a process that began in 1542: the acquisition of control over the countryside and the total breakdown of village autonomy" (Handy 1984:255).

By 1983, the military had killed an estimated 100,000 to 140,000 Guatemalans (mostly civilians), "disappeared" some 40,000 more, razed over 440 villages, and generated close to a million internal and external refugees; the majority of these politically motivated actions occurred between 1977 and 1983. Conservative and urban-biased data gathered by the U.S. embassy estimated that political assassinations were 30 per month in 1971, 75 per month in 1975, and 303 per month in 1982 (Booth and Walker 1989:110). By the mid-1980s, the Guatemalan military had successfully forced any semblance of popular civil society underground and had developed a surveillance apparatus particularly pervasive in the countryside.

If the Costa Rican PLN successfully cultivated an electoral presence in all of Costa Rica's cantons, the Guatemalan military successfully developed an institutional apparatus that penetrated the countryside to a similar degree—although clearly through different means. During the administration of Ríos Montt, the general dismissed 324 village mayors and replaced them with appointed officials. Moreover, he established military zones in each of the country's 22 departments to replace the nine military zones that had existed before that (Handy 1984:261). It was difficult to drive through the Guatemalan countryside without taking note of the military presence in nearly every town and village. The military established barracks throughout the country, developing the impression of a country under siege—in this case by its own army.

In the zones of greatest conflict, the military developed model villages.[16] Throughout the countryside, it also implemented Patrullas de Autodefensa Civil (PACs), or civil defense patrols. In theory the PACs provided the communities with an apparatus to monitor subversion. With this system, men of a certain age (generally sixteen and older) could volunteer to observe and tally movements by outsiders to and from their community. These men, who were usually armed, provided this information to the military, which could then use it to control rural movements. While voluntary on paper, the PACs became required in practice, and the failure to participate incurred charges of subversion. The military, therefore, effectively militarized the communities on a village-by-village basis. PACs also served to inhibit any other kind of associational development—also for fear that this would be seen as subversive. At their peak in the mid-1980s, the PACs involved an estimated 900,000 men (Dunkerley 1988:496). One volume on rural violence in Guatemala reported, "The civil patrol system, which the Guatemalan army established as the cornerstone of its rural counterinsurgency program in the early 1980s, stands out as the dominant institutional legacy of the period

of violence in rural Guatemala" (Carmack 1988:27). While it was contested, the Guatemalan military would remain dominant and hegemonic precisely because Guatemala's traditional elites depended on it to
control the countryside and because the military effectively lived up to
this challenge through the 1980s and early 1990s.

Comparative Overview

Guatemala and Costa Rica adopted two radically different responses
to the onset of mass politics, but in both cases the regime-founding
coalitions strengthened their organizational capacity and secured their
dominant political position by gaining control over and regulating the
countryside. Whereas as the Guatemalan military resorted to coercion
to delimit and restrict political participation, the Costa Rican PLN relied
on electoral politics to incorporate and channel participation. The Costa
Rican politicians of the PSD and the Guatemalan military, therefore,
curtailed prospects for their respective traditional elites to rule as a
dominant and unified force.

While control of the countryside did not ensure endurance, no regime
in twentieth-century Latin America endured without both a weakened
traditional elite and institutional control of the rural poor. In this sense,
contemporary Costa Rica and Guatemala contrast with the failed democratic examples analyzed in this book as well as with a broader set of
Latin American cases. The political instability of South America's political regimes can be partially attributed to this failure to control the
countryside. Collier and Collier (1991) compare the polarizing political
cycles in Argentina, Peru, Uruguay, Colombia, Brazil, and Chile and the
more enduring regimes of Mexico and Venezuela. While they primarily
focus on labor incorporation to explain varied party-system outcomes,
their analysis also supports the argument that, where the traditional oligarchy remained strong and political parties organized urban labor alone,
regimes did not endure.[17] This was true in the first six cases mentioned.
Conversely, Mexico and Venezuela share with Costa Rica and Guatemala
a pattern where the governing coalition strengthened its organizational
capacity and successfully dominated the countryside—albeit through
different mechanisms.

Mexico's hybrid electoral-authoritarian regime, for example, has endured longer than any other regime in Latin America.[18] Founded in the
turbulent decades following the 1910 revolution, the Mexican constitution promised land reform, which was implemented most effectively

during the administration of Lázaro Cárdenas (1934–40). The revolution broke the political back of Mexico's agrarian elite while the land reforms greatly weakened their economic control over rural production.[19] Cárdenas also institutionalized support from the rural poor by incorporating the peasantry into the governing party (which would become the hegemonic Partido Revolucionario Institucional—PRI) and cementing that support with (promises of) land reform and protection of communal lands.[20] The PRI developed a one-party-dominant regime that has governed since. The PRI's decision in 1991 to reform Article 27 of the Mexican constitution effectively withdrew the state's responsibility to protect communal lands and renounced the party's historic blend of political incorporation and economic patronage in the countryside. Fox (1994b) has demonstrated that the persistence of authoritarian enclaves in rural areas enables the PRI to guarantee electoral outcomes in its favor, even if it loses support in the city. But electoral success has not translated into continued control or support of the rural areas, as illustrated by the Chiapas rebellion in 1994. The decision to reverse protection of communal lands has contributed since 1994 to the rise in rural protest, posing the greatest sustained challenge to the regime. The PRI's ability to address these rural challenges has proven central to the endurance of Mexico's hybrid electoral-authoritarian regime.

Like Costa Rica and Mexico, Venezuela's governing coalition came to control the countryside and depend on it during elections. By the middle of the twentieth century, Venezuela's traditional agrarian elite was quite weak, surpassed in power by a new elite that had developed with the discovery of oil. Acción Democrática and Comité de Organización Política, Venezuela's dominant parties, cogoverned, therefore, without the potential threat of an agrarian elite. These parties secured their position in part by mobilizing and incorporating the rural poor with the (oft-forsaken) promise of land reforms and social services. Many authors have explained the endurance of Venezuelan democracy by highlighting some combination of the following factors: the nature of the 1958 transition to democracy, which occurred with the making of political pacts that protected elite interests and restricted political participation; the strength of the post-1958 party system; and the oil boom that generated wealth and state revenue. The framework developed here, however, anticipates the need to explain institutional endurance by incorporating an analysis of social sectors—those willing to agree at one moment to a pact and then subsequently to abide by it.[21]

The Costa Rican, Guatemalan, Mexican, and Venezuelan cases are salient reminders of a diverse set of enduring political regimes in which the governing institutions or parties developed organizational capacity, autonomy from the agrarian elite, and control over the countryside. This pattern is not unique to Latin America, but also resonates in Japan, which is among East Asia's most enduring political regimes.[22] Following defeat in World War II, Japan had little choice but to found a democracy under the directives of the United States. Japan not only repressed communist-based labor movements, as occurred in most of postwar Latin America, but the wartime government also implemented a far-reaching land reform that formalized exclusion of landed elites. In essence, Japan destroyed its landed class and diluted the elite's capacity to challenge the regime, dictate policy, or control the rural areas. Taking advantage of a weakened agrarian elite, Japan's dominant party, the Liberal Democratic Party (LDP), successfully cultivated a base of electoral support in the countryside in exchange for agricultural subsidies, border protection, and state-supported prices (Bullock, forthcoming). The rural areas have maintained disproportionate weight in electoral calculations, which has benefited the LDP for most of the post–World War II decades, allowing it to dominate national politics and stabilize the regime accordingly.

Scholars of Asia, in general, have argued that regime stability has rested quite squarely with the politics of the countryside. In cases as diverse as China, India, South Korea, Taiwan, Malaysia, and Indonesia, regimes have sustained political stability, in the face of quite different social structures and varying political regimes, by subordinating rural elites to the state. In some cases this was facilitated by comprehensive land reforms, in others by varying forms of state patronage. But in each case the state diminished the political autonomy of its rural elites and successfully incorporated and/or repressed its rural poor with the extension of state subsidies and/or state coercion (Meisner 1977; Amsden 1979; Rudolph and Rudolph 1987; Hart, Turton, and White 1989; Brass 1994; Bellow and Rosenfeld 1990; Varshney 1995; Bullock, forthcoming and n.d.).

This brief comparative overview is meant to highlight the need for regime scholars to reincorporate the countryside into their analyses. The countryside, however, is no intellectual panacea. Studies of it alone cannot explain regime endurance if they are not part of a historically grounded analysis of governing coalitions; for the organization and interests of traditional elites, the rural poor, and governing coalitions are historically constituted and vary by country, as we have seen in Costa Rica and Guatemala. Moreover, studies of the countryside generally entail the difficult process of gathering, scouring, and analyzing comparative data that is often hard to come by. Nonetheless, the analysis presented here suggests that in the absence of assessing the rural bases of political regimes—the coalitions that direct them, the sectors that support them, and the forces that can disrupt them—we will not be able to explain the conditions under which newly founded regimes endure.

Demanding Democracy

This chapter has focused on regime endurance. It has argued that the failure of the contemporary regime literature to address the rural basis of regimes limits its ability not only to explain the conditions under which regimes are founded but also the conditions under which they can endure. This argument calls for future research to incorporate the politics of the countryside back into these studies, whether they focus on the coalitions that found regimes or the ones that are strong enough to sustain them.

But endurance is not always a morally preferable outcome. While the endurance of democratic regimes is a valuable and desirable end, the endurance of authoritarian regimes cannot be applauded. This is not least because efforts to control the countryside—whether successful or not—have all too often resulted in widespread human rights abuses. Recent events in Guatemala, El Salvador, Cambodia, Vietnam, and China offer vivid reminders of the atrocities that have been committed in the countryside as authoritarian governing coalitions have attempted to institutionalize their control. It is against this backdrop of repressive control of the countryside that demands for democracy remain most challenging.

Under what conditions, therefore, can actors found enduring democracies? The comparative historical analysis developed in this book suggests that without a publicly expressed division within the traditional elites over authoritarian practices, in conjunction with a rise in popular organization, prospects for a democratizing coalition in Guatemala, as elsewhere, appear dim. This same comparative historical analysis suggests that in the absence of diluting entrenched military and elite power and of incorporating the peasantry into a governing political party, democracies rarely endure.

Thus we return to the dilemma posed in Chapter 1: How can newly founded democracies endure if they inherit a powerful agrarian elite that is likely to be antagonistic to the procedures and the substance of democracy? Contrary to prevailing wisdom—that reform should come sequentially and slowly—the cases studied here suggest that new democracies endured when they implemented rapid and bounded redistributive reforms at the moment of political transition. Rapid reforms enabled democratizing coalitions to dilute economic power precisely when affected elites did not have the organizational capacity or political allies to challenge the new regime. Bounded reforms tempered and circumscribed elite opposition with the promise that the democratic regime would subsequently protect property rights and the elite's participation in the policy process. In sum, the failed and successful examples of reform analyzed here suggest that far-reaching social and economic reforms have been feasible precisely when they have been initiated in tandem with democratic transitions.

Yet many newly founded democracies in Latin America have failed to do precisely that. Rather than implement redistributive economic reforms that both weaken traditional elites and subordinate them to the rule of law, they have left rural structures—including authoritarian institutions and practices—largely intact. A promising round of research on states and citizenship has analyzed the obstacles to democracy in the contemporary Latin American countryside (Fox 1994a, and 1994b; O'Donnell 1993, and 1994). These studies reveal the varied ways in which democracy is practiced or subverted in rural areas. In many of these areas, states have limited institutional capacity and elites remain unaccountable. These are claims that resonate in many developing countries with recently founded democracies, as clientelism and patronage subvert democratic citizenship in rural areas. These studies have cautioned against smug and self-congratulatory remarks about democracy when its scope is largely circumscribed to urban areas. O'Donnell (1993) cautions that this kind of low-intensity citizenship can endure with national democratic institutions for a long time.

The conclusion here is different. This book concludes that the quality of democracy and the conditions for its endurance are related. The comparative historical study of Costa Rica and Guatemala suggests that the endurance of democracy in an age of mass politics requires governing coalitions to democratize the politics of the countryside. States need to penetrate the countryside and subvert traditional elites. They need to find mechanisms to incorporate the rural poor. And they need to sustain that support with access to political and economic resources. While rural citizenship might be low-intensity, it cannot be nonexistent. The study here poses the question as to whether national democratic regimes can endure in the absence of a concerted effort to incorporate the rural poor, to dilute traditional elite power over local government, and to create more capable democratic states. At the time of this writing, these are questions that Central American states face squarely as they negotiate the end to civil wars and attempt to consolidate the fragile social bases of democracy. As the Guatemalan military and guerilla forces negotiate an end to civil war, the ways in which they address these questions of power will affect not only the quality of the democracy that they seek to construct, but possibilities for it to endure.

Reference Matter

Notes

Chapter One

1. Collier and Collier (1991) and Scully (1992) draw on a large body of comparative historical studies. They begin with the premise that historical structures and institutions condition political choices and seek to explain the conditions under which political choices generate new institutional legacies. From this perspective, democracy and authoritarianism are explained as outcomes of historically constituted political paths. Moore (1966), Stinchcombe (1968), Rustow (1970), Skocpol (1979), Krasner (1982 and 1983), P. A. Hall (1986), Luebbert (1991), Rueschemeyer, Stephens, and Stephens (1992), and Putnam (1993), for example, have all highlighted the ways in which historical legacies (institutional, ideational, or cultural) shape contemporary politics. All of these authors view political development as a discontinuous process characterized by critical junctures and historical legacies; actors attempt to resolve politically salient conflicts at these critical junctures and, in the process, consolidate new political, economic, and social institutions. Thereafter, these institutions sustain a historical legacy by shaping as well as constraining subsequent action and discourse. The ability of actors to transform these institutions fundamentally occurs infrequently.

2. For discussions of the political violence in Guatemala, see Aguilera Peralta, Romero Imery, et al. (1981), Black (1984), Handy (1984), McClintock (1985), Aguilera Peralta (1988), Carmack (1988), Dunkerley (1988), Manz (1988), Smith (1990b), Jonas (1991), Bastos and Camus (1993), Trudeau (1993), Amnesty International (1993 and 1995).

3. There are some notable exceptions to this observation. Linz and Stepan (1978) argue that political leaders were largely responsible for democratic breakdowns. Moreover, some observers within the modernization tradition argue that a set of structural prerequisites is necessary for democracy.

4. See Osegueda (1955 and 1958), Cardoza y Aragón (1955a and 1955b), Toriello (1955), Bauer Paiz (1956), and Jonas and Tobis (1974) for arguments of this type. See Handy (1994) for a competing argument that begins with the premise that one cannot understand Guatemala's history through the lens of U.S. foreign policy or dependency theory.

5. See Bethell and Roxborough (1988) and R. Collier (1993) for a discussion of Latin America in the period immediately following World War II.

6. This definition of state building draws on Weber's (1946) classic definition of the state. For particularly suggestive theories of state building, see P. Anderson (1974) and Tilly (1985 and 1990) on Western Europe; Skowronek (1982) on the United States; and Migdal (1988) and Cohen, Brown, and Organski (1981) on what was once called the Third World.

7. See Polanyi (1944), Gerschenkron (1962), O'Donnell (1993), and Chaudhry (1993) for the argument that markets depend on state intervention and regulation.

8. A long tradition of scholars has concluded that the nature of elite power affects the types of political coalitions that are formed. Moore (1966), Gerschenkron (1962), Paige (1975), and Stephens (1989) typically argue that a system in which agriculture was labor repressive naturally forged a coalition between landowning elites and political or military elites that was difficult to dissolve and particularly inimical to democracy; see Huber and Safford (1995) for a reevaluation of this argument as it applies to Latin America. Downing (1992) has argued that where a strong military state developed, a military-elite alliance proved inimical to democratic regimes in early modern Europe. Those seeking explanations of policy making have also fruitfully adopted a coalitional perspective to explain the conditions under which certain policies are pursued and struggles over policy take place. In particular, see Lowi (1964), Hirschman (1965), Ascher (1984), Gourevitch (1986), Rogowski (1989), Katzenstein (1985), and Weir (1992: 194). This body of literature has insightfully delineated the ways in which political institutions, policy packaging, and crises points shape and often reshape the interests and, hence, coalitions that are likely to form. These authors, however, do not directly refer to the conditions leading to democratization as much as to the process of struggling over, adjudicating between, and choosing particular policy outcomes.

9. Luebbert (1991: 314) found a similar pattern with the rise of mass politics in Europe. Efforts by elites to restrict mass participation before the rise of mass organizations were widely unsuccessful. In fact, it was through the rise of mass organizations and debate about the social question that stabilizing democratic institutions were constructed in Europe.

10. Przeworski and the regulationists have argued that the primary class compromise in Europe is between capital and labor. In Latin America, this class compromise has appeared most viable when it has taken place between a divided oligarchic class and increasingly organized middle sectors, in the

context of an increasingly organized working class; see Collier and Collier (1991), and Rueschemeyer, Stephens, and Stephens (1992).

11. The classic argument about civil society and its relationship to democracy may be found in Tocqueville's (1969) discussion of the United States. An argument put forth during the 1960s, 1970s, and 1980s suggested that a hypermobilized civil society provokes political, economic, and military elites to topple democracy, because they fear the rising chaos, decline of profits, and so forth. See, for example, Huntington (1968) and O'Donnell (1973). See Keane (1988) and Cohen and Arato (1992) for excellent overviews and interpretations of the burgeoning literature on civil society.

12. Cited in Mainwaring, O'Donnell, and Valenzuela (1992: 13) in their introductory summary of Przeworski's argument in the same volume.

13. See Karl's (1986) discussion of Venezuela; Hagopian's (1990) discussion of Brazil.

14. The recent literature on democratization overwhelmingly suggests that one needs to consolidate democratic institutions and stabilize economies before one can look at what are often considered second-order questions of economic access and equity. Eastern European policy makers in the 1980s and early 1990s largely followed mainstream economists' advice that rapid stabilization, relatively rapid liberalization, and slow redistribution were the order of the day. The academic debate over the wisdom of this advice has flourished, as critics question the harshness of stabilization and liberalization measures. These scholars argue that such measures have negative effects both for the future of nascent democracies (because they weaken democratic institutions and faith in their administrative capacity) and for the direction of the economy. These critics, however, have not questioned the assumption that new democracies should wait before they push forward redistributive measures because, they contend, such measures will overburden budgets and polarize politics in ways that could precipitate a coup. See Przeworski (1991), Haggard and Kaufman (1992), Bresser Pereira, Maravall, and Przeworski (1993), Schmitter (1994). Also see collection of essays in *Journal of Democracy* (October 1994).

Chapter Two

1. By the end of the nineteenth century, Liberals had reassumed office throughout the Central American isthmus, beginning with Costa Rica (1870) and followed by Guatemala (1871), El Salvador (1871), Honduras (1876), and Nicaragua (1893). Throughout Latin America, Liberals had struggled with Conservatives to shape the roles and jurisdiction of newly independent states, the appropriate types of markets for and political mechanisms of growth, and the appropriate spaces for civic participation.

2. Costa Rican coffee production began almost four decades prior to the Liberal reforms. Consequently, whereas the Guatemalan Liberal reforms initiated and consolidated the development of coffee as the basis of agrarian

capitalism, the Costa Rican Liberal reforms promoted and consolidated an already-developing coffee export economy. However, as discussed in Chapter 2, the Liberal reforms in both cases reinforced the ability of the respective elites to accumulate capital in the coffee economy. Consequently, this chapter focuses on the interaction of the Liberal reforms with regimes of accumulation rather than arguing that it was the sequencing of coffee production and state reform that explains the different political outcomes.

3. See Jessop (1990b) for his review of the literature on regimes of accumulation. Also see Lipietz (1989: 1–3) for a particularly clear overview of what constitutes a regime of accumulation.

4. Paige (1987: 151) also argues that one needs to look at the different forms of capital accumulation and labor control as a way to delineate, first, the different bases of economic, political, and social power of the coffee elites and class relations; second, the role, the growth, and increasing autonomy of the state in promoting agrarian capitalism and in shaping and/or inhibiting the growth of civil society; and third, state-society relations. Coffee elites seeking to compete on the international market confronted four problems that the Liberal governments sought to address: "1) acquisition and control over land, 2) organization and rationalization of production, 3) mechanization and finance of processing, and 4) finance of and control over exports" (Paige 1987: 144). In the process, Liberals constructed and/or consolidated varied regimes of capital accumulation and labor control.

5. Paige (1975) made a similar observation in his study of agrarian conflict.

6. The argument developed in this chapter challenges two prevailing analyses of the 1930s. The first contends that a dramatic *regime change* occurred throughout nearly all of Central America during this decade, the second that Costa Rica followed a *different* pattern from the rest of the isthmus. Regarding the first point, Baloyra Herp (1983) and Bulmer-Thomas (1987) have argued that new caudillo regimes emerged in the 1930s to replace the Liberal oligarchic states. This chapter argues, however, in accord with Woodward (1985: 215), that practices adopted in the 1930s paralleled those employed by nineteenth-century Liberal reformers. With regard to the second point, Baloyra Herp (1983), Bulmer-Thomas (1987), and Woodward (1985) all argue that Costa Rica followed a different pattern from that of the rest of the isthmus. Indeed, Costa Rica did not install a dictator. This chapter illustrates, however, that Costa Rica followed a pattern similar to that of the rest of the isthmus. It adopted political measures in the 1930s that, in fact, derived from Liberal political institutions and practices established in the late nineteenth and early twentieth centuries.

7. The initial Liberal victory gave way to divisions within the Liberal camp. García Granados assumed political leadership in 1871 and spoke for the new merchant class. The merchants hoped to do away with the commercial privileges extended by Conservatives to the more established commercial elite and to liberalize trade. They did not seek substantial social and economic change but, in fact, hoped to work with the Conservatives whom

they had defeated (Kauck 1988: 145; McCreery 1994: 172–73). Barrios, who had engineered the military victory, mobilized a different coalition—coffee farmers from the western provinces and urban and middle-class sectors—which sought rapid legislation to "modernize the economy," regardless of Conservative demands. The group that had mobilized behind Barrios did not want to adopt a conciliatory position with Conservatives, whom they felt had legislated unnecessary commercial and political restrictions; nor did they seek to undermine the latter's economic livelihood. Rather, this second group of Liberals called for active state intervention, cheap land and labor, and credit. Confronted with the threat of another military uprising by the opposing Liberal faction, García Granados acquiesced to elections in 1873 and was defeated by Barrios (Cambranes 1985: 247; Dunkerley 1988: 25; McCreery 1994: 173).

8. This was not the first time that Guatemalan Liberals had expelled the archbishop. Following independence in 1821, the archbishop had gone into exile and religious orders were expelled. These earlier Liberals also assumed responsibility for overseeing the rituals associated with marriage, birth, and death, and, as they would in the 1870s, they confiscated church lands (McCreery 1994: 132–33).

9. There is little dispute over measures to improve the training, capacity, and presence of the Guatemalan military, yet surprisingly little is written about it. My efforts to secure materials from the archives at the Escuela Politécnica were thwarted in 1989 and 1990. State documents issued on the centennial of the school's founding present its basic chronology but provide little exact data or comparative analysis of the military.

10. Guatemalan elites in the first half of the nineteenth century had primarily produced the raw materials for the dyes indigo and cochineal. The latter is brilliant red, produced from female cochineal insects grown on the nopal cactus, then crushed.

11. Prior to the Liberal period, the state licensed a private firm, the Consulado de Comercio, to build and maintain infrastructure. Apparently cochineal producers dominated the Consulado; they had considered the existing roads sufficient for the transport of cochineal and found little reason to spend limited monies on building infrastructure to facilitate the transport (and indirectly the expansion) of coffee (McCreery 1994: 170).

12. This land reform did not initially have a substantial effect on the highlands where the majority of the Indian population lived, except for parts of Huehuetenango, Quiché, the Verapaces, and Chiquimula (Pérez Brignoli 1989: 84; McCreery 1990: 107). It is difficult, however, to assess the exact impact of these decrees (Dunkerley 1988: 27–28; McCreery 1990: 97) because the figures available are incomplete and, thus, do not accurately reflect net losses by communities and/or individuals. McCreery (1990, and 1994, ch. 8), who has assiduously researched land tenure in Guatemala, cautions us, therefore, not to describe what happened in the late nineteenth century in apocalyptic terms.

13. Guatemala's land area is about 26,906,880 acres, an estimated 42,042 square miles, or an estimated 109,000 square kilometers (Stone 1982: 27; Dunkerley 1991: 119).

14. The coffee plantations used labor only on a seasonal basis. Therefore it was to the coffee elites' advantage for indigenous communities to possess the resources to sustain themselves during the non–harvest period, to reproduce future seasonal labor, and to produce food for domestic consumption. The law encouraged political leaders to ensure that municipalities that had historically relied on communal property maintained sufficient communal lands for these purposes, particularly if there was competition for this land. Consequently, at times the local authorities helped poor communities to acquire more land (McCreery 1983: 739, and 1990: 106–7). Leaving the communal lands in the hands of the communities, however, was not a functionally determined outcome. The exploitation of agricultural populations can take many forms; indeed, the plantation owners could have turned the majority of the labor force into sharecroppers or tenants-at-will on the remaining land, or forced the peasant population to become increasingly dependent on them for subsistence throughout the rest of the year. One way of explaining the particular form that labor exploitation took in Guatemala is to highlight the fear of Indian rebellion. Liberal (and Conservative) leaders feared that if they confiscated communal lands they would incite rebellion. Related to this is the likelihood that creole landowners preferred geographical segregation except during the harvest, when indigenous peasant labor was called for. I thank Arun Swamy for his insight into this matter.

15. DZA Potsdam, A.A., No. 12436, Bergen to Bulow, Nov. 15, 1877, cited in Cambranes 1985: 302.

16. As discussed in Chapter 1, I do not elaborate on the United States' near monopoly in the banana industry, shipping, and railways, because it does not contribute to the argument of regime trajectories. Guatemalan dictator Estrada Cabrera extended concessions to the railroad that included, among other things, monopoly rights over rail service, a 99-year tax exemption, and free land. The Guatemalan Liberals extended further concessions to the United Fruit Company in 1924, 1930, and 1936. By the 1930s substantial international capital investment had created a U.S.-owned banana enclave in both countries; in Guatemala the United States also came to own and control basic infrastructure, including railroads, electrical plants, and ports. This chapter focuses, however, on the development and organization of the domestic coffee economy, which dominated exports in Guatemala and Costa Rica through the mid-twentieth century. The organization of coffee production had a substantial impact on the nature of the Liberal oligarchic state, rural class relations, and the formation of the mid-twentieth-century coalitions and reform periods. The U.S.-owned banana enclaves have been studied extensively; for an overview, see Handy (1984: 78–88), Skidmore and Smith (1984), Woodward (1985: 177–214), Dunkerley (1988), Edelman and Kenen (1989: 52–54), Chomsky (1990), Dosal (1993). For further discussion see Kepner and Soothill (1949), León Aragón (1950), and May and Plaza (1958).

17. The legislation of forced wage labor was not new. Nineteenth-century labor legislation fluctuated between the abolition and reinstatement of various forms of forced labor. Both 1820s Liberals and mid-nineteenth-century Conservatives had employed forced wage labor. Popular resistance and non-systematic implementation, however, had curtailed its effectiveness and scope. With the boom in cochineal production in the mid-nineteenth century, the resort to forced labor had lapsed (McCreery 1983: 741, and 1994, chs. 3–4, 180–81). The late-nineteenth-century Liberal reforms, however, created a more coercive labor market in response to coffee-elite demands for guaranteed access to labor. The resulting systems of forced labor did not include poor ladinos as part of this labor reserve, unlike those of prior governments. Indeed, the reforms reinforced the segmented labor market whereby rural workers were predominantly indigenous (McCreery 1983 and 1990; Dunkerley 1988: 26). See Gordon, Edwards, and Reich (1982) for a discussion of segmented labor markets.

18. Quote from *Recopilación de las leyes emitidas por el gobierno democrático de la república de Guatemala por la Asamblea Nacional Legislativa*, 1881, vol. 1, pp. 457–58, cited in McCreery (1976: 456). The experience of land-labor legislation coupled with indigenous resistance to assimilation prevented the homogenization of Guatemalan cultures desired by Liberal intellectuals (Palmer 1990, ch. 6).

19. For a discussion of Decrees 177 (1877) and 243 (1894), see McCreery (1983: 742–43); Handy (1984: 66–67); Cambranes (1985: 183); Pérez Brignoli (1985: 76–77); Dunkerley (1988: 26–29). Barrios legislated the first comprehensive rural labor code, Decree 177, on April 3, 1877. Decree 177 contained measures that resurrected debt peonage and obliged communities to provide temporary work for the plantations. The decree elaborated one kind of resident worker and two kinds of day workers. It also regulated the rights and responsibilities of, as well as the relationship between, the plantation owner, resident workers, and day workers. Military service or forced work in public projects awaited those who could not pay taxes or were not indebted.

20. Debt was incurred through various mechanisms. Labor contractors, called *habilitadores*, traveled to indigenous communities to lend money when crops were scarce and during religious festivals. When most of these peasants could not generate enough capital to pay these "loans," they were forced to work on the plantations to pay their debts. Labor contractors took responsibility not only for the peasants incurring debt but also for assuring the arrival of the indebted to the plantations. They were accountable to the plantation owners and at times had to absorb the cost of those who did not arrive. *Habilitadores*, therefore, worked closely with police forces to track down those who were committed to debt peonage or those who had fled. Plantation owners also indebted highland peasants with the *fincas de mozos*, leasing portions of land in the highlands to campesinos in return for their wage labor in the coffee piedmont during the harvest season. This practice was not widespread and little is known about it (Dunkerley 1988: 28–29).

21. The oligarchy sought to secure seasonal labor at harvest time, leaving

the coffee worker responsible for him- or herself, and relieving the coffee planters of the expense of supporting their workers with a living wage, the rest of the year. Consequently, Guatemala developed a "classic" minifundio-latifundio relationship. Coffee dominated Guatemala's exports in 1920 but claimed about one-fifth of the total cultivated land mass. Corn grown largely for domestic consumption claimed, by contrast, one-half the total cultivated land mass (McCreery 1994: 201).

22. President José María Reyna Barrios revised the rural labor laws in 1893 and 1894. This second round of labor legislation abolished the system of conscripted labor gangs in May 1894 with Decree 243. The measures contained in this decree maintained that those who could demonstrate employment on another plantation were exempt from labor on the public-works projects and/or from serving in the military. The measure also exempted peasants with land sufficient to pay real-estate taxes, literate Indians who promised to abandon their indigenous ethnic identity, or anyone who could pay 15 pesos every year to the state (McCreery 1983: 743; Cambranes 1985: 224, 228).

23. See Scott (1990) for a discussion of everyday forms of resistance.

24. In the 1926 election, in which the Liberal Party had been divided, Ubico ran with the support of the progressive youth and student faction. After his loss, he distanced himself from this sector and ran in the 1931 race with the support of the oligarchy. Subsequently, he enacted measures that betrayed the goals of the students. Throughout the course of his dictatorship, he made clear his loathing for intellectuals and workers.

25. There is remarkably little written on Manuel Estrada Cabrera. See *El Señor Presidente*, a novel by Miguel Angel Asturias (1988), which describes the pervasive and perverse social control during the Cabrera period.

26. Ubico steered Guatemala out of the Great Depression by using the most orthodox economic policies in the region, including balancing the budget and reducing public employment in various sectors such as finance and customs. In Guatemala, and in El Salvador, wages were cut by 30 percent (Dunkerley 1988: 92–93). Ubico also developed a General Directory of Banks in October 1931 in order to create a centralized, uniform, systematic apparatus that could coordinate, investigate, and plan the operations of various financial institutions. He sought also to provide credit and ensure bank deposits in order to promote financial stability, create faith in the financial institutions and markets, and increase monetary circulation. Through measures such as these, Ubico balanced the budget, maintained monetary stability, and paid off outstanding government debts (Grieb 1979: 59–60; Dunkerley 1988: 92–93; Gleijeses 1989a: 31; McCreery 1994: 314–16).

27. Those who did not cultivate any land of their own were required to work 150 days out of the year on a plantation; those who cultivated less than one and five-sixteenths of a *manzana* of their own had to work for 100 days out of the year on a plantation (Grieb 1979: 39; McCreery 1983: 757, and 1994: 316–22).

28. Ubico extended the advantageous terms of a previous contract established by Estrada Cabrera and suspended UFCO's contract obligations to the Guatemalan state (Grieb 1979, ch. 12). Ubico also cancelled UFCO's obligations, as contracted in 1930, to build a Pacific port and accompanying rail facilities in exchange for a few agreements that clearly benefited the United Fruit Company.

29. See Grieb (1979: 184–87) for a description of the contract and terms negotiated and renegotiated in 1924, 1930, and 1936. By 1934, UFCO claimed title to 3.5 million acres of Guatemalan land; it cultivated fewer than 115,000 acres (Handy 1984: 82; Woodward 1985).

30. See Vega Carballo (1981: 308) for the distribution of public expenses between 1890 and 1930.

31. Guardia's successor, General Próspero Fernández Oreamuno, persecuted the Catholic Church with authorization from Congress. In subsequent years, the government and media challenged the Church's control over education, marriage, and burials. Fernández Oreamuno expelled Bishop Thiel and the Jesuits. Moreover, he oversaw the secularization of cemeteries, prohibition of religious education as well as religious and monastic orders, the derogation of the *Concordato*, the outlawing of alms collection without government authorization, and restrictions on religious processions. Three years later, the state legalized divorce and civil marriages (Oconitrillo 1981: 12; Stone 1982: 267; Salazar 1987a: 96; P. Williams 1989: 101). Philip Williams (1989: 101) contends that these decrees grew out of personal animosities between General Fernández Oreamuno and the bishop and the Jesuits rather than anticlerical positions articulated by the Liberals. Animosity certainly existed. Nonetheless, anticlerical behavior was consistent with the tenets of Liberalism, and similar, if harsher, measures were implemented elsewhere. Indeed, religious opposition to these reforms resulted in the formation of the Partido Unión Católica del Clero, which ran in municipal and legislative elections in the early 1880s. Anticlerical sentiment found expression even after the government of Fernández Oreamuno, as evidenced by the presidential election of Rafael Iglesias Castro (1894–1902) whose Partido Civilista was unabashedly Liberal and anticlerical. And, in 1895, the Congress responded by passing a constitutional reform prohibiting the invocation of religious justification in political campaigns. This reform attacked the very rationale of the short-lived Partido Unión Católica del Clero (Oconitrillo 1981: 22–27).

32. Cited in Edelman and Kenen (1989: 58). Echoing Rodrigo Facio, Vega Carballo (1981: 251, 265–68) argues that Guardia's success in undermining other military coup attempts and power bases created the basis for a democratic resurgence. This position is hard to sustain. It rests on a mythology of Costa Rica's prior democratic history. Moreover, it is not entirely clear why a dictator's success in routing his military competitors would lead to a democratic resurgence. Alternatively, one could argue that it reinforced a practice of resorting to military power to consolidate political power.

33. Archivos Nacionales de Costa Rica, Congreso Constitucional 19570, *Acuerdo* 3, August 24, 1940. Also see Vega Carballo (1981) and Muñoz Guillén (1990).

34. Costa Rica did not develop a strong or vital economy prior to the introduction of coffee agriculture. Despite Costa Rica's name, "rich coast," the country's agriculture before the mid-nineteenth century had not successfully produced or exported any particular crop. See MacLeod (1973); I. Cohen (1980); C. Hall (1982: 34); Stone (1982); Dunkerley (1988: 21); and Winson (1989).

35. See Polanyi's (1944) classic discussion of the role of the state in shaping markets. See Chaudhry (1993) for a contemporary discussion of Polanyi and the role of the state in constructing markets in the developing world.

36. The absence of a comparatively strong oligarchy prior to the introduction of coffee cultivation has contributed to divergent interpretations and a rather vitriolic debate within Costa Rican historiography about the nature of socioeconomic stratification prior to the introduction of coffee. Traditional historiography has promulgated the notion that Costa Rica's pre-coffee political economy was a rural democracy characterized by equitable land distribution worked by yeoman farmers. Costa Rican and U.S. authors who have promoted this general view include, among others, Rodrigo Facio Brenes, Eugenio Rodríguez Vega, Carlos Monge Alfaro, and Mitchell Seligson. See Gudmundson (1986a: 173–78) for an excellent summary of the different positions on this debate. These scholars blame the introduction of coffee, in one way or another, for undermining equitable economic relations. They maintain that coffee production heightened the concentration of landholdings and increased the number of landless peasants, a process similar to that in Guatemala. Revisionist historians have convincingly demonstrated that traditional references to Costa Rica's historical rural democracy are not based on fact and belie Costa Rica's pre-coffee inequalities, comparatively mild though they were. According to this second approach, pre-coffee Costa Rica was not an egalitarian society that the coffee economy later subverted and destroyed. Costa Rican and foreign historians, including Mario Samper and Lowell Gudmundson, have individually questioned that view and have argued that the introduction of coffee did not subvert an ideal rural democracy for which there is little evidence but, rather, initially advanced the more equitable land tenure and wages that traditional historians had attributed to the pre-coffee era. Only later, in the nineteenth and twentieth centuries, did coffee production lead to an economic decline for the vast number of Costa Rican peasants and wage laborers. Coffee, therefore, did not destroy a rural democracy of land tenure. Nonetheless, the initial success of coffee production did lead to a changed conception of land and property rights. With the development of coffee, land assumed the characteristic of property invested with capital and labor. Land values increased almost twentyfold over a 30-year period, reaching higher levels than in the other Central American countries (Dunkerley 1988: 22). Throughout the nineteenth century Costa Rica experienced a steady privatization of previously unclaimed or unsettled

lands (Acuña Ortega 1986: 53). Robert Williams (1994: 41–53), citing unpublished data gathered by Mario Samper, observes that the areas with the greatest land concentration coincided with those areas that had had more inequitable land tenure during the colonial period.

37. The introduction of coffee cultivation and the subsequent growth of a related economic elite in Costa Rica in the mid-1800s occurred with relatively minimal conflict, insofar as coffee production did not strategically challenge patterns of land use or spark a struggle between relative traditional and commercial elites, as it did in Guatemala and in El Salvador. In the 1820s and 1830s, Costa Rica's weak state assumed an ad hoc role to facilitate coffee growers' acquisition of *terrenos baldíos* (public or waste lands) free of charge, as well as their cheap purchase of other public lands (C. Cardoso 1977: 170). Municipal governments took the lead in promoting access to land (R. Williams 1994: 44). In 1821, the Municipality of San José decided to distribute free land to those who said that they would grow coffee. This led to an outward migration of potential laborers from the *meseta central* to regions outside of the central province, a pattern that contrasted with that in Guatemala, where the state often confiscated lands and regulated labor flows. In 1825 Costa Rica's central government exempted producers from paying the *diezmo*, a tithe, for coffee and other products, and later abolished it for all crops (C. Cardoso 1977; Hall 1982: 35). Carolyn Hall (1982: 35) notes that following independence from Spain, municipal governments initially assumed an unwitting if active role in promoting the production of coffee; these initial efforts—tax exemptions and efforts to give away land in outlying regions—applied to many crops besides coffee (C. Hall 1982: 36). In 1831, the government declared that those who cultivated certain products—including coffee, sugar, cotton, cacao, yucca, and bananas—on state lands would become the owners of that land after five years (Stone 1982: 78, 133; C. Hall 1982: 35–36). In 1832, the government agreed to subsidize some coffee growers (C. Cardoso 1977: 170). The government also passed a series of land grants and homestead acts encouraging outward migration from the central valley (Seligson 1975; C. Cardoso 1977: 172; Samper 1990: 53; Edelman 1992: 168–75).

38. Figures calculated from C. Cardoso 1977: 172, Table 3.

39. Samper (1990), however, cautions against the idea that all land became dedicated to coffee cultivation.

40. In Costa Rica, processors employed sophisticated technology and machinery, which surpassed those used in Guatemala, and employed the "wet method," which required larger capital investment (Paige 1987; Winson 1989: 21). Processing in Costa Rica tended to be geographically separate from the production process, which emphasized the differentiation of economic power between small and large producers versus the processors (C. Hall 1982; Stone 1982; Paige 1987: 174). In Guatemala, by contrast, the coffee oligarchy created a vertically integrated economy; those with large landholdings developed their own *beneficios*, physically concentrating the entire production process from planting to harvest to processing. The Guatemalan pro-

246 *Notes to Pages 63–70*

cessing operation was not only linked to production but also employed a less sophisticated, labor-intensive, processing method (Paige 1987: 169–81).

41. See Carlos Luis Fallas's classic novel, *Mamita Yunai*, for a firsthand discussion of the organizing efforts for the banana strike and the ensuing government repression.

42. Costa Rica, like El Salvador, responded to the Depression by implementing a heterodox rather than orthodox set of policy initiatives, including debt default, debt moratoria, and exchange-rate depreciation (Bulmer-Thomas 1987: 83). Costa Rica's economic response included state intervention to counter the macroeconomic crisis as well as to moderate rising rural conflict between the small and medium-sized producers versus the processors, exporters, and financiers of coffee. Costa Rica sought, as did Guatemala, to bolster the basis for coffee production, but the Costa Rican response was not as coercive. Whereas Guatemala engaged in budgetary balancing, Costa Rica's budget deficit continued to rise (Vega Carballo 1986: 316). And, whereas Guatemala created institutions to repress and suppress rural conflict, Costa Rica largely built state institutions to moderate conflict. The Liberal regime also cut wages by 15 percent, although President Jiménez did set a minimum wage in the early 1930s (Stone 1982: 298). These stabilizing economic measures coincided with a commitment of resources to increasing public works. Public-work expenditures more than tripled between 1932 and 1939 (Bulmer-Thomas 1987: 71). The regime also renewed projects for infrastructure development in the 1930s, although not to the same degree Guatemala had.

43. IDECAFE represented the Costa Rican oligarchy in international negotiations that attempted to address plummeting coffee prices following the Brazilian government's announcement it would no longer regulate its coffee industry against overproduction. IDECAFE also helped to alleviate problems resulting from the outbreak of World War II and the contraction of markets (C. Hall 1982: 154).

44. See Goodwin and Skocpol (1989), who argue that organizing revolutionary multiclass coalitions is, at one level, easier in situations where there is what they call neo-patrimonial rule, as was the case in Guatemala in the 1930s. In Costa Rica, by contrast, the existence of formal democratic procedures, despite an antidemocratic context, inhibited the development of a multiclass coalition composed of the middle and working classes. I elaborate on this point in the next chapter.

Chapter 3

1. See Bethell and Roxborough (1988, and 1992) for a thorough and concise statement of this position. R. Collier (1993) highlights the primacy of domestic factors, particularly the incorporation of labor, to explain political trajectories in Latin America. See Rock (1994) for an edited volume presenting different positions on this debate.

2. The dominant position in the democratization literature of the 1980s,

represented by O'Donnell and Schmitter (1986), argues that one needs to look at the emergence of hardliners and softliners in the state and in civil society. If hardliners in the state ally with moderates in the civic opposition, democratization is more likely. While the argument I develop in this chapter shares the idea that one needs to look at coalition politics, it differs in the following ways. First, I analyze the class composition of the coalitions that emerge and stress that democratization could not occur in the face of elite unity. Second, I situate this discussion in its historically embedded context, stressing the ways in which regimes of accumulation shaped policy conflicts, how the prior state response to rural conflict shaped coalition partners, and how the depth of civil society influenced counterreform outcomes. Third, I analyze the ways in which the balance of power within the coalition shaped the stability of the reform coalition and the scope of subsequent reforms.

3. Despite the development of civil and political society in Costa Rica and its near absence in Guatemala, it is difficult to deduce from these conditions the stability versus fluidity of reform coalitions. While it seems logical and likely that the lack of a Guatemalan civil society during the Liberal period would explain the fluidity of its political coalitions during the reform period, as its political parties and civil society began to develop, it seems harder to argue that the stability of the Costa Rican alliance does derive from a more developed civil society.

4. While it is widely acknowledged that Calderón did not support Otto Cortés, the source of his hostility with former president Cortés and his son remains unclear. See, for example, Rodríguez V. (1980: 35), who was a student political activist of the time and is now a Costa Rican intellectual. Also see Lehoucq (1992: 165–66), who cites U.S. State Department records, and Creedman (1971: 88–112). They argue that while Cortés had supported Calderón in the prior election, his support had been lukewarm; at the end of 1940, a rumor floated that Calderón would dismiss Cortés's relatives who held political office or force them to resign; five did lose office.

5. In Calderón's first year of office, he did not act against the population of German descent. Schifter (1986, ch. 3) notes that Calderón himself had made antisemitic statements.

6. A signal that Calderón would side with the Allies against the Axis powers occurred in the spring of 1941. Costa Rica had recently signed international treaties that dictated that Axis ships in the ports of signatories should be confiscated. When a German and an Italian ship docked in Costa Rica in April of that year, the crews learned that the Costa Rican government intended to comply with the treaties. In response to this news, the Axis crews set these two ships on fire, then blamed the Costa Rican government for arson. As a result, pro-Nazi propaganda in Costa Rica increased. Efforts to diminish the tension and to end the conflict as quickly as possible led to an informal agreement to save face for all involved, which rested on the decision to send the German and Italian crews to Japan. However, without Costa Rican consent, they ended up in the United States. The German government and population subsequently became more actively hostile to the Calderón

government. Following the ship incident, rapprochement increased between Costa Rica and the United States while antagonism increased between the Costa Rican government and the German nationals living in Costa Rica (Schifter 1986: 126–35).

7. Nazi sympathizers had attained some influence in the Costa Rican government and economy during León Cortés's administration (Schifter 1986: 57; Cerdas Cruz 1991: 281–82). Germans influenced some areas of policy making, such as the successful pursuit of antisemitic legislation, particularly in the areas of commerce and immigration. Following the outbreak of World War II, the Nazi party in Costa Rica, led by Karl Bayer and Max Effinger, claimed approximately 50 members (Schifter 1986, ch. 3; Cerdas Cruz 1991).

8. Few studies of this time period refer to the fate of Costa Ricans of Italian and Japanese descent. These communities were smaller and less economically powerful than the Germans, who held key positions in finance, commerce, export, and processing.

9. Whereas Cortés, the outgoing president, seemed to have left Costa Rica fiscally sound, the first few years of Calderón's administration were stricken with financial difficulties. There are contradictory estimates about the state of the economy in the last years of Cortés's government; some argue that there was a fiscal surplus equaling about one-tenth of government revenues. Indeed, there were fiscal surpluses throughout Central America in these years (Bulmer-Thomas 1987: 96–97). Schifter (1986: 107–8) argues, however, that even if there was an increase in export earnings, they parallelled an increase in government spending such that Calderón, in fact, inherited a debt of 2,239,100.43 colones in 1940. Regardless of whether or not Cortés left the fiscal house in order, there is agreement that under Calderón's administration, Costa Rica, in contrast to the rest of the region, did not run a fiscal surplus and experienced high inflation.

10. See Edelman and Kenen (1989: 74–76) for a reprint of the Communist Party's 1932 minimum program.

11. Quote from Manuel Mora, cited in Contreras and Cerdas (1988: 47).

12. Alicia Cerdas's grandfather had been an Italian anarchist who had traveled to Costa Rica to work on the railroad. Her father, by contrast, was a prominent politician in the official party, Partido Republicano Nacional. Interview with Alicia Cerdas, July 7, 1990.

13. By 1937, the Costa Rican CP's platform in fact coincided with the Comintern line: nationalism; nonviolence; improving the economic and political situation of urban and rural workers.

14. See Ferreto (1984) for an autobiographical discussion of his role in the communist party from the 1930s through the early 1950s.

15. The Costa Rican communists had adopted the popular front strategy in the late 1930s, but its use was interrupted by the announcement of the Hitler-Stalin pact in 1939. After the 1941 invasion of Russia by Germany, however, antifascist forces allied once again to revive the popular front strategy.

16. For references to this alleged coup and the populist alliance that grew out of it, see Aguilar Bulgarelli (1983: 55–66, 489–91); Contreras and Cerdas (1988: 84–114). This story originates with Manuel Mora, who recounted it in a July 28, 1990, interview.

17. Not everyone who remained in the ruling party, however, sanctioned this informal alliance between the PRN and the CP. For example, in the beginning of 1943, the secretary of education tried to prevent the distribution of the communist party newspaper to the public libraries, a clear affront to an alleged friend of the ruling party and government (Contreras and Cerdas 1988: 96).

18. Calderón's statement may be found in Soto Harrison (1991: 49–50).

19. Each letter has been reprinted in Soto Harrison (1991: 85–91).

20. *La Tribuna*, June 20, 1943, cited in Rodríguez V. (1980: 77).

21. Mora indicated that Teodoro Picado, the president of the legislature and Calderón's chosen "heir" for the presidency, sought to distance himself from the communists; Picado had hoped to regain capitalist support that Calderón had definitively lost. In 1943, Picado attempted to reform the electoral law so that the responsibility for scrutinizing the votes for president would be transferred from the *juntas receptoras* to the Congress (Rodríguez V. 1980: 70–72). The communist party, the (upper-) middle-class Centro, and the elite opposition rallied against this reform law, suspicious of the increased room for fraud. Mora argued that Picado sought to assure his victory without having to sustain relations with the communist party or to promote additional social reforms; the elite opposition thought Picado's move was to assure Cortés's loss. Picado failed to reform the electoral law and, subsequently, accepted the reform alliance with the communist PVP.

22. Rodríguez V. (1980: 82–83), citing information taken from the *Diario de Costa Rica*, Sept. 24, 1943.

23. See Creedman (1971: 253–63) for an account of the violence that occurred around the 1944 elections.

24. See Scott (1990) and Corradi, Fagen, and Garretón (1992) for discussions of the varied ways in which, and places where, people organize when confronted with fear.

25. From Carlos Samayoa Chinchilla, *El Dictador y Yo*, cited by Dunkerley (1991: 126).

26. For a discussion of how the Salvadoran uprising influenced the Guatemalan students, see Morales de la Cruz (1944: 11–12); Oscar de León Aragón's article in *El Imparcial*, (Oct. 26, 1945); Galich (1977: 244–59).

27. Germans had assumed a predominant role among coffee producers in Guatemala (and Costa Rica). By the end of the nineteenth century they owned the largest and most productive coffee-producing lands, totaling one-quarter of all coffee plantations and generating about two-thirds of the country's coffee production and an even greater percentage of exports (Paige 1987: 150). While the percentage of estates owned by Germans declined in the early twentieth century (to just under 10 percent in 1913), by the 1920s they still controlled four of the six largest coffee operations and accounted for

35.8 million pounds (or roughly 68 percent) out of total coffee exports of 52.5 million pounds (Handy 1984: 66; Dunkerley 1988: 29; McCreery 1994: 233–34). The increasingly powerful German coffee plantation owners did not really intermingle with the Guatemalan coffee elites but remained an introverted economic, political, and social group (Handy 1984: 66). Most maintained their German citizenship. They created networks that until the 1940s controlled a good part of the economic operations in the capital as well as most economic transactions in Alta Verapaz.

28. Ubico had always felt antipathy for Germans and had considered Hitler a peasant, although he sympathized with and praised the fascist regimes in Italy and Spain (Grieb 1979: 249); Guatemala was the first country officially to recognize Franco's Spain. Nonetheless, the administration had denied registration in 1934 to the National Socialist Party. It had temporarily closed down a German school in 1935, claiming that it used propaganda in the curriculum (Grieb 1979: 250). Later, Ubico severely restricted and monitored foreigners' ability to maneuver in Guatemala and stripped them of the right to hold dual citizenship (Grieb 1979: 255): "A frequently repeated story in Guatemala City was that even if the Germans managed to organize a fifth column in the country, it would not matter, since General Ubico had a firm control of the other four columns" (Grieb 1979: 254).

29. See Huntington (1991: 120–21) for an overview of dictators who tried to remain in power in the late 1970s and 1980s but either died in office, were overthrown, or lost an election that they believed they would win.

30. Gleijeses (1991: 26), citing U.S. archival documents from Ambassador Long to the secretary of state.

31. The military academy, or Escuela Politécnica, had a series of foreign directors, including a U.S. officer in the 1930s. The symbolism of U.S. influence over Guatemala was not lost on a generation of Guatemalan nationalists, which sought to decrease U.S. influence over important issue areas in the economy and polity. These nationalists never really attempted, however, to decrease U.S. influence over the Escuela Politécnica.

32. AEU students, the reform party Frente Popular Libertador (FPL), and professional groups had attempted to organize a nationwide general strike in conjunction with simultaneous uprisings throughout the country as a means to overthrow the regime. The police discovered this plan and arrested those involved (Petersen 1969: 87; Interview with Anonymous A, Jan. 31, 1990, a 1940s activist and later a distinguished diplomat who preferred to remain anonymous).

33. Petersen 1969: 87; Grieb 1976: 540; Handy 1984: 104–6; Albizures 1989a: 43; Gleijeses 1991: 28–29, also based on Toriello nd.; Interview with Paz Tejada, Aug. 11, 18, 1990; Interview with Jorge Toriello, Mar. 30, 1994.

34. Ubico left Guatemala for the United States after the October Revolution. Upon his departure, he was certain that the Guatemalan people would call for his return. He died two years later, in 1946, in the United States. In 1963, his body was returned to Guatemala for burial (Grieb 1979: 278).

35. Anti-Arévalo political forces tried to discredit his campaign by claim-

ing that while in Argentina he had been a fascist. Pictures of him campaigning with a fascist-like salute were clever political ploys, but the claims remained unsubstantiated. Some of these pictures can be found in AGCA, Hermeroteca, *Hojas Sueltas*, 1944.

36. In the 1944 presidential elections, for example, the parties and university student association formed an electoral front, Frente Unido de Partidos y Asociaciones Cívicas Independientes, which included the Frente Popular Libertador (FPL), Renovación Nacional (RN), Partido Centroamericanista, Concordia Centroamericana, Unión Cívica, and the Asociación de Estudiantes Universitarios (AEU) (Petersen 1969: 89–90). The 1944 electoral coalition was the most cohesive one formed during the reform period insofar as there was near universal support within reform circles for Arévalo, who had come to represent the move from authoritarianism to democracy. Similarly, the reform parties formed an electoral coalition for the 1950 presidential elections in which Jacobo Arbenz Guzmán won. The front included the Partido de Integridad Nacional (PIN), which had launched his campaign, Partido de Acción Revolucionaria (PAR), Renovación Nacional (RN), Partido Comunista (PC), Partido de la Revolución Guatemalteca (PRG),part of the FPL, and the Comité Político de los Trabajadores (Gutiérrez Alvarez 1985: 186–87).

37. The FPL, for example, was one of the first reform parties; however, it sometimes sidestepped informal congressional alliances and voted with the opposition. In the 1950 presidential elections, the FPL was the only reform party that did not support Arbenz's presidential candidacy (Handy 1985: 122–23, 146). PIN, FPL, RN, and the Partido Socialista (PS) refused to enter into an alliance with the PGT. Handy (1985: 179) writes that attempts at coalition building between the reform parties (1951–52) often collapsed over issues of communism: "Most often these [attempts] floundered on the shores of anti-communist feeling on the part of the PIN, FPL, and sometimes the RN and the Socialist Party. These parties steadfastly refused to join a coalition which included the Communist party." Yet despite this conflict among the reform parties it became increasingly apparent in 1952, once the rural sector had become mobilized, that these reform parties needed to provide a more united front to implement the reforms as well as to ward off the threat of an opposition coup. In this spirit, the PAR, PS, RN, FPL, and PIN dissolved themselves and formed a new party, the Partido de la Revolución Guatemalteca (PRG) in July 1952; but by the end of the month the PAR and RN had left (Handy 1985: 181–82). During this period of alliance making and breaking, the communist PGT tried to form broader electoral alliances and worked closely with President Arbenz.

Chapter Four

1. The reformers did pass limited measures to advance the political and social rights of women and Costa Rica's small indigenous and black populations. Social security legislation passed in the reform period included clauses extending coverage for maternity care. A law for the protection of Indians,

which affected around 3,000 persons, also passed; this law sought to provide Indians with increases in infrastructure, medical services, and potable water, but it received minimal attention (Bell 1971: 33). Neither women, Indians, nor blacks, however, gained substantive economic or political rights.

2. Exact figures for wage levels and numbers working at the rates set by the social insurance legislation are not available, and records for 1940 salaries are unreliable. However, a 1950 study demonstrated that the average monthly salary for public and private workers combined was 145 colones (Rosenberg 1983: 60). Given that the average salary for public and private employees was below 400 colones, it is not unreasonable to assume that the reformers did, in fact, intend to cover a majority of employees.

3. A debate exists over who was responsible for the ideas embodied in the labor code. While the communists argue that the ideas and political pressure for the code came from them, Barahona Streber contends that Calderón proposed the idea for these reforms based on his commitment to social Christian ideas promoted by Cardinal Mercier—ideas to which Calderón had access when training in Belgium. According to Barahona Streber, he and Calderón had a series of discussions about the form that these reforms should take. There is no debate, however, over the fact that Oscar Barahona Streber drafted the code.

4. See Costa Rica (1943), Articles 12 and 31 of the Labor Code; Interview with Barahona Streber, Aug. 23, 1994. Also see Lehoucq (1992: 197) for a discussion of the limitations of the labor code.

5. Picado's administration did propose a reform to the labor code. The administration set out to create three commissions to establish minimum wages for agriculture, industry, and commerce, respectively, in each province. Representatives from both capital and labor were to participate in these commissions (Picado 1945: 27–28).

6. The communist party's propaganda stated its commitment to organizing in the rural areas. However, the CP did not make this a priority, as confirmed in interviews with Arnoldo Ferreto on July 8 and 10, 1990, Eduardo Mora on June 25, 1990, and Manuel Mora on July 12, 25, and 28, 1990.

7. The letter was published in August 1943 and included signatures from José Joaquín Alfaro, Tomás Malavassi, Mariano Cortés Castro, Fausto Coto Monge, and Walter Dittel (Lehoucq 1992: 131).

8. Lehoucq (1992: 226–36) has written the most detailed discussion of the positions, debates, and voting tallies of legislators who voted on the 1946 electoral reform. Soto Harrison (1991), minister of the interior during these debates, includes a collection of reprinted newspaper reports that highlight the political mudslinging that took place. Soto Harrison discussed this episode in an interview on Aug. 25, 1994.

9. Extremely limited official documentation exists to corroborate arguments about the implementation and successes of these reforms. Similarly, limited personal recollection by reform or opposition actors in interviews conducted in 1990 and 1994 indicate that the reforms—regardless of whether

they were implemented—elicited minimal response either from the reform or opposition leaders; objection to the reforms seems to have resulted in non-compliance but not active or violent efforts to overturn the laws themselves. Despite minimal attention given in the literature on the Costa Rican reform period, the government did legislate a number of piecemeal rural reforms to distribute land, regulate prices, and increase access to credit for smallholders. The Calderón reform administration passed a 1942 squatters' law, *Ley de Parásitos*, that provided rural workers with the right to cultivate and take possession of uncultivated lands (Calderón 1944: 22). The state assumed responsibility for compensating owners whose land was affected (Bell 1971: 8). The administration created a Ministry of Agriculture and Livestock, which had an Office of Colonization and Distribution of State Lands (Seligson 1978: 4). In July 1943 the administration legislated Law 23, which called for regulating sales of agricultural goods and provided norms to avoid speculation. The Inspección General de Hacienda assumed responsibility for implementing this law (Calderón 1944: 20). The administration passed Law 34, six days later, to control commercial speculation (Calderón 1944: 8). The government also authorized the National Bank of Costa Rica later in the summer of 1943 to import all types of implements and to sell them cheaply to farmers and rural workers (Calderón 1944: 20). The regime attempted to improve access to credit by extending the National Bank's services beyond the central valley to facilitate access to capital in the outlying regions of the country (Bell 1971: 32). And the administration passed the Law of Harvest (March 1944), which prohibited landowners from requiring a tenant to pay more than 20 percent of the crop value or 8 percent of the value of the lands leased (Salazar 1981: 95). President Picado (1944–48) continued efforts to improve the situation of smallholders by providing fairer prices to small and medium-sized farmers. The legislature passed two laws (110 and 36) in the first year of his term that guaranteed prices for agricultural products and provided easier access to rural credit through the establishment of *juntas rurales de crédito* (rural credit boards). The Centro noted that the *juntas rurales de crédito* displaced the usurers insofar as they provided cheaper and less onerous loans. The usurers, in response, began to use their capital to buy lands, thus displacing small producers. Consequently, the small producers would take out cheap loans from the *juntas* but then had to pay rent to the usurers for land that had previously been theirs (*Surco*, year 2, no. 24, June 1, 1942: 9–10). The state also guaranteed prices for corn, rice, and beans—although not for coffee—so as to prevent speculation by intermediaries (Picado 1947b: 11–12). Actual implementation of these rural reform policies was sabotaged, however, by many Costa Rican agricultural elites (Mora 1980: 182).

10. Manuel Mora (1980: 171) made a 1942 radio speech in which he stated the need to pass an income tax to increase state revenues.

11. Otilio Ulate, important newspaper publisher and 1948 presidential candidate, created the term *civil oligarchy* to describe the rise of a group of political officials who promoted presidential campaigns and used presidents

to meet the group's ends (Interview with Rodríguez, July 27, 1990). The term highlighted the opposition's fear of an autonomous state and autonomous state officials.

12. A preparatory commission prepared a working draft for the constituent assembly. The commission was composed of men from across the political spectrum, including three leftists, three social democrats, six liberal democrats, six centrists, and three rightists (Silvert 1969: 53).

13. The discussion lasted from November 1944 to March 1945. See the minutes from the Constituent Assembly as well as Guatemala, *Diario de Sesiones Constituyente: Comisión de los 15*. Also see national newspapers (Nov. 1944–Mar. 1945) including *La Hora, Nuestro Diario*, and *El Imparcial*.

14. Guatemala, *Diario de Sesiones Constituyente: Comisión de los 15*: 86. Also refer to *El Imparcial*, July 24, Nov. 3, Nov. 8, 1944, Jan. 26, 1945.

15. See Article 9 of the 1945 Guatemalan constitution.

16. As mentioned in Chapter 2, the rural communities had preserved limited autonomy from central rule. Although the state had penetrated these communities with increased military presence and the creation of various mechanisms to deliver labor to the coffee plantations, its control over daily life was impeded by the lack of infrastructure and communication. Consequently, the indigenous communities had sustained pockets of autonomy despite general military control and economic exploitation (Silvert 1969: 192–93; Smith 1984).

17. The new military's official publication, *La Revista Militar* (1945–54), highlights this new image. See "El Nuevo Ejército," *La Revista Militar* 4–5 (Mar.–May 1945): 14–15. Also see the March 1953 issue of *Revista Militar* for the 1953 congressional address by the chief of the armed forces, and *El Imparcial* (1945–49) for repeated statements by Chief of the Armed Forces Francisco Arana about the apolitical nature of the National Military of the Revolution.

18. At the time of the signing of the Constituent Assembly in March 1945, the Guatemalan reformers had not completed the demilitarization process. Accordingly, the 1945 Constitutive Law of the Army stated that "the President of the Republic will demilitarize, in the best way possible, civilian services that at the time of this law are still militarized." *Ley Constitutiva del Ejército* 1945, *Disposiciones Transitorios*, Article 2: 71.

19. The military zones were also responsible for providing individual soldiers with additional skills that would be useful to them and to society after completion of their required military service. To this end, the military zones were supposed to establish agricultural centers, small schools, and small industries. Guatemala (1946: 4).

20. See "Discurso del Jefe de las Fuerzas Armadas entre el Congreso de la República." *Revista Militar* (Jan.–Mar. 1953): 136–39. In February 1990 I tried to gain access to information on the educational reforms at the Escuela Politécnica. The archivist and military officers at the school alleged that this information had been burned in a fire.

21. The junta purged the military twice more, after the unsuccessful Arana revolt of 1949 and Castillo Armas revolt of 1950 (Handy 1986: 396).

22. Cruz Salazar (1972: 84) argues that the creation of a minister of defense and a chief of armed forces reflected dissent within the revolutionary junta. With the clear victory of Juan José Arévalo as president, junta member Francisco Arana became dissatisfied; he did not support Arévalo and reasonably concluded that Arévalo would not appoint him to an important position in the next administration. To appease Arana, the reformers created two positions, one for Arbenz as a defense minister who would participate in political affairs and one for Arana as head of the military. I have found no evidence to corroborate or contradict this reasonable argument.

23. See Cruz Salazar (1972, and 1987) for a similar argument. He was one of the key figures of those in the military who organized against the reform coalition and briefly assumed political office in the counterreform period.

24. The labor code differentiated between day and night workers. Nighttime workers did not have to work more than 6 hours a night or 36 hours a week.

25. The legalization of common-law marriage with Decree 444 in 1947 also increased financial protection for women, ladina and indigenous, who had been deserted by a male spouse. Legislators argued that cohabitation was common practice among poor urban ladinos and that women often were left without economic recourse if and when their spouses left them. The legislation argued that these women and their children should have the same rights as married women, provided that the couple had been public about its relationship and that the women did not develop a sexual relationship with another man. Common-law marriage also acknowledged the constitutional rights of indigenous couples, giving them the same rights as those married by civil and/or Christian law. See *La Hora* (Feb. 21, 1945), *Nuestro Diario* (Feb. 21, Feb. 22, 1945), and *El Imparcial* (Jan. 22, Feb. 21, 1945) for a discussion of the debates over the family and common-law marriage. Articles 72–78 of Decree 444 outlined ideas regarding the family, maternity, and marriage. Also see *El Imparcial* (Sept. 6, Sept. 9, Oct. 13, Oct. 28, Oct. 29, Oct. 30, 1947) and *Mujeres* (Aug., Sept. 1952). *El Imparcial* (Oct. 2, 1947) also announced that the Ministry of Economy and Labor was engaged in a study of alternatives for prostitution.

26. See *El Imparcial* (Jan. 10, 1953) for discussion of the number of labor disputes registered in 1952.

27. The reform coalition did not initially challenge the vagrancy law for fear of upsetting the national economy, which had been based on oppressive labor control, and for fear of alienating the oligarchy. For newspaper articles that report on the need to make rural work mandatory and/or regulated, see, for example, *El Imparcial* (Jan. 22, 1945), *Diario de Centro América* (Feb. 26, 1945), and *Nuestro Diario* (Jan. 27, 1945: 9, and Mar. 14, 1945: 9). The reform administration overturned the vagrancy law, however, in 1947. Smith (1984) argues that the change in labor laws had a minimal effect. The labor control

laws of the Liberal period had been established to confront a situation of labor scarcity. By the mid-1940s, however, the rural population had grown significantly, so that market forces themselves could ensure a sufficiently cheap and constant labor supply. Whether or not this was actually the case, it is clear that the dissolution of the vagrancy law diminished an institutional justification and mechanism for state control of rural labor markets as well as oligarchic dependence on the state for assuring capital accumulation. In conjunction with the demilitarization of rural areas, the dissolution of the vagrancy law willfully diminished state capacity to control patterns of labor migration in the rural areas.

28. Arévalo committed substantial resources and propaganda to education, particularly to literacy programs. Hence, the reformers were creating the conditions that would indirectly allow for an increase in rural organizing. The literacy programs, however, were only mildly successful.

29. During Arévalo's administration, development plans included strengthening the state's capacity in the areas of banking and credit, agricultural and industrial development, and housing. The reformers replaced Liberal era ministries with other state institutions, including the Ministry of Economy and Labor, the Central Bank, the Institute of Development and Production (INFOP), and the Department of Cooperative Development (Bauer Paiz 1974: 62–64; Monteforte Toledo 1975: 15; Handy 1984: 109; Dunkerley 1988; Dosal 1988: 323). In 1947, Arévalo identified industrialization as a "national emergency" and passed Decree 459, the Law of Industrial Development (Dosal 1988: 323). The legislation offered concrete incentives and advantages to new industries (García Bauer 1948: 106). The industrialization strategy undergirding this decree did not differ substantially from that of most of the preceding Liberal leaders, who had employed fiscal incentives and tariff protection to spur select industries. The mid-twentieth-century reformers, however, enacted these policies more systematically and regularly than their Liberal predecessors (Guerra Borges 1971: 123–32; Dosal 1988: 328). Ultimately, industrialization efforts were moderately successful but failed to create or sustain support among either veteran or newly established industrialists, who felt alienated by the social policies that followed. Efforts at increasing the state's capacity to intervene and spur the economy during the Arévalo administration had mixed results, often proving more successful in urban than in rural areas.

30. Reprinted in *El Imparcial* (Apr. 4, 1945: 7) from an interview in the Mexican newspaper *Excelsior* (Mar. 23, 1945).

31. In the initial years of the Arévalo administration the government passed a series of ad hoc measures to increase access to and productivity of land; it sidestepped, however, questions of actual land distribution. In 1947, the reform coalition promoted the formation of an agrarian studies commission with the mandate to analyze the country's land tenure and the land reform experiences in Switzerland, Italy, Mexico, and Romania (Melville and Melville 1971: 33; Handy 1984: 109 and 1994: 80; García Añoveros 1987: 162; Interview with Paz Tejada, on Aug. 11, 18, 1990). The decrees of forced

rental passed in the last years of the Arévalo administration (1949 and 1951) were precursors of more comprehensive redistributive reforms implemented in the 1950s. These decrees represented the first real action by the reformers to address the issue of access to land. They were intended to increase the rural poor's access to unused lands and to ensure that land rents were not exorbitant (García Añoveros 1987: 162–63; Guerra Borges 1987: 140; Handy 1984: 109–10; Dunkerley 1991: 132).

32. See *El Imparcial* (Mar. 21, 1950, and May 7, 1952) and Handy (1994: 86–87), who cites at least six proposals.

33. The value of the bonds corresponded to land values declared in the May 1952 tax receipts. The bonds offered 3 percent interest, and their maturity ranged from 2 to 25 years, depending on the estimated value of the property (Paredes 1964; Handy 1988a: 684; Gleijeses 1989b: 459–60; Interview with Capuano, August 9, 14, 15, and 16, 1990).

34. An older analysis states that the law affected 1,799 individual property owners and 90 corporate entities leading to the expropriation of 866,344 *manzanas* on 1,284 farms; only 11 farms were expropriated in their totality (Paredes 1964: 16). Handy (1988a: 687), in a more recent analysis of the land reform records, which he observes are incomplete, calculated that almost 800 private estates, totaling 765,233 *manzanas*, were expropriated, with an additional 189,803 *manzanas* pending expropriation.

35. See for example articles in the communist newspaper *Tribuna Popular* (Aug. 15, Oct. 27, Dec. 29, 1953, Jan. 9, Jan. 12, Jan. 20, 1954). See also Handy (1994), who has most thoroughly analyzed the rural conflicts that emerged, as well as García Añoveros (1987: 172–73) and Gleijeses (1989b: 453).

36. UFCO and its subsidiaries had received preferential treatment during the Liberal period, during which time it had received land grants and long-term tax exemptions, which minimized its responsibility to the Guatemalan state or Guatemala's economic development. UFCO cried that the expropriated lands were valued at $19,355,000. UFCO and the U.S. State Department, which backed these demands for increased compensation, did not respond to the fact that UFCO therefore owed the Guatemalan state decades of back taxes because it had previously undervalued its land to minimize tax payments.

37. The recipient of private property would pay 5 percent of the annual crop value over a course of 25 years. The recipient of land in lifetime usufruct would pay 3 percent of the annual crop value over a course of 25 years. State-owned lands could not be sold. Thus the *fincas nacionales* could only be redistributed as cooperatives for lifetime tenure. Under the terms of the agrarian reform law, this redistribution could take place only if the majority of the workers on the *finca* voted in favor of it (Handy 1988a: 685; Gleijeses 1989b: 460).

38. This information comes from Comité Interamericano de Desarollo Agrícola (1965), which also claims that 90 percent of the loans made by this institution in 1953 were repaid. Also see Gleijeses 1989b: 467.

39. The inauguration of the National Agrarian Bank was announced in *El Imparcial* (Oct. 21, 1953) and the *Unidad Organo Central de la CGTG* (the national labor federation newspaper), year 2, no. 15, Oct. 31, 1953.

40. The agrarian reform law and the corresponding creation of state institutions, however, did not unambiguously benefit the rural communities. The creation of local agrarian institutions and the ensuing proliferation of national peasant unions challenged local indigenous forms of political and spiritual governance, most notably that of the elders and *cofradías* (religious brotherhoods), which had held political and moral sway over their respective communities. Furthermore, as Chapter 5 highlights, ladino reformers sought to incorporate peasants into the reform coalition by appropriating their indigenous mythology, culture, and history while simultaneously attempting to assimilate the indigenous into existing ladino culture.

41. The desire to cultivate additional lands to prevent expropriation cannot explain the increase in coffee yield, given that the turnaround for coffee, from planting to the first harvest, takes several years. However, the high production did demonstrate that the reform did not prove detrimental to coffee production in the short run.

42. In the final months of the reform period, Guatemala also started to debate an income-tax bill, which passed the first of three readings needed to approve it. The June 1954 coup occurred before the bill could be passed (Handy 1985: 153 n. 16; Gleijeses 1989b: 478–79). This final development might suggest that elite opposition to income tax in both Costa Rica and Guatemala sparked the respective civil wars. However, I argue that in order to understand the oligarchic opposition, one needs to consider the differential bases of capital accumulation in each country's coffee economy and the challenges in the 1940s and 1950s to reform these bases. In Costa Rica, the legislation of income tax challenged the oligarchy's previous absolute discretion to control its finance and investment; land reform was on the agenda but was not a priority for either reformers or the coffee elites. By contrast, in Guatemala, the redistributive issue that was of central concern for reformers and nonreformers alike was land ownership and the sanctity of private property; income tax was important but, again, not the priority issue.

Chapter Five

1. See Collier and Collier (1991) for a conceptual discussion of labor incorporation as well as a systematic comparison of the incorporation periods of eight Latin American countries. The 1940s and 1950s social reforms in Costa Rica and Guatemala initiated periods of labor incorporation insofar as labor achieved basic political rights and social services, gained an increased influence over the direction of policy, and constituted an important support base for the reform coalition. Within the Collier and Collier framework, Costa Rica's reform period would be populist and Guatemala's would be radical populist. However, their typology does not help to explain why both

countries in this study would found enduring regimes in the aftermath of labor incorporation, a point discussed further in Chapter 7.

2. Aguilar (1989: 21), Picado (1946, 1947b), and Miller (1993: 519) present different data about levels of union registration and grievances filed. Discrepancies, however, are slight.

3. By the end of the reform period, the communist party itself claimed 12,000 members (Rojas Bolaños 1986: 23). Miller (1993: 519, 525), citing 1945 U.S. embassy reports, suggests that at the height of organizing, the CTCR claimed 30,000 members and that the CP claimed 3,000 party members.

4. During these years, the CTAL followed the Browder line articulated by the U.S. Communist Party, which essentially called for communists to subordinate socialist struggles to a joint rally against fascism. This led to the de facto dissolution of some communist parties in Latin America (Aguilar 1989: 30; Interview with Ferreto, July 8, 10, 1990; Interview with E. Mora, June 25, 1990; Interview with M. Mora, July 12, 25, 28, 1990).

5. The Costa Rican communist party also founded schools to train or recruit cadre. Other political parties did not dedicate similar resources to education; traditional politicians generated votes through patronage rather than through political programmes and/or analysis. To cultivate this worker identity, the CP had organized education sessions in the 1930s, but it increased the scope of this education and outreach in the 1940s (Interview with A. Cerdas, June 25, 1990; Interview with E. Mora, June 25, 1990). Curricula in the communist-run schools covered the tenets of Marxism-Leninism and the history and analysis of Costa Rica. The schools sought to create consciousness about contemporary ills and the need for social change. Arnoldo Ferreto argued that this theoretical training was imperative because Costa Rica did not really have a large proletariat class. Consequently, communist party members and workers needed to be taught what they could not learn through experience; they needed "proletarian educational theory" (Interview with Ferreto, July 7, 1990).

6. The first two organizations, Liga and JOC, sought to provide spiritual guidance for workers; JOC also sought to provide technical training. The Liga and JOC, however, did not successfully put forth a message that resonated with workers. Leadership rivalries and poor organization further obstructed the work of the Liga and JOC (See Backer 1978; and P. J. Williams 1989).

7. The Church founded CCTRN five years after the communists founded the Comité Sindical de Enlace and a couple of months after the Church said that its members could support Vanguardia Popular, the communist party. The Church, however, founded the CCTRN before either the final legislation of the labor code or before the Comité Sindical was transformed into the CTCR.

8. While announced in 1943, the CTCR was officially registered at the Ministry of Labor on May 1, 1945 (Miller 1993: 518).

9. I thank Patricia Badilla and her M.A. students for sharing their work on Costa Rica's rural areas in the 1940s.

10. The cost of living rose throughout the reform period. Using 1936 figures to establish a base of 100, the cost of living index rose to 229.49 by 1948 (Aguilar 1989: 16).

11. P. J. Williams (1989: 115) claims that the CCTRN was not founded to compete with the CTCR but to provide the means for an independent Catholic movement. The decision to create a Catholic labor movement, however, resulted from dissatisfaction with the existing labor movement and the hope to provide a better alternative, an inherently competitive position.

12. The phrase "triumph of civic consciousness" was evoked in my 1989–90 interviews with original participants as well as written in primary and secondary documents, including *El Imparcial*, July 3, 4, 1944, Galich (1977), and Obando Sánchez (1978: 134–35).

13. Three labor representatives, Carlos Manuel Pellecer, Humberto Sosa, and Eduardo Arriola, participated in the Constituent Assembly, which lasted from November 1944 to March 1945. Thirteen labor leaders were elected to Congress between 1945 and 1954 and various unions formed political committees to support certain legislation and candidates (Gutiérrez G. 1964: 39–40).

14. Teachers first organized in the Asociación Nacional de Maestros in July 1944, which shortly thereafter became STEG. SAMF had been a mutual aid society before the October Revolution, but emerged with a union organization, demands, and responsibilities in July 1944 (Bishop 1959: 9). Workers also organized trade unions in the United Fruit Company, print shops, bakeries, commerce, and industries that manufactured shoes and furniture. See *El Imparcial*, July 1944.

15. Many teachers who belonged to the teachers union, STEG, were women who believed that they had a mission to foster a democratic and national consciousness among Guatemalans. Teachers from this time period elaborated on their duty or mission as teachers, women, and mothers. Julia Meléndez de León, a teacher and partisan of the reform party FPL, indicated that she, like the women she worked with, felt like soldiers and custodians of change during the reform period (Interview with Meléndez de León, Jan. 5, 1990). Politicians and artists, in turn, began to refer publicly to women's social role and political duty as mothers at large, teachers, and spiritual soldiers with a responsibility to nurture a democratic society and Guatemalan nation in the home and in the classroom (e.g., Rolz Bennett 1949: 51). The irony in the presupposition that women could cultivate a new democratic person but might not themselves have the ability to vote "responsibly" was a contradiction that was played out in the Constituent Assembly and in the newspapers.

Furthermore, the writers and artists of two intellectual journals, *Saker-Ti* and *Revista de Guatemala*, mirrored the members of STEG in their efforts to foster a new democratic culture that would provide the basis for a new Guatemala. Their efforts to create a new national identity paralleled the state's to cultivate a national civic identity, which often used working-class imagery. President Arévalo, a pedagogue himself, took an active interest in supporting the newly reopened Universidad Popular, which provided basic skills to enhance job opportunity for men and women in the working class (Interview with Amado Herrera, March 10, 1990. Also see *El Imparcial,* Mar. 24, 25, 1947, Feb. 2, Dec. 15, 1952).

16. The CTG founded Escuela Claridad in 1945 to create a proletarian consciousness and to train union leaders for the labor movement. Escuela Claridad organized workshops and conferences. Teachers active in the reform parties and/or old-time labor activists who had survived the 1930s—many in exile in Mexico—discussed a range of general topics, including economics, politics, history, mathematics, and Spanish, and labor-specific issues, including labor rights and union training (*Claridad,* Nov. 18, 1945; Obando Sánchez 1978: 123). The school's motto embodied the labor leaders' vision in 1945: "A la liberación de los trabajadores por su capacitación ["Worker liberation through education]" (*Claridad,* July 28, 1945). To this end, in July 1945, the CTG executive decided that each of the member unions was responsible for sending at least four people to the school in order to gain the general knowledge and organizing skills necessary for a successful union movement (García L. 1952; Bishop 1959: 17–18). The incipient Guatemalan labor movement divided over Escuela Claridad's relationship to the CTG. Escuela Claridad had official representation and, therefore, voting privileges in the CTG's executive committee. This status motivated the more moderate unions of the CTG, including printers, barbers, and mechanics, to organize against the school's status in the CTG. The CTG executive rejected this demand, although it did ultimately take away Escuela Claridad's vote in the executive committee. Ten dissenting unions withdrew from the CTG in November 1945 (*El Imparcial,* Nov. 6, 1945; Cardoza y Aragón 1955a: 97; Bishop 1959: 17–20).

17. The administration's fear of communist infiltration and of the attempt to make Marxist thought hegemonic, at least within workers' circles, led the Arévalo administration to expel suspected communists in 1946 and 1948 (Monteforte Toledo 1965: 292). Another contentious effort to educate and politicize workers occurred in 1950 with Escuela Jacobo Sánchez, which met the same fate as Escuela Claridad. In September of 1950, within less than a month of its founding, the Ministry of the Interior closed the school because of its Marxist orientation. The school in fact was founded by the future editor of the communist daily. José Manuel Fortuny stated that Escuela Jacobo Sánchez focused on teaching Marxism; while the attendance was paltry, the reaction was vehement (Interview with Fortuny, Aug. 10, 1990). President Arévalo's administration also closed down the communist weekly newspaper *Octubre* as well as a falangist paper, *Acción Social Cristiana* (*El Imparcial,* Sept. 28, 1950). Despite this order, at the end of September, Escuela Jacobo Sánchez held classes, after which students were detained for five hours before they were released (*El Imparcial,* Sept. 30, 1950).

Arévalo also adopted more subtle forms of assuaging labor radicalism, such as assigning radical labor leaders to diplomatic posts abroad. Overall, given Arévalo's identification with the transition to democracy and his support for historic social reforms, organized labor and Arévalo sustained a basic relationship of mutual support (Bishop 1959: 26–27), increasingly so with the secular trend toward political polarization.

18. CTG and FSG were the most significant labor federations in terms of numbers and influence. After the initial division, some fifteen of the best-organized moderate unions in Guatemala founded the FSG in January 1946, preeminent among them the SAMF (*El Imparcial*, Jan. 28, Feb. 7, 1946). FSG developed a more moderate and "apolitical" line than that articulated by the CTG, and sought to promote "harmony" between capital and labor, rejecting international ideologies and ties (*El Imparcial*, Jan. 30, Feb. 1, 9, 1946). By 1949, the FSG had attained a more powerful position than that of the CTG; the former had 58 unions and 54,000 members by 1949. Ironically, the SAMF, which had mobilized for the formation of the FSG because of the CTG's overly radical position, left the FSG in 1950 because of the latter's increasingly radical positions (*El Imparcial*, Sept. 22, Oct. 1, 3, 23, 1950; Bishop 1959: 131–32). SAMF's departure severely weakened the FSG but also decreased tension between FSG and CTG. Subsequently, FSG joined the Latin American international, CTAL, headed by Lombardo Toledano, in January 1950; SAMF had opposed joining the CTAL (Schneider 1958: 129; Bishop 1959: 97–99, 103, 130–35; García Añoveros 1987: 136). FRCT formed in 1945 and later changed its name to Federación Laboral Autónoma de Guatemala (FLAG) (López Larrave 1976: 32). It did not wield much power during the reform period.

19. In 1948, the Guatemalan CTG voiced support for the Costa Rican labor organizations, which were confronted with rising opposition from the counterreform coalition led by Otilio Ulate. The CTG said, "The attack on the Costa Rican government will be like an attack on the government of President Arévalo and on the Guatemalan workers, on the part of the enemies of the October Revolution" (*El Imparcial*, Apr. 1, 1948).

20. Politicians and labor activists from the reform period have noted that, of the three centrals, the CTG, which assumed the more radical position, most consistently supported the governing reform coalition and most closely identified with the Partido Acción Revolucionaria (PAR) (*El Imparcial*, Jan. 4, 1946). In the 1946 elections for deputies, for example, the CTG stated that it would rally behind the PAR with the proviso that the PAR present a candidate list for the province of Guatemala, in which two out of four proposed candidates came from the CTG; the CTG, however, tried to maintain autonomy from the PAR (*El Imparcial*, Jan. 4, 1946, Mar. 10, 1947; Handy 1985: 115, n. 70). In turn, the PAR at times invited labor leaders to join its electoral slates. Consequently, labor organizing and partisan work at times became intertwined, with one person occasionally fulfilling two missions—those of labor and partisan representative (Bishop 1959: 77, 110–12). See AGCA, Hemeroteca, *Hojas Sueltas*, 1947, "Manifiesto de la Confederación de Trabajadores Guatemaltecos." This manifesto claims that the PAR is the most progressive of the parties but that the CTG does not have any organic ties to any political parties: "The CTG is an allied organization of the PAR but maintains an independent position from all political groups."

21. *El Imparcial* (Aug. 4, 1947) outlines the CNUS's plan of action, including reforms to the labor code to advance rural workers' rights, further study of the social security laws, legalization of various unions, and agrarian reform.

22. Even SAMF, which had withdrawn from the CTG and the FSG, joined the confederation with the stipulation that the CGTG not join the CTAL or the World Federation of Trade Unions. The CGTG postponed its decision, but eventually joined the international labor organization in 1953 (*El Imparcial*, Aug. 19, 1953; Bishop 1959).

23. As always, union figures vary. According to the official CGTG paper, the CGTG claimed 12 legal federations and 6 federations whose juridical status was pending; it had 380 inscribed unions with 78 unions still waiting for their juridical status, with a total of 104,392 union members (*Unidad Organo Central de la CGTG*, Aug. 31, 1953). Also see *Tribuna Popular* (Aug. 21, 1953). José Alberto Cardoza, national deputy and member of the executive board of the CGTG, stated that the CGTG claimed 521 unions, 440 of which had juridical personality, totalling 110,000 members (*El Imparcial*, Dec. 14, 1953).

24. The rise in labor unity did not mean that some of the previous labor leaders and organizations did not create dissension within the CGTG or split off; see *El Imparcial* (Apr. 9, 1952). However, by the early 1950s, the majority of the urban labor force belonged to the CGTG, which had developed strong working relations with the peasant unions.

25. The CTG saw the CNCG as a divisive organization that had emerged to satisfy Castillo Flores's opportunism, anticommunism, and desire to split the popular movement. Castillo Flores, on behalf of the CNCG, responded that the CNCG was, in fact, organizing a different social base than that previously mobilized by the CTG (*El Imparcial*, May 31, June 3, 1950; López Larrave 1976: 35; Interview with Fortuny, Aug. 3, 1990).

26. Also see *Tribuna Popular* and *Acción Campesina*, 1952–54.

27. See *Tribuna Popular* (Feb. 23, 1954). The CNCG held a congress in 1954 in which it protested sectarianism related to the implementation of the agrarian reform.

28. The congress brought together 290 delegates and organized five commissions which covered women's civil and political rights, women and the agrarian reform, defense and protection for women workers, and women in the struggle for peace and national sovereignty. Señora María Villanova de Arbenz, the first lady (1951–54) spoke, and the congress concluded with demands for the extension of suffrage to illiterate women, women's right to demand land and credit, and equal pay for equal work. See *Tribuna Popular*, Aug. 16, Nov. 14, 26, 28, Dec. 2, 1953; *Unidad Organo Central de la CGTG*, Nov. 15, 1953. See Yashar (1992, ch. 6) for an elaboration of the gendered nature of some of the political organizing during the mid-twentieth-century reform period.

29. Handy (1985: 293) notes that the PGT split over the land invasions, with communist leaders Pellecer and Fortuny pushing for increasing class

conflict and others renouncing this strategy. With the clear threat of a coup in 1954, the party adopted a less combative position and tried to limit land invasions.

30. The following discussion of efforts to assimilate and praise indigenous communities draws from *Saker-Ti, Revista de Guatemala, El Campesino,* and *El Imparcial* (covering 1944–54), as well as documents from the Instituto Indigenista Nacional and its educational materials. I also draw from Interview with Anonymous B, May 19, 1990.

31. Also see *Tribuna Popular* (Oct. 29, 1953). To this day, it is not uncommon for Guatemalans to highlight their ancestral blood and connections to the *Popul Vuj* while in the same breath making derogatory comments about contemporary Indian culture and practice.

32. This fear is illustrated by two different responses to Indian mobilization. In the first incident, a large group of Indians demonstrated in September 1944 in the capital in support of Ponce, who had promised them land; newspaper coverage assumed a fearful, if condescending tone, describing the demonstrators as unruly, drunk Indians with machetes in their hands. In the second incident, two days after the overthrow of Ponce, Indians rose up in Patzicia out of fear that they would not receive the land he had promised them; around twenty ladinos were said to have been killed. This in turn led the government to order the indiscriminate shooting of Indians in the area. Carlos Paz Tejada stated that the ladino community was prepared to retaliate and had rounded up and was prepared to shoot all Indians found in the town. Paz Tejada was able to avert a bloodbath by bringing the Indians to another town (*El Imparcial*, Sept. 19, 1944; Silvert 1969: 38; Albizures 1988, 1989a, and 1989b; Adams 1990; Interview with Paz Tejada, Aug. 11, 1990).

33. Manuel Galich, then Minister of Public Education, who supported the founding of the Instituto Indigenista Nacional, stated that ladinos did not understand or know indigenous life and culture (Galich 1945: 83). *Saker-Ti* contained an article that disputed the idea that there was an "Indian problem" and argued that it was in fact a ladino problem (*Saker-Ti* 2, no. 3 [Jan.-Feb.] 1948). However, the reformers generally perceived the survival of indigenous communities as a problem.

34. During his term at the IIN, Goubaud initiated investigations concerning indigenous communities and Guatemala's regional markets, made a map illustrating Guatemala's indigenous languages, and developed an alphabet for 4 out of Guatemala's 21 indigenous languages: Quiche, Cakchiquel, Mam, and Kekchi (Arriola n.d.: 4–5).

35. La Alameda, a school in Chimaltenango, trained a few indigenous teachers so that they in turn could coordinate educational programs in their communities. This effort to redress rural problems through education and spiritual "development" characterized the policies undertaken by Arévalo. Nonetheless, despite the tremendous fanfare around education, the campaign to increase literacy, train teachers, and increase the number of students receiving higher levels of training was only partially successful.

36. See *El Campesino* (Aug. 5, 1945) for a story that implies that Juan

Chapín's education results in more hygenic children, increased productivity, higher rates of savings, improved standard of living and conditions for the internal market, cooperation with the government, and the state's legalization of his marriage. Also see *El Campesino*, Jan.-Feb. 1947. While the reformers legalized common law marriage, with Decree 444 in 1947, they also promoted state or Catholic marriages in journals targeting rural indigenous areas.

37. Also see *El Campesino* 39, 40 (July-Aug. 1948).

38. *Tribuna Popular* (Jan.–June 1954) reported on efforts to unify the popular movement in defense of the regime.

Chapter Six

1. While precise data regarding rural support are lacking, interviews with people representing different sides of this debate indicate that Cortés had a large following in the rural areas. Interviewees also agreed that peasants and rural workers tended to vote in accord with their rural patron for political and economic reasons (Interview with Azofeifa, Aug. 18, 1994; Interview with Soto Harrison, August 16, 1994; Interview with Monge, August 26, 1994). I also thank Patricia Badilla for sharing her work in progress, which includes oral histories with Costa Rican peasants who participated in the political struggles of the 1940s.

2. The social reforms passed during the prior period had garnered urban working-class support. Cortés did not publicly oppose the social reforms but remained silent on the matter. When the Congress voted on the labor code, only one *cortesista* voted to pass it. The other six did not attend the session, highlighting their contempt for the law and for Calderón. This silence on the reforms compelled many to assume Cortés's opposition to the social legislation (Creedman 1971: 224; Rodríguez V. 1980: 83, 85).

3. Students of law also formed the Costa Rican Communist Party in 1931, the Guatemalan revolutionary student movement in 1944, and parts of the Guatemalan counterreform movement.

4. See Yashar (1995) for the impact of the Centro on the evolution of the PSD and the subsequent party system in Costa Rica.

5. This discussion of the Centro is based on interviews with Isaac Felipe Azofeifa (June 1990) and Eugenio Rodríguez (July 27, 1990), both members of the Centro, as well as from an analysis of *Surco*, the newspaper published by the Centro. Secondary resources on the Centro are Rodríguez V. (1980) and Aguilar Bulgarelli (1983), among others. I confirmed this secondary information with Azofeifa during interviews on August 18, 19, and 25, 1994.

6. The Centro also attacked the communist party for its subsequent conciliation with the government that the CP had so bitterly opposed in the 1940 elections. The Centro correctly observed the about-face made by the communist party, which initially berated the Calderón government only to ally with it later; however, the Centro itself later made alliances that seemed to contradict its previously stated ideological position. In the second half of

the 1940s, the Centro allied with the very conservative oligarchic faction that it opposed ideologically.

7. Isaac Felipe Azofeifa (Interview, June 13, 21, 1990) and Rodríguez (Interview, July 27, 1990) commented on the international ideological currents that influenced the thinking of those in the Centro; also see Rodríguez V. (1980: 24–25).

8. The Centro disseminated its views through its newspaper, *Surco*, although Creedman (1971) claims that *Surco* did not distribute over 500 copies. Some of its members became editors of Ulate's newspaper in February 1944. Through the media, they attempted to reshape public discourse (Gardner 1971: 49).

9. The Centro did not set up a local chapter in the province of Limón, which, along with Guanacaste, has always been marginalized from Costa Rican politics and policy. The communists organized their first successful strike in Limón and maintained a strong base there until the mid-1980s.

10. Creedman (1971: 179) questions the argument that the Centro supported reform legislation: "A reading of the various issues of *Surco* gives the impression that the Center was not firmly in favor of the social legislation of Calderón Guardia. As Isaac Felipe Azofeifa said, they were '. . . like embarrassed conservatives, saying that the measure was acceptable in principle, but in reality opposing it by saying that it needed more study'" (Interview). Otón Acosta flatly declared that they were a group of middle-class youths who opposed the social reforms (Interview). In May 1942, Oscar Barahona Streber, the principal author of the Labor Law and an important collaborator in the Social Security Act, said that the Center, instead of helping Calderón enact the reforms, "in reality opposed them." However, in interviews twenty years later, members from the Centro and Calderón's party stated that the Centro did support the broad outlines of reforms. What is indisputable is that the Centro joined the opposition, which created more impediments than not for the implementation of the reforms.

11. During the time I was doing research for this project, Alberto Martén was the only surviving member of this trio. In interviews (July 13, 1990, Aug. 17, 22, 1994), Martén provided the historical background on AD. On two occasions he presented the story of its founding. Luis Alberto Monge, then a member of AD, corroborated this story (Interview, Aug. 26, 1994).

12. The reform alliance in 1946 essentially promised the votes of cadre in Partido Vanguardia Popular (communist) to the Partido Republicano (the official party). In the capital of San José, however, the PVP ran independently (Aguilar Bulgarelli 1983: 177).

13. In the opposition convention following Cortés's death, each opposition party put forth a candidate. No one candidate won a majority in the first round. The PSD candidate, Figueres, who emerged in 1948 as the leader of the armed rebellion, came in last, highlighting the limited resonance of both his persona and the PSD during the reform period. In the second round, the opposition elected Ulate (PUN).

14. Despite provisions in the electoral code prohibiting political demon-

strations during the campaign for the 1948 elections, the opposition organized a march for July 21, 1947, which took place following an exchange of letters with the administration. At the end of the march, the opposition presidential candidate, Ulate, called for a strike in San José and Cartago, which was approved the following night and announced by Ulate and Figueres on July 23. In fact, disturbances started on July 19 in Cartago, a few days before the opposition declared the strike. For further information see Fernández Durán (1953); Salazar (1981: 123); Aguilar Bulgarelli (1983: 201–37); Rojas Bolaños (1986: 141); Schifter (1986: 217–21). The *huelga de los brazos caídos* was discussed during each Costa Rican interview for this book.

15. In another example of the increasing polarization between Benjamín Núñez and Archbishop Sanabria, the former organized a demonstration in October 1947 despite the archbishop's initial attempt to dissuade him (Miller 1993: 533–34).

16. Many of these banana workers were of Jamaican and Nicaraguan descent. This population had been excluded from the legal and discursive changes of the reform period, the implementation of which had primarily benefited white workers in the capital. Throughout the reform period, blacks remained politically and geographically marginalized, without the right to vote or to enter the capital of San José. A 1942 presidential decree poignantly highlighted the fact that neither the counterreform movement nor the reform coalition as a whole considered blacks or other people of color as part of or suitable members of the polity. See *International Labour Review* 46, no. 4 (Oct. 1942): 489, which reprints a presidential message from the Costa Rican newspaper *La Gaceta*, May 5, 1942.

17. In almost every interview I conducted during the summer of 1990 and August 1994 with noncommunist activists and politicians, the interviewees referred to the *brigadas* and the random violence they engendered, such as fist fights and raucous behavior. In a few of these discussions, interviewees mentioned the bomb attempt.

18. Cited in Miller (1993: 533) and mentioned in an interview with Manuel Mora (July 1990).

19. The U.S. embassy advocated finding a candidate on whom both Calderón and Ulate could agree (Schifter 1986: 258, 263). By 1948 the United States did seek to weaken the communists but did not advocate a military solution, nor did it promote Figueres. Indeed, the United States did not distinguish between different factions within the opposition and developed ties largely with Ulate (Schifter 1986: 274–76).

20. The Caribbean Legion included a group of revolutionaries committed to overthrowing dictatorships in Central America and the Caribbean, particularly Trujillo of the Dominican Republic and Somoza of Nicaragua. Figueres joined the legion relatively late in the process but convinced it that once it had helped topple the Costa Rican government, it could use Costa Rican territory as a base to overthrow Somoza. Figueres misled the legion on two fronts: first, he misrepresented the situation in Costa Rica, which was

far from a dictatorship; second, he ultimately retracted his help and his commitment to allow the members of the league to operate in Costa Rica in preparation for invading Nicaragua. A number of those involved in the Caribbean Legion subsequently distanced themselves from Figueres.

21. In contrast to their Guatemalan counterparts, Costa Rican peasants and rural workers did not side with the reform government, which had not provided them with the benefits extended to workers in the urban areas. Moreover, the rural sector had developed a relationship of self-described benign dependence on the Costa Rican oligarchy and depended on local elites for credit, patronage, and information. Finally, the Costa Rican peasantry had already been incorporated in the 1930s through the creation of IDECAFE and, therefore, had already achieved partial access to and participation in the state. Already incorporated, it was not available for mobilization by the 1940s reform coalition and looked on its actions with suspicion. Under these conditions, the propaganda of anticommunism found fertile ground and motivated rural workers and peasants to join the opposition armed forces led by Figueres (Interview with Azofeifa, Aug. 18, 1994; Interview with Soto Harrison, Aug. 16, 25, 1994; Interview with Monge, July 25, 1994; also, Patricia Badilla's unpublished work).

22. Although Father Núñez signed an agreement at the Mexican embassy in which respect for the reforms and labor rights were ensured, it appears that he did not have Figueres's authority to do so. Consequently, when the post-1948 regime discriminated against and persecuted communists and organized labor, Figueres denied that the junta had reneged on an official agreement. A second controversy exists over whether or not Figueres and Mora signed another pact, this one in the hills of Ochomogo, where Núñez arranged for Mora to meet with Figueres. During these negotiations, Mora voiced concern for ensuring respect for the social reforms and the advances achieved by the workers. Both sides now agree that Figueres assured Mora that the armed opposition was not against the reforms and would advance them further once in power. Debate, however, exists over whether or not Figueres and Mora consummated this discussion with the signing of a pact of Ochomogo. Mora says they did. Figueres denies this.

23. Other unions began to emerge in the 1950s, but their membership rate was unimpressive and their influence very limited. The establishment of unions in the post-1948 period, however, does not necessarily indicate an increase in the organization of labor, for the economic sectors most represented by unions today are professionals and technocrats. By the late 1970s, 1 out of 10 workers was unionized, but only 1 out of 20 industrial workers and 1 out of 50 small rural producers were unionized. See Palma (1980: 194) and Schifter (1983: 224–29).

24. See Palma (1980: 194); Schifter (1983: 224–29); Rovira Mas (1985); Rojas Bolaños (1989a: 158); *Tico Times* (Costa Rica), May 18, 1990; "La OIT y el Solidarismo," *La República*, July 24, 1990. *Solidarismo*, an idea first articulated by Alberto Martén in a 1947 pamphlet, has replaced many labor unions. As an antidote to communism and labor unions in the workplace, Martén argued that workers and owners needed to establish a new relation-

ship to replace the antagonistic one that prevailed at the time. He suggested that owners and workers develop a form of joint ownership, making everyone a capitalist invested in the growth of the given business. Martén argued that this would not only undermine the basis for radical organizing on the left and right, but would also improve workers' conditions. To develop this sense of ownership, he proposed the creation of savings-and-loan credit groups to which workers and owners alike would contribute. This idea gained ground domestically and internationally in the 1970s and 1980s. In practice, however, *solidarismo* has served to undermine further existing labor unions. The International Labour Office stated in July 1990 that in fact, *solidarismo* had placed obstacles before the free organization of unions. Others studies have noted that many businesses require workers to sign a contract to join *solidarista* organizations and not to join labor unions.

25. These nationalized banks joined the Banco Nacional de Costa Rica, the national bank that was responsible for issuing currency and overseeing the private banks that had previously maintained a certain degree of autonomy from state control. The joint announcement of Decrees 70 and 71 had unintended consequences. "The two measures together tied up the bank deposits of investors for some time. . . . No one had much money available except as bank deposits, and the tax was therefore impossible to collect as deposits were frozen. The government could not collect directly from the bank accounts since Costa Rican accounts are numbered and secret" (Gardner 1971: 359). Ulate later overturned this decree, which had proven ineffective because of massive tax evasion (Gardner 1971: 293, 359, 427).

26. See Gardner (1971: 283–90) for a discussion of development projects initiated or sanctioned by the junta.

27. To name the four directors of each bank, Martén had originally proposed that the chambers of commerce, industry, and agriculture, as well as the Catholic labor union Rerum Novarum and the bankers association, would all propose a list of candidates to the government. The government would choose at least one candidate from each list for a total of 28 directors (Interview with Martén, Aug. 17, 22, 1994). Martén said, "I asked the chambers to send me lists of names to choose the directors of the banks. Therefore, the chambers more than anything gained power [as a result of the nationalization of the banks] to name the directors of the banks. . . . Hence, I offered a directorship to Jaime Solera and to Manuel Jiménez, two of the richest men in the country, and most important financiers in the country. Manuel Jiménez accepted it. But Jaime Solera answered, 'I do not want to be steward of my own house.' He did not accept."

28. See Muñoz Guillén (1990) for a discussion of Costa Rica's pre-1949 military.

29. The much weaker and incipient commercial and industrial sectors formed the Comité de Comerciantes e Industriales de Guatemala (CCIG) and the Asociación General de Industriales de Guatemala (AGIG). AGIG was a splinter group from CCIG formed in 1948. The CCIG and AGIG did not necessarily present a united front (Gleijeses 1991: 209). After the 1952 agrarian

reform law, the AGIG tried to hold discussions with the government while the CCIG refused contact.

30. Similar labor legislation in Costa Rica elicited similar criticisms. However, Costa Rican labor legislation and proposed land reforms were more moderate challenges to the capacity of that country's oligarchy to accumulate capital, given that it had profited largely from control over finance, commerce, and processing. The 1947 income tax law, which challenged the Costa Rican oligarchy's freedom over capital, however, generated a violent response, as discussed earlier.

31. The government generally failed to prosecute this illegal practice (Gleijeses 1991: 46; Handy 1994: 102–3). Gleijeses draws this conclusion from documents in the Guatemalan archives (AGCA), Bush (1950), and Bishop (1959).

32. See for example *El Imparcial* (Dec. 9, 1946, Mar. 17, 1950, June 3, 1952). "The leadership has persisted in fomenting a class struggle that in our latitudes becomes a much more serious struggle, that is to say a racial fight. This struggle is already producing its fruits of social disaggregation, which will finish with nationality, carrying us to anarchic chaos, which is advantageous to the unspeakable ends which antipatriotic elements are propounding" (*El Imparcial*, Mar. 17, 1950).

33. In fact, the land reform led to an increase in productivity, as owners began to cultivate their previously fallow lands and the beneficiaries of the land reform began to cultivate their newly acquired land, as discussed in Chapter 5.

34. The archives of the Guatemalan Catholic Church house excellent sources for social historians interested in the years prior to the reform period. According to the caretakers of the archives, however, Archbishop Rossell y Arellano stated in his will that the records from 1944 to 1954, and his personal correspondence, would not be available until 50 years after his death, to protect the reputation of anyone who might have been implicated in these materials.

35. Also see *Acción Social Cristiana*, Sept. 4, 1952, for a similar type of statement.

36. See *El Imparcial*, Aug. 20–23, 26, 1946, which reported on a demonstration to protest anticlerical and communist influence. The Church declared that it was not responsible for calling the protest, which had been organized by the political parties. Nonetheless, the archbishop made clear that, while he did not condone or condemn the demonstration, Christians could attend and belong to political parties as long as this did not contradict Christian ideals (*El Imparcial*, Aug. 24, 1946).

37. Archbishop Rossell y Arellano had wanted to travel with the original Black Christ. The inhabitants of Esquipulas, however, protested. The archbishop therefore commissioned a replica.

38. The full text of "De la Carta Pastoral del Excmo. y Revmo. Sr. Don Mariano Rossell y Arellano Arzobispo de Guatemala sobre los Avances del

Comunismo en Guatemala" may be found in AGCA, Hermeroteca, *Hojas Sueltas*, 1954. This translation is from Gleijeses (1991: 287).

39. This discussion of the market women compiles information gathered in interviews, particularly with Concha Estévez (Mar. 10, 1994), Archbishop Próspero Penados (Feb. 16, 1990), Leonora Paz y Paz (Feb. 13, 19, 1990), and Carmén Yolanda Chavarría de Ponce (Feb. 26, 1990). Also see *Tribuna Popular* (1952–54) and *El Imparcial* (June 20, Oct. 6, 1952, Mar. 21, 24, July 11, 1953).

40. Estévez also noted that popular mobilization in the late 1980s was also opening the doors to communism. An old campaign poster for the now defunct Partido de Unificación Anticomunista leaned against the wall of her small market stall, highlighting that the reform and counterreform struggles still resonated politically for her.

41. Archbishop Próspero Penados recounted this story in an interview (Feb. 16, 1990) during which he highlighted the Church's constant fear of persecution by the presumed Marxist government.

42. Congressional seats were distributed in the following manner after the January 1953 elections: PAR, 22; PRG, 16; RN, 7; PGT, 4; opposition, 5; progovernment independents, 2 (Gleijeses 1991: 182).

43. Some interviewees denied that AGA provided financial support to the opposition, but most—representatives of different political tendencies—stated that the AGA did help finance efforts to overthrow the democratic regime and reverse the course of the social reform period.

44. For example, see *El Imparcial* and *La Hora* (Jan.–June, 1954).

45. Castillo Armas wrote the first article in the first *Revista Militar* after Ubico's overthrow in which he discussed the dawn of a new democratic period and the need for the military to adopt a new role in this process. Ironically, he later became the leader of the 1954 invasion that overthrew the democratic regime.

46. Handy (1994: 185) refers to a similar example.

47. For example, see *El Imparcial* (Nov. 27, 1944, Dec. 22, 1944, Mar. 11, 30, Apr. 29, 1947, June 14, 1950); *Diario de Centro América* (Nov. 27, 1944).

48. I was denied access to military education records from the period 1944–54. Officers at the military academy claimed that these records "had been lost" or had been burned in a fire in the late 1970s. However, Paz Tejada indicated that the military officers always suspected the reform leaders (Interview, Aug. 11, 18, 1990). Four Guatemalan military officers, who preferred to remain anonymous, confirmed this and emphasized the general concern about rising communism in these years in a joint interview (Mar. 29, 1994).

49. Paz Tejada recounted a gathering of military men in late 1948 or early 1949. Officials including chiefs from barracks from all of the military zones in the country attended the event. The evening turned to politics and all present, including Francisco Javier Arana, who had been part of the revolutionary junta and was then the chief of the armed forces, criticized the Arévalo government. Someone stated that the high command was worried about the political and military disaster the government was precipitating

and that it was time for the military to act. When Paz Tejada was asked his opinion, he claims to have deflected the rebellious mood with a personal story used to highlight the advances rather than the limitations of the reform period. He later learned that the evening had been organized, in part, to ascertain whether a military coup was possible. The high command had wanted to hear Paz Tejada's perspective, given his influence over the junior officers, ranks whose support would be necessary in the event that they initiated a coup. According to Paz Tejada, his response dissuaded them from attempting a coup at that point. Paz Tejada recounted this story to highlight internal dissension within the military high command, active efforts to plot coups, and anticommunism in the military ranks (Interview with Paz Tejada, Aug. 11, 1990; also see Cáceres 1980: 411–43; Gleijeses 1991: 60).

50. The government cancelled the Partido de Unificación Anticomunista's registration in August 1950 following the "Minutes of Silence" protest that had been organized by the opposition to commemorate the death of former Chief of the Armed Services Francisco Javier Arana and to accuse the government of having masterminded his assassination. The PUA registered again in 1952.

51. These four arguments were made in an interview with four anonymous retired military officers (Mar. 29, 1994) and an interview with Lt. Colonel Cruz Salazar (Mar. 2, 1990), who betrayed Arbenz and participated in the post-reform military junta.

52. The United States' pervasive role in orchestrating the June 1954 invasion by Castillo Armas has been convincingly and amply documented. See, for example, Osegueda (1955), Jonas and Tobis (1974), Jonas (1981), Immerman (1982), Schlesinger and Kinzer (1982), and Gleijeses (1991).

53. The Guatemalan government discovered this agreement in January 1954, less than six months before the actual invasion. This discovery both led to an outcry of support for the regime and increased fear of an international conspiracy to overthrow it.

54. The ban was successful. Guatemala was unable to buy arms from the West and in the last instance bought them from Czechoslovakia. When the United States and domestic Guatemalan opposition learned of the arrival of Czech arms, they pointed to it as an example of communist control over Guatemala.

55. Gleijeses (1991) has argued that the Guatemalan military did not defend the regime for fear of a U.S. invasion. At one level, this argument seems compelling. However, it sidesteps first the fact that the Guatemalan military had already voiced its own opposition to the regime prior to and independent of the United States; second, that former military men were themselves active in organizing the invasion; and, third, the conditions under which militaries in fact do not act in accord with U.S. principles or threats, as in the cases of Guatemala in the 1980s, Nicaragua in the 1980s, and Cuba from the 1960s on. While the latter two cases were different kinds of regimes from that of Guatemala from 1944 to 1954, they both included cases where the threat of U.S. invasion was real but the military leaders appeared to have re-

mained relatively steadfast in their support for the respective regime. These observations suggest that one needs to analyze the domestic situation to understand the conditions in which militaries respond to or reject international threats.

56. Castillo Armas later showcased the 1956 land reform. While this was largely for appearances' sake, Bulmer-Thomas (1987: 166) points out that Guatemala's remained the only land reform passed in Central America in the 1950s. The regime also did not close down the Guatemalan Social Security Institute, and even improved its coverage of the labor force, until by the late 1950s it was operating at a level almost as high as that in Costa Rica.

57. In 1990, members of the teachers' union, STEG, who had been active during the 1940s and 1950s, initiated a legal proceeding to reclaim the bank accounts and property seized in the counterreform period (Interview with Anonymous B, March 19, 1990).

58. Bishop (1959: 284–85) argues that the labor movement suffered such great blows because of its dependence on the communist PGT, its position as an official labor movement tied to the state apparatus, and its subsequent failure to build a grassroots base.

59. While the Guatemalan elite has diversified its crop production in the second half of the twentieth century to include cotton, cattle, and sugar, it continues to rely on concentrated landholdings and repressive labor relations. Official agricultural census data revealed in 1979 that 1 percent of all farms claimed 22 percent of all cultivated land, while 87 percent of all farms claimed 16 percent of cultivated land (Dunkerley 1991: 146). Peasant organizations continue to document and protest the sub-subsistence wages provided and the repressive working conditions.

Chapter Seven

1. Levine (1988) criticized the first round of democratization studies included in O'Donnell, Schmitter, and Whitehead (1986) for not taking into account the social forces that uphold and support democracy. My approach shares with Levine's the need to root institutional questions of how democratic regimes endure in the social forces that uphold them, but it differs with his injunction to analyze social support, per se. Indeed, there are too many cases where broad-based support for democracy gave way to more powerful efforts to overthrow it—as in Guatemala 1954. Rather, I argue that we need to look at the social groups that can disrupt democracy and why they would agree to a system that diminishes their capacity to make decisions that influence economic production, local governance, and national policy.

2. See, for example, Bates (1981 and 1989); Janvry (1981); Johnston and Clark (1982); Grindle (1986); Prosterman and Riedinger (1987); and Timmer (1991) for development studies that underscore the centrality of the politics of the countryside. Most of these authors, however, do not attempt to explain democracy or authoritarianism, but focus on development as an outcome. See R. Williams (1986, and 1994); Brockett (1988); Dunkerley (1988);

and Roseberry, Gudmundson, and Samper (1995) for examples of Central American studies that emphasize the importance of the countryside for national outcomes. See Hopkins (1995), who explores the argument that the terms of agricultural development are related to democratic outcomes. See Fox (1990) for the argument that the transition to democracy does not necessarily democratize rural relations.

3. In comparing the political economy of development literature on Latin America and Asia, Evans (1987: 214, 221) notes that while the latter pays great attention to the role of rural elites, the former largely ignores it. He urges Latin Americanists focusing on development to pay great attention to the politics of the countryside, particularly insofar as Latin American rural elites have subverted development and growth patterns. This is a plea that regime scholars should also heed if they are interested in explaining not only the conditions in which democracies are founded but also the conditions in which they endure.

4. Stephens (1989) and Collier and Collier (1991) incorporate the countryside into their analyses, but it is not a dominant focus of their explanations. Stephens notes that a weakened landed elite engaged in non-labor-intensive agriculture proved most auspicious for democracy. She explores this argument further in her co-edited volume (Huber [Stephens] and Safford 1995). Collier and Collier highlight how a weak oligarchy and radical labor incorporation (urban and rural) led to more integrative political party systems.

5. The following discussion on Costa Rica draws in summarized fashion from Yashar (1995).

6. The two oligarchic parties (PRN and PUN) that had run against one another in the 1948 elections that sparked the civil war joined political forces following the founding of the Partido Liberación Nacional (PLN). Electoral alliances between the opposition parties have changed names throughout the postwar decades from Unificación Nacional (National Unification) to Coalición Unidad (United Coalition) to Partido Unidad Social Cristiana (United Social Christian Party, PUSC). Despite changes in name, this coalition has been able to call support from around 40 percent of the national electorate (Hernand 1986: 305). The conservative alliances have commanded multiclass electoral support from the most economically and politically conservative agro-export elites, neoliberal ideologues, parts of the urban working class, and rural banana workers. Jiménez Castro's two-part analysis of Costa Rican elections has shown that between 1953 and 1978 this conservative alliance received the majority of the votes in most of the cantons of the metropolitan area (Jiménez Castro 1977: 26–33). In contrast to previous electoral alliances, the PUSC, formed in December 1983 as a merger of various elite parties, has demonstrated the potential to become a permanent, nationally organized party, rather than just an electoral coalition. The PUSC, which seems to have engaged in serious party outreach, has made steady electoral gains throughout the 1980s. In the 1986 elections, it gained control of more than 25 percent of the municipalities (versus 2 percent in the previous elections), and it gained an additional 7 seats in the national legislature,

for a total of 25 out of the 57 seats. In the 1990 elections, it upset PLN legislative hegemony and won 29 seats, assuming the majority.

7. See Yashar (1995) for a discussion of the different branches of Costa Rican government. The executive was weakened after the 1948 civil war in exchange for a strengthened legislature. It is important, therefore, to evaluate political strength on the basis of who dominates the legislature and not, as is often customary, on presidential victories.

8. Carazo, who won the 1978 presidential elections, was a PLN leader who left the party shortly before the 1978 elections, ran for the opposition coalition, and split the PLN vote. The 1978 election was the first time in the postwar period that the PLN lost its majority in the legislature.

9. Between 1948 and 1978, infant mortality was reduced from 117 to 17 per thousand, life expectancy increased from 60 to more than 74 years of age, illiteracy practically disappeared, and the university population reached 2.5 percent of the total population. "Between 1961 and 1980, Costa Rican social security expenditures in relation to GDP rose almost five times (from 2 percent to 9 percent) and in relation to fiscal expenditure grew almost three times (from 13 percent to 36 percent), without a doubt the most significant increase in the region" (Mesa-Lago 1989: 62–63).

10. Studies of these rural policies suggest that they were not as generous as is often asserted. Landed peasants, it appears, have benefited more from these programs than their landless counterparts; larger landholders have benefited most of all (Seligson 1980: 123–25; González-Vega and Céspedes 1993: 92, 114–16). Studies of these programs indicate that they provided the advantage to the landed and not the landless peasants. Moreover, while land reform programs were developed in the 1960s, they were accompanied by increasing land concentration during that same time period (Seligson 1980: 137).

11. The economic crisis of the 1980s challenged this postwar exchange. Confronted with an exhausted economic model and the mandates of the international lending and aid agencies, the PLN adopted neoliberal policies. The rural sectors shifted their support from the PLN to the conservative alliance, PUSC, in the 1990 elections. These reforms were also accompanied by a rise in protest, particularly in the countryside (Edelman 1983: 166–80; Gudmundson 1989b; L. Anderson 1991: 171).

12. By 1979, agriculture constituted 28.4 percent of GDP and manufacturing constituted 15.1 percent of GDP in Guatemala. Agriculture as a percentage of GDP in Latin American countries was higher only in Nicaragua and Paraguay in 1979. Manufacturing as a percentage of GDP in 1979 was lower only in Panama and Venezuela (Grindle 1986: 49–50).

13. In the years immediately following the 1954 coup, the United States increased military aid to Guatemala. Until 1972, Guatemala's military aid far outpaced that in the rest of Central America. Booth and Walker (1993: 177) report that Guatemala received an annual average of $1.5 to $1.66 million between 1945 and 1990. Guatemala received the following annual averages, in millions of dollars, for the following dates: 1953–61: $0.19; 1962–

72: $3.31; 1973–82: $0.38; 1983–86: $1.48; 1987–90: $6.9. Aid increased following the Cuban and Nicaraguan revolutions. The Carter administration suspended military aid in the late 1970s. The Bush administration suspended $3.3 million of military assistance because of human rights abuses.

14. The military attempted to create a hegemonic party system, drawing on the model offered by the Partido Revolucíonario Institucional (PRI) in Mexico. To this end, it founded the Partido Institucional Democrático (PID).

15. The military changed the electoral laws to give the advantage to the PID by making it more difficult for other parties to register. The new regulations developed by the military had the unintended consequence, however, of encouraging more reformist factions to coalesce around the moderate candidacy of Mario Méndez Montenegro of the Partido Revolucionario (PR), the one reform party allowed to register for the elections. Brothers Mario and Julio César Méndez Montenegro had participated in reform politics in the 1940s and 1950s. However, following the 1954 coup, Mario assumed a more moderate position and in 1958 founded the Partido Revolucionario. Shortly before the elections, Mario died and Julio César ran and won with a sizable plurality. The PID-dominated legislature had to approve his victory before he could take office and, therefore, compelled him to agree to its terms before it would do so. From 1954 to 1985, Julio César Méndez Montenegro was the only elected civilian president.

16. The model villages are comparable to those established in Vietnam. In the hope of controlling subversive activities, Guatemala's military relocated peasants into more concentrated areas, thus gaining the capacity to monitor their movements.

17. Colombia is the partial exception to this argument. While Colombia has sustained a formal political democracy since 1958, its continuing suspension of civil liberties, restrictions on political participation, human rights abuses, and civil war make it difficult to type it either as a case of enduring democracy or authoritarian rule.

18. There is a rich literature on Mexican politics. The argument developed here has been particularly influenced by Eckstein (1977); Grindle (1977, and 1986); Hamilton (1982); Hellman (1983); Collier and Collier (1991); and Rueschemeyer, Stephens, and Stephens (1992).

19. Recent historiography has revealed that this challenge to Mexico's elite was less extensive than previously presented, given the uneven patterns of land distribution that occurred, the conservative retreat of the administration that followed Cárdenas, and the reemergence of new elites. Nonetheless, it is still commonly noted that Mexico's twentieth-century agrarian elites were both weaker than in the prior century and significantly weaker than most of their Latin American counterparts.

20. Considerable debate has emerged over the intent and extent of Mexico's land reform. While the land reform was not implemented equally in all regions, it did change the ownership of land and offered a symbol of the PRI's commitment to the peasantry.

21. Discussions of Venezuela include Roseberry (1982); Levine (1973);

Peeler (1985); Karl (1986); Stephens (1989: 298, 312–13); Collier and Collier (1991); Coppedge (1994); and Kornblith and Levine (1995).

22. It is commonly noted that Japan's Liberal Democratic Party created and sustained a one-party regime with the support of the countryside. See Donnelly (1977); Pempel (1978); George (1981); and Inoguchi (1990). See Bullock (forthcoming), for a systematic analysis of the LDP's ties to the countryside and the consequences for Japanese political stability.

Bibliography

Archival Sources

ARCHIVES AND NEWSPAPER DEPOSITORIES

Archivo General de Centroamérica (AGCA), Guatemala City, Guatemala
Archivos Nacionales de Costa Rica, San José, Costa Rica
Archivo Nacional de la Asamblea Legislativa, San José, Costa Rica
Biblioteca Nacional, Hermeroteca, San José, Costa Rica
Biblioteca Nacional, Hermeroteca, Guatemala City, Guatemala

COSTA RICAN NEWSPAPERS

Acción Social Cristiana
La República
Surco (1942–45)
Tico Times

GUATEMALAN NEWSPAPERS, JOURNALS, BULLETINS, AND
POLITICAL PARAPHERNALIA

Acción Campesina (1952–54)
Boletín de la AGA (1945–50)
Boletín de la sección departamental de Guatemala del STEG (1946–47)
Boletín Mensual del Comité Ejecutivo Nacional del STEG (1952)
El Campesino (1946–48; 1952–54)
Claridad (1945)
Diario de Centro América (Jan.–Mar. 1945)
Economía (IIES), nos. 12–97
Hojas Sueltas (1944–54), looseleaf papers catalogued by year at the Hermeroteca at AGCA

La Hora (Jan.–Mar. 1945)
El Imparcial (1944–53)
Lanzas y Letras (1958–62)
Mujeres (Aug.–Sept. 1952)
Nuestro Diario (Jan.–Mar. 1945)
Octubre (Nov. 1951–Apr. 1953)
Revista Cafetalera de Guatemala (1944–53)
Revista de Economía, Ministerio de Economía y Trabajo (1947–54)
Revista de la Facultad de Ciencias Jurídicas y Sociales de Guatemala (1945–46)
Revista de Guatemala (1945–53)
Revista de Maestros (1946–52)
Revista Militar, Organo de Publicidad del Ejército Nacional de la Revolución (1944–54)
Saker-Ti (1947–51)
Tribuna Popular (Aug. 1953–June 1954)
Unidad Organo Central de la CGTG (1953)

Interviews

COSTA RICA

Azofeifa, Isaac Felipe. Founding member of Centro, Partido Social Demócrata, and poet. June 13, 21, 29, 1990; Aug. 18, 19, 25, 1994.

Barahona Streber, Oscar. Drafted social legislation in Costa Rica and Guatemala in the 1940s. August 23, 1994.

Cerdas, Alicia. Member of Partido Vanguardia Popular (communist party). July 7, 1990.

Cerdas, Fernando. Member of Partido Vanguardia Popular (communist party). July 7, 1990.

Ferreto, Arnoldo. Leader of Partido Vanguardia Popular (communist party). July 8, 10, 1990.

Martén, Alberto. Member of Acción Demócrata and Partido Social Demócrata. July 13, 1990; Aug. 17, 22, 1994.

Monge, Luis Alberto. Member of Acción Demócrata and former president of Costa Rica (1982–86). Aug. 26, 1994.

Mora Valverde, Eduardo. Member of Partido Vanguardia Popular (communist party). June 25, 1990.

Mora Valverde, Manuel. Secretary general of Partido Vanguardia Popular (communist party). July 12, 25, and 28, 1990.

Núñez, Benjamín. Priest, labor organizer, and former minister of labor. Aug. 17, 1994.

Rodríguez, Efraín. Union activist in CTCR and labor organizer in Costa Rica since the 1930s. July 3, 1990.

Rodríguez, Eugenio. Member of Partido Social Demócrata. July 27, 1990.

Soto Harrison, Fernando. Secretary of the interior in the first part of the Picado administration. June 3, 1990; Aug. 16, 25, 1994.

Torres Rivas, Edelberto. Guatemalan student activist in 1954 and sociologist. June 4, June 22, 1990.

GUATEMALA

Amado Herrera, Eloy. Director of Universidad Popular. March 10, 1990.
Chavarría de Ponce, Carmen Yolanda. Lawyer. Feb. 26, 1990.
Cruz Salazar, José Luis. Military officer and participant in 1954 junta that took power after overthrow of President Arbenz; also political scientist. Mar. 2, 1990.
Enríquez Morales, Coronel Mario René. Director of the Escuela Politécnica. Feb. 27, 1990.
Estévez, Concha. President of Comité Locatarias Anticomunistas. Mar. 10, 1990.
Gramajo, Hector. Former defense minister. Mar. 19, 1990; Mar. 29, 1994.
Meléndez de León, Julia. Teacher and member of STEG. Jan. 5, 1990.
Morales, Walter René. Officer at Escuela Politécnica. Feb. 27, 1990.
Osegueda, Raúl. Former minister of education. Mar. 2, 1990.
Paz y Paz, Leonora. Political activist for women's rights. Feb. 13, 19, 1990.
Penados del Barrio, Próspero. Archbishop of Guatemala City. Feb. 16, 1990; Mar. 19, 1990.
Toriello, Jorge. One of three members of 1944 revolutionary junta. Mar. 30, 1994.
Vela, David. Editor of *El Imparcial*. Jan. 20, 1990; Mar. 14, 1990.
Villamar Contreras, Marco Antonio. Student activist in 1944 and reform politician. Oct. 27, 1989; Feb. 12, 23, 1990.
Anonymous A. Educator and former diplomat. Jan. 31, 1990.
Anonymous B. Teachers from STEG. Mar. 19, 1990.
Anonymous C. Four Guatemalan military officers. Mar. 29, 1994.

MEXICO

Capuano, Ernesto. Senior official of Guatemala's National Agrarian Bank. Aug. 9, 14, 15, 16, 1990.
Fortuny, José Manuel. Secretary general of the Partido Guatemalteco del Trabajo (Guatemalan communist party). Aug. 3, 10, 1990.
Guerra Borges, Alfredo. Member of the secretariat of the Partido Guatemalteco del Trabajo (Guatemalan communist party). Aug. 8, 1990.
Paz Tejada, Carlos. Former Guatemalan military officer. Aug. 11, 18, 1990.

Books and Articles

AGA and CCIG. 1948. *Opinión patronal sobre reformas al código de trabajo*. Publicaciones de la Asociación General de Agricultores y de la Cámara de Comercio e Industria de Guatemala. Guatemala City: Unión Tipográfica.
Acuña Ortega, Víctor H. 1987. "La ideología de los pequeños y medianos productores cafetaleros costarricenses (1900–1961)." *Avances de Investi-*

gación, no. 23. Universidad de Costa Rica: Centro de Investigaciones Históricas.

———. 1986. "El desarrollo del capitalismo en Costa Rica: 1821–1930." In Víctor H. Acuña Ortega and Iván Molina Jiménez, eds., *El desarrollo económico y social de Costa Rica: de la colonia a la crisis de 1930*. San José, Costa Rica: Alma Mater.

———. 1985. "Clases sociales y conflicto social en la economía cafetalera costarricense: productores contra beneficiadores: 1932–1936." *Revista de Historia*. Número Especial, Simposio: Historia, problemas y perspectiva agraria en Costa Rica. Heredia, Costa Rica, pp. 181–206.

Acuña V., Miguel. 1974. *El 48*. San José, Costa Rica: Librería, Imprenta y Litografía Lehmann.

Adams, Richard. 1990. "Ethnic Images and Strategies in 1944." In Carol A. Smith, ed., *Guatemalan Indians and the State, 1540 to 1988*. Austin: University of Texas Press.

———. 1970. *Crucifixion by Power: Essays on Guatemalan Social Structure, 1944–1966*. Austin: University of Texas Press.

———. 1969. "El problema del desarrollo político a la luz de la reciente historia sociopolítica de Guatemala." Buenos Aires: Instituto Torcuato Di Tella, Centro de Investigaciones Sociales.

Aguilar, Marielos H. 1989. *Clase trabajadora y organización sindical en Costa Rica*. San José, Costa Rica: Editorial Porvenir.

———. 1983. *Carlos Luis Fallas: su época y sus luchas*. San José, Costa Rica: Editorial Porvenir.

Aguilar Bulgarelli, Oscar. 1986. *La Constitución de 1949: antecedentes y proyecciones*. San José: Editorial Costa Rica.

———. 1983. *Costa Rica y sus hechos políticos de 1948: problemática de una década*. San José: Editorial Costa Rica.

Aguilera Peralta, Gabriel. 1983. "Le Procéssus de Militarisation de l'Etat Guatémaltèque." *Nordsur* 8, no. 15: 59–81.

———. 1988. "The Hidden War: Guatemala's Counterinsurgency." In Nora Hamilton, Jeffry A. Frieden, Linda Fuller, and Manuel Pastor, Jr., eds., *Crisis in Central America: Regional Dynamics and U.S. Policy in the 1980s*. Boulder, Colo.: Westview Press.

Aguilera Peralta, Gabriel, Jorge Romero Imery, et al. 1981. *Dialéctica del terror en Guatemala*. Ciudad Universitaria Rodrigo Facio, Costa Rica: Editorial Universitaria Centroamericana.

Alba, Victor. 1968. *Politics and the Labor Movement in Latin America*. Stanford, Calif.: Stanford University Press.

Albizures, Miguel Angel. 1988, 1989a & 1989b. "Recuerdos de la Revolución I, II, & III: Entrevista con el Coronel Carlos Paz Tejada." *Otra Guatemala*. Año 1, no.4 (September); Año 2, no. 5 (January); Año 2, nos. 7–8 (July).

Almond, Gabriel A., and Stephen J. Genco. 1978. "Clouds, Clocks, and the Study of Politics." *World Politics* 29, no. 4 (July): 489–522.

Althusser, Louis. 1979. *For Marx*. London: Verso.

Alvarado, Humberto. 1953. *Por una arte: nacional, democrática y realista.* Guatemala: Ediciones Saker-Ti.

Ameringer, Charles D. 1982. *Democracy in Costa Rica.* New York: Praeger Publishers.

Amnesty International. *1995 Report.* London: Amnesty International Publications.

———. 1993. *Guatemala: Impunity — A Question of Political Will.* New York: Amnesty International U.S.A.

Amsden, Alice H. 1979. "Taiwan's Economic History: A Case of Etatisme and a Challenge to Dependency Theory." *Modern China* 5, no. 3 (July): 341–80.

Anderson, Leslie. 1991. "Mixed Blessings: Disruption and Organization among Peasant Unions in Costa Rica." *Latin American Research Review* 26, no. 1: 111–43.

Anderson, Perry. 1974. *Lineages of the Absolutist State.* London: Verso.

Anderson, Thomas P. 1982. *Politics in Central America: Guatemala, El Salvador and Nicaragua.* New York: Praeger Publishers.

Aníbal González, Mario. 1986. "Los Alemanes en Quetzaltenango." *La Hora,* Feb. 7.

———. 1986. "Recuerdos de la Dictadura del Gobierno Jorge Ubico" (editorial). *La Hora,* Feb. 15.

Arévalo Martínez, Rafael. 1984. *Ubico.* Guatemala: Tipografía Nacional.

Arias, Arturo. 1979. *Ideologías, literatura y sociedad durante la revolución guatemalteca.* Havana: Casa de las Américas.

Armstrong, Rosalie, and Warwick Armstrong. 1983. "The Rural Roots of Social Struggle: The Peasantry in Guatemala, El Salvador and Nicaragua." *NorthSouth* 8, no. 15.

Arriola, Aura Marina. n.d. "Los indígenas y la política indigenista en Guatemala." Manuscript.

Arriola Avendaño, Carlos Enrique. 1987. "La lucha de clase en torno a la política agraria. Guatemala: 1944–1954." Thesis, Universidad de San Carlos, Guatemala.

Ascher, William. 1984. *Scheming for the Poor: The Politics of Redistribution in Latin America.* Cambridge, Mass.: Harvard University Press.

Asturias, Miguel Angel. 1988. *El Señor Presidente.* San José, Costa Rica: Editorial Universitaria Centroamericana.

Backer, James. 1978. *La Iglesia y el sindicalismo en Costa Rica.* San José, Costa Rica: Editorial Costa Rica.

Baloyra Herp, Enrique A. 1983. "Reactionary Despotism in Central America." *Journal of Latin American Studies* 15: 295–313.

Bardhan, Pranab. 1984. *Land, Labor, and Rural Poverty: Essays in Development Economics.* Delhi: Oxford University Press.

Bastos, Santiago, and Manuela Camus. 1993. *Quebrando el silencio: organizaciones del pueblo maya y sus demandas (1986–1992).* Guatemala: FLACSO.

Bates, Robert H. 1989. *Beyond the Miracle of the Market: The Political Economy of Agrarian Development in Kenya.* Cambridge, Eng.: Cambridge University Press.

———. 1981. *Markets and States in Tropical Africa: The Political Basis of Agricultural Policies.* Berkeley: University of California Press.

Bauer Paiz, Alfonso. 1974. "La revolución guatemalteca del 20 de octubre de 1944 y sus proyecciones económicas-sociales." *Alero* 8: 58–70.

———. 1956. *Como opera el capital yanqui en Centroamérica: el caso de Guatemala.* Mexico: Editorial Ibero-Mexicana.

Bell, John Patrick. 1971. *Costa Rica: The 1948 Revolution.* Austin: University of Texas Press.

Bello, Walden F., and Stephanie Rosenfeld. 1990. *Dragons in Distress: Asia's Miracle Economies in Crisis.* San Francisco: Institute for Food and Development Policy.

Bendix, Reinhard. 1964. *Nation-Building and Citizenship.* Berkeley: University of California Press.

Bennett, Douglas, and Kenneth Sharp. 1980. "The State as Banker and Entrepreneur: The Last Resort Character of the Mexican State's Economic Intervention, 1917–76." *Comparative Politics* 12 (Jan.): 165–89.

Bethell, Leslie, ed. 1991. *Central America Since Independence.* Cambridge, Eng.: Cambridge University Press.

Bethell, Leslie, and Ian Roxborough. 1992. *Latin America Between the Second World War and the Cold War, 1944–1948.* Cambridge, Eng.: Cambridge University Press.

———. 1988. "Latin America Between the Second World War and the Cold War: Some Reflections on the 1945–8 Conjuncture." *Journal of Latin American Studies* 20: 167–89.

Bishop, Edwin Warren. 1959. "The Guatemalan Labor Movement, 1944–1959." Ph.D. diss., University of Wisconsin.

Black, George, with Milton Jamail and Norma Stoltz Chinchilla. 1984. *Garrison Guatemala.* London: Zed Press.

Blasier, Cole. 1985. *The Hovering Giant: U.S. Responses to Revolutionary Change in Latin America, 1910–1985.* Rev. ed. Pittsburgh, Pa.: University of Pittsburgh Press.

Bobbio, Norberto. 1989. *Democracy and Dictatorship.* Minneapolis: University of Minnesota Press.

Booth, John A. 1989. "Costa Rica: The Roots of Democracy." In Larry Diamond, Juan J. Linz, and Seymour Martin Lipset, eds., *Democracy in Developing Countries: Latin America.* Boulder, Colo.: Lynne Reinner.

———. 1987. "Costa Rica." In Gerald Michael Greenfield and Sheldon L. Maram, eds., *Latin American Labor Organizations.* New York: Greenwood Press.

Booth, John A., and Mitchell A. Seligson. 1989. *Elections and Democracy in Central America.* Chapel Hill: University of North Carolina Press.

Booth, John A., and Thomas W. Walker. 1989. *Understanding Central America.* Boulder, Colo.: Westview Press.

Bourgois, Philippe I. 1989. *Ethnicity at Work: Divided Labor on a Central American Banana Plantation.* Baltimore: Johns Hopkins University Press.

Bouchez, L. Francis, and Alberto M. Piedra. 1980. *Guatemala: A Promise for Peril.* Washington, D.C.: Council for Inter-American Security.

Bowen, Gordon L. 1984. "Guatemala: The Origins and Development of State Terrorism." In Donald E. Schulz and Douglas H. Graham, eds., *Revolution and Counterrevolution in Central America and the Caribbean.* Boulder, Colo.: Westview Press.

Brass, Paul R. 1994. *The Politics of India Since Independence.* 2nd ed. Cambridge, Eng.: Cambridge University Press.

Bresser Pereira, Luis Carlos, José Carlos Maravall, and Adam Przeworski. 1993. *Economic Reforms in New Democracies: A Social-Democratic Approach.* Cambridge, Eng.: Cambridge University Press.

Brockett, Charles D. 1988. *Land, Power, and Poverty: Agrarian Transformation and Political Conflict in Central America.* Boston: Unwin Hyman.

Buhrer, J. C., and C. Levenson. 1980. *Le Guatemala et ses Populations.* Brussels: Editions Complexes.

Bullock, Robert. Forthcoming. "The Social Bases of the Development State: Agriculture and the Conservative Coalition in Postwar Japan, 1955–1993." Ph.D. diss. University of California, Berkeley.

———. n.d. "Agricultural Development in Korea and Taiwan." Manuscript, University of California, Berkeley.

Bulmer-Thomas, Victor. 1987. *The Political Economy of Central America Since 1920.* Cambridge, Eng.: Cambridge University Press.

———. 1983. "Economic Development Over the Long Run—Central America Since 1920." *Journal of Latin American Studies* 15: 269–94.

Bush, Archer C. 1950. "Organized Labor in Guatemala, 1944–1949: A Case Study of an Adolescent Labor Movement in an Underdeveloped Country." M.A. thesis, Colgate University.

Cáceres, Carlos. 1980. *Aproximación a Guatemala.* Culiacan: Universidad Autónoma de Sinaloa.

Calder, Bruce Johnson. 1970. *Crecimiento y cambio de la iglesia católica guatemalteca, 1944–1966.* Guatemala City: Editorial José de Pineda Ibarra, Seminario de Integración Social Guatemalteca.

Calderón Guardia, Rafael Angel. 1944. *Mensaje de la República Doctor Don R. A. Calderón Guardia presentado al Congreso Constitucional el 1 de mayo.* Costa Rican National Library.

Cambranes, J. C. 1985. *Coffee and Peasants: The Origins of the Modern Plantation Economy in Guatemala, 1853–1897.* Stockholm: Institute of Latin American Studies.

———. 1984. "Origins of the Crisis of the Established Order in Guatemala." In Steve C. Ropp and James A. Morris, eds., *Central America: Crisis and Adaptation.* Albuquerque: University of New Mexico Press.

Capuano, Ernesto. 1988. "El movimiento sindical guatemalteco y sus relaciones con la Confederación de Trabajadores de América Latina, CTAL." Manuscript, Mexico City.

Cardoso, Ciro F. S. 1991. "The Liberal Era, c. 1870–1930." In Leslie Bethell, ed., *Central America Since Independence*. Cambridge, Eng.: Cambridge University Press.

———. 1977. "The Formation of the Coffee Estate in Nineteenth-century Costa Rica." In K. Duncan and I. Rutledge, eds., *Land and Labour in Latin America*. Cambridge, Eng.: Cambridge University Press.

———. 1975. "Historia económica del café en Centroamérica (siglo XIX): Estudio comparativo." *Estudios Sociales Centroamericanos* 4, no. 10 (Jan.–Apr.): 9–55.

Cardoso, Fernando Henrique. 1979. "On the Characterization of Authoritarian Regimes in Latin America." In David Collier, ed., *The New Authoritarianism*. Princeton, N.J.: Princeton University Press.

Cardoso, Fernando Henrique, and Enzo Faletto. 1979. *Dependency and Development in Latin America*. Berkeley: University of California Press.

Cardoza, José Alberto. 1990. "El día del tipógrafo: la huelga." *Otra Guatemala* 3, no. 11 (May).

Cardoza y Aragón, Luis. 1955a. *La revolución guatemalteca*. Mexico City: Cuadernos Americanos.

———. 1955b. *Guatemala: las líneas de su mano*. Mexico City: Fondo de Cultura Económica.

Carmack, Robert M., ed. 1988. *Harvest of Violence: The Maya Indians and the Guatemalan Crisis*. Norman: University of Oklahoma Press.

Carvajal Herrera, Mario. 1978. *Actitudes políticos del costarricense*. San José, Costa Rica: Editorial Costa Rica.

Cehelsky, Marta. 1974. "Habla Arbenz." *Alero* 8: 116–24. Tercera Epóca.

Cerdas Cruz, Rodolfo. 1991. "Costa Rica Since 1930." In Leslie Bethell, ed., *Central America Since Independence*. Cambridge, Eng.: Cambridge University Press.

Chea Urruela, José Luis. 1988. *Guatemala: la cruz fragmentada*. San José, Costa Rica: Editorial DEI.

Chaudhry, Kiren. 1993. "The Myths of the Market and the Common History of Late Developers." *Politics and Society* 21, no. 3 (Sept.): 245–74.

Chomsky, Aviva. 1990. "Plantation Society, Land and Labor on Costa Rica's Atlantic Coast, 1870–1940." Ph.D. diss., University of California, Berkeley.

Cohen, Isaac. 1980. "Notas sobre el trasfondo histórico del desarrollo centroamericano." Mexico City: Naciones Unidas, Comisión Económica para América Latina.

Cohen, Jean, and Andrew Arato. 1992. *Civil Society and Political Theory*. Cambridge, Mass.: MIT Press.

Cohen, Youssef, Brian R. Brown, and A. F. K. Organski. 1981. "The Paradoxical Nature of State-Making." *American Political Science Review* 75, no. 4 (Dec.): 901–10.

Collier, David, ed. 1979. *The New Authoritarianism in Latin America*. Princeton, N.J.: Princeton University Press.

Collier, Ruth Berins. 1993. "Combining Alternative Perspectives: Internal

Trajectories versus External Influences as Explanations of Latin American Politics in the 1940s." *Comparative Politics* 26, no. 1 (Oct.): 1–30.

———. 1982. "Popular Sector Incorporation and Political Supremacy: Regime Evolution in Brazil and Mexico." In Sylvia Ann Hewlett and Richard S. Weinhart, eds., *Brazil and Mexico: Patterns in Late Development*. Philadelphia: Institute for the Study of Human Issues.

Collier, Ruth Berins, and David Collier. 1991. *Shaping the Political Arena: Critical Junctures, the Labor Movement, and Regime Dynamics in Latin America*. Princeton, N.J.: Princeton University Press.

———. 1979. "Inducements versus Constraints: Disaggregating Corporatism." *American Political Science Review* 73, no. 4 (Dec.): 967–86.

Comité Interamericano de Desarollo Agrícola. 1965. *Tenencia de la tierra y desarollo socioeconómico del sector agrícola*. Washington, D.C.

Concerned Guatemalan Scholars. 1982. *Guatemala: Dare to Struggle, Dare to Win*. New York: Solidarity Publications.

Connolly, William E. 1983. *The Terms of Political Discourse*. 2nd. ed. Princeton, N.J.: Princeton University Press.

Contreras, Gerardo, and José Manuel Cerdas. 1988. *Los años 40: historia de una política de alianzas*. San José, Costa Rica: Editorial Porvenir.

Cooperative Oral History Project. 1970a. "Interview with Alberto Martén Chavarría." July 7. Manuscript, University of Kansas.

———. 1970b. "Interview with Padre Benjamín Núñez." July 7. Manuscript, University of Kansas.

———. 1970c. "Interview with Otilio Ulate." July 16. Manuscript, University of Kansas.

Coppedge, Michael. 1994. *Strong Parties and Lame Ducks: Presidential Partyarchy and Factionalism in Venezuela*. Stanford, Calif.: Stanford University Press.

Corradi, Juan E., Patricia Weiss Fagen, and Manuel Antonio Garretón, eds. 1992. *Fear at the Edge: State, Terror, and Resistance in Latin America*. Berkeley: University of California Press.

Costa Rica. 1951. *Asamblea Nacional Constituyente de 1949*. Vols. 1–3. San José, Costa Rica: Imprenta Nacional.

Costa Rica. 1944, 1946, 1948. Costa Rican National Archives, Secretaría de Gobernación. Carteros, Secretaría de Agricultura.

Costa Rica. 1943. *Código de Trabajo*. Alvaro Ruíz Valverde, comp. San José, Costa Rica: n.p.

Creedman, Theodore S. 1971. "The Political Development of Costa Rica, 1936–1944: Politics of an Emerging Welfare State in a Patriarchal Society." Ph.D. diss., University of Maryland.

Cruz, Vladimir de la. 1986. "Notas para la historia del movimiento campesino en Costa Rica." In Carmen Lila Gómez et al., *Las instituciones costarricenses del siglo XX*. San José, Costa Rica: Editorial Costa Rica.

Cruz Salazar, José Luis. 1987. *El carácter revolucionario del movimiento de octubre de 1944*. Guatemala: Asociación de Investigaciones y Estudios Sociales.

———. 1972. "El Ejército como una fuerza política." *Estudios Sociales*, no. 6. Guatemala City: Universidad Rafael Landívar.

Dahl, Robert A. 1989. *Democracy and Its Critics*. New Haven, Conn.: Yale University Press.

———. 1971. *Polyarchy: Participation and Opposition*. New Haven, Conn.: Yale University Press.

Davis, Shelton H. 1983. "State Violence and Agrarian Crisis in Guatemala: The Roots of the Indian-Peasant Rebellion." In Martin Diskin, ed., *Trouble in Our Own Backyard: Central America and the U.S. in the 1980s*. New York: Pantheon.

Denton, Charles F. 1971. *Patterns of Costa Rican Politics*. Boston: Allyn and Bacon.

Di Palma, Giuseppe. 1990. *To Craft Democracies: An Essay on Democratic Transitions*. Berkeley: University of California Press.

Di Palma, Giuseppe, and Laurence Whitehead, eds. 1986. *The Central American Impasse*. London: Croom Helm.

Díaz Castillo, Roberto. 1978. "Víctor Manuel Gutiérrez y el problema indígena." *La Tradición Popular* 19. Guatemala City: Universidad de San Carlos, Centro de Estudios Folklóricos.

Díaz Rozzotto, Jaime. 1958. *El carácter de la revolución guatemalteca: ocaso de la revolución democrático-burguesa corriente*. Mexico City: Ediciones Revista Horizonte.

Dion, Marie Berthe. 1958. *Las ideas sociales y políticas de Arévalo*. Mexico City: Editorial América Nueva.

Domínguez, Jorge I. 1980. *Insurrection or Loyalty: The Breakdown of the Spanish American Empire*. Cambridge, Mass.: Harvard University Press.

Donnelly, Michael W. 1977. "Setting the Price of Rice: A Study in Political Decision-Making." In T. J. Pempel, ed., *Policymaking in Contemporary Japan*. Ithaca, N.Y.: Cornell University Press.

Dosal, Paul J. 1993. *Doing Business with the Dictators: A Political History of United Fruit in Guatemala, 1899–1944*. Wilmington, Del.: Scholarly Resources.

———. 1988. "The Political Economy of Guatemalan Industrialization, 1871–1948: The Career of Carlos P. Novella." *Hispanic American Historical Review* 68, no. 2 (May): 321–58.

Downing, Brian M. 1992. *The Military Revolution and Political Change: Origins of Democracy and Autocracy in Early Modern Europe*. Princeton, N.J.: Princeton University Press.

Dunkerley, James. 1991. "Guatemala Since 1930." In Leslie Bethell, ed., *Central America Since Independence*. Cambridge, Eng.: Cambridge University Press.

———. 1988. *Power in the Isthmus: A Political History of Modern Central America*. New York: Verso.

Eckstein, Susan. 1977. *The Poverty of Revolution: The State and the Urban Poor in Mexico*. Princeton, N.J.: Princeton University Press.

Economic Commission for Latin America and the Caribbean [ECLAC]. 1995.

Statistical Yearbook for Latin America and the Caribbean. 1994 ed. Chile: United Nations Publication.

Edelman, Marc. 1992. *The Logic of the Latifundio: The Large Estates of Northwestern Costa Rica Since the Late Nineteenth Century*. Stanford, Calif.: Stanford University Press.

———. 1983. "Recent Literature on Costa Rica's Economic Crisis." *Latin American Research Review* 18, no. 2: 166–80.

Edelman, Marc, and Joanne Kenen, eds. 1989. *The Costa Rica Reader*. New York: Grove Weidenfeld.

Elster, Jon. 1988. "Introduction." In Jon Elster and Rune Slagstad, eds., *Constitutionalism and Democracy*. Cambridge, Eng.: Cambridge University Press.

English, Burt H. 1971. *Liberación Nacional in Costa Rica: The Development of a Political Party in a Transitional Society*. Gainesville: University of Florida Press.

Erlan López, Matilde. 1948. *Revista de Guatemala* 9, no. 1 (July–Sept.): 48–68.

Evans, Peter. 1992. "The State as Problem and Solution: Predation, Embedded Autonomy, and Structural Change." In Stephan Haggard and Robert R. Kaufman, eds., *The Politics of Economic Adjustment: International Constraints, Distributive Conflicts, and the State*. Princeton, N.J.: Princeton University Press.

———. 1987. "Class, State, and Dependence in East Asia: Lessons for Latin Americanists." In Frederick C. Deyo, ed., *The Political Economy of the New Asian Industrialism*. Ithaca, N.Y.: Cornell University Press.

Evans, Peter B., Dietrich Rueschemeyer, and Theda Skocpol, eds. 1985. *Bringing the State Back In*. Cambridge, Eng.: Cambridge University Press.

Evans, Peter, and John D. Stephens. 1988. "Studying development since the sixties: The emergence of a new comparative political economy." *Theory and Society* 17: 713–45.

Facio, Rodrigo. 1973. *La moneda y la Banca Central en Costa Rica*. San José, Costa Rica: Editorial Costa Rica.

———. 1943. *El Centro ante las garantías sociales*. San José, Costa Rica: Imprenta Borrase.

Falla, Ricardo. 1978. *Quiché Rebelde*. Guatemala City: Editorial Universitaria.

Fallas, Carlos Luis. 1986. *Mamita Yunai*. San José, Costa Rica: Editorial Costa Rica.

Fallas, Carlos Luis, Eduardo Mora V., and Arnoldo Ferreto. n.d. *Calderón Guardia, José Figueres y Otilio Ulate. A la luz de los últimos acontecimientos políticos*. San José, Costa Rica.

Fernández Durán, Roberto. 1953. *La huelga de brazos caídos*. San José, Costa Rica: Editorial Liberación Nacional.

Fernández Vásquez, Rodrigo. 1982. "Costa Rica: interpretación histórica sobre reforma social y acción eclesiástica, 1940–1982." *Estudios Sociales Centroamericanos* 33 (Sept.–Dec.): 221–47.

Ferreto, Arnoldo. 1984. *Vida Militante*. San José, Costa Rica: Editorial Presbere.

Figueres Ferrer, José. 1987. *El Espíritu del 48*. San José, Costa Rica: Editorial Costa Rica.

———. 1986. *José Figueres. Escritos y Discursos, 1942–1962*. San José, Costa Rica: Editorial Costa Rica.

Figueroa Ibarra, Carlos. 1980. *El proletariado rural en el agro guatemalteco*. Guatemala City: Editorial Universitaria.

Fischel, Astrid. 1987. *Consenso y represíon: una interpretacíon socio-política de la educación costarricense*. San José, Costa Rica: Editorial de Costa Rica.

Fox, Jonathan. 1994a. "The Difficult Transition from Clientelism to Citizenship: Lessons from Mexico." *World Politics* 46, no. 2 (Jan.): 151–84.

———. 1994b. "Latin America's Emerging Local Politics." *Journal of Democracy* 5, no. 2 (Apr.): 105–16.

———, ed. 1990. Special issue: The Challenge of Rural Democratisation: Perspectives from Latin America and the Philippines. *The Journal of Development Studies* 26, no. 4 (July).

Frankel, Anita. 1969. "Political Development in Guatemala, 1944–1954: The Impact of Foreign, Military and Religious Elites." Ph.D. diss., University of Connecticut.

Galeano, Eduardo H. 1988. *Memory of Fire: Century of the Wind*, vol. 3. Cedric Belfrage, trans. New York: Pantheon.

Galich, Manuel. 1977. *Del pánico al ataque*. Guatemala City: Editorial Universitaria.

———. 1945. "Discurso del Ministro de Educación Pública, Bachiller Manuel Galich." *Universidad de San Carlos* 1 (Oct.–Dec.): 75–85.

Gallie, W. B. 1956. "Essentially Contested Concepts." In *Aristotelian Society*, vol. 51. London: Harrison.

García Añoveros, Jesús. 1987. *La reforma agraria de Arbenz en Guatemala*. Instituto de Cooperación Iberoamericana. Madrid: Ediciones Cultura Hispánica.

———. 1978. "El Caso Guatemala (junio de 1954): La Universidad y el Campesinado." *Alero* 28: 133–234.

García Bauer, José. 1948. *Nuestra Revolución Legislativa*. Guatemala City: n.p.

García L., Graciela. 1952. *Las luchas revolucionarias de la nueva Guatemala*. Mexico City: n.p.

Gardner, John W. 1971. "The Costa Rican Junta of 1948–1949." Ph.D. diss., St. John's University.

Geiger, Theodore. 1953. *Communism Versus Progress in Guatemala*. Planning Pamphlets, no. 85. Washington, D.C.: National Planning Committee on International Policy.

George, Aurelia D. 1981. "The Japanese Farm Lobby and Agricultural Policy-Making." *Pacific Affairs* 54, no. 3 (fall): 409–30.

Gerschenkron, Alexander. 1962. *Economic Backwardness in Historical Perspective: A Book of Essays*. Cambridge, Mass.: Belknap Press.

Gleijeses, Piero. 1991. *Shattered Hope: The Guatemalan Revolution and the United States, 1944–1954*. Princeton, N.J.: Princeton University Press.

———. 1989a. "La aldea de Ubico: Guatemala, 1931–1940." *Mesoamérica* 17 (June): 25–59.

———. 1989b. "The Agrarian Reform of Jacobo Arbenz." *Journal of Latin American Studies* 21 (Oct.): 453–80.

Gómez Padilla, Julio. 1980. "Cambios en las relaciones de producción en el movimiento revolucionaria de 1944–1945." *Economía* 63 (Jan.–Mar.): 27–53.

González-Vega, Claudio, and Víctor Céspedes. 1993. "Costa Rica." In Simon Rottenberg, ed., *The Political Economy of Poverty, Equity, and Growth: Costa Rica and Uruguay*. Oxford: Oxford University Press.

González-Víquez, Cleto. 1978. *El sufragio en Costa Rica ante la historia y la legislación*. San José, Costa Rica: Editorial Costa Rica.

Goodwin, Jeff, and Theda Skocpol. 1989. "Explaining Revolutions in the Contemporary Third World." *Politics and Society* 17, no. 4 (Dec.): 489–509.

Gordon, David M., Richard Edwards, and Michael Reich. 1982. *Segmented Work, Divided Workers: The Historical Transformation of Labor in the United States*. New York: Cambridge University Press.

Goubaud Carrera, Antonio. 1945. "Discurso del Director del Instituto Indigenista Nacional, Licenciado Antonio Goubaud Carrera." *Universidad de San Carlos* 1 (Oct.–Dec.): 86–99.

Gourevitch, Peter. 1986. *Politics in Hard Times*. Ithaca, N.Y.: Cornell University Press.

Grieb, Kenneth J. 1979. *Guatemalan Caudillo: The Regime of Jorge Ubico, Guatemala 1931–1944*. Athens: Ohio University Press.

———. 1978. "The Myth of a Central American Dictators' League." *Journal of Latin American Studies* 10, no. 2: 329–45.

———. 1976. "The Guatemalan Military and the Revolution of 1944." *The Americas* 32, no. 4 (Apr.): 524–43.

Grindle, Merilee S. 1986. *State and Countryside: Development Policy and Agrarian Politics in Latin America*. Baltimore: Johns Hopkins University Press.

———. 1977. *Bureaucrats, Politicians, and Peasants in Mexico: A Case Study in Public Policy*. Berkeley: University of California Press.

Guatemala. 1954. *Boletines Informativos del Ejército* (June 22–25). Relaciones Públicas del Ejército.

Guatemala. 1947–51. Departamento de Fomento Cooperativo. *Memoria de las Labores Desarolladas Durante el Año 1947, 1948, 1949, 1950, 1951*.

Guatemala. 1946. *Memoria de las Labores del Organismo Ejecutivo en el Ramo de la Defensa Nacional Durante el Año Administrativo de 1944 presentada al Congreso de la República en sus Sesiones Ordinarios de 1946*. Guatemala City.

Guatemala. 1945. Constitución de la República de Guatemala. Decretada y sancionada por la Asamblea Constituyente de Guatemala el 11 de marzo de 1945. *Revista de la Facultad de Ciencias Jurídicas y Sociales de Guatemala*, nos. 1-2 (May–Aug.): 35–79.

Guatemala. 1945. *Diario de Sesiones Constituyente Comisión de los 15.* Guatemala City: Tipografía Nacional.

Guatemala. 1945. *Ley Constitutiva del Ejército.* Reglamentos Generales. Ejército Nacional de la Revolución Ministerio de la Defensa. Guatemala City: Tipografía Nacional.

Guatemala. 1945. *Memoria de las Labores del Organismo Ejecutivo en el Ramo de la Defensa Nacional Durante el Año Administrativo de 1944 presentada al Congreso de la República en sus Sesiones Ordinarios de 1945.* Guatemala City.

Guatemala. 1944. *Anales de la Escuela Politécnica.*

Gudmundson, Lowell. 1995. "Lord and Peasant in the Making of Modern Central America." In Evelyne Huber and Frank Safford, eds., *Agrarian Structure and Political Power: Landlord and Peasant in the Making of Latin America*, pp. 151–76. Pittsburgh: University of Pittsburgh Press.

————. 1989a. "Peasant, Farmer, Proletarian: Class Formation in a Smallholder Coffee Economy, 1850–1950." *Hispanic American Historical Review* 69, no. 2 (May): 221–57.

————. 1989b. "Costa Rica." In Abraham F. Lowenthal, ed., *Latin America and Caribbean Contemporary Record*, vol. 5. New York: Holmes and Meier.

————. 1986a. *Costa Rica Before Coffee: Society and Economy on the Eve of the Export Boom.* Baton Rouge: Louisiana State University Press.

————. 1986b. "La Costa Rica cafetalera en contexto comparado." *Revista de Historia* 14 (July–Dec.): 11–23.

————. 1979. "El campesino y el capitalismo agrario de Costa Rica: una crítica de ideología como historia." *Revista de Historia* 8 (Jan.–July): 59–81.

Guerra Borges, Alfredo. 1988. "Apuntes para una interpretación de la Revolución Guatemalteca y de su derrota en 1954." *Anuario de Estudios Centroamericanos* 14: 109–20.

————. 1987. "Guatemala: tres tiempos de un historia inconclusa." In María Teresa Gutiérrez-Haces et al., eds., *Centroamérica: una historia sin retoque.* Mexico City: Sociedad Cooperativa de Publicaciones Mexicanas.

————. 1971. *Evaluación de la política de fomento industrial en Guatemala.* Guatemala City: n.p.

Gutiérrez Alvarez, Coralia. 1985. "Los trabajadores del campo y la política agraria en la revolución guatemalteca de 1944–1954." Thesis, Universidad Nacional Autónoma de México.

Gutiérrez G., V. Manuel. 1964. *Breve historia del movimiento sindical de Guatemala.* Mexico City: n.p.

Gúzman Bockler, Carlos, and Jean-Loup Herbert. 1970. *Guatemala: una interpretación histórico-social.* Mexico City: Siglo Veintiuno Editores.

Haggard, Stephan, and Robert R. Kaufman. 1992. *The Politics of Economic Adjustment: International Constraints, Distributive Conflicts, and the State.* Princeton, N.J.: Princeton University Press.

Hagopian, Frances. 1990. "Democracy by Undemocratic Means: Elite Pacts in Brazil." *Comparative Political Studies* 23, no. 2: 147–70.

Hall, Carolyn. 1982. *El café y el desarrollo histórico-geográfico de Costa Rica.* San José, Costa Rica: Editorial Costa Rica.

Hall, Peter A. 1986. *Governing the Economy: The Politics of State Intervention in Britain and France.* New York: Oxford University Press.

Hamilton, Nora. 1982. *The Limits of State Autonomy: Post-Revolutionary Mexico.* Princeton, N.J.: Princeton University Press.

Handy, Jim. 1994. *Revolution in the Countryside: Rural Conflict and Agrarian Reform in Guatemala, 1944–1954.* Chapel Hill: University of North Carolina Press.

———. 1992. "Reforma y contrareforma: la política agraria en Guatemala, 1952–1957." In Julio Castellano Cambranes, ed., *500 Años de lucha por la tierra: estudios sobre propiedad rural y reforma agraria en Guatemala.* Guatemala City: FLACSO.

———. 1988a. "The Most Precious Fruit of the Revolution: The Guatemalan Agrarian Reform, 1952–1954." *Hispanic American Historical Review* 68, no. 4: 675–705.

———. 1988b. "National Policy, Agrarian Reform, and the Corporate Community During the Guatemalan Revolution, 1944–1954." *Comparative Studies in Society and History* 30, no. 4 (Oct.): 698–724.

———. 1986. "Resurgent Democracy and the Guatemalan Military." *Journal of Latin American Studies* 18: 383–408.

———. 1985. "Revolution and Reaction: National Policy and Rural Politics in Guatemala, 1944–1954." Ph.D. diss., University of Toronto.

———. 1984. *Gift of the Devil: A History of Guatemala.* Boston: South End Press.

Harrison, Lawrence. 1985. *Underdevelopment Is a State of Mind: The Latin American Cases.* Center for International Affairs, Harvard University. Lanham, Md.: University Press of America.

Hart, Gillian, Andrew Turton, and Benjamin White. 1989. *Agrarian Transformations and the State in Southeast Asia.* Berkeley: University of California Press.

Held, David. 1987. *Models of Democracy.* Stanford, Calif.: Stanford University Press.

Hellman, Judith. 1983. *Mexico in Crisis.* 2nd ed. New York: Holmes and Meier.

Hernand, Rubén. 1986. "Elecciones generales de Costa Rica." In *Sistemas Electorales y Representación Política en Latinoamérica.* Madrid: Fundación Friedrich Ebert.

Herrera, Tomás. 1986. *Guatemala: Revolución de Octubre.* Ciudad Universitaria Rodrigo Facio: Editorial Universitaria Centroamericana.

———. 1977. "Guatemala: del gobierno de 'mano fuerte' de Ubico al gobierno del 'socialismo espiritual' de Arévalo." *Estudios Sociales Centroamericanos* 16 (Jan.–Apr.): 168–94.

Higley, John, and Richard Gunther, eds. 1992. *Elites and Democratic Consolidation in Latin America and Southern Europe.* Cambridge, Eng.: Cambridge University Press.

Hirschman, Albert O. 1965. *Journeys Towards Progress: Studies of Economic Policy Making in Latin America.* Garden City, N.J.: Doubleday.

Holleran, Mary. 1949. *Church and State in Guatemala.* New York: Columbia University Press.

Honig, Bonnie. 1993. *Political Theory and the Displacement of Politics.* Ithaca, N.Y.: Cornell University Press.

Hopkins, Raymond. 1995. "Agriculture and Democracy." Paper prepared for the annual meeting of the American Political Science Association, Chicago, Aug. 31–Sept. 3, 1995.

Huber, Evelyne, and Frank Safford, eds. 1995. *Agrarian Structure and Political Power: Landlord and Peasant in the Making of Latin America.* Pittsburgh: University of Pittsburgh Press.

Huntington, Samuel P. 1991. *The Third Wave: Democratization in the Late Twentieth Century.* Norman: University of Oklahoma Press.

———. 1968. *Political Order in Changing Societies.* New Haven, Conn.: Yale University Press.

Immerman, Richard. 1982. *The CIA in Guatemala: The Foreign Policy of Intervention.* Austin: University of Texas Press.

Inoguchi, Takashi. 1990. "The Political Economy of Conservative Resurgence under Recession: Public Policies and Political Support in Japan, 1977–1983." In T. J. Pempel, ed., *Uncommon Democracies: The One-Party Dominant Regimes.* Ithaca, N.Y.: Cornell University Press.

Inter-American Development Bank. 1994. *Economic and Social Progress in Latin America: 1994 Report.* Baltimore: Johns Hopkins University Press.

International Labour Office (ILO). 1941–44. *International Labour Review.*

Jamail, Milton Henry. 1972. "Guatemala 1944–1972: The Politics of Aborted Revolution." Ph.D. diss., University of Arizona.

Janvry, Alain de. 1981. *The Agrarian Question and Reformism in Latin America.* Baltimore: Johns Hopkins University Press.

Jessop, Bob. 1990a. *State Theory: Putting Capitalist States in Their Place.* University Park: Pennsylvania State University Press.

———. 1990b. "Regulation Theories in Retrospect and Prospect." *Economy and Society* 19, no. 2 (May): 153–216.

Jiménez Castro, Wilberg. 1986. *Genesis del gobierno de Costa Rica.* Vol. 1. San José, Costa Rica: Alma Mater Ciudad Universitaria "Rodrigo Facio," Universidad de Costa Rica.

———. 1977, 1981. *Análisis electoral de una democracia: estudio del comportamiento político costarricense durante el período 1953–1975.* San José, Costa Rica Editorial Costa Rica.

Johnston, Bruce, and William Clark. 1982. *Redesigning Rural Development*. Baltimore: Johns Hopkins University Press.

Jonas, Susanne. 1991. *Battle for Guatemala: Rebels, Death Squads, and U.S. Power*. Boulder, Colo.: Westview Press.

———. 1981. *Plan piloto para el continente*. San José, Costa Rica: Editorial Universitaria.

Jonas, Susanne, and David Tobis, eds. 1974, 1976. *Guatemala: una historia inmediata*. Berkeley, Calif: North American Congress on Latin America.

Jones, Chester Lloyd. 1970. *Guatemala: Past and Present*. Minneapolis: University of Minnesota Press.

Journal of Democracy. 1992. Special issue: Capitalism, Socialism, and Democracy. Vol. 3, no. 3 (July).

Journal of Democracy. 1994. Special issue: Economic Reform and Democracy. Vol. 5, no. 4 (Oct.).

Karl, Terry Lynn. 1990. "Dilemmas of Democratization in Latin America." *Comparative Politics* 23, no. 1 (Oct.): 1–21.

———. 1986. "Petroleum and Political Pacts: The Transition to Democracy in Venezuela." In Guillermo O'Donnell, Philippe C. Schmitter, and Laurence Whitehead, eds., *Transitions from Authoritarian Rule*. Baltimore: Johns Hopkins University Press.

Katzenstein, Peter. 1985. *Small States in World Markets: Industrial Policy in Europe*. Ithaca, N.Y.: Cornell University Press.

Kauck, David M. 1988. "Agricultural Commercialization and State Development in Central America: The Political Economy of the Coffee Industry from 1838 to 1940." Ph.D. diss., University of Washington.

Kaufman, Robert R. 1972. *The Politics of Land Reform in Chile, 1950–1970: Public Policy, Political Institutions and Social Change*. Cambridge, Mass.: Harvard University Press.

Keane, John. 1988. *Democracy and Civil Society*. London: Verso.

Kepner, Charles David, Jr., and Jay Henry Soothill. 1949. *El imperio del banano: Las compañías bananeras contra la soberanía de las naciones del Caribe*. Mexico City: Ediciones del Caribe.

Kitschelt, Herbert. 1992. "Review Essay: Structure and Process Driven Explanations of Political Regime Change." *American Political Science Review* 86, no. 4 (Dec.): 1028–34.

Kornblith, Miriam, and Daniel H. Levine. 1995. "Venezuela: The Life and Times of the Party System." In Scott Mainwaring and Timothy R. Scully. eds., *Building Democratic Institutions: Party Systems in Latin America*. Stanford, Calif.: Stanford University Press.

Krasner, Stephen D. 1983. *International Regimes*. Ithaca, N.Y.: Cornell University Press.

———. 1982. "Punctuated Equilibrium: An Approach to the Evolution of State-Society Relations." Manuscript, Department of Political Science, Stanford University.

Kuznesof, Elizabeth. 1986. "Comentarios sobre 'La Costa Rica cafetalera:

economía, sociedad y estructuras de poder.'" *Revista de Historia* 14 (July–Dec.): 31–39.

Lafeber, Walter. 1983. *Inevitable Revolutions: The U.S. in Central America.* New York: W. W. Norton.

Lapp, Nancy. 1994. "Expansion of Suffrage and the Timing of Land Reform in Latin America." Paper prepared for the 18th International Congress of the Latin American Studies Association, Atlanta, Ga., Mar. 10–12.

Leal, Héctor Alfonso. 1955. *Tierra de liberación para el campesino.* Guatemala City: Tipografía Nacional.

LeGrand, Catherine. 1986. "Comentarios sobre 'La Costa Rica cafetalera en contexto comparado,' de Lowell Gudmundson." *Revista de Historia* 14 (July–Dec.): 41–52.

Lehman, David, ed., 1974. *Peasants, Landlords and Governments: Agrarian Reform in the Third World.* New York: Holmes & Meier.

Lehoucq, Fabrice Edouard. 1992. "The Origins of Democracy in Costa Rica in Comparative Perspective." Ph.D. diss., Duke University.

———. 1991. "Class Conflict, Political Crisis, and the Breakdown of Democratic Practices in Costa Rica: Reassessing the Origins of the 1948 Civil War." *Journal of Latin American Studies* 23, no. 1 (Feb.): 37–60.

León Aragón, Oscar de. 1950. *Los contratos de la United Fruit Company y las compañías muelleras en Guatemala: Estudio histórico-jurídico.* Guatemala City: Editorial del Ministerio de Educación Pública.

Levine, Daniel. 1988. "Paradigm Lost: Dependence to Democracy." *World Politics* 15, no. 3 (Apr.): 377–94.

———. 1973. *Conflict and Political Change in Venezuela.* Princeton, N.J.: Princeton University Press.

Linz, Juan J. 1978. *The Breakdown of Democratic Regimes: Crisis, Breakdown, and Reequilibration.* Baltimore: Johns Hopkins University Press.

———. 1975. "Totalitarian and Authoritarian Regimes." In F. Greenstein and N. Polsby, eds., *Handbook of Political Science*, vol. 3. Reading, Pa.: Addison-Wesley.

Linz, Juan J., and Alfred Stepan. 1978. *The Breakdown of Democratic Regimes.* Baltimore: Johns Hopkins University Press.

Linz, Juan J., and Arturo Valenzuela. 1994. *The Failure of Presidential Democracy.* Baltimore: Johns Hopkins University Press.

Lipietz, Alain. 1989. *Towards a New Economic Order: Postfordism, Ecology, and Democracy.* Oxford: Oxford University Press.

———. 1987. *Mirages and Miracles: The Crises of Global Fordism.* London: Verso.

Lipset, Seymour Martin, and Stein Rokkan. 1967. "Cleavage Structures, Party Systems and Voter Alignments: An Introduction." In Lipset and Rokkan, eds., *Party Systems and Voter Alignments: Cross-National Perspectives.* New York: Free Press.

López, Matilde Elena. 1948. "Balance del Primer Congreso Interamericano de Mujeres." *Revista de Guatemala* 9, no. 1, (July–Sept.): 48–68.

López Larrave, Mario. 1976. *Breve historia del movimiento sindical guatemalteco*. Guatemala City: Editorial Universitaria.

Loveman, Brian. 1976. *Struggle in the Countryside*. Bloomington: Indiana University Press.

Lowi, Theodore J. 1964. "American Business, Public Policy, Case Studies, and Political Theory." *World Politics* 16, no. 4 (July): 677–715.

Luebbert, Gregory M. 1991. *Liberalism, Fascism, or Social Democracy: Social Classes and the Political Origins of Regimes in Interwar Europe*. New York: Cambridge University Press.

———. 1987. "Social Foundations of Political Order in Interwar Europe." *World Politics* 39, no. 4 (July): 449–78.

McClintock, Michael. 1985. *The American Connection*. Vol. 2, *State Terror and Popular Resistance in Guatemala*. London: Zed Press.

McCreery, David. 1994. *Rural Guatemala, 1760–1940*. Stanford, Calif.: Stanford University Press.

———. 1990. "State Power, Indigenous Communities, and Land in Nineteenth-Century Guatemala, 1820–1920." In Carol A. Smith, ed., *Guatemalan Indians and the State, 1540 to 1988*. Austin: University of Texas Press.

———. 1983. "Debt Servitude in Rural Guatemala." *Hispanic American Historical Review* 63, no. 4: 735–59.

———. 1976. "Coffee and Class: The Structure of Development in Liberal Guatemala." *Hispanic American Historical Review* 56, no. 3: 438–60.

MacLeod, Murdo J. 1973. *Spanish Central America: A Socioeconomic History 1520–1720*. Berkeley: University of California Press.

Mainwaring, Scott, Guillermo O'Donnell, and J. Samuel Valenzuela, eds. 1992. *Issues in Democratic Consolidation: The New South American Democracies in Comparative Perspective*. Notre Dame, Ind.: University of Notre Dame Press.

Mainwaring, Scott, and Timothy R. Scully, eds. 1995. *Building Democratic Institutions: Party Systems in Latin America*. Stanford, Calif.: Stanford University Press.

Malloy, James M., and Mitchell A. Seligson. 1987. *Authoritarians and Democrats: Regime Transitions in Latin America*. Pittsburgh, Pa.: University of Pittsburgh Press.

Manz, Beatriz. 1988. *Refugees of a Hidden War: The Aftermath of Counterinsurgency in Guatemala*. Albany: State University of New York.

Martz, John D. 1967. "Costa Rican Electoral Trends, 1953–1966." *The Western Political Quarterly* 20, no. 4 (Dec.): 888–909.

Marshall, T. H. 1963. *Class, Citizenship, and Social Development*. Chicago: University of Chicago Press.

Marx, Karl. 1978. "The Eighteenth Brumaire of Louis Bonaparte." In Robert C. Tucker, ed., *The Marx-Engels Reader*. 2nd ed. New York: W. W. Norton.

May, Stacy, and Galo Plaza. 1958. *United States Business Performance*

Abroad: The Case Study of the United Fruit Company in Latin America. Washington, D.C.: National Planning Association.

Meisner, Maurice. 1977. *Mao's China: A History of the People's Republic.* New York: Free Press.

Mejía, Medardo. 1949. *El movimiento obrero en la revolución de octubre.* Guatemala City: Tipografía Nacional.

Melville, Thomas, and Marjorie Melville. 1971. *Guatemala: The Politics of Land Ownership.* New York: Free Press.

Memoria del Primer Congreso Interamericano de Mujeres. 1947. Celebrado en la capital de Guatemala, del 21 al 27 de agosto de 1947. Guatemala City: Tipografía Nacional.

Mesa-Lago, Carmelo. 1989. *Ascent to Bankruptcy: Financing Social Security in Latin America.* Pittsburgh, Pa.: University of Pittsburgh Press.

Migdal, Joel. 1988. *Strong Societies and Weak States: State-Society Relations and State Capabilities in the Third World.* Princeton, N.J.: Princeton University Press.

―――. 1987. "Strong States, Weak States: Power and Accommodation." In Myron Weiner and Samuel Huntington, eds., *Understanding Political Development.* Boston: Little, Brown.

Miller, Eugene D. 1993. "Labour and the War-Time Alliance in Costa Rica, 1943–1948." *Journal of Latin American Studies* 25, no. 3 (Oct.): 515–42.

Ministerio de Educación Pública (and Universidad de Costa Rica). 1994. *El Significado de la Legislación Social de los Cuarenta en Costa Rica.* San José, Costa Rica: Ministerio de Educación Pública.

Monge, Luis Alberto. 1976a. "Informe del Partido Liberación Nacional de Costa Rica." In *Socialismo Democrático en Costa Rica y Venezuela: Los Partidos Liberación Nacional y Acción Democrática.* San José, Costa Rica: CEDAL.

―――. 1976b. "Evolución de la Idea Social Demócrata en América Latina." In *Socialismo Democrático en Costa Rica y Venezuela: Los Partidos Liberación Nacional y Acción Democrática.* San José, Costa Rica: CEDAL.

Monteforte Toledo, Mario. 1975. *La revolución de Guatemala, 1944–1954.* Guatemala City: Editorial Universitaria.

―――. 1965. *Guatemala: monografía sociológica.* 2nd ed. Mexico City: Instituto de Investigaciones Sociales, UNAM.

Moore, Barrington. 1966. *Social Origins of Dictatorship and Democracy: Lord and Peasant in the Making of the Modern World.* Boston: Beacon Press.

Mora Valverde, Manuel. 1980. *Discursos, 1934–1979.* San José, Costa Rica: Editorial Presbere.

Morales de la Cruz, Baltasar. 1944. *La caída de Jorge Ubico: Derrocamiento de una tiranía: Reseña de la gesta cívica de junio de 1944.* Guatemala City: Tipografía Sánchez & de Guise.

Munck, Ronaldo. 1989. *Latin America: The Transition to Democracy.* London: Zed Books.

Muñoz Guillén, Mercedes. 1990. *El estado y la abolición del ejército, 1914–1949.* San José, Costa Rica: Editorial Porvenir.

Newbold, Stokes [Richard Adams]. 1957. "Receptivity to Communist Fomented Agitation in Rural Guatemala." *Economic Development and Cultural Change* 5 (July): 338–61.

Obando Sánchez, Antonio. 1978. *Memorias: la historia del movimiento obrero en Guatemala en este siglo.* Guatemala City: Editorial Universitaria Guatemala.

Ochoa, Enrique A. 1987. "The Rapid Expansion of Voter Participation in Latin America: Presidential Elections, 1845–1986." In James W. Wilkie and David Lorey, eds., *Statistical Abstract of Latin America*, vol. 25. Los Angeles: UCLA Latin American Center Publications, University of California.

Oconitrillo, Eduardo. 1981. *Un siglo de política costarricense: Crónica de 23 campañas presidenciales.* San José, Costa Rica: Editorial Universidad Estatal a Distancia.

O'Donnell, Guillermo. 1994. "Delegative Democracy." *Journal of Democracy* 5 (Jan.): 55–69.

———. 1993."On the State, Democratization and Some Conceptual Problems: A Latin American View with Glances at Some Postcommunist Countries." *World Development* 21, no. 8, (Aug.): 1355–70.

———. 1979. "Tensions in the Bureaucratic-Authoritarian State and the Question of Democracy." In David Collier, ed., *The New Authoritarianism in Latin America.* Princeton, N.J.: Princeton University Press.

———. 1977. "Corporatism and the Question of the State." In James M. Malloy, ed., *Authoritarianism and Corporatism in Latin America.* Pittsburgh, Pa.: University of Pittsburgh Press.

———. 1973. *Modernization and Bureaucratic-Authoritarianism: Studies in South American Politics.* Berkeley: Institute of International Studies, University of California.

O'Donnell, Guillermo A., and Philippe C. Schmitter. 1986. *Transitions from Authoritarian Rule: Tentative Conclusions About Uncertain Democracies.* Baltimore: Johns Hopkins University Press.

O'Donnell, Guillermo A., Philippe C. Schmitter, and Laurence Whitehead, eds. 1986. *Transitions from Authoritarian Rule: Prospects for Democracy.* Baltimore: Johns Hopkins University Press.

Osegueda, Raul. 1958. *Operación Centroamérica £$ OK £$.* Santiago, Chile: Prensa Latinoamericana.

———. 1955. *Operación Guatemala $$ OK $$.* Mexico City: Editorial América Nueva.

PGT. 1953. "La dirección colectiva y el reforzamiento de la disciplina." Informe al pleno ampliado del Comité Central del Partido Guatemalteco del Trabajo, presentado por Bernardo Alvarado Monzón, 16, 17, 18 (Oct.).

———. 1952. "La situación política nacional, las tareas inmediatas de la revolución y la actividad del Partido Comunista de Guatemala." Informe del secretario general, José Manuel Fortuny, al pleno ampliado del Comité Central del Partido (Feb.).

Paige, Jeffery M. 1990. "The Social Origins of Dictatorship, Democracy and Socialist Revolution in Central America." *Journal of Developing Societies* 6:37–42.

———. 1987. "Coffee and Politics in Central America." In Richard Tardenico, ed., *Crises in the Caribbean Basin*. Beverly Hills, Calif.: Sage Publications.

———. 1975. *Agrarian Revolution: Social Movements and Export Agriculture in the Underdeveloped World*. New York: Free Press.

Palacios, Julio E. 1950. *La Huelga de 1944*. Guatemala City: Editorial del Ministerio de Educación Pública.

Palma, Diego. 1980. "El estado y la demovilización social en Costa Rica." *Estudios Sociales Centroamericanos* 27 (Sept.–Dec.): 183–206.

Palmer, Steven. 1990. "A Liberal Discipline: Inventing Nations in Guatemala and Costa Rica, 1870–1900." Ph.D. diss., Columbia University.

———. 1988. "Un paso adelante, dos atrás: una crítica de 'consenso y represión.'" *Revista de Historia* 18 (July–Dec.): 227–42.

Paredes Moreira, José Luis. 1964. *Aplicación del Decreto 900: estudios sobre reforma agraria en Guatemala*. Guatemala City: Facultad de Ciencias Económicas, Instituto de Investigaciones Económicas y Sociales, Universidad de San Carlos.

Peeler, John A. 1985. *Latin American Democracies: Colombia, Costa Rica, and Venezuela*. Chapel Hill: University of North Carolina Press.

Pempel, T. J. 1978. "Japanese Foreign Economic Policy: The Domestic Bases for International Behavior." In Peter J. Katzenstein, ed., *Between Power and Plenty: Foreign Economic Policies of Advanced Industrial States*. Madison: University of Wisconsin Press.

Pérez Brignoli, Héctor. 1989. *A Brief History of Central America*. Ricardo B. Sawrey A. and Susana Stettri de Sawrey, trans. Berkeley: University of California Press.

———. 1985. *Breve historia de Centroamérica*. Madrid: Alianza Editorial.

Petersen, John Holger. 1969. "The Political Role of University Students in Guatemala: 1944–1968." Ph.D. diss., University of Pittsburgh.

Picado, Teodoro. 1947a. *Una carta y cinco reportajes: Impuesto sobre la renta*. San José, Costa Rica: Imprenta Nacional.

———. 1947b. *Mensaje del Señor Presidente de la República, Licenciado don Teodoro Picado presentado al Congreso Constitucional el 1 de mayo de 1947*. San José, Costa Rica: Imprenta Nacional.

———. 1946. *Mensaje del Señor Presidente de la República presentado al Congreso Constitucional el 1 de mayo de 1946*. San José, Costa Rica: Imprenta Nacional.

———. 1945. *Mensaje del Señor Presidente de la República presentado al Congreso Constitucional el 1 de mayo de 1945*. San José, Costa Rica: Imprenta Nacional.

Poitevin, René. 1977. *El proceso de industrialización en Guatemala*. San José, Costa Rica: Editorial Universitario Centroamericana.

Polanyi, Karl. 1944. *The Great Transformation*. Boston: Beacon Press.

Prosterman, Roy L., and Jeffrey M. Riedinger. 1987. *Land Reform and Democratic Development*. Baltimore: Johns Hopkins University Press.

Przeworski, Adam. 1991. *Democracy and the Market: Political and Economic Reforms in Eastern Europe and Latin America*. Cambridge, Eng.: Cambridge University Press.

———. 1988. "Democracy as a Contingent Outcome of Conflicts." In Jon Elster and Rune Slagstad, eds., *Constitutionalism and Democracy*. Cambridge, Eng.: Cambridge University Press.

———. 1986. "Some Problems in the Study of the Transition to Democracy." In Guillermo O'Donnell, Philippe Schmitter, and Laurence Whitehead, eds., *Transitions from Authoritarian Rule*. Baltimore: Johns Hopkins University Press.

———. 1980. "Material Bases of Consent: Politics and Economics in a Hegemonic System." *Political Power and Social Theory* 1: 23–68.

Przeworski, Adam, Pranab Bardhan, Luis Carlos Bresser Pereira, László Bruszt, et al. 1995. *Sustainable Democracy*. Cambridge, Eng.: Cambridge University Press.

Putnam, Robert D. 1993. *Making Democracy Work: Civic Traditions in Modern Italy*. Princeton, N.J.: Princeton University Press.

Quan, Stella. 1972. *Guatemala: una cultura de ignominia*. Mexico City: Escuela Nacional de Antropología e Historia.

Remmer, Karen. 1991. "New Wine or Old Bottlenecks: The Study of Latin American Democracy." *Comparative Politics* 23, no. 4 (July): 479–95.

Rock, David. 1994. *Latin America in the 1940s: War and Postwar Transitions*. Berkeley: University of California Press.

Rodríguez Sáenz, Eugenia. 1988. "Las interpretaciones sobre la expansión del café en Costa Rica y el papel jugado por el crédito." *Revista de Historia* 18 (July–Dec.): 163–86.

Rodríguez V., Eugenio. 1980. *De Calderón a Figueres*. San José, Costa Rica: Editorial Universidad Estatal a Distancia.

Rogowski, Ronald. 1989. *Commerce and Coalitions: How Trade Affects Domestic Political Realignments*. Princeton, N.J.: Princeton University Press.

Rojas Bolaños, Manuel. 1989a. "The Solidarismo Movement." In Marc Edelman and Joanne Kenen, eds., *The Costa Rican Reader*. New York: Grove Weidenfeld.

———. 1989b. "El proceso democrático en Costa Rica." In Manuel Rojas Bolaños, ed., *Costa Rica: la democracia inconclusa*. San José, Costa Rica: Editorial Departamento Ecuménico de Investigaciones.

———. 1986. *Lucha social y guerra civil en Costa Rica, 1940–1948*. San José, Costa Rica: Alma Mater.

———. 1978. "El desarrollo del movimiento obrero en Costa Rica: un intento de periodización." *Revista de Ciencias Sociales* 15–16 (Mar.–Oct.): 13–31.

Rolz Bennett, José. 1949. "Mujer, Universidad, Patria y Cultura." *Universidad de San Carlos XVII* (Oct.–Dec.): 43–56.

Romero, Carmen María. 1984. "Las transformaciones recientes del estado costarricense y las políticas reformistas." *Estudios Sociales Centroamericanos* 13, no.38 (May–Aug.): 41–53.

Rosada Granados, Héctor. 1992. "Parties, Transitions, and the Political System in Guatemala." In Louis W. Goodman, William M. LeoGrande, and Johanna Mendelson Forman, eds., *Political Parties and Democracy in Central America*. Boulder, Colo.: Westview Press.

Roseberry, William. 1986. "Hacia un análisis comparativo de los países cafetaleros." *Revista de Historia* 14 (July–Dec.): 25–29.

———. 1982. "Peasants, Proletarians, and Politics in Venezuela, 1875–1975." In Robert P. Weller and Scott E. Guggenheim, eds., *Power and Protest in the Countryside*. Durham, N.C.: Duke University Press.

Roseberry, William, Lowell Gudmundson, and Mario Samper Kutschbach, eds. 1995. *Coffee, Society, and Power in Latin America*. Baltimore: Johns Hopkins University Press.

Rosenberg, Mark. 1983. *Las luchas por el seguro social en Costa Rica*. San José: Editorial Costa Rica.

Rovira Mas, Jorge. 1988. *Estado y política en Costa Rica, 1948–1970*. San José, Costa Rica: Editorial Porvenir.

———. 1985. "Del desarrollo de Costa Rica y su crisis en el período de postguerra: 1948–1984." *Anuario de Estudios Centroamericanos* 11, no. 1: 23–42.

Ruddle, Kenneth, and Philip Gilette, eds. 1972. *Latin American Political Statistics: Supplement to the Statistical Abstract of Latin America*. Los Angeles: University of California.

Rudolph, Lloyd I., and Susanne Hoeber Rudolph. 1987. *In Pursuit of Lakshmi: The Political Economy of the Indian State*. Chicago: University of Chicago Press.

Rueschemeyer, Dietrich, Evelyne Huber Stephens, and John D. Stephens. 1992. *Capitalism Development & Democracy*. Chicago: University of Chicago Press.

Rueschemeyer, Dietrich, and Peter B. Evans. 1985. "The State and Economic Transformation: Toward an Analysis of the Conditions Underlying Effective Intervention." In Peter B. Evans, Dietrich Rueschemeyer, and Theda Skocpol, eds., *Bringing the State Back In*. Cambridge, Eng.: Cambridge University Press.

Rustow, Dankwart A. 1970. "Transitions to Democracy: Toward a Dynamic Model." *Comparative Politics* 2, no. 3 (Apr.): 337–63.

Salazar, Jorge Mario. 1987a. "Estado liberal y luchas sociales en Costa Rica (1870–1920)." *Revista de Ciencias Sociales* 36 (June): 91–102.

———. 1987b. "Luchas sociales e intervencionismo estatal en Costa Rica (1920–1940)." *Revista de Ciencias Sociales* 37–38 (Sept.–Dec.): 61–69.

———. 1981. *Política y reforma en Costa Rica: 1914–1958*. San José, Costa Rica: Editorial Porvenir.

———. 1980. *Calderón Guardia*. San José, Costa Rica: Ministerio de Cultura, Juventud y Deportes, Dirección de Publicaciones.

Samper K., Mario. 1990. *Generations of Settlers: Rural Households and Mar-*

kets on the Costa Rican Frontier, 1850–1935. Dellplain Latin American Studies, no. 26. Boulder, Colo.: Westview Press.

———. 1988. "Fuerzas sociopolíticas y procesos electorales en Costa Rica, 1921–1936." *Revista de Historia*, special issue: 157–222.

Schifter, Jacobo. 1986. *Las alianzas conflictivas*. San José, Costa Rica: Libro Libre.

———. 1983. "La Democracia en Costa Rica como producto de la neutralización de clases." In Chester Zelaya, et al., eds., *Democracia en Costa Rica: cinco opiniones polémicas*. San José, Costa Rica: Editorial Universidad Estatal a Distancia.

———. 1981. *La fase oculta de la guerra civil en Costa Rica*. San José, Costa Rica: EDUCA.

Schlesinger, Stephen, and Stephen Kinzer. 1982. *Bitter Fruit: The Untold Story of the American Coup in Guatemala*. Garden City, N.Y.: Anchor Press.

Schmitter, Philippe. 1994. "Dangers and Dilemmas of Democracy." *Journal of Democracy* 5, no. 2 (Apr.): 57–74.

Schmitter, Philippe C. with Terry Lynn Karl. 1994. "The Conceptual Travels of Transitologists and Consolidologists: How Far to the East Should They Attempt to Go?" *Slavic Review* 53, no. 1 (spring): 173–85.

Schneider, Ronald M. 1958. *Communism in Guatemala, 1944–1954*. Foreign Policy Research Institute Series, University of Pennsylvania, no. 7. New York: Praeger Publishers.

Scott, James. 1990. *Domination and the Arts of Resistance: Hidden Transcripts*. New Haven, Conn.: Yale University Press.

Scully, Timothy R. 1992. *Rethinking the Center: Party Politics in Nineteenth- and Twentieth-Century Chile*. Stanford, Calif.: Stanford University Press.

Seligson, Mitchell A. 1987. "Costa Rica and Jamaica." In Myron Weiner and Ergun Ozbudun, eds., *Competitive Elections in Developing Countries*. Durham, N.C.: Duke University Press.

———. 1980. *Peasants of Costa Rica and the Development of Agrarian Capitalism*. Madison: University of Wisconsin Press.

———. 1978. "Agrarian Reform in Costa Rica, 1942–1976: The Evolution of a Program." Land Tenure Center, no. 115. Madison: University of Wisconsin.

———. 1975. "Agrarian Capitalism and the Transformation of Peasant Society: Coffee in Costa Rica." Council on International Studies, Special Studies, no. 69. Buffalo: State University of New York.

Seligson, Mitchell A., and Miguel Gómez B. 1989. "Ordinary Elections in Extraordinary Times: The Political Economy of Voting in Costa Rica." In John A. Booth and Mitchell A. Seligson, eds., *Elections and Democracy in Central America*. Chapel Hill: University of North Carolina Press.

Silva Girón, César Augusto. 1987. *Cuando gobiernan las armas*. Guatemala City: Coronel de Infantería Improset.

Silvert, Kalman H. 1969. *Un estudio de gobierno: Guatemala*. Seminario de

Integración Social Guatemalteca: Publicación no. 26. Guatemala City: Editorial "José de Pineda Ibarra."

Skidmore, Thomas E., and Peter H. Smith. 1984. *Modern Latin America.* New York: Oxford University Press.

Skocpol, Theda. 1979. *States and Social Revolutions: A Comparative Analysis of France, Russia, and China.* Cambridge, Eng.: Cambridge University Press.

Skowronek, Stephen. 1982. *Building a New American State: The Expansion of National Administrative Capacities, 1877–1920.* Cambridge, Eng.: Cambridge University Press.

Smith, Carol A. 1990a. *Guatemalan Indians and the State, 1540 to 1988.* Austin: University of Texas.

———. 1990b. "The Militarization of Civil Society in Guatemala: Economic Reorganization as a Continuation of War." *Latin American Perspectives* 17, no. 4 (fall): 8–41.

———. 1984. "Local History in Global Context: Social and Economic Transitions in Western Guatemala." *Comparative Studies in Society and History* 26, no. 2: 193–228.

Solórzano, Alfonso. 1974. "Factores económicos y corrientes ideológicas en el movimiento de octubre de 1944." *Alero* 8 (Sept.–Oct.): 77–80.

Soto Harrison, Fernando. 1991. *Qué pasó en los años 40.* San José, Costa Rica: Editorial Universidad Estatal a Distancia.

Steinmo, Sven, Kathleen Thelen, and Frank Longstreth. 1992. *Structuring Politics: Historical Institutionalism in Comparative Analysis.* Cambridge, Eng.: Cambridge University Press.

Stephens, Evelyne Huber. 1989. "Capitalist Development and Democracy in South America." *Politics and Society* 17, no. 3 (Sept.): 281–352.

Stinchcombe, Arthur L. 1968. *Constructing Social Theories.* New York: Harcourt, Brace and World.

Stone, Samuel. 1983. "Production and Politics in Central America's Convulsions." *Journal of Latin American Studies* 15, no. 2 (Nov.): 453–69.

———. 1982. *La dinastía de los conquistadores: la crisis del poder en la Costa Rica contemporánea.* San José, Costa Rica: Editorial Universitaria Centroamericana.

Surco. 1943. *Ideario costarricense. Resultado de una encuesta nacional.* No. 2. San José, Costa Rica: Editorial Surco.

Suslow, Leo A. 1949. "Aspects of Social Reforms in Guatemala, 1944–1949: Problems of Planned Social Change in an Underdeveloped Country." Hamilton, N.Y.: Colgate University Area Studies, Latin American Seminar Reports, no. 1.

Taracena Arriola, Arturo. 1989. "El primer partido comunista de Guatemala (1922–1932): diez años de una historia olvidada." *Anuario de Estudios Centroamericanos* 15: 49–63.

———. 1988. "Presencia Anarquista en Guatemala entre 1920 y 1932." *Mesoamérica* 9, no. 15 (June): 1–23.

Thorp, Rosemary. 1984. *Latin America in the 1930s: The Role of the Periphery in World Crisis*. London: Macmillan.

Tilly, Charles. 1990. *Coercion, Capital, and European States, AD 990-1990*. Oxford: Basil Blackwell Press.

———. 1985. "War Making and State Making as Organized Crime." In Peter B. Evans, Dietrich Rueschemeyer, and Theda Skocpol, eds., *Bringing the State Back In*, pp. 169–89. Cambridge, Eng.: Cambridge University Press.

Timmer, Peter C. 1991. *Agriculture and the State*. Ithaca, N.Y.: Cornell University Press.

Tocqueville, Alexis de. 1969. *Democracy in America*. J. P. Mayer, ed., George Lawrence, trans. Garden City, N.Y.: Anchor Books.

Toriello, Guillermo. 1955. *La Batalla de Guatemala*. Santiago: Editorial Universitaria.

Toriello Garrido, Jorge. n.d. "Acontecimientos de la revolución del 20 de octubre de 1944." Manuscript.

Torres, José Luis. 1986. *Otilio Ulate: su partido y sus luchas*. San José: Editorial Costa Rica.

Torres Rivas, Edelberto. 1991. "Crisis and Conflict, 1930s to the Present." In Leslie Bethell, ed., *Central America Since Independence*. Cambridge, Eng.: Cambridge University Press.

———. 1984. "The Beginning of Industrialization in Central America." Latin American Program, no. 141. Washington, D.C.: The Woodrow Wilson International Center for Scholars.

———. 1977. "Crisis y coyuntura crítica: la caída de Arbenz y los contratiempos de la revolución burguesa." *Política y Sociedad* 4, (July–Dec.): 53–83.

———. n.d. "University Students in the 1944–54 Process." Mexico City: Enfoprensa, Agencia Centroamericana de Noticias.

Trudeau, Robert H. 1993. *Guatemalan Politics: The Popular Struggle for Democracy*. Boulder, Colo.: Lynne Rienner.

U.S. Department of State. 1954. *Intervention of International Communism in Guatemala*. Department of State Publication 5556, Inter-American Series 48. Washington, D.C.

Varshney, Ashutosh. 1995. *Democracy, Development, and the Countryside: Urban-Rural Struggles in India*. Cambridge, Eng.: Cambridge University Press.

Vega Carballo, José Luis. 1986. *Hacia una interpretación del desarrollo costarricense: ensayo sociológico*. 5th ed. San José, Costa Rica: Editorial Porvenir.

———. 1982. *Poder político y democracia en Costa Rica*. San José, Costa Rica: Editorial Porvenir.

———. 1981. *Orden y progreso: la formación del estado nacional en Costa Rica*. San José, Costa Rica: Instituto Centroamericano de Administración Pública.

Villagrán Kramer, Francisco. 1993. *Biografía política de Guatemala: los pac-*

tos políticos de 1944 a 1970. Guatemala City: Facultad Latinoamericana de Ciencias Sociales.

―――. 1975. "1945: Institucionalización Revolucionaria." *Alero* 12 (May–June): 102–8.

Villamar Contreras, Marco Antonio. 1985. "El rol de los partidos políticos: testimonio I." In *El rol de los partidos políticos en Guatemala.* Guatemala City: Asociación de Investigación y Estudios Sociales.

―――. 1960. "La encrucijada de la economía guatemalteca." *Lanzas y Letras* 21–22 (Jan.–Feb.): 20.

Wasserstrom, Robert. 1975. "Revolution in Guatemala: Peasants and Politics Under the Arbenz Government." *Comparative Studies in Society and History* 17, no. 4 (Oct.): 443–78.

Weber, Max. 1946. "Politics as a Vocation." In H. H. Gerth and C. Wright Mills, eds., *From Max Weber: Essays in Sociology,* pp. 77–128. New York: Oxford University Press.

Weeks, John. 1985. *The Economies of Central America.* New York: Holmes and Meier.

Weir, Margaret. 1992. "Ideas and the Politics of Bounded Innovation." In Sven Steinmo, Kathleen Thelen, and Frank Longstreth, eds., *Structuring Politics: Historical Institutionalism in Comparative Analysis.* Cambridge, Eng.: Cambridge University Press.

Weller, Robert P., and Scott E. Guggenheim, eds. 1982. *Power and Protest in the Countryside.* Durham, N.C.: Duke University Press.

Williams, Philip J. 1989. *The Catholic Church and Politics in Nicaragua and Costa Rica.* Pittsburgh, Pa.: University of Pittsburgh Press.

Williams, Robert G. 1994. *States and Social Evolution: Coffee and the Rise of National Governments in Central America.* Chapel Hill: University of North Carolina Press.

―――. 1986. *Export Agriculture and the Crisis in Central America.* Chapel Hill: University of North Carolina Press.

Winson, Anthony. 1989. *Coffee and Democracy in Modern Costa Rica.* London: Macmillan.

―――. 1978. "Class Structure in Agrarian Transition in Central America." *Latin American Perspectives* 5, no. 4, issue 19 (fall): 27–48.

Woodward, Ralph Lee, Jr. 1985. *Central America: A Nation Divided.* New York: Oxford University Press.

Yashar, Deborah J. Forthcoming. "The Quetzal Is Red: Political Liberalization, Participation, and Violence in Guatemala." In Douglas A. Chalmers et al., eds., *The New Politics of Inequality in Latin America: Rethinking Participation and Representation.* Oxford: Oxford University Press.

―――. 1996. "Rehaciendo la política: Costa Rica y Guatemala a mediados del siglo xx (Recasting politics: Costa Rica and Guatemala in the Mid-Twentieth Century)." *Mesoamérica* 17, no. 31 (June): 57–98.

―――. 1995. "Civil War and Social Welfare: The Origins of Costa Rica's Competitive Party System." In Scott Mainwaring and Timothy R. Scully, eds., *Building Democratic Institutions: Parties and Party Systems in Latin America*. Stanford, Calif.: Stanford University Press.

———. 1992. "Demanding Democracy: Reform and Reaction in Costa Rica and Guatemala, 1870s–1950s." Ph.D. diss., University of California, Berkeley.

Zea González, Emilio. 1989. "El espejismo de la democracia en Guatemala." Guatemala City.

Index

In this index "f" after a number indicates a separate reference on the next page, and "ff" indicates separate references on the next two pages. A continuous discussion over two or more pages is indicated by a span of numbers. *Passim* is used for a cluster of references in close but not consecutive sequence.

Library of Congress Cataloging-in-Publication Data

Yashar, Deborah J.
    Demanding democracy : reform and reaction in Costa Rica and
Guatemala, 1870s–1950s / Deborah J. Yashar.
        p.   cm.
    Includes bibliograhical references (p. 279) and index.
    ISBN 0-8047-2790-2 (cloth : alk. paper). — ISBN 0-8047-2873-9
(paperback : alk. paper)
    1. Democracy—Costa Rica. 2. Costa Rica—Politics and government.
3. Authoritarianism—Costa Rica. 4. Democracy—Guatemala.
5. Guatemala—Politics and government. 6. Authoritarianism—
Guatemala. I. Title.
JL 1456.Y37 1997
320.97286—dc20   96-31846
                                                                CIP

⊗ This book is printed on acid-free, recycled paper.

Original printing 1997

Last figure below indicates year of this printing:

06 05 04 03 02 01 00 99 98 97